The Last Great Frontier

Essays on Muslim Evangelism

Compiled by Phil Parshall

OPEN DOORS WITH BROTHER ANDREW

The Last Great Frontier
Copyright © 2000 by Dr. Phil Parshall

Published (2000) in the Philippines by
OPEN DOORS WITH BROTHER ANDREW
Southeast Asia Region
PO Box 1573-1155 QCCPO Main
1100 Quezon City

Reprinted — 2001

ISBN 971-8635-01-7

Printed in the Philippines

To the "new wave" of Filipinos

who have become motivated

to share their faith

with the Sons of Ishmael

as found throughout the world.

Contents

FOREWORD

Where does one go for some basic information on Islam? Things like, in which countries of the globe are there significant numbers of Muslims? What simple Arabic words can we learn as we begin to befriend a Muslim? What teaching about God do we have in common with Islam? What does the Quran say about Jesus? What does the Quran say about the Bible? How important is power encounter in evangelizing Muslims? What are the issues in contextualization in Muslim evangelization? How risky is it to evangelize Muslims? What qualities are needed by a missionary to Muslims? Should the missionary keep the Muslim fast of Ramadan?

Dr. Phil Parshall, veteran missionary to Muslims, Islamic scholar, and visiting professor at Asian Theological Seminary, has put together a *Reader on Islam* that answers all the questions raised above, and more. His annotated bibliography of books on Islam is worth the price of the book. There is a great deal more. Many of the articles he includes in the *Reader* were written by him but there are also materials from Ashkenaz Asif, Howard Brant, Clyde Cook, Dean Gilliland, Charles Kraft, John Speers, John Travis, Dudley Woodberry, and Tom Wright. There are even articles from Muslim critics of Christian missionaries!

I learned a great deal in perusing this Reader. I look forward to studying it more carefully. I commend it to anyone who has even the faintest desire that the world's one billion Muslims will come to hear and know of Jesus, the only name given under heaven among men by whom we can be saved.

DR. ISABELO F. MAGALIT
President
Asian Theological Seminary
Manila, Philippines

INTRODUCTION

Over the years I have assigned this compilation of articles to my seminar and seminary students. There has been a great deal of expressed enthusiasm that such material has been gathered into one collection that could be easily photocopied. Most of the overhead transparencies that I use in my classes have also been included.

This selection comes from varied sources and touches upon a wide range of topics. The majority of the articles deal with Islam in some form. However, I have added a few writings that relate to the Christian walk of the full-time minister. In these days of repeated moral failure such an emphasis seems warranted.

The reasons I included Ahmed Deedat's booklet on questioning the validity of the Bible are: 1) the widespread dissemination of this material and 2) the need for missionaries to prepare themselves adequately for theological attacks on the veracity of the Bible as God's word.

A number of my articles are included in this compilation. These are about issues I have not dealt with in the books I have written thus far. Nine of the inclusions are reprints from *Evangelical Missions Quarterly*, America's foremost journal for missionary practitioners.

My thanks to each contributor, especially to OPEN DOORS WITH BROTHER ANDREW (Southeast Asia Region), for their editorial and financial assistance in making this book become a reality.

PHIL PARSHALL

PART ONE

TRENDS AND PERSPECTIVES FOR THE 21ST CENTURY

MISSIOLOGICAL ISSUES FOR THE NEW MILLENNIUM

by Phil Parshall

What seer is competent to peer into the new millennium and postulate definitive happenings? At best, we see through a glass darkly. Yet, in the interest of missiological stewardship, it behooves us within the missionary community to at least let our minds ramble through the options, alternatives, and potentials. Any student of history early on observes the fickleness of human activity. The only predictable constant is that there is no absolute "You-can-count-on-it" surety.

Having covered my prophetic inadequacies by the above statement, I still am somewhat seduced by a strange, mystical moment that will occur at midnight December 31, 1999. How few humans have ever lived to see the inauguration of a new millennium! It will truly be a unique happening on planet earth, celebrated even by those such as our Muslim friends who maintain an allegiance to a lunar-based calendar initiated in 622 A.D.

As I pause to consider missiologically this universal event, I really do wonder if the turning of a calendar page will precipitate any earth-shattering, cataclysmic occurrence. After all, this past decade is a hard act to follow. The opening of the Communist world to the Gospel has been a miracle only to be compared to a yet to be realized mass turning of Muslims to Christ.

It seems to me that most issues in the future will be contiguous and therefore somewhat similar in nature to that which we are presently experiencing. But I do see an enhancement of trends that we can even now empirically identify. To the exposition of these issues I now turn my attention. They will be addressed under four major headings: (1) sending country perspectives; (2) field issues with a missionary focus; (3) field issues with a ministry focus; and (4) overall trends of danger to the cause of missions.

SENDING COUNTRY PERSPECTIVES

Missionary activity is integrally related to the sending church. On this front, there are a number of indications that are causing alarm among missionaries. It appears Sunday and Wednesday night services will soon disappear from the land-scape of evangelical church life. We have already crossed the threshold of dedicated Christians not feeling guilty for omitting these meetings from their weekly schedule. What this does is drastically reduce the missionary's exposure within the church. At best, many can only hope for a testimony "update" during Sunday morning services.

Sunday school classes are still an open venue for ministry. However, the week-long missionary conference will soon be but a fragrant memory of the past. Weekend "mission exposures" are the wave of the future. Innovative drama and fast-paced multi-media presentations will be needed to capture the attention of increasingly lethargic congregations.

Church mission committees will continue to ask hard questions regarding support issues. There will be a great reluctance to send out a family with four or more children as opposed to a newly married couple. Perhaps my most "infamous" writing was an article published in 1977 in *Evangelical Missions Quarterly* in which I proposed a voluntary limiting by missionary families to only two children. Interestingly, the article is still photocopied and circulated by certain mission leaders. Needless to say, I have had my share of criticism for daring to advance such an intensely personal postulate.

Geographic considerations will continue to be a support-related issue. There will be serious questions concerning the feasibility of financing a family in Tokyo with an annual need of $100,000. Other high cost urban areas of the world will come under the critical scrutiny of church mission committees.

All of the above will open the door to the support of national evangelists. They are, after all, linguistically and ministerially competent. For a fraction of the cost of supporting a Western missionary, a national family can be sent forth into productive ministry. We can expect a number of new societies to emerge that will specialize in this type of outreach. Increasingly, missions will be compelled to defend their traditional *modus operandi*. Some will switch to a dual track which will allow Western-supported national missionaries to minister in their own countries.

There will be no letting up in involvement in supporting relief and development projects. Physical needs of the oppressed will continue to attract more attention and resource sharing than will the appeal to consider the eternal state of lost souls. Therefore, missions will be forced into a larger involvement in developmental outreach. Unless great care is exercised, this will become the tail that wags the dog.

Young people, as never before, will be turned on to short-term mission exposures. Their love of travel and adventure fits nicely into a "spiritual experience." Recruiters applaud and emphatically state this is a proven method of recruiting long-term missionaries. Field personnel groan as they contemplate the care and processing of energetic young novices who absorb their limited time and energy.

Unfortunately, the field missionary loses on this one. Few will be the candidates of the future who will make a long-term commitment to missions without a two-week to two-year exposure that allows for a bail out without negative overtones. Accommodation for this paradigm shift must be made on the field level. If this is not done, the potential long-term candidate will just go to a group who only specializes in abbreviated ministry tours abroad. The young person will then complete his or her mission foray without an in-depth consideration of a professional missionary career. Traditional mission societies, as we now know them, would then begin to die off for lack of new recruits.

Home boards face perplexing and, at times, seemingly irresolvable conflicts in regard to internationalization issues. As the global community continues to shrink, we find young people caught in cultural binds. Should the Korean join a British-based missionary society or instead, insist on membership in a mono cultural Korean mission? Should IFMA/EFMA-related organizations be pro-active or pro-inactive as regards recruitment of Africans and South Americans?

17

Is achieving the goal of integration worth the hassles encountered in regard to working through cultural, financial, and linguistic distinctives?

Increasingly, I see Asians opting for their own mission structures. This is prompted by their nationalistic spirit, financial ability, and administrative acumen. There is hesitation to adjust to a Western-dominated leadership. The exceptions relate to countries which, as yet, have inadequate resources to pull off a totally indigenous effort.

From all countries there will continue to be a steady flow of tentmakers going forth. Quasi-tentmaking missions like Frontiers will attract those who desire a dual secular-religious identity and function. As never before, this resource of people will be better trained, and thus become more effective in the field.

A limited amount of mission mergers can be anticipated. It is extremely difficult to allow one's personal and corporate identity to die. In 1989 my mission, International Christian Fellowship did just that as we merged with the much larger SIM International. It has been a happy marriage, though not without some measure of emotional trauma. On a pragmatic basis, such mergers make a great deal of sense.

FIELD ISSUES WITH A MISSIONARY FOCUS

Vividly, I recall my then field director speaking about my job performance to friends. He was complimentary but ended up by saying, "Of course, Phil still has feet of clay." It was an uncomfortable reminder that others were aware of my inadequacies. As we move toward the year 2000, it appears to me that the new millennium missionary will have strong weaknesses as well as commendable strengths. Both traits need to be recognized. The following are a few prophetical observations somewhat based on extrapolation from current realities.

a) Weaknesses

As never before, mission boards are recruiting from a pool of young people who have been emotionally wounded during their early years of life. My empathy for these strugglers is enhanced by the fact that I too am a product of a dysfunctional home. My alcoholic father, who could not hold down a steady job, was a constant source of deep embarrassment to me. As a family, in the dead of night, we frequently loaded up all of our belongings in our dilapidated car and "escaped" to an adjacent town. The bill collectors, arriving the next morning would, I'm sure, curse their gods for ever allowing them to have an encounter with Phil Parshall, Sr.

The emotional trauma of those years played havoc on my nervous system from 1959 to 1973. By God's grace I survived. Many were the days during our first decade in Bangladesh that I was not at all sure God's grace would be sufficient. But it was!

Not all missionary problems can be laid at the feet of parental inadequacies. Genetic and cultural influences bear down strongly on the formation of our behavior. Needless to say, our own propensity toward sin actually is the root cause of most of our conflicts.

So where does all of this lead us? These are some areas of concern:

- Western culture places a major emphasis on self-fulfillment. The church seldom preaches anymore on the "crucified life." Out of this milieu comes the youthful missionary who has been shaped and formed through media and peers to expect a situation in which self will be pampered and coddled.

  Major conflicts erupt as the new recruit's expectations clash, sometimes violently, with the senior field missionary's expectations. Relationships become strained which often leads to a high level of emotional tension. This has a direct bearing on what has been and most likely will continue to be an unacceptable rate of attrition of first term missionaries.

  In recent months, the secular world has promoted the importance of having a well-adjusted EQ (emotional quotient) in addition to an adequate IQ (intelligence quotient). To this I would add FQ (functional quotient). The missionary of the future would do well to concentrate on academic preparation (IQ), relationship building (EQ), and competence in job performance (FQ). Permeating all of the above should be a strong, virile spiritual quotient (SQ).

- The cross-cultural missionary of the year 2000 and beyond will gravitate toward the cities of the unreached world. Though hundreds of millions of the lost reside in rural settings, the modern missionary, in most instances, simply cannot make the necessary lifestyle adjustments to survive incarnationally in primitive environs.

  But problems will persist even in the urban areas. Nationals will continue to criticize the missionary's choice of housing which at times is even ostentatious There are those who have chosen to live in guarded subdivisions. Others have private swimming pools. The $20,000 vehicles of some contrast sharply with the 25 cent fare a national pastor may give to a bus conductor to enable him to have a hot, polluted ride across town. Resentment builds up.

Internationalness brings with it an additional component of tension. In one mission station there was a discussion of who should be assigned the larger home. A Western lady suggested their family should have the commodious place as their Asian colleagues were more accustomed to living in cramped conditions in their own country, and could therefore easily adjust to the smaller house. As the Asian told me this story I could see in her eyes, not anger, but deep hurt.

In a gathering of mission leaders in which I was present, a senior missionary stood and said that the query had been raised, "Are we racist?" We were all shocked by the question. But many of us, upon reflection, had to respond with a qualified affirmative answer.

The struggle goes on in multiple areas. Lifestyle issues will be a continuing point of conflict as the gap between the relative wealth of the foreign missionary and the near poverty level of some national pastors becomes greater not less. Interestingly, this problem now also extends to the more affluent Asian missionary ministering in poverty-stricken Third World nations. It is no longer just a Western problem.

Family concerns dominate the potential recruit's thinking. What medical facilities are available? Will their house be screened? Is nutritious food available in the market? What schooling options are there? Does the mission object to home schooling? Are there reasonable recreational facilities nearby?

What a startling contrast to the questions we asked (or did not ask) when we were recruited for village work in primitive Bangladesh in 1961. Are today's and tomorrow's missionaries any less spiritual for asking about such concerns? At times, we graying "seniors" want to answer with a resounding "Yes." But then we are tempered a bit.

It is natural to want to love and protect one's family. It is even spiritual and biblical to have such a focus. "Just have faith and trust the Lord" somehow has a different ring to it in the year 2000 than it did in 1961. We must not condemn outright the products of a modern protective and maximally insulated-from-pain society.

However, the call for balance must go forth. Tomorrow's recruits are to be confronted lovingly, yet firmly, with a call to discipleship that necessarily involves some measure of risk. Reasonable precautions will be made for the comfort and safety of missionary families. But this wall of protection will, of necessity, not be absolute.

• Perhaps, it is appropriate to list the communication explosion under this category.

Without doubt, faxes, e-mail, and other upcoming computer-related discoveries are extremely helpful to the mission enterprise. Keeping in touch with family, supporters, and relatives has become efficient, speedy, and relatively cheap.

The down side relates to "computer obsessionism." Missionaries who, in the near past, could not be persuaded to touch a typewriter key now gleefully punch away at the same letters by the hour. Some type of magical metamorphosis has taken place which has made the information gathering and communication process a compulsive activity.

So what's wrong? The answer is not in what is being done but rather in what is being left undone. The orphans of the computer age are people. Missionaries find it much more compatible to interact with an obedient (most of the time!) keyboard than with Christian and non-Christian nationals who can, at times, be rude and uncooperative. How terribly easy to lock oneself away in a room and rationalize that computer ministry is people ministry.

I protest! There needs to be a ceiling on computer time that ends up negating people time. By the year 2000, most every missionary who steps off the plane in his or her designated country of ministry will carefully cuddle in his/her arms the latest laptop filled to the brim with the most up to date software. May there be a firm commitment to the prior commitment of homo sapiens over computer chips.

Recently, in an Asian country, a missionary family arrived in the field with a 55 gallon drum filled with videos. In a South American country a video store operator was converted to Christ. He told my friend how amazed he was that missionaries rented the same kind of sex-violence oriented films that non-Christians did. One new recruit became discouraged with language study. He then began to spend most of every day in an air-conditioned room watching the latest Hollywood flicks. Internet the world over offers sexual temptations of a most explicit nature in the privacy of the missionary's home.

Everyone needs some type of break from the intensity of missionary life. Unfortunately, most of the choices are less than spiritually healthy. Many of the old barriers (legalisms?) have been dropped as regards unacceptable modes of entertainment. Free choice without guilt will increasingly be the order of the day. There is and will continue to be a need for close spiritual accountability in this area.

- Great hopes were raised as a consortium of missions came together with the expressed aim of impacting unreached Muslims with the Gospel in an Asian country. Resources were marshaled from near and far. A significant amount of money was spent to ensure the viability of the team. Spiritual dynamics were emphasized.

Twenty-one missionaries actually became residents in that Muslim area over a ten-year period. By the end of the decade the number of personnel had dwindled to four and the consortium was disbanded. Six of the missionaries had been redeployed in non-Muslim ministries in other areas of the country. But eleven had left permanently, of whom only one couple had served more than six years.

Reasons? There were the usual physical hassles. A visiting missionary in the area was killed by a Muslim high on drugs. That incident added a heavy fear component to the context. The few who tried to live in the more rural settings found the lifestyle trying. The weather was hot and humidity high. Conflict with Islam and Muslims seemed to be a serious spiritual drain on the missionaries. There were no conversions. The administrative structure was inadequate. All of this contributed to serious inner-team friction. Criticism became the order of the day. Instead of pulling together in times of adversity, they were pulling apart. Disintegration was the inevitable result.

But was it "inevitable?" In our Bangladesh team, we had nowhere near that attrition rate during a twenty-year span of time. Can it be that the missionaries of this day, and by extrapolation, the missionaries of the next millennium have been culturally conditioned to short term activity always with a live "cut and run" option tucked away in their minds? No longer is the missionary call put forth as "lifetime" but rather as "long term." Even that is slowly dissolving into "short term."

Change is a Western societal norm. There no longer is any real guilt associated with "not making it" on the field. Not that I am in favor of guilt trips, but I do question the whole process of diminished expectations as regards the staying power of the modern missionary.

All of the above leads to a frustration voiced by a field director of a large mission. Repeatedly, he urged the home councils to raise the standards of the candidates they were accepting. So many of the new missionaries he was receiving were creating massive problems, and not a few were calling it quits after a few years. Meanwhile the time and financial input into these lives were overwhelming.

But he wasn't being heard. It seemed the focus of his board was more on quantity than quality. In desperation, he wrote to the home leadership, "Okay, you just keep on sending out inadequate missionaries . . . and I will just keep on shipping them back to you."

Is there not a better way forward? A few suggestions:

1   Require a difficult short-term involvement in a Third World country. My two-month summer foray into Mexico with Operation Mobilization in 1960 gave me a tremendous insight into the problems of heat, non-responsiveness to the Gospel, team frictions, and discouragement. Too many short-term trips these days are sanitized adventure tours. As a minimum, candidates should spend time in inner-city urban ministry.

2   Home leadership must put more emphasis on psychological testing and interviews. Where there are obvious problems, the mission must not hesitate to hold people back until some resolution occurs.

3   A more thorough investigation of the candidate's background should take place. Perhaps actual interviews with the reference and home pastors would facilitate this process.

4   It is legitimate to question whether adequate field care is being provided for missionaries. As emotional needs will be greater in future years, now is the time to recruit special care-givers who could be regionally placed in various areas of the world. They would be a part of an "on the field" team which would be accessible to hurting missionaries.

The bottom line is that there is no fool-proof *modus operandi* which assures that only well-adjusted and low-risk missionaries actually reach and remain on the field. But if mission societies are to be innovative and effectively ongoing, now is the time to address these issues.

b) Strengths

Fortunately the picture is not all grim. There are some very positive things concerning missionaries about which to prognosticate.

- Without doubt today's overseas minister is better trained than any in the history of the missionary movement. Avant-garde institutions throughout the world are emphasizing relevant subjects within the disciplines of Missiology, Theology, and the social sciences. Tent-makers are exceedingly well-prepared to compete in the marketplace in their chosen vocation.

  Creative options are being offered for in-service training. Study can be carried out through extension courses. Two-week modules are offered periodically during the year. Many of these are now taught by the new breed of "jet set professors" who fly out and conduct courses on the field on a regional basis.

  The Internet will open up a whole new dimension to further study. It is a cheap and immediate way to communicate with the training institution. I foresee a 50 to 75 percent rise in the number of missionaries taking extension courses on the field by the year 2005. Third World nationals will find this option attractive. It allows them to remain in their country, and continue to be active in ministry while working toward an advanced degree from a prestigious institution.

- In recent years we have seen fresh missiological initiatives launched. "A.D. 2000 and Beyond," and the emphasis on the "10-40 Window" are just two of the high profile emphases that indicate missionaries are still in a visionary mode. Critics scoff that such are nothing more than "flavor-of-the-month" efforts aimed at promotion and mobilization. No more than just a reflection of the need to cater to the Western desire to get excited about that which is sensational and has an exciting twist to it.

  Granted that there is definitely a PR component to these missiological creations. However, behind all of this, I see minds at work which are dedicated to our Lord. One illustration of an innovation of eye-catching magnitude is Greg Livingstone's founding of the mission, Frontiers. This fifteen-year-old group has placed over 600 missionaries throughout the Muslim world.

These quasi-tentmaker types with their emphasis on team formation have broken new ground among evangelical mission societies. Loose in structure but tight in focus, these visionaries have corporately produced probably the largest mission ever to target just Muslims.

There will most likely be a multiplication of new concepts placed before the believing public as we push into the new millennium. Each one will have the designer's assurance that God's imprimatur is securely tagged to his or her product. It will be up to the discerning Christian to accept or reject such claims.

• Sitting in a relaxed mode by the seashore, I was intrigued to listen as an intelligent young missionary shared with me his testimony of receiving a spiritual revolution in his life through the "Toronto Blessing." He had attended what was then the Toronto Vineyard Church as an agnostic. The emotional intensity of the leaders and congregation somewhat turned him off. But then most unexpectedly, he found himself overwhelmed by the Spirit of God. He quickly crossed the line from skeptical observer to believing participant. With enthusiasm, he related all the positive spiritual benefits he had received since that initial experience.

A few months later, I sat among one thousand Filipinos as they were mesmerized by a visiting "Blessing" speaker. Some of the believers engaged in hilarious laughing for the entire 3½ hours. As the preacher from the West crawled over the benches he would mystically wave his hand over a row of people. Down they went as if struck by a horizontal flash of lightning. It was like a gala fiesta full of emotional exuberance.

Have we now come to the ultimate spiritual experience? Or can we expect the year 2000 to usher in a new dynamic exposure to God that some will unhesitatingly embrace while others scoff? These are difficult issues as we find dedicated saints on both sides of the fence. Many Pentecostals are pondering, with serious reservation, what they regard as the emotional excesses of the "Blessing" phenomenon. And privately they are questioning the legitimacy of the very movement to which they themselves can be considered parents or at least step-parents.

Then there are other more relatively subdued spiritual movements such as prayer walks and intercession for the "100 gateway cities." Even the variety of power encounter ministries which once caused an outcry of criticism have pretty well been accepted into the mainstream. Respected leaders like Neil Anderson, Tim Warner, and Philip Steyne have contributed to this metamorphosis.

It took Bill Bright to successfully emphasize and popularize a juices-only-forty-day fast. As one who has personally benefited from the experience, I can only express appreciation for a fresh emphasis that this ancient spiritual discipline has received in our evangelical community.

It will take a unique person to come up with, and then implement an unheard of spiritual experience for the upcoming decades. But, successful or not, I'm sure there will be some who will give it a try. And if there are those in the Body of Christ who therefore receive a fresh touch from the Lord, then perhaps the onlooking agnostics should at least be moderate in the tone of their criticism. The commendable thing is that there is a viable and active pursuit of a new reality in Christ. And that, indeed, is a positive missiological trend.

- Missionaries of tomorrow will demonstrate a more egalitarian attitude toward the nationals among whom they labor. The context of the colonialism of their elders will basically be unknown to them. Missionaries coming from wealthy countries to minister among the poor and oppressed will, nevertheless, have to exercise constant vigilance over attitudes of superiority. This especially relates to the critical spirit that develops when dealing with corrupt officials who demand bribes as an incentive to perform their appointed tasks.

- Lastly, there will continue to be a flow of ministers who are willing to undergo the rigors of life in the rural communities of the Third World. This will be a lessening number, but it will still have significance. In my travels, particularly in Africa, I have been deeply challenged by observing missionaries in basic living conditions. Their compelling concern is for the millions outside of the reach of the evangelistic opportunities that are so prolific in the cities.

FIELD ISSUES WITH A MINISTRY FOCUS

Geographical Considerations

This past decade has brought about cataclysmic changes in the political landscape of our planet. All of these shifts in governments have greatly impacted the direction of various mission boards. This reorientation of missiological strategy will continue to be carried into the coming years.

As long as conditions permit, the missionary emphasis on the Common-wealth of Independent States will be expanded. Asia in general and China in particular will draw those societies which have a focus on evangelizing the masses. Four regions will begin to register a definite decline in foreign missionaries. They are:

1   WESTERN EUROPE They have heard and they have rejected. Hearts are open to materialism and closed to spirituality. So goes the rationale that will peripherize Western Europe to new missionary thrusts of signifi-cance.

2   AFRICA The Western church is experiencing compassion fatigue as they receive never-ending appeals for an area of the world where tribalism and power intrigues seem, at least in certain places, to negate the impact of the Gospel. Countries like Somalia, Sudan, Liberia, and Rwanda cast a pall of hopelessness over the African continent.

3   JAPAN No one doubts the spiritual need of this heavily populated coun-try. However, little fruit for a half century of intense Gospel propagation has caused discouragement. Added to this is the extremely high support figure required to labor in Japan.

4   SOUTH AMERICA Much is heard about the vitality of the church in South America. There is now a strong current of thinking that says foreign involvement is no longer needed. This will affect missionary recruit-ment in future years.

Islam

Whither Muslim evangelism in the 2000's? There was a day when it was "cool" to be heavily engaged in ministry to Muslims. My amazement knew no bounds in the 80's when it was the "in" thing to be a missionary in an Islamic nation. But I had little confidence that such a miraculous event would be long standing. Now, as we move into the latter half of the 1990's, we see a definite pattern of lessening emphasis on Islam. The CIS and China are picking up the slack. Muslim think tanks are sailing through rough waters. Enrollment in seminary and Bible college courses on Islam is down, even to the point of having classes canceled due to below minimum registration. Recruitment for Muslim outreach through traditional mission societies is less than in the 80's.

There are, however, a few bright spots. Fuller Seminary continues to do well in its Islamic program that offers both masters and doctorate degrees. Columbia International University has initiated an MA in Muslim studies. Frontiers is encouraged in its recruiting efforts. Groups like Operation Mobilization and Youth with a Mission maintain their commitment to Muslim outreach. Hopefully, these institutions and mission societies will retain and expand their focus on Islam.

Islamic violence will continue and even increase. There will always be a "cause" or a grudge for them to settle. The Quran and Hadith give adequate room for these disagreements to be mediated through terroristic activities that supposedly are sanctioned by Allah. The fundamentalist fringe has a built-in hard core following of the "defenders of the faith and guardians of the *ummah* (community)."

Islam is perhaps the fastest growing religion in the world. Much of this growth is attributable to the Muslims' refusal to utilize birth control methods. But by no means is this the total picture. In many countries of Africa Muslim propagation is extremely effective. Reputable sources now place the Islamic population of America at six million. By the new millennium Islam is expected to replace Judaism as the religion with the second greatest number of adherents in the United States. Most of Europe is seeing a large rise in their Muslim population. This comes from a high birth rate of Muslim citizens, increased immigration (legal and illegal), and successful evangelization of the local people.

Bangladesh, Indonesia, and parts of Africa like Ethiopia will continue to see Muslim-convert churches formed. But these efforts will increasingly be contested by fundamentalist Muslims whose influence cannot be expected to decrease. Soon the role of "missionary" in the majority of Islamic nations will be virtually non-existent. Mission boards must adequately prepare for that day by initiating non-traditional entry strategies. Frontiers has been in the forefront of such innovations though SIM along with other groups is now putting emphasis in that direction.

Various Projections

High-tech methodology in Gospel propagation is sure to be an important part of our future. Billy Graham and others have already put their organizations right at the cutting edge of new technology. Satellites are the brave new frontier of missions. Soon a number of these will be totally Christian-owned. High quality pictures and excellent content programs will be raining down on the most impenetrable countries. Internet with cheap voice contact will make it possible to web out the Gospel to even places like Saudi Arabia. The downside will be the difficulty of engaging in person-to-person follow-up.

The current Catholic-Evangelical dialogue is going to have a long-term effect on field ministries. When reputable leaders issue calls for close cooperation with Catholics, the natural outcome is to question the need for evangelizing this segment of "Christianity." This will lead to Catholic countries like those found in South America and parts of Europe being placed outside of the evangelistic priorities of some mission boards.

By the new millennium, or soon thereafter, there will be a significant "changing of the guards" of powerful mission leadership. Donald McGavran has already received his well-deserved promotion to heaven. Ralph Winter, Loren Cunningham, Brother Andrew, Bill Bright, and Billy Graham have all begun the process of transition in their ministries. One could experience a moment of apprehension seeing these giants of the faith begin to move off the missions scene. Yet, the God of Moses, Joshua, of Elijah and Elisha still reigns.

Missionaries or tentmakers are presently serving in every country in the world. This means they may be residents in areas of physical danger. At times there will arise the option of fleeing violence as has been the case in a number of African countries recently. In most instances, Western governments make provision for the necessary evacuation of their citizens. And usually this offer is accepted.

But who then gets left behind? There is a growing sentiment among national Christians that they, in such instances, are being forsaken by their spiritual guides. They have been told to trust the Lord in times of danger. And that is precisely what they have to do. But unfortunately, it appears the fleeing missionaries are placing their trust in helicopter evacuations. As they lift off, their final shouted words to terrified nationals is an assurance of prayer for them but to be done in some distant safe haven.

In 1971 in Bangladesh, I went through the trauma of deciding to stay in Dhaka during the East Pakistan nine-month civil war. About 90 percent of the missionary community evacuated. In this instance hostilities were not aimed at the foreigners. Our danger was in being caught in the crossfire. How the nationals—Muslim and Christians alike—so appreciated our presence. Conversely, a great deal of hurt was experienced by the nationals who felt abandoned by their missionary colleagues who opted for evacuation.

How will this play out in future years? Certainly, the prognosis is for civil wars and violence to escalate. Mission boards should be encouraged to draw up contingency plans that would allow volunteers to stay behind and walk through the crucible with their national brethren. This sharing of trials would seem to be an appropriate Christian response.

SIX OVERALL TRENDS OF DANGER
TO THE CAUSE OF MISSIONS

1 Pluralism

Incoming students at a conservative, missions-minded Bible college were questioned regarding their belief concerning the uniqueness of Christ. Twenty-five percent of the freshmen did not affirm Jesus as the exclusive path to God. I am confident this number would be considerably greater among first year students at some other American Christian colleges and universities.

Our Western culture promotes a pluralistic world view. Dogmatism is deemed to be synonymous with bigotry. And who wants to be accused of being a bigot? Therefore, the road to social acceptance lies in being broad and congenial to varying views and opinions. The only person you are allowed to oppose dogmatically is the person who is dogmatic.

All of this has had a dramatic effect on biblical hermeneutics. In order to appear loving and non-judgmental, Christians have gone out of their way to avoid Bible verses that point to an exclusive salvation in Christ. Hell is seldom the subject of a Sunday morning sermon. The fate of the Christ-rejecter is, at best, dwelt upon once a year in a weekend missions·conference. Even reputed theologian John Stott has questioned whether everlasting punishment is truly everlasting.

This inclusivistic trend will unfortunately escalate in the coming years. It has everything going for it . . . except a biblical basis. Missions therefore takes a direct hit. Many Christians will be hesitant to support evangelism. Social development projects that assist people in this life will be preferred. Young people, who are not motivated by the strong biblical teaching on the destiny of the lost, will not give serious consideration to missions involvement.

Is there an answer to this dilemma? Certainly biblical teaching on the subject must be put forth in unequivocal terms. Churches and Christian schools should interact with their constituency. The major problem seems to be lack of communication and biblical exegesis. A dedicated effort must be launched to overcome a deficiency that, if not dealt with on a sustained basis, will undermine the cause of church growth worldwide.

2 Syncretism

It has been my privilege to have been deeply involved with contextualization as a missiological principle for the past two decades. I have always been keenly aware that the distance between proper contextualization and improper syncretism is rather minimal. So easily religious syncretism can win the day. My book, *New Paths In Muslim Evangelism*, published in 1980 has a section dealing with this missiological problem.

Recently an instructive survey was made among Muslim converts living in an Islamic nation in Asia.[1] The following are the responses given by 72 believers, of whom 36 are leaders of convert congregations. The respondents may well be representative of over 4000 professing believers.

- 76% meet together in homes in Christian worship once a week
- 16% meet more than once a week
- 50% go to the traditional mosque once a week and do the standard Arabic prayers that affirm Muhammad as a prophet of God
- 66% read or listen to the Gospels daily
- None read or listen to the Quran (other than when in the mosque)
- 96% affirm the Old Testament, New Testament, and the Quran
- 66% say the Quran is the greatest book
- 55% affirm God as Father, Son, and Holy Spirit
- 97% declare Jesus to be the only Savior
- 93% agree with the statement, "God loves and forgives because Jesus gave His life for me."
- 100% believe that "People can be saved from evil spirits and Jinn (mystical spirits of power) through faith in Jesus."
- 100% pray to Jesus for forgiveness of sin
- 97% declare they are not saved because of Muhammad's prayers
- 100% find peace and closeness to God when reading the Gospels

Are we looking at a dynamic, biblically-informed, contextualized Muslim convert church? Or are we pondering on what a half-breed syncretistic expres-

---

[1] Research conducted by the Fuller School of World Mission

sion of Christianity looks like? Most of us will tend to highlight the obvious problems like mosque attendance, belief in the Quran, and the fact that only 55 percent affirm God as Father, Son, and Holy Spirit.

But what about the other data that reveal frequent cell-type worship gatherings, a high rate of daily Bible reading, and affirmation of Jesus as both Savior and deliverer? Most of these, almost all men, have been professing believers between six and ten years. Some have had to endure persecution from fellow Muslims, even to the point of fleeing to an adjacent country and remaining there for a period of time. Presently, it appears this opposition is muted, perhaps stemming from the fact that many are now actively participating in mosque worship.

Are these "followers of Jesus" in a process of spiritual maturing that will soon bring them to total cognitive as well as behavioral orthodoxy? Or is this a powerful case study of how excessive contextualization ends up with an unacceptable Christian-Islamic syncretism? The Evangelicals who spent a great deal of time and money in carrying out the field interviews noted all the concerns herein expressed and then concluded, "An objective look at the data, reveals that there has been a real work of God among Muslims in this movement."

As we progress toward the future, there will undoubtedly be many such dilemmas that will arise. From the earliest moments of Gospel propagation, especially in the contextualized mode, we must make every effort to clarify biblical truth as well as biblical behavior. The drift toward a theological syncretism of the old and the new must be resisted with vigor.

3 Materialism

The perennial quest of humankind toward riches goes on unabated. By some, the motivation is need; by most, it is simply greed. Along the way spirituality is the loser. How easy for fleshly comforts to dominate one's complete being. The things of the Spirit compete on an uneven playing field. Immediate self-gratification is a powerful motivation in the lives of men and women worldwide.

When my wife and I visited Moscow in 1978, we saw deprivation on the streets and in the shops. How different today where, from Russia, we see TV pictures of stores packed with merchandise. Unfortunately, a materialistic orientation toward life is fast becoming the new god of the masses. The *mafia* and the street gangs along with high priced prostitutes are out in force. Progress toward affluence, yes, but at what price?

It is no great mystery why Jesus was so down on the wealthy. Riches seduce one's spirit. Spirituality becomes neutralized. And missions become a mega loser.

I still find myself overwhelmed by the amount Christians spend on luxuries compared to donations to charitable causes. Missions will have to struggle increasingly with this problem as we march into the new age where there will most likely be even more wealth, at least in the more developed countries of the world.

4 Nationalism

A high degree of nationalistic pride is another enemy of missions. One would like to think we are moving toward a commonwealth of nations in which there is equal respect for all people. The reality is that societal divisions based on creed, ideology, religion, race, and tribal divisions are rampant throughout the world. Each ethnic group or political entity is convinced of its superiority and by extension, the inadequacy of other peoples. There are exceptions, but overall, nationalism has exceeded responsible limits.

Enter into the scene the foreign missionary. A major factor in getting a hearing for the Gospel relates to his or her citizenship. This style of racism will probably become greater over the next decade. Much will depend on the maturity and broad-mindedness of influential leaders within each country as to whether it all adversely affects the cause of missions.

5 Ethnocentrism

My concern here relates to the attitude of the missionary who goes forth into an alien setting. A number of books have been written on this subject. In theory, there should be no insensitive attitudes or actions on the part of the missionary which offend the people of the host country.

Unfortunately, that is often not the case. Much cultural baggage continues to be an integral part of the foreign missionary's life and ministry. This has been and will continue to be a Westerner's problem. More specifically, my empirical research indicates that those of us who are Americans must struggle the most with this issue of ethnocentrism. Our culture has strongly promoted the false premise that in most every area of life the American way is the best way.

But, interestingly, the new wave of Asian missionaries are now locked into the same problem. They are moving into developing countries with a conviction that results will follow if the national there will just do things like they do in their homeland. A considerable amount of money is expended in order to make things happen quickly. Bible colleges and seminaries are established without reference to existing institutions. Free trips are offered to the missionary's home country so the nationals can be better equipped to do things the "proper" way.

Most of these men and women are sincere zealots. In some instances they are responsive to guidance. But this is not always the case. Without doubt, this movement of Third World missionaries will expand tremendously as we enter the new millennium. This inevitability is to be welcomed. It is only to be hoped the new can learn sensitivity from the old, and the old can learn zeal from the new. Above all, we together as representatives of the broken Body of Christ, need to crucify maximally the tendency toward an ethnocentric orientation to ministry.

6 Immorality

A journal article I wrote some years ago was entitled, "Missionaries and Morality." The editor in refusing the article explained that pastors and laymen reading it might be a bit overwhelmed by realizing that such a problem could possibly exist among God's special servants.

Some of my greatest disappointments in life relate to this embarrassing issue. Consider the following (with pseudonyms):

- Two ladies feeling the deep loneliness stemming from life on an isolated mission station begin to find emotional and physical release in each other's arms.

- The defeat Tom felt as he struggled with first year language study was excruciating. He found refuge in sexy novels purchased at the local marketplace. One late night, in a moment of debilitating depression, Tom went into the bedroom and began to strangle his wife. By God's grace, she awakened. Her shouts brought him back to sanity and heartfelt repentance.

- In 1974 at the Lausanne Congress, Matt, a very accomplished and well-known missionary, told me of his watching two X-rated movies. Today, Matt is divorced and out of the ministry.

- Ed was physically and compulsively drawn toward the attractive maid who worked in the home. After some time, he succumbed to have sex with her while his family was away leading Bible studies.

- It was with great excitement that I learned I would be ministering at a large conference with a renowned missionary. At the last moment Sam canceled out. Later, I heard he had been discovered having relations with a woman who was on his ministry team.

I could go on but it would serve no real purpose. One of the disquieting aspects of this problem is that I personally know of no Christian worker who, out of a strong sense of guilt and repentance, confessed to his or her immorality without first being apprehended. This leads me to ponder how many there are that are ensnared in the entangling net of sexual sin who have not yet been caught and revealed to the trusting public.

Is this an issue of missiological concern for the new millennium? For sure! Sexual temptations have never been stronger. Satan has probably never had so many victories in defeating God's servants through moral sins as he is presently having. And it has all the potential of escalation. Mission boards must have frank discussions with candidates and deal with sexual aberrations before they are allowed to proceed to the field. Then, after arrival, there must be an adequate counseling and accountability procedure in place. No one, not even the strongest among us, is invulnerable to sexual sin.

Conclusion

The new millennium looks missiologically exciting. There will be lots of challenges. Some of these will lead to defeat but I am confident that, over all, we are going to see stunning victories in our battles. No longer is the mission enterprise a Western-centric operation. How thrilling to see our "children" from the Third World rising up and leading the charge. May we all join hands, hearts, and resources to march into the new millennium full of faith and spiritual vitality.

Lead on, O King Eternal!

METHODOLOGICAL OPTIONS FOR MUSLIM EVANGELISM*

by Phil Parshall

Jay Smith's provocative postulate endorsing confrontational debate with Muslims really does not represent a new paradigm. Rather, it is a rehash of that which has been tried, tested, and found wanting. Even in contemporary times, we have had Anis Shorrosh boldly taking on Ahmed Deedat in a debate provocatively entitled, "The Quran or the Bible: Which is God's Word?" Some 12,000, mostly Muslims, gathered in Birmingham, England on August 7, 1988 for this highly animated face-off. Shorrosh took off his kid gloves and sought to academically undermine Quranic authority.

Perhaps, he was too "successful." For in July 1990, Shorrosh journeyed to Deedat's home turf in South Africa only to be met with a wildly antagonistic and

---

* Reprinted by permission of *Evangelical Missions Quarterly* (Box 794, Wheaton, IL, 60189, USA)

even violent response from the local Muslims. An article in the Durban newspaper headlined their news report, "Controversial Christian Theologian Leaves the Country After Death Threats." Both England and South Africa are nominally Christian countries. But even in those contexts Muslims were highly offended by being forced to endure a type of harsh criticism of their revered holy book. This, in spite of the fact that Deedat has long been the master of scorn and ridicule aimed so provocatively against our Bible.

But do we have a trade-off? Are there specific conversions emanating from the Smith-Shorrosh polemical approach? Both men have been engaged in their ministries of undercutting Islam for some years. However, to my knowledge neither of them have seen Muslims come to Christ, at least not in any significant numbers. Conversely, a great deal of antagonism has been generated. If this is where all of this leads, it is only fair to question seriously the validity of their strategy.

Are there alternative methodologies that should be examined? The following are some suggestions, most of which has been tested in varying contexts.

1 Interaction not Confrontation

"Will you come and participate in our Muslim-Christian interaction?" The intelligent, young Filipino convert from Seventh Day Adventism to Islam put this unique proposition to me. He requested I simply give a 20-minute testimony of what Christ means to me. After being assured that this would not be in a debate format, I accepted the invitation. Once before, I had observed their interaction in which only about forty people were in attendance.

On the appointed evening, I approached the band shell in Rizal Park. To my considerable consternation, I was confronted with a sea of 700, almost all Muslim faces. Many were in full Islamic dress. On the well-lit platform were two posters proclaiming, "Dr. Phil Parshall — Special Speaker on the subject, 'Is the Bible the Word of God?'" As I walked up I heard a young Filipino at the microphone forcefully explaining why he, as a Baptist pastor, had renounced Christianity and become a Muslim. Quite an introduction for me. I had been duped!

Nevertheless, I proceeded to give a clear testimony of my conversion and the rationale for my biblically-based faith. Microphones had been set up in the audience and for the next two hours Muslims questioned me regarding biblical authority and other "easy" issues like the Trinity and how the crucifixion can affect mankind today. When the audience didn't appreciate my answer, the cry of "Allahu Akbar" (God is great) rolled over the band shell!

At the end, a group of Muslims came up and said they had never heard Christianity explained in such a manner. The next day a Pakistani and a Saudi who had been in the meeting came to my Reading Center. They were most gracious and concluded our time together by purchasing a Bible which the Saudi assured me he would be taking shortly with him back to his homeland.

In my talk I never once denigrated Islam. My presentation was a positive affirmation of my Christian faith. Somehow, I managed to be gracious to my Muslim host, even though I admit to a bit of anger against him for his duplicity.

Perhaps this format could be successfully utilized in a public setting. One word of warning. Some Filipino pastors have engaged in these interactions and done very poorly. Only those trained in Christian theology and in Islamics should attempt this method of evangelism. The Muslims have been schooled in Deedat style argumentation and know how to play hard ball.

2   Bookrooms

During the mid 70's, I had the privilege of being part of a team which pioneered a contextualized approach to evangelism in a Southeast Asian country. As a result of this applied methodology, thousands of Muslims have become Christians. This outreach is ongoing and is now being utilized by many different groups within that country.

One of our most successful venues for making contacts with Muslims was through bookrooms or reading centers. In 1980, my wife and I were part of a team of four couples who went to pioneer in a district of one and a half million Muslims. To our knowledge, there had never been a convert in that area. Our team rented small rooms in rural village markets where the people would congregate weekly to buy and sell goods.

The centers were set up to be religiously attractive to Muslims. Scripture verses in Arabic were hung on the walls. We wore clothes appreciated by Muslims. Sitting on mats on the floor, we projected an image of a "holy man" or a religious teacher. Contextual literature was shared with the visitors. At first Muslims would drop in out of curiosity. But soon meaningful conversations took place. Within six months we began to harvest the firstfruits of our labors. Today there are over 500 baptized Muslim background believers in just that one area.

For the past 13 years, I have had a bookroom bordering the Islamic community in inner city Manila. This Reading Center is likewise attractively decorated with Islamic art decor. But, as is appropriate in the city, simple chairs and stools are provided. I show the "Jesus" film in Muslim dialects four afternoons a week. Two tables of literature are set up on the sidewalk just outside the Center.

Hundreds of Muslims have watched the film. Many have been deeply touched, especially by the crucifixion reenactment. A great deal of literature has been distributed. Visible fruit has been minimal, although perhaps the number one witnessing convert in all of the Philippines commenced her spiritual pilgrimage as she stepped into the Center and was befriended by an OMF missionary lady who led her to Christ and discipled her.

In restrictive Islamic countries it may not be possible to have a book-room outreach. But among minority Muslim populations and in more open societies like Pakistan, Indonesia, and a number of South Sahara countries, such centers are a valid option. This would be true throughout Europe as well. Each context would call for a unique approach that would be appreciated by the target community.

3 Tentmaking

The major impact in mission to Muslims in the new millennium will be, of necessity, related to tentmaking strategies. By the year 2000, few Islamic nations will be granting visas to openly declared missionaries. In extreme fundamentalist countries even Christian lay missionaries who are overt in witness will find themselves declared *persona non grata*, or worse yet, as with Filipinos in Saudi Arabia, some will end up with extended prison terms.

Yet, the nature of the Great Commission demands an inclusion of the 1.2 billion Muslim population of the world. Political and religious barriers must be looked upon as challenges rather than closed doors. There will always be "means" available to somehow penetrate even the most difficult of Islamic lands. Many evangelical missions have now launched "alternative ministries" departments which address the need for creative entry strategies into Muslim countries.

Frontiers has fielded probably the largest force specifically targeting the world of Islam. Their team-based approach has given them maximum flexibility in professional options. Minimal bureaucracy within Frontiers has had a compelling appeal to the younger generation of X'ers and boomers. Few of their secularly well-trained personnel have had extensive preparation in theology and Islamics. Yet, in Frontiers' 15 years of existence they have fielded over 600 staff and have seen scores of small Muslim background believer fellowships come into being.

Islam, in its early years, was propagated through the influence of a dedicated network of laypeople. This army of traveling businessmen took every opportunity to share their faith with those they met. This is why Asia today embraces almost two thirds of the Muslim population of the world. The tentmakers were amazingly successful. It is now the *"Kairos"* for Christians to implement a similar strategy for impacting the Islamic world. These approaches will need to be characterized by a spirit of innovation as well as flexibility.

4 Radio

It would be my considered opinion that we have not begun to experiment adequately with contextual radio programming for the Islamic world. Much of the present effort is wrapped in Western dress and filled with Christian clichés which are unintelligible to the average Muslim listener. Felt needs are not a focus.

Sensitive programming could include: talk shows on issues relevant to Muslims, health hints, poetry, Scripture quizzes, reading from dramatic books, a soap opera with a compelling, emotional type presentation, biographical drama, chanting of the Arabic Bible, talks on moral issues, discussion of the spirit world, farming information, nutrition helps, relevant indigenous music (both vocal and instrumental), question and answer interaction, relaying of personal messages, marital counseling, on-site interviews of interesting people, and finally, the offer of a free Bible correspondence lesson for all who request it. Most of these ideas could be incorporated into a low key one hour daily program presented in a Muslim dialect.

Dr. Ross James, in cooperation with FEBC and SIM, is developing radio programs that have a focus on assisting rural people in the area of health needs. There is considerable potential for such programming in the Muslim world. Where medium wave broadcasting is not allowed, short-wave is always an option.

Television is being considered by some entrepreneurs as a method to present Christ to Muslims. If this comes to pass, I can only hope the programming will be culturally and religiously relevant to the Muslim mind. My fear is it might be but a rehash of Western Christian TV presentations. That would be sad indeed.

5 Spiritual Dynamics

The Western missionary is a specialist in methodology. We have our *gurus* like Ralph Winter who is perhaps the world's greatest living missiologist. And we pay him due respect for his amazing innovation and productivity.

But what about a missionary *guru* known solely for spirituality? Can there be a consensus that such a man or woman exists? Oh, yes, we may have our individual nominations, but I doubt if anyone would garner over 50 votes. There appears to be no living missionary in the lineage of a spiritually intense Hudson Taylor or Adoniram Judson.

Why is this so? Have our families, churches, Bible schools, and even missions misdirected our steps? Why all the emphasis on statistics and success? Is this now what drives our mission community? "Doing" has somehow overshadowed, and in some cases obliterated, "being." Is this a possible reason for our general impotence as we stand before the world of a nearly impregnable Islam?

Recently, Jim Plueddemann, general director of SIM, called together all of the leadership of the mission for a gathering in London. The most pungent part of that consultation was the morning hours when Jim led us into a time of deep spiritual soul searching. On our knees we sought the living Lord for forgiveness, humility, purity, and empowerment. It was a time few of us will ever be able to forget.

Bill Bright, in his seventh decade of life, issued a call for Christians to be involved in a 40-day-juices-only fast and time of prayer. He has set a personal example by keeping this fast for the past three years.

In 1996, a group of 13 of us in the Philippines who are involved in Muslim evangelism also followed this style of fast. Our two-fold focus was personal holiness and a breakthrough in Muslim evangelism. We fasted during the 30-day Ramadan Fast and then for an extended 10 days. Each of us testified to a new spiritual sensitivity as a result of self-deprivation. A few had a major revolution in their personal walk with the Lord. There were some gains in Muslim outreach as well.

I realize the brief confines of this article does not allow for a thorough presentation of all of the missiological options for Muslim evangelism. Others can fill in the blanks. But I would conclude by emphasizing the absolute imperative of prioritizing a "classic" approach to a revitalization of spiritual reality among us missionaries who are called to be light and salt to the "Sons of Ishmael."

PART TWO

CONTEXTUALIZATION:
CLOSING THE GAP
OF SPIRITUAL AND
CULTURAL BARRIERS

S I M

GUIDELINES FOR
MUSLIM MINISTRY

In January 1987, twenty-two Society for International Ministries (SIM) mission-aries and seven consultants met in Monrovia, Liberia to discuss SIM's on-going commitment to Muslim evangelism. After listening to a number of position papers and after spending several days working on statements which would be agreeable to all participants, the following recommendations were submitted to the SIM General Director. These recommendations were ratified by the May 1988 SIM International Council and are to be implemented by each Area Director where SIM is engaged in Muslim outreach.

SIM GENERAL RESOLUTION

We reaffirm the unceasing responsibility of the SIM to press on with the mandate of proclaiming the Gospel to all people until the return of Jesus Christ.

Recognizing that the numerous Muslim people groups have formed a united wall of resistance toward the Gospel and acknowledging that existing Christian agencies (be they church or mission) have not always responded as they should to bridge the deep chasm of spiritual and cultural barriers to those who have been Islamized, we recommend that SIM strengthen its resolve to evangelize Muslim people groups.

THE SPIRITUAL NATURE OF OUR CONFLICT

In our outreach to Muslims, we are engaged, first and foremost, in a spiritual conflict. As we are involved in spiritual warfare, SIM will consciously maintain its spiritual dynamism as the focus of our Mission. This will involve:

a) Requiring our missionaries to have solid Bible training before going into ministry to Muslims.

b) Pastoral ministry to missionaries working with Muslims to encourage them in their walk with God.

c) Annual conferences with a biblical and spiritual emphasis.

d) Continued emphasis on prayer as the chief weapon against our enemy.

CONTEXTUALIZATION: ITS NEED AND MEANING

We also recognize that there are sociocultural factors which affect our ministry to Muslims. For this reason, we adhere to the principle of contextualization. As this word "contextualization" has been used in a variety of ways, we define its meaning for our intended use.

By the term "contextualization," we mean:

> Meaningful and appropriate cross-cultural transmission of biblical truth which is faithful to its original intent and sensitive to culture.

"Enculturation" and "cultural sensitivity" are other terms which convey a similar meaning.

We recognize this term may be used in ways which we do not intend. There are several interpretations which we explicitly do *not* attribute to the term "contextualization."

1   Passive acceptance of any cultural forms and lifestyles, apart from the judgment of Scripture on them.

2   Religious syncretism in any of its forms.

3   Construction of any "theology" to serve as a philosophical underpinning for the violent and illegal overthrow of political and social structures in a particular geopolitical context (e.g., "Black Theology" or "Liberation Theology").

CONTEXTUALIZATION: GUIDELINES FOR ITS USE

a) Implementation of contextualization in each SIM area

The intention of this section is to provide guidelines to SIM Areas involved in Muslim ministry. It is understood that as each Area will face slightly different situations these guidelines will assist Administration in the formation of Area policy Muslim outreach.

Each Area Council will be responsible in implementing these measures in a way appropriate to their need. These Areas should be responsible for relaying their Area policies to the National (Home) Offices for new personnel to consider before coming to the field.

b) Principles for application

The following general guidelines are submitted as principles for adopting, adapting or rejecting any particular issue of contextualized practice:

1   The Bible is totally sufficient. All considerations must be subjected to its test.

2   Ask "Is there a specific command/principle/example in Scripture?"

3   Scriptural injunctions must not be sacrificed to harmonize with culture/ society.

4   Consider the risk of minimizing important theological differences.

5   Consider long-range ramifications.

6   Seek to determine if adopting traditional religious/cultural forms promotes or impedes acceptance of the biblical message.

7   Look for legitimate functional substitutes.

8   Recognize that in Islam form is meaning.

9   Consider each cultural form carefully before discarding it. Unnecessary removal of legitimate items from the cultural network may impede the spread of the Gospel.

c) Contextualizing our message

We hold to these cardinal truths:

> The Bible is the inerrant, authoritative Word of God.
>   It is the only revelation from God that speaks authoritatively on the issues of sin, salvation, sanctification, and reconciliation of man with God.
>   Furthermore, we believe that Jesus Christ is the only way to God. He is the ultimate in God's revelation to mankind, fully God and fully man, God incarnated into humanity.

Therefore, we acknowledge that Christian and Islamic theologies are irreconcilable. But, as Christian missionaries to Muslims, we want to be understood. We are obliged to communicate the Christian message as clearly as possible.

Therefore, we should utilize theological bridges to the Muslim mind. This could involve:

1   Studies of personalities common to both the Bible and the Koran—men and women of faith who followed the will of God.

2   Teaching on covenants.

3   Teaching on redemption in the Old Testament.

4   Fulfillment of Old Testament prophecy in the New Testament.

5   In Muslim evangelism, we must build relationships over a long period of time. The importance of a chronological approach using Bible stories that gradually lead people to an understanding of the Gospel can not be overemphasized. The aim is to convey the cardinal truths that are necessary for a Muslim to understand the Gospel. Examples of this type of approach would be the methods suggested in *Let's Help the Fulani* by Gerry Swank, SIM; and *Chronological Approach to Evangelism* by New Tribes Mission.

d) Contextualization of missionary lifestyle and approach

We recognize that many Western missionaries offend Muslims unknowingly because of their dress or mannerisms. The contextualization of the missionary lifestyle is important, both in narrowing the communication gap between the missionary and the Muslim and in avoiding unnecessary offense.

Therefore, missionaries to Muslims should adapt their lifestyles to that of the people to whom they minister in the following ways:

1   Avoid food or drink offensive to those to whom we minister.

2   Readily partake of the hospitality of the people, and extend hospitality to them.

3   Wear culturally modest clothes (both men and women), and learn to wear the costume of the local people where appropriate.

4   Learn and adapt culturally appropriate mannerisms in social interaction.

5   Participate in appropriate rites of passage.

6   Avoid ostentatious living.

7   Maintain consistency, particularly in team ministries.

e) Contextualization of training and care given to new Muslim converts

Wishing to avoid the frequent difficulties resulting from extractionism, ministry should be oriented towards the family or social group. We should seek to provide Bible training at the level of the people and in their context.

We recognize that local Muslim teachers can sometimes provide us with useful role models for teaching and discipling new converts from Islam. This may vary, however, from country to country, and depend upon the type of Muslim and tribal culture.

We may also look at the former religious practices of converts from Islam as we teach them the biblical practices which correspond to the same needs.

We should introduce new believers into Christian forms of communal experience (*ummah*), teaching mutual interdependence and corporate dependence on God.

f) Contextualization of church forms appropriate for Muslim converts

SIM missionaries, in consultation with field leadership, will be given freedom to use culturally appropriate church forms which maintain the dynamism of the people group in which they are planting that church, while changing that which is biblically unacceptable through the teaching of the Word of God.

We are not insisting on ethnically homogenous churches, but we recognize that the believer in this type of church feels more at home and is a more effective witness to his people. Therefore, at the inception, freedom will be given for homogenous groups to form and develop along socio-cultural lines. At the same time there should be teaching on the organic unity of the Body of Christ.

For the training of Muslim converts, culturally-sensitive Bible training programs must be adopted. In evangelism/church planting ministry among Muslims, we recommend that Muslim converts be given freedom and encouragement to form their own church within biblical parameters.

g) Helping the national churches contextualize their approach

Inasmuch as contextualization is recognized as an important principle in church planting among Muslims, this principle needs to be understood by the existing

SIM-related churches and their developing missionary societies (e.g., Evangelical Missionary Society). If contextualized models are adopted without the consensus of other related church bodies, there could be serious misunderstanding.

Accordingly, top SIM leadership will communicate with national church leadership in Africa to encourage the discussion of this principle through the Evangel Fellowship.

STRATEGY CONSIDERATIONS

There are presently 93 million Muslims in SIM's area of activity. This figure will become even larger in the future. This figure includes numerous Muslim people groups and many major urban centers either in areas where SIM presently works or contiguous to them (e.g., Senegal, Mali, Chad, Cameroon, Malawi, Tanzania, Mozambique).

To meet this awesome challenge, SIM will need to recruit a minimum of 670 new Muslim workers within the next decade. These will be assigned to rural, urban, and nomadic situations. If certain politically sensitive areas should become open, this requirement would increase. This also assumes there will be cooperation with indigenous missionary agencies.

Every effort will be made to strengthen existing SIM-related national churches in their missionary responsibility to Muslims.

Furthermore, SIM seeks greater cooperation with other like-minded missions and churches seeking to minister to Muslims

a) Strategy for research

SIM will conduct research among Muslim people groups at two levels:

Level #1   A broad-based survey of sub-Saharan Africa, using Larry Vanderaa's 1984 survey of Franco-phone West Africa as a model.

Level #2   A detailed research of specific prioritized people groups following the model of MARC's *That Everyone May Hear.*

We recommend that the respective Directors appoint someone to carry out the broad-based survey as soon as possible. It is envisioned that the Area Muslim Coordinators would coordinate this research into the specific people groups (see p. 62, M).

b) Classification for use in identifying target groups

We will use the following classification of target groups:

Class A — Those people groups with whom SIM is already working, but the evangelizing and church planting are still in an early phase.

Class B — Those people groups who are in the same country where SIM is working, but are not being reached by SIM. They are contiguous to SIM work.

Class C — Those people groups with whom SIM is working, but who are also found in countries where SIM has no work.

Class D — Those people groups who lie outside SIM influence in that we do not work among them or in any country where they live.

c) Guidelines on rural outreach

There are still vast populations of unreached Muslims in rural areas. SIM will strengthen its efforts to reach out to rural Muslim people groups by establishing teams to plant churches among them.

As we think of entering these Muslim groups, a major point of strategy will be to select first those groups which demonstrate a receptivity to the Gospel or have high potential in influencing other contiguous people groups.

d) Guidelines on nomadic outreach

Drought conditions have dislodged many of the nomadic peoples of Africa, and they are presently going through a period of social upheaval. As a result, they are more open to religious change and Christian witness. Now is the strategic time to concentrate our efforts in reaching them.

Therefore, we will strengthen our efforts to evangelize nomadic groups among whom we already have personnel, e.g., Tuaregs, Fulanis, Borans, etc., as well as recruiting for those untouched, such as the Arabs, Tubus, Tuaregs in Mali, etc.

e) Recommendation on urban outreach

Due to the large rapidly growing urban areas all over Africa, we must give special attention to urban Muslims. We must reorient our thinking to include a strong emphasis on these urban areas.

Where appropriate, rural ethnic groups will be linked in ministry with the same ethnic group in the urban centers.

In areas where evangelical churches already exist, we will seek to cooperate with them in meeting this overwhelming challenge.

SIM will use every means possible in media, prayer groups, and publicity of all types to emphasize Muslim urban outreach in the home countries. This should result in the recruiting of personnel to meet the challenge of the mushrooming cities such as Abidjan, Lagos, Ibadan, Accra, Kumasi, Cotonou, Porto Novo, Mombassa, Monrovia, Conakry, Niamey, Ouagadougou, etc.

f) Strategy for media outreach

WHEREAS, the harvest is great—millions of Muslims in the present and projected areas of SIM ministry—and the laborers are few (too few SIM missionaries are involved in some way in Muslim outreach), and

WHEREAS the Muslims are utilizing mass media in concentrated efforts to propagate and defend their religion and to attack Christianity, and

WHEREAS the Lord has provided mass media to multiply the efforts of His laborers in the harvest:

1 Mass media will be made an integral part of ministries to Muslims, with appropriate staffing needs listed on the personnel needs list.

   a) Mass media is defined as literature, audio/cassette, video-cassette, radio, TV and films.

b) Mass media must be considered and integrated where appropriate when strategy is laid for entry into new ethnic groups.

c) A reevaluation of the utilization of mass media must be made for current outreach to Muslims.

2 High priority will be given to the recruitment of personnel with media skills for ministry to Muslims.

3 Current missionary staff who feel the leading of the Holy Spirit to work in media will be given the freedom to do so within the context of the ethnic group in which they labor.

g) Literature to counter Muslim polemicists

Given that Muslim polemicists are currently producing highly provocative material against Christianity, and that these are being distributed in areas where SIM ministers, an investigation will be made of available literature and other media which counter the efforts of Muslim polemicists, and this literature will be made available through selected channels to strengthen the faith and witness of Christians to Muslims.

It is envisioned that SIM will establish a central repository for information on Muslims, which will function both as a dissemination point for information, literature and other resources for Muslim outreach.

SIM will attempt to second a person or persons to the Fellowship of Faith for · Muslims (FFM) to help bolster their staff in needed administration and business functions, and seek funding to assist FFM in the collection, production, and distribution of effective literature for Muslim outreach.

h) Strategy on physical ministries

Recognizing our desire to reach Muslims for Christ, we also empathize with them in a wide range of physical and social needs. In an attempt to meet some of these needs as a legitimate expression of Christian compassion, we recognize the need to avoid the twin pitfalls of creating dependency on the one hand, and offering inducements to Christianize, on the other hand.

Accordingly, these guidelines will be followed for physical ministries:

1 Thorough research will be made to identify legitimate felt needs.

2   Guidelines and criteria will be established for avoiding the problems alluded to above.

3   Appropriate low profile physical ministries will be identified to meet one or more of the legitimate felt needs.

4   Strategies integrating physical ministries into Muslim outreach will be developed.

5   Muslim-oriented missionaries, respected community leaders, and if possible, a Christian anthropologist will provide inputs and on-going guidance to the project.

6   Where natural disaster makes immediate relief essential in a Muslim society, highest priority should be given to the inclusion of an administrator who understands Islam and the local culture.

i) Team strategies

In view of the pressure on missionaries working among Muslims, our emphasis will be toward team ministry. This means that those working on the team should be encouraged to function as a body, with all their ministries focused toward their common task. A team leader will work to bring coordination to the work and encourage other members. Teamwork includes input and support from the leadership (Area Director) down to the grass-roots missionary.

A team approach is important for:

1   Mentoring of new personnel.

2   Continuity of ministry.

3   Mutual strengthening of team members through prayer and encouragement.

4   Opportunity for the varying gifts of personnel to complement each other in church planting.

5   Stronger presence for more effective witness.

Therefore, more planning and research will be done on preparing teams for ministry to Muslims. This approach is important in both rural and urban outreach.

j) Motivation of the indigenous church for Muslim evangelism

Given that foreign missionaries will never be able to meet the challenge of Islam alone, it is considered our highest priority to work with and support our related national churches in Muslim evangelism.

Special report will be made to encourage the church in Africa to initiate or increase its outreach to Muslims by helping train them in appropriate ways of evangelizing Muslims and establishing culturally relevant fellowships and churches.

This will be implemented by:

1   Holding seminars for church leaders and laity that will sensitize them to the cultural differences between Christian and Muslim mindsets, and promote understanding and evangelistic concern.

2   Initiating outreach programs involving trainees in practical use of newly-acquired skills.

3   Identifying potential trainers from the seminars and outreach programs who could receive advance training for extending indigenous church outreach to Muslims.

k) Recommendation on training for Muslim outreach

1   Program will be instituted at two levels:

Level A   Seminars for lay persons on how to witness to Muslims with a view to organizing them for united outreach.

Level B   Advanced programs for those who will work with Muslims on an ongoing basis with particular emphasis on preparing those who can train others for outreach to Muslims.

2   SIM will encourage the Accrediting Council for Theological Education in Africa to emphasize the need for Bible colleges and seminaries to provide specialized training in Muslim ministries.

3   SIM will encourage Evangelical African writers to produce materials for use in Muslim ministries.

l) Muslim information network

The International Media Department is requested to select a suitable staff person who could:

1   Prepare articles on Muslim evangelism for *SIM Now*.

2   Produce an in-house bulletin for SIM missionaries who work with Muslims.

3   Prepare materials for sharing with a wider network of non-SIM people and agencies who may be interested in SIM's Muslim outreach.

4   Distribute videos and literature which relate to Muslim outreach.

m) Coordinators for Islamic ministries

In order to implement and coordinate outreach to Muslims at the local level, we recommend that involved Area Councils appoint a coordinator (who would be on full time if possible) to assist the Area Director in the following responsibilities:

1   Motivating and stimulating Muslim awareness

2   Networking information

3   Literature and resource distribution

4   Facilitating training and coordinating seminars

5   Recommending study programs

6   Coordinating research

7   Formulating strategy

8   Promoting cooperation

The Area Coordinators will also work with the International Outreach Coordinator, and each Area engaged in Muslim outreach will work out its policies in regard to contextualization using the guidelines provided in this document as well as in the paper "Towards an SIM Position on Contextualization."

RECRUITMENT AND TRAINING OF PERSONNEL

a) Area policy manuals for Muslim outreach

A strategy/policy manual for Muslim outreach will be prepared for every SIM Area. A public version of this (without sensitive material) should be available to the recruiting staff in each National Office. This material should also be used as a basis to identify and recruit missionaries for specific categories of Muslim outreach:

1   Urban
2   Rural (settled)
3   Rural (nomadic)
4   Muslim elite (urban and rural)

b) Reorganization of regional representation in home countries

Consideration should be given to reorganizing our system of regional representation in order to make better use of specialized gifts. For example, it might be possible to enlarge existing regions with a view toward teaming up individuals with different ministry gifts to share joint responsibility for that larger region. A major goal would be to have someone designated specifically to recruit for Muslim ministries.

c) Recruitment priority for Muslim workers

Recruitment of workers specifically for Muslim outreach will be given top priority at all levels to insure finding and training suitable recruits for Muslim outreach. The following means are suggested:

1 Treat recruitment more functionally, rather than as one of the many responsibilities carried on by regional representatives/director. Organize recruitment teams aimed at recruiting workers for Muslim outreach.

2 Maintain an effective presence at strategic centers of missiological research and Bible training, possibly with missionaries-in-residence who are presently in home countries.

3 Send out small teams of potential recruits for a focused and well-prepared cross-cultural learning experience under a proven SIM leader. It may be possible to incorporate this as part of an accredited educational program at certain Christian colleges.

d) Recruitment of short and long term workers

While short terms are valuable recruiting and training programs, every effort must be made to communicate the need for long-term commitment by those entering Muslim ministries.

e) Screening process for Muslim workers

1 Our screening process for Muslim outreach should clearly communicate the harshness, difficulties, and aspects of spiritual warfare inherent in this effort, and the qualities necessary to function well in it.

2 It should be communicated to potential recruits that pre-field internship is required of all missionaries entering full-time Muslim outreach. This internship should be strongly recommended for all others ministering in Muslim contexts.

3 In view of frequent attacks of Satan experienced by workers in Muslim evangelism, and the effect that this can have on interpersonal relationships, potential recruits should be expected to have lived and worked effectively in some form of Christian community (such as a residential college or church internship) for a sufficient time to enable a good testimony to be established.

f) Training of new personnel

1 New missionaries who are going into Muslim ministry may be required to participate in an approved specialized training course/internship in Islamics (of approximately three months duration) prior to leaving for field assignment. Further specialized training should be encouraged as necessary, including cross-cultural studies and Arabic.

2 Advanced training programs to assist experienced missionaries in specialized outreach to Muslims (urban, rural, nomadic) will be sought. This might take place at locations in proximity to the most successful kinds of outreach models which exist within or outside of SIM.

3 Each National Office should consider making "training requirements" a fixed item within the category of outgoing expenses which must be raised before departure. Doing this broadly, as opposed to doing it on an individual basis, would tend to ease the burden by averaging down the cost. Other financing options are, of course, the prerogative of each National Office.

4 National Offices are encouraged to find means whereby appointees may receive benefits usually reserved for "active" missionaries to facilitate special Islamic training/internships.

PUBLICITY CONSIDERATIONS

In publicity matters, there are three areas of concern. First, it is necessary to have accurate information from the field for publicity purposes. Second, we need to find adequate means to produce and distribute appropriate information to potential candidates, supporters and prayer partners. Third, because Muslims monitor all publications for information on what missions like SIM are doing, there is need for information control.

a) Getting information from the field

The appointment of full-time information officers on every field should be a priority. Multi-nation and larger Areas should appoint part-time assistant information officers.

b) Distribution of information

1   Use polemic Islamic videos and literature to stir interest and involvement on campuses of theological institutions.

2   Prepare response video to the materials mentioned above, using the most effective Christian apologists to Islam available.

3   Prepare a colorful article/booklet describing our founders' broad vision for outreach to Muslims; add the extent of the fulfillment of that vision today (simple, emotive).

4   Prepare effective videos/literature to counteract the view being propagated in Africa that Christianity is a colonial import and not indigenous to Africa.

c) Information control

1   Make a major effort in our unrestricted publicity channels such as *SIM Now* and prayer letters to address the facts concerning SIM's historic involvement and vision for outreach to Muslims, as well as the extent and aggressiveness of Islam in Africa and our home countries.

2   Channel more specific but still safely printable information (excluding names, for example) to prayer groups specifically raised to support SIM or other Islamic ministries. Appropriate videos could also be channeled to these groups.

3   Channel explicit or sensitive information to Mission representatives for word-of-mouth recruitment efforts only.

MINISTERING IN HOME COUNTRIES

a) Encourage existing policy

Develop a specifically Muslim outreach/church planting effort in home countries in line with the stated objective of the *SIM Manual*, pp. 61-62, sec. 2,d; and employing appropriate strategy guidelines as stated on p. 62, sec. 3.

b) Use of African Christians

It is suggested that SIM consider enlisting the help of African Christians to assist in outreach to Muslims in SIM home countries.

c) Cooperation with existing agencies

Outreach to Muslims should be pursued on a broad inter-denominational basis, with SIM promoting interest and involvement on the part of existing churches. Fellowships established through such efforts would choose their own affiliations, and SIM would not seek to form such groups into an SIM denomination.

d) Targeting specific locations in home countries

SIM National Offices should seek, where possible, to target one or more specific cities/areas for Muslim outreach efforts.

TOWARDS AN SIM POSITION ON CONTEXTUALIZATION

The term "contextualization" includes the ideas inherent in words like "indigenization" or "enculturation." The term indigenization asks, "Who owns the program?" The term enculturation asks, "Does it fit the culture?" Contextualization combines those two thoughts and asks, "How do you transfer what God has said through 'holy men of old' who lived in an ancient cultural context, into the language of people who live in a very different one, through the medium of translators who live in yet another context—today's space age?" This tri-cultural obstacle is the most complex of all.

Definition

Accordingly, we define contextualization as meaningful and appropriate cross-cultural transmission of biblical truth which is faithful to its original intent and sensitive to culture.

Assumptions

There are several assumptions which lie behind our idea of appropriate contextualization:

1 Biblical truth is absolute and defines the essence of the Gospel and the Church. These truths cannot be compromised in any way.

2 There are, however, various legitimate ways in which these same truths can be expressed and applied in different cultures. These expressions and applications must be consistent with principles of biblical interpretation.

3 As every culture contextualizes the Gospel and the Church, missionaries come to new cultures already biased towards their own home culture. To transmit this would be theological imperialism. It leads to the confusion of the Gospel and the planting of a foreign church.

4 A contextualized Gospel and church which are faithful to Scripture and sensitive to culture must be worked out for each culture being entered. This insures that the issues which must be decided for someone to be converted are the core (and not subsidiary) issues. It allows flexibility in forms of expression which are meaningful to the new church within its culture.

5 A contextualized church will be better able to maintain its unity, sustain its purity, and witness to its own community. Having experienced the process of contextualization, it will be better equipped to transmit biblical truth to other cultures. It may result in increased receptivity.

Areas of application

Contextualization should be applied to areas such as the following:

1 Dress, behavior, and lifestyle of the missionary.

2 Types of development projects which, if inappropriate, might be interpreted as "inducements" by the non-Christian community.

3   Language, including the Scripture translation, used in evangelism and worship.

4   Thought patterns and communication style, as found in the new culture (e.g. story-telling or use of indigenous music).

5   Initial selection, sequence, and emphasis of certain aspects of the Gospel relevant to any culture (e.g. the different way the early apostles shared the Gospel with Jews versus the way they shared it with Gentiles).

6   Worship posture and expression in prayer, music or formal discourse, allowing for various forms. We need to be careful, however, that we do not overlook the delicate relationship between form and meaning. We should avoid inadvertently encouraging a form or practice which is perceived by the worshiper or his unconverted acquaintances as having a meaning which is in conflict with biblical truth. (e.g. Certain kinds of music in African culture are related to evil practices. The posture of prayer may be much more significant for a Muslim than for a former Catholic.)

7   Discipling and training methods, keeping in mind the past experiences and future needs of new converts.

8   Church organization and government, allowing various forms.

NOTE: The process of contextualization should be perpetuated not only by example but through teaching as a discipline among national pastors, missionaries, and church leaders.

Problems with contextualization

1   In the rush to contextualize some may attempt to lessen the demands of the Gospel or sacrifice biblical truth to make the Gospel or Church more acceptable. This may lead to syncretism.

Accordingly, we in SIM limit the use of contextualization to those means and methods which are in harmony with the Word of God, our final authority. Scripture must be the final judge of every culture.

2   Missionaries may not always understand the meaning behind forms which they either allow or disallow in the church. Accordingly, the best ones to

decide what is appropriate are well-taught believers who can speak to their own culture.

3   Some theologians, arguing that the method of interpretation used by Evangelicals is often dictated by their cultural mindset, produce new theologies based on different hermeneutical systems—all in the name of contextualization (e.g. "black theology" or "liberation theology").

We, however, define our hermeneutics as the grammatico-historical interpretation of Scripture, which states that the meaning of any Scripture is defined by the intent of the author, which in turn, can only be determined by the language he used and the historical context in which he wrote. Thus, while there can be only one meaning, there may be numerous applications.

LESSONS LEARNED
IN DOING
CONTEXTUALIZATION

by Phil Parshall

There is a certain amount of presumption embodied in the topic I was assigned for this Consultation. Is it possible for anyone to claim the status of having "learned contextualization?" I would emphatically place myself in the learner category rather than take my seat among the "pseudos" who brazenly claim to have absolutized even a small segment of the rich treasures of human-divine knowledge. In the Islamic realm of applied contextualization, we who are beginner-practitioners are in the stage of hypothesis and experimentation rather than that of confirmation and dogmatic pronouncement.

Yet, there are small slivers of light breaking forth and piercing the stygian darkness of the pre-dawn morning. Never before in thirteen centuries of Muslim-Christian relations has there been such a mobilization of resources for the task of confronting the Sons of Ishmael with the liberating Gospel of Jesus Christ. True, the Crusaders mobilized *en masse*, but it was with a sword of death, not a sword of Spirit and Life.

Can one imagine a mission executive stating that his society must consider immediately opening a Muslim front in their outreach because "Young people today seem only interested in going to Islamic countries?" As commendatory as this "new wave" is, I cannot help but ponder on the potential contradictory influence of contemporary headlines vis-à-vis that of the Holy Spirit. Is all of this activity generated by a deep love for Christ and Muslims, or have young people been seduced by a passing fad—a spotlight status—a romantic illusion? Only time will reveal whether we are in a pop or a classic mode. In the meantime we press on!

This paper will focus on five areas of relevance to the contextualization issue. Many of the anecdotes come from my personal involvement and observation. There are included, however, some second-hand accounts which are from reputable sources. More than once I have been forced to resort to the use of pseudonyms in order to protect those ministering in sensitive situations—or to spare embarrassment to certain individuals. It is obvious that I will not be able to give more than a cursory treatment to a number of complex issues that are raised in this paper. I refer the interested reader to my previous writings for further understanding of my missiological positions.

THEOLOGICAL DIVERSITY

One time honored and emotionally preserved ethos of Evangelicals is an unswerving commitment to non-essential theology and practice. How else could we ever have come to a place where opinions on pre/mid/post become a test of whether one is an Evangelical? Illustrations could go on *ad infinitum*. This propensity toward a sharp delineation of minutiae has affected the courage of innovators who otherwise would be eager to wade out into the sea of the unexplored Probing, persistent questions relating to one's support base militate against an enthusiastic plunge into the unknown.

Lest I be misunderstood, I am unequivocally an Evangelical. However, my reservation relates to people who are so dichotomistic in hermeneutics that they can only ever see theology in terms of sharply delineated black and white. Some of us have been forced to deal with Third World cultures and non-Christian religions. We, at times, find ourselves awash in a sea of murky gray.

Even with total commitment to biblical faith, a contextualist is still extremely vulnerable to the surging waves of personal and institutional criticism. It was not easy for me to receive a copy of a mimeographed negative critique of my evangelistic methodology which ends up asking if I am not on a path which will lead to a denial of the work of the Cross. This was written by an esteemed friend who has spent many years ministering in a Muslim country. At least two churches (from the far right) have dropped our support, though several others have commenced giving to us. I recall one sleepless night tossing and turning ensnared in a web of conflicting emotions towards a prominent person who had targeted my ministry as an example of unacceptable theological accommodation.

Still, through it all, I am a total convert to contextualization. Without doubt, my writings and articulated thoughts are errant in numerous places and in need of correction. And so, in my more rational moments, I welcome the navigational correctives that keep the ship on course.

A few of the theological controversies in the contextualization debate are as follows:

Baptism

A prominent missiologist has been widely quoted as saying a close biblical equivalent to New Testament baptism would be to have a coffin in front of the church. A new convert would lie down in the coffin and then the lid would be closed and reopened. The new believer would rise from the coffin signifying death to the old life and resurrection to the new life in Christ. As far as I can ascertain, the coffin would not be filled with water.

No other postulate of mine has aroused the purists as much as my statement in *New Paths in Muslims Evangelism* that I would be interested in seeing experimentation done in the area of a functional substitute for baptism. The reason for my suggestion (not a dictum or even a conviction) relates to the Muslim view that baptism is the severing of one's link with the Islamic community. Baptism has often been the seal of alienation and commencement of an extraction syndrome.

Thus, the appeal for a different type of initiatory rite that could be known more for its religious significance than for its negative sociological impact. Perhaps the missiologist's proposal of a waterless coffin did not get wide enough exposure to provoke a counter-attack. But my suggestion certainly managed to stir some of the saints to an impassioned defense of the baptistry. To me this is not worth a confrontation. The Bible clearly teaches **water** baptism and it is also a universal, historical practice of the Church. Let us continue the sacrament in undiluted form and seek to interpret this ceremony to Muslims in a clear biblical manner.

Homogeneity

Donald McGavran opened Pandora's box when he took a quietly practiced missiological strategy and went on to institutionalize it as a church growth principle. The flak has not abated nor are there signs of any real reconciliation between protagonists and antagonists.

There are many who feel a homogeneous convert church is the only practical way to bring Muslims to faith in Christ and at the same time see them remain within the general sociological boundaries of Islamic society. In most countries, Muslims view the Christian church as a foreign entity to be ridiculed, not respected. Its forms, procedures, creeds, architecture, and articulation are totally alien.

To circumvent such antagonism the formation of loosely structured, culturally relevant, and biblically oriented convert fellowships has been the focus of a growing number of missionaries. As yet, it is impossible to give a thorough evaluation of the effort. But it is fair to say that initial reports have been favorable. Converts are appreciative of the opportunity to worship with others from an Islamic background. Biblical forms of prostration, chanting God's Word, fasting, and use of familiar words have all contributed to believers making a smooth transition to the new community. And, most importantly, in many of the researched fellowships, converts have remained as salt and light among their Muslim relatives and friends. They have not become the typical extracted, persecuted ones and twos that make exciting biography, but are dead-ends as far as church growth potential is concerned.

The effort has just begun—but it is a worthy involvement.

Terminology

Somewhat nervously, I sat in the home of missionaries in an ancient city of North Africa. Within a few minutes the "consultation" began with a fellow servant of Christ on the subject of proper terminology to use in Muslim evangelism. His pressing concern related to Christians using the Quranic *Isa* as the word for Jesus. My response was to ask why Christians use *Allah* for God throughout the Middle East and Indonesia. This is the Quranic word for God and yet fully accepted by all Arab Christians. Is there not an inconsistency to feel comfortable with *Allah* and yet be so antagonistic toward *Isa*?

Some Christians in Asia have forcefully opposed using *Allah* as the word for God. They can only think in terms of post-seventh century Islamic linguistic forms. Historical research indicates *Allah* was not only a common poetic word for God among Arabs in pre-Muhammad times, but that Arab Christians also used *Allah* as a biblical word in the centuries before Islam was launched.

Language usage is much more than a cognitive exercise of communication. Words are emotionally powerful. We must continue to probe for appropriate linguistic forms to reach both the heart and the mind of our Muslim friends.

Fasting

Does the Bible allow for fasting in the prescribed Muslim form? Dogmatic answers abound. In North Africa the answer among missionaries has been consistently negative. Others, elsewhere, are not so sure.

I personally have kept the Ramadan Fast according to the prohibitions of Islam in 1982 and 1985. According to my admittedly limited knowledge, I only know of one other missionary who has kept the entire Fast. But missionaries from five different missions, who are working among Muslims in the Philippines, kept at least part of the 1986 Ramadan Fast.

Our observations lead us to conclude that our Muslim neighbors have appreciated our following their fasting ritual. For a number of the missionaries, fasting has been a positive spiritual experience. To all, there has come a new appreciation of the discipline and rigor demanded by a month of daytime abstinence from food and water. It is my considered opinion that dogmatism and legalism is not called for. Rather, there should be an open climate of freedom on the subject, unencumbered with any hypocritical value judgments toward either the doers or the abstainers.

Supernatural experiences

Enter John Wimber, the intelligent, articulate advocate for hands-on healing. His books and tapes continue to cause a rippling effect among Christians around the world. After listening to some twenty hours of his teaching on tape, I conclude there is much of what he says that has direct potential for good in our contextualized ministry. We are often dealing with folk Muslims who are more interested in Elijah-type confrontations than in an academic exposition of the book of Romans. "Where is the God of the Bible," they ask. "Show Him—not just declare Him—and I will believe!"

What is our response? More talk about the lame man made to walk, the blind man made to see, the issue of blood healed, the demons exorcised . . . more talk, more exposition, more cognition . . . but no demonstrations, no signs,

71

no healings?

A challenge to faith. Is it not appropriate to pray for a reinstatement of Old and New Testament miracles, healings, visions, and dreams? Not for the purpose of self-aggrandizement or personal kingdom building, but purely for the glory of God to be revealed in the lives of Muslims.

To conclude this section let me emphatically affirm the need for a careful, considered, mature risk-taking. Reading John F. Kennedy's *Profiles In Courage* makes one realize the cost of moving out into the unknown. It seems to me Christians should be in the front ranks of courageous innovation.

LIFESTYLE AND FINANCES

"At times it has been hard, not least because of the resistance and skepticism of our colleagues. One fellow missionary is praying that we shall see the light and move. Discouraging, isn't it?"

This recently received letter is from an extremely gracious and sensitive missionary wife. She and her husband had made the decision to "go national." They have adopted local Muslim garb and live in a very simple home completely surrounded by Muslims. Their neighbors accept them as one of their own, while at least some of their co-workers across town in the missionary compound direct devastating criticism at them.

A basic cause of this type of alienation is the clash between the older and the newer breed of missionary. I am constantly amazed at the number of missionary compounds still intact throughout Africa and Asia. There, for decades, dedicated servants of Christ have found a relatively safe haven of Western-style existence that many have felt essential to their emotional and physical well-being. In these clustered communities, houses can be built to Western specifications, dogs are kept as pets, and even pork can be enjoyed.

The new missionary arrives and, in protest, insists on renting a small facility among Muslims. Almost invariably, this leads to friction with a frequent result, being either the new recruit capitulates or he endures until his first furlough and then calls it quits. In this ongoing scenario the status quo is maintained.

I was saddened to observe how deeply the compound mentality can also affect nationals. In a small town heavily populated by Muslims, there is an excellent Christian hospital. A missionary leader decided to assist the national Christian staff in moving off the compound and into rented houses in various parts of the town. The purpose of this move was to diffuse the Christian witness out among Muslims. In a short time, the staff insisted that the mission acquire a large tract of land, and allow them to purchase plots and build homes. As I stood in the middle of the highway of that town, I saw the hospital on one side with all the nationals' homes in an adjacent plot, and on the other side of the road was a sea of Muslim homes. Western mentality had been exported, accepted, and applied. How sad!

But there are positive developments. In a paper delivered at SIM's Consultation of Muslim Evangelism held in January 1987 in Monrovia, Liberia, John Miller stated:

> The example of a missionary who contextualizes his lifestyle will encourage converts to retain what is good or neutral in their cultural background. This will help the convert church to appear less foreign, and may make it easier for other Muslims to give serious consideration to the Gospel. . . . My wife has worn the black veil while visiting Arabs. . . . Another lady missionary, in trying to make contacts to practice her Swahili, found that wearing the veil greatly facilitated her access to the people.

In the southern Philippines, I met two American Wycliffe ladies living in a simple wood frame house in the home of the Muslim vice-mayor of the town. These young women had been warmly accepted into the household as family members. Their privacy was restricted to a small partitioned room on one side of the house. In another area of the Philippines, a SEND International missionary has moved into a home with very poor Muslims, thus incarnating his faith in a lifestyle that would be impossible for most Westerners to even consider.

There does need to be balance. In one Islamic country a very sharp missionary couple with small children took up residence in a tiny bamboo house in a village setting. Some of the Muslim neighbors felt the Westerners were a bit odd. They could not understand why Americans would deprive themselves in such an extreme manner.

Contextualized lifestyle must be cognizant of local norms, expectations, and preferences. Adaptations will vary greatly according to these considerations as well as health and emotional concerns.

And now to finances. The temptation in Muslim work is to become involved in some type of assistance ministry which requires significant monetary input. Missionaries see this as an expression of physical and spiritual concern for Muslims. It also is said to soften the ground for the proclamation of the Gospel.

Muslims, on the other hand, frequently see ministries such as hospitals, schools, orphanages, self-help programs, and agricultural projects as blatant, immoral, unethical inducements toward proselytization. They feel violated when they are forced to sit through a Gospel indoctrination before receiving an out-patient checkup at the nearby Christian clinic. Whenever foreign money is introduced into the community by missionaries, Muslims feel intimidated. An example of this tension occurred recently in a strong Muslim area as reported in a Christian newsletter.

> The Gospel work was going on smoothly. Souls were being saved and converts publicly identified themselves with Isa Almasih in water baptism. The clamor of the believers was for a place of worship because no house in the village was large enough to accommodate a Christian service. So the committee (of a foreign relief and development agency) decided to provide them with a church building. When the set of posts were completed, the lay leader was summoned by the local political head, and there interrogated by him and one hundred Muslims. When he confessed he was a follower of Isa Almasih as taught in the Bible, he was requested to bring a translated Bible portion. Those who could read it said it is a good book while the illiterate ones condemned it and confiscated all the copies. At intervals, words such as these were heard, "Let's shoot him . . . Let's cut off his head." Other sympathizers suggested releasing him with a stern warning to stop the spread of this new religion. The posts then could be utilized for a school building.
> The lay leader had to evacuate with his family to another town.

At the point where external funds were utilized for the construction of a high profile building, Muslims began to direct severe opposition toward the small emerging group of converts. The result was the cessation of the work.

This whole area of finance and assistance requires a great deal of prayerful consultation. It is possible to destroy, almost overnight, the careful ministry of years. I particularly recall our anxiety in one situation where a sister mission decided to set up a large agricultural project adjacent to an area where we had labored intensively over the past five years. We envisioned the new believers in Christ immediately going to that large mission and requesting assistance and employment. This would have undercut all of our efforts for the converts to remain financially indigenous and in their pre-conversion employment.

As soon as we came to know of the mission's plans, we made a representation to their leadership to consider another location for their project. Unknown to us, they had already paid a non-refundable deposit on the property. Their mission committee met and decided to honor our request, and in so doing lost a considerable amount of money. I will always remember this magnanimous act with a deep sense of gratitude.

In a number of my writings I have sought to propose creative alternatives to our past *modus operandi* in assisting Muslims financially. I will not repeat those suggestions in this paper. However, I would urge all agencies and missions involved in Muslim ministry not just to take the easy road of distributing assistance whenever there is a need. We must carefully calculate and project the long-term effects of our help.

CRITIQUE OF ISLAM

Quite unintentionally, a book which included a few sentences critical of Muhammad was introduced on the shelf of a Christian bookstore inside a hospital compound in a rural setting. A Muslim secured the book, and roused the entire surrounding community to a feverish pitch of emotional opposition. Even though the hospital was the only adequate medical facility for many miles around, yet the Muslims made plans to burn it down. A military helicopter was sent to protect the compound. Only after a great deal of negotiation and conciliation were the Muslims pacified.

Due to the nature of Islamic belief and Muslim temperament, it behooves the Christian to exercise extreme caution in witness. Most of my missionary career I have felt I am sitting on top of the proverbial powder keg. One false move, and I'm in trouble.

So it is at this point that the Christian is in conflict. Does he go for presence, proclamation, or persuasion? How much can he affirm when constantly asked of his opinion of Muhammad? Are we obligated to point out the inadequacies of Islam, or is a positive witness for Christ sufficient?

It has been somewhat amusing, and at times disconcerting, to be accused by some as being too harsh, and by others as being overly sympathetic toward Islam. Perhaps I have been somewhat successful in finding a balance between the extremes. One person writes me as soon as he discovers something in my prayer letter which he considers derogatory toward Islam. Another friend said he was concerned that *Beyond the Mosque* was overly sympathetic to Muslims. But then he got to the last chapter, and felt I had achieved parity!

Kenneth Cragg is often criticized by Evangelicals for being soft on Muslims. Yet his recent book, *Muhammad and the Christian* was negatively reviewed in the Islamic journal, *Arabia*. The Muslim reviewer was particularly displeased that Cragg was distressed over Islam's propensity toward violence.

Arabia, incidentally, is a relatively fair and widely circulated magazine representing a broad range of Muslim viewpoints. They have twice printed my "letter to the editor" taking issue on (1) the reported conversion of Neil Armstrong to Islam, and (2) the twice-stated assertion that one million Muslims have converted to Christianity in Bangladesh in the past decade. These denials were thus able to effectively penetrate every Muslim country.

Not only is Islamic theology a sensitive issue, but the Palestinian Diaspora remains a question of burning significance.

Throughout the Islamic world, most Muslims give at least verbal assent to the "Palestinian cause." To be critical of the Muslim position is to insure a negative response to one's attempts toward communication and friendship.

My understanding of the Muslim stand has been enhanced by the careful reading of Colin Chapman's *Whose Promised Land*. This excellent book succeeds in highlighting the biblical, quranic, historical, and practical aspects of the ownership of the Holy Land. Both sides are given fair treatment.

In a more personal manner, I have been enriched by my friendship with Riad and Izdehar Kassis, Syrian Christians presently studying in the Alliance Biblical Seminary in Manila, Philippines. Riad is a strong Syrian nationalist who supports the Palestinian cause and yet a Christian who dearly loves our Lord. His insights on the terribly complex Jewish-Muslim-Christian controversy have been most helpful.

Some well-intentioned Christians have felt free to enter into well-publicized debates with Muslim orator *par excellence*, Ahmed Deedat. Deedat is an Indian now resident in South Africa who has made a thorough study of certain aspects of Christianity. He delights to forcefully and eloquently point out supposed contradictions in biblical passages. His tapes and books are in great demand throughout the Muslim world.

John Gilchrist has authored several good responses to Deedat's attacks. To me this is a much more valid rebuttal to Deedat than taking him on in a debate hall filled with several thousand emotionally charged Muslims.

It is important for Christians not to overly emphasize the view that Islam is a Satanic counterfeit and Muslims are demon-possessed. This type of thinking leads to aloofness for, after all, who wants to embrace a demon or greet Satan with a bestowal of peace? Without compromise, we can appreciate the good in Islam, affirm the theology which agrees with the Bible and unreservedly love the individual Muslim.

INCARNATED SPIRITUALITY

This subject has been much on my mind as I have been researching and writing a book on this theme for the past two years. *The Dove and the Crescent—Reflections on Christian-Muslim Spirituality* [published as *The Cross and the Crescent*] will be an interaction between the spiritual beliefs and practices of the world's two largest monotheistic religions. It is my conviction that the mutual ethos of Islam and Christianity lie in the realm of the spirit. In Muslim thought, Allah is as much a spirit as in biblical theology.

Do Muslims desire to be "spiritual?" Are they gripped with a sense of sin and guilt? Is God real to Muslims? What does a religion built on faith and works produce in the way of godly people? Why are there significant distinctions in religious practice between the Orthodox Saudi and the Sufi Bangladeshi? These are questions I am probing. I invite the input of others in this quest for a fuller understanding of Islamic spirituality.

My specific concern in this paper is to explore issues relating to the goal of Christians effectively and dynamically incarnating godly lives within a Muslim community. Followers of Islam must see a qualitative difference in the behavior of Christians before they will deem Christianity worthy of serious investigation. They must be convinced the rituals followed by Christians to assist them in knowing God are indeed superior to their own highly formalized and ritualized system of religious expression.

So, how are we doing? In seeking an answer to this question I prepared a questionnaire on spirituality and sent it to eight hundred missionaries. Three-hundred-ninety of them serving in 32 different countries with 37 mission societies responded. Forty-six percent of the respondents were under 40 years of age. Seventy-six percent of them were married. An equal number of men and women returned the form. The following are a few excerpts from the computerized findings of the survey.

- The greatest spiritual struggle in life is in the area of having adequate devotions.

- The *least liked* aspect of being a Christian is the ongoing battle with sin.

- Eighty-seven percent spend less than 30 minutes in prayer on a daily basis. Twenty-seven percent of them pray under 10 minutes a day.

- Eighty-eight percent read the Bible less than 30 minutes daily.

- Only 23 percent stated Bible reading is always a joy to them.

- Thirty-two percent are frequently tense; while 64 percent are tense on an infrequent basis.

- Seventy-one percent experience a problem with lust.

- On a monthly basis, 44 percent read one Christian book; while 21 percent read none.

- Alcoholic beverages are imbibed by 26 percent while 20 percent have taken tranquilizers since becoming missionaries.

In a recent conversation with a well-known mission executive I was amazed at the intensely personal questions he asks each of his missionaries during private interviews. I queried as to the response he found in regard to time spent in personal devotions. He replied that the norm was between 15 and 30 minutes. This was a deep concern to the mission leader, particularly in light of the fact that most of these missionaries are ministering among Muslims.

Are missionaries in Islamic countries facing more sexual temptation than those working among other people? A young lady missionary met a married Muslim in a public market and commenced a relationship that only ceased when she was sent back to her home country. An American church leader in a Muslim setting succumbed to the temptation of an affair with a maid in his home. This led to his divorce and subsequent marriage to the Asian lady who is many years his junior. Loneliness led to two missionary women engaging in a homosexual relationship resulting in a great deal of trauma, both for them and for their mission leadership.

Satan attacks in areas of vulnerability. Loneliness, sexual drive, depression, moodiness, and tiredness provide easy access to Satan's powerful influence on a man or woman of God. Mission societies must be more sensitive to the spiritual needs of their missionaries. This can be accomplished by prayer retreats, book reading facilities, inner-team counseling, tape lending libraries, adequate vacation breaks, as well as a constant emphasis (with accountability procedures) on personal devotions.

One is gripped by reading the biographies of Jonathan Goforth, Hudson Taylor, and Adoniram Judson. These men were permeated by spiritual priorities. Their lives were a penetrating reflection of their relationship with Christ. Perhaps our technological age has seduced us into thinking contextualized methodology is a more pressing area of emphasis than is our spiritual encounter with our Lord.

When the devout Muslim asks us if we pray five times a day, do we have an answer of spiritual equivalence? Are we somewhat embarrassed when requested to share details of our fasting belief and **practice**? Do we treat our Bible with the same respect the Muslim does his Quran? In sensitivity to the Muslim, can we assure him we do not eat pork or drink alcoholic beverages?

Perhaps we need to ponder deeply what it means to be "all things to all men" as we confront the issue of incarnated spirituality. Whatever else it means, the bottom line is that Muslims must experience Jesus when they experience us!

WHITHER CONTEXTUALIZATION?

I am encouraged. Never before have missionaries to Islam been so sensitized to cross-cultural issues. Yet, we have just begun. Mission leadership must constantly, with gentleness, prod older field missionaries into dreaming new dreams and seeing new visions. Team seminars should struggle with localized issues regarding the implementation of contextualization.

A few specifics of encouragement:

- Biola University, Columbia Graduate School, Fuller Theological Seminary, Trinity Evangelical Divinity School, and Wheaton Graduate School have all offered credit courses on a contextualized approach to Muslim evangelism.

- The following mission societies have had some direct involvement in contextualized ministry to Muslims: International Christian Fellowship, Frontiers, SIM International, International Missions Incorporated, Assemblies of God, Navigators, Overseas Missionary Fellowship, SEND

International, Youth With a Mission, Operation Mobilization, and Australian Baptist Missionary Society. Inclusion in this list does not indicate an official mission-wide policy nor even of total agreement within a specified field. It simply means individuals within these missions have made some definite move toward applied contextualization.

- The United Bible Societies have issued some very attractive and relevant biblical texts for vernacular Muslim audiences. The most outstanding of these is the Muslim Bengali New Testament done in cooperation with Dr. Viggo Olsen in Bangladesh. This very attractive production has become the number one bestseller of all books in Bangladesh.

- Other contextual literature has been marketed with local Muslim artwork and design. David Owen's Arabic harmony of the Gospels is an outstanding example of linguistic and stylistic adaptation to Muslim thought. This harmony is framed in rhythmic and poetic form similar to that which is found in the Quran.

- Frank Gray, overseas director of programming for Far Eastern Broadcasting Corporation, has engaged in creative thought in regard to contextual radio broadcasts. He, along with others, may soon spearhead a significant new wave in mass media effectiveness.

- Zwemer Institute of Muslim Studies, under Dr. Robert Douglas, continues on the cutting edge of promoting Muslim evangelism. Fuller Theological Seminary has now initiated MA and Ph.D. programs in Islamics under Dr. Dudley Woodberry. This is a much needed addition to formal training for Muslim ministry.

- And, most importantly, Muslims are actually accepting Christ and being baptized. Fellowships of believers are being formed in many Muslim countries.

Twenty-five years ago, my wife (of eight months) and I took an overnight steamer journey from Dhaka to Manikganj, Bangladesh. I entered that small village as bereft of knowledge of Islam as the town was of electricity, running water, and paved roads. Sixty-two months later I emerged with a somewhat sane mind and body, but basically as ignorant of Islam as I had been when I initially set foot in our tin "honeymoon shack." I had not seen one Muslim come to Christ.

How typical this testimony is of so many missionaries. We have gone forth with the Word of God and faith, but with a woefully inadequate understanding of Islam. The situation has improved. Missionaries are now a new breed of probers and innovators. But are they in it for the long haul? One of my great disappointments in life has been to see sharp, well-educated missionaries with great potential call it quits after only one or two terms. Effective Muslim evangelism simply cannot be accomplished within minimal time commitments.

These are just a few reflections on lessons "being learned." My final summary statement is that all of the hassles and heartaches of these many years have been eminently worthwhile in light of the end result of seeing the lineage of the firstborn of Abraham grafted into the Body of Christ. These special believers are, to me, much more precious than fine gold or precious jewels!

CHAPTER 6

CONTEXTUALIZED EVANGELISM AMONG MUSLIMS: A CRITIQUE

by Phil Parshall

Through the decades, tantalizing references to a more contextualized out-reach to Muslims have surfaced in Christian publications. The earliest evangelical reference to such an approach that I have been able to pinpoint is Baptist James Barton's seminal work printed in 1918 under the title, *The Christian Approach to Islam*. Regrettably, I have not been able to document more than postulate. It seems much easier to dream dreams than to slug it out in the trenches and do the tough work of activating theory.

A MODEL BIRTHED

Islamistan* is a third world nation of over 90 million Muslims. The country's very small Christian community has its roots in the conversion process from a

---

* A pseudonym for a majority Muslim country.

minority non-Muslim religion. Only a handful of Muslims have converted to Christ over the centuries in this country.

In 1975, our team of 27 International Christian Fellowship (now merged with SIM since 1989) missionaries launched what became known as a contextualized approach to Muslim evangelism. Hundreds of hours of intense research went into the formation of our *modus operandi*. The academic disciplines of anthropology and sociology were utilized as hand-maids, but the constant focus of the team was theological orthodoxy. Each new item of strategy was thoroughly scrutinized and prayed over in direct relationship to our mission's evangelical Statement of Faith. Our missionaries represented six countries and several denominations. We insisted that the Lord give us one mind before we implemented any point of experimental strategy. This was followed by a thorough review of the results. In this way, the team inched forward, carefully but boldly. It was all very much a collective effort.

Early on, we decided to de-westernize maximally the Gospel and seek to make the Word of God come alive within a Muslim context. Easier said than done! Some of the strategy we decided on are as follows:

a) Adoption of a simple lifestyle for our missionaries. National dress was worn.

b) Muslim dietary practices were followed.

c) At the time of Friday worship shoes were removed, believers sat on the floor, Bibles were placed on folding stands, Muslim-style religious vocabulary was utilized, chanting of God's Word was practiced, Muslim tunes were linked to Christian words, corporate prayer while kneeling was emphasized, and worshipers embraced in Eastern fashion.

d) Fasting was presented as an area of liberty, but it was continually impressed on the believers that legalistic, meritorious, and Pharisaical type-fasting is not biblical.

e) The convert's Muslim name was retained.

f) Baptism was performed by nationals and never by foreign missionaries.

g) Formation of house churches of converts was the goal from the outset. A large organizational structure was avoided.

h) Constant emphasis was given to let converts stay within their Muslim society. "Extraction evangelism" was to be avoided maximally.

i) Attractive evangelistic literature with Muslim art design was produced and distributed.

j) Minimum financial assistance was given to new believers.

The results of this effort have been exciting. Today, several thousand former Muslims are redeemed children of God, made anew through the blood of Christ. House churches have been formed throughout the country. Several missions are now participating in this approach. National converts are largely replacing missionaries as both primary evangelizers and group leaders. Literally, none of this had taken place prior to 1975.

There have been adjustments made to the above list of methodology whenever the situation has called for change. An illustration of this has been the necessity (placed upon them by the government) for the missionaries to pull back from more direct evangelism. They are now primarily engaged in discipleship, literature production, and government-mandated social ministries.

PROBLEM AREAS IN ISLAMISTAN

The results detailed above have not come without frustration, perplexity, pain, and loss. To illustrate some of the problems, let us look at various reactions to this contextualized approach.

a) Muslims who convert

They are enthusiastic about being able to work out their new faith in Christ within a milieu of familiarity. Continuity with the former makes for less trauma as the new is adopted into the very core of their being. They are agreeable and anxious to remain as salt and light among their own friends and relatives.

b) Muslims who do not convert

The "secular" or non-religious Muslim is not at all belligerent. Most authorities fit into this category. But they are forced to act if there is a serious complaint lodged by the devout or fanatical fringe of Islamic society.

There has been a moderate outcry by the very religious leaders of Islamistan. Articles of protest about the "deceitful methods of missionaries" have appeared in national newspapers. Serious pressure has been put on immigration officials to reduce the number of missionary visas. This has, to some extent, been successful. Converts have been investigated by police. This type of harassment has been expected. There is a general feeling that things may well get worse if the number of converts continues to escalate. But, given the Islamic theological perspective on *jihad*, Muslim response could have indeed been much worse.

c) Non-Muslim-background church

The traditional church in Islamistan, at first, reacted very strongly against the new contextualized outreach. Their own worship liturgy, linguistic usage, and Christian cultural distinctives were being threatened. What right did foreigners have to introduce a radical new form of Christian expression into the country? Also, such evangelistic efforts would redirect missionary staff and funding from being involved with the present church. Then, there was the question of whether a flood of Muslim converts would simply overwhelm their church and render them irrelevant. An objective hearing of these concerns show they had some real validity.

SIM sought to liaison with evangelical church leaders on these issues. Progress was slow. Alienation and hurt was the price paid for forward movement in those early days. Only as several missions began to see specific results did the traditional church begin to be open to serious dialogue. One denominational organization opted to bring Muslim converts into the church. This helped ease the tension considerably. Today, as never before in its history, the church is more accepting of and involved in Muslim evangelism. This does not mean that everyone is yet on the bandwagon!

d) Involved missionaries

There has been no disenchantment with the contextual model on the part of those actually doing the work. Conversely, there is a sense of awe at what the Lord is doing in what was once a rocky, barren, unproductive field of God's vineyard.

As would be expected, there have been "casualties" along the way. After visiting fifty countries, it would be my considered opinion that Islamistan is one of the most difficult places on planet earth for Westerners to live. Yet, there are many missionaries who are still plugging away who were present at the commencement of the new thrust in 1975.

e) Uninvolved missionaries

One of the exciting and reinforcing aspects of this ministry has been the absence of missionaries from any of the 25 different organizations taking a negative stance on the contextualized outreach. They have been tremendously supportive and gracious. This affirmation extends to that which was received from homeside administrators who would visit Islamistan, and warmly extend their positive encouragement to what was being done. If this latter group of men had not stood with us, especially in our early efforts, I doubt whether we could have pressed forward.

OTHER PROBLEM AREAS IN AND BEYOND ISLAMISTAN

To a greater or lesser extent, many of the above hassles have been encountered wherever contextualized Muslim evangelism has been attempted. In this section I will address other problems people have faced when they have implemented this approach. It is best to be discreet and avoid names and specific geographical designations.

The "panacea proclamation" has greatly annoyed senior missionaries in various countries. These dedicated long-term ministers of the Gospel in harsh lands suddenly find a young, brash, and very inexperienced missionary arriving on the field bringing with him the latest article or book on contextualization. Very quickly, the overt or implied criticism begins. The old way is passe'. Little results can be shown for decades of labor. Let us launch out into a proven model and make things happen . . . quickly. CONFLICT!

Or perhaps it is a gentle missionary who is committed to not rocking the boat. He simply wants to move off the large mission compound and live in a Muslim context totally immersed in Islamic culture and lifestyle. The senior folk are quick to point out things have never been done in this way—no, not in decades of missionary work. The new recruit quietly acquiesces, puts in his time in the compound, and then resigns during his first furlough. A person of great potential is lost to God's work.

In the above scenario the more common reality is the motivated missionary who becomes absorbed into the norm. His vision and cutting-edge desire is muted as he is integrated into a tightly knit system of perpetuating that which has always been.

I continue to be concerned about financial and employment assistance given to inquirers or converts. Muslims have every right to protest what they regard as "inducements" given to people of their community. They declare so-called Muslim conversions to Christ to be no more than selling one's soul for material gain. Much more deliberation needs to be directed toward this problem. Integrity is an absolute necessity in our ministry to Muslims.

In a very few cases, contextualization has been blamed for immorality. The close proximity of a missionary couple to a Muslim family has supposedly been the cause of the wife committing adultery with a married Muslim man. Fortunately, this type of occurrence has been extremely rare, and root causes can be identified far removed from that of living a contextual lifestyle.

Honest and sincere theological disagreements occur in regard to contextualization. These are understandable and should be addressed and worked through with a maximum spirit of graciousness and humility. Some of the more common differences of opinion relate to:

a) Linguistic usage

How can Allah and Isa be used as names for God and Jesus? Sitting in a home in Casablanca, Morocco, I had a long discussion with a devoted missionary who took great exception to my usage of Isa for Jesus. However, he was happy for Allah to be used for God in his Arabic Bible. This seemed a contradiction to me.

b) Practices

Recently, in a meeting, a missionary gave a praise item for how his keeping of the Ramadan Fast opened up new friendships for him among his Muslim neighbors. Following this, a fellow missionary requested prayer that the Lord would overrule a Satanic spirit that could be sensed within the system of Islamic fasting!

In an early writing, I proposed that someone could experiment with an alternative for water baptism along the lines of a public profession of faith akin to an initiatory rite. This suggestion created waves of protest. Water baptism is biblical, historical, and universal. I agree. SIM always has and continues to teach and practice water baptism.

The idea of Friday worship replacing Sunday church has been considered heretical by a small minority. Biblically, Sunday is a precedent, not a command.

Formation of homogeneous Muslim convert churches has been a problem to some. The point has been missed that all are welcome. Traditional Christians, Hindus, Animists, and Westerners—all can feel free to attend a contextualized service. But the flavor and style of the worship is geared toward those who are Muslim in background.

c) Syncretism

This is definitely a danger. Have the converts really understood the Gospel? Are they making a clear break with Islamic beliefs that contradict biblical truth? Will second generation believers become religious half-breeds? What about very independent-minded convert leaders who insist on keeping too close to Islam that the result is biblical compromise?

These are serious issues that demand maximum attention by giving clear and repetitive Bible teaching to all converts and their children. But, to be fair, I think the dangers are no more compelling than the syncretism I see Christians in the West making with the world, the flesh, and the devil.

There is a simple way to neutralize all these stated problems. We can choose to be safe and avoid all experimentation. But as I study and meditate on the life of Paul, I cannot help but feel, if he were alive today, he would be right with us on the cutting edge of innovation, seeking to apply carefully contextual principles to the evangelization of Muslims.

TRANSFER POTENTIAL

One of the false ideas concerning contextualization is that it is a pre-packaged methodology ready to be applied in total in any given Muslim context. Nothing could be further from the truth. Let me illustrate from my own experience.

It was a privilege to be a missionary in Islamistan for twenty years. I was part of the team who formulated and implemented contextual strategy in that land. Recently, I visited throughout Islamistan and was again overwhelmed at what the Lord has done.

But, for the past eight years, I have been a missionary working among Muslims in another third-world country. It has been my earnest desire to see a repetition of the great things experienced in Islamistan. However, laboring for these years with a team of missionaries and nationals has produced minimal fruit. We have found that we face a very different set of circumstances and challenges. Instead of working with a more mystical-type Islam, we are rather brought into confrontation with a strong animistic-based set of beliefs and practices. Islam is but a top layer which, nevertheless, creates a sociological bond of almost impregnable unity among adherents.

Missionaries here continue in the process of investigating what specific keys to this "context" will open the door of resistance and allow the Gospel to flow freely. The "power" gifts of exorcism and healing seem to be important in meeting areas of felt need. Muslims want to see a demonstration of the power of Truth rather than a cognitive definition of Truth. Many evangelical missionaries feel more comfortable with the latter rather than the former.

Contextualization is open-ended. It is not a neat and well-defined conceptual framework just waiting to be successfully applied in all situations. At times, contextualization appears to be fluid, evasive, and ill-defined. But I would contend it is imperative that we struggle with these concepts if we are to maximize success in building a truly indigenous church.

Islam has been offended by nominal Christians down through the centuries. The Crusades are a vivid historical reality to many Muslims. Millions of Sons of Ishmael are alive today who actually experienced the latter years of Western colonial domination in their beloved homeland. Current political and religious strains between Islam and Christianity make it essential for our witness to be both sensitive and relevant.

Our obligation is to study contextual models, decide what may be applicable and then carefully experiment and evaluate. Along with this, research should be commenced toward discovery of entirely new innovations which may be appropriate to our situation.

Our final goal is to see the Word of God come alive in its unhindered power and authority. Contextual principles, I am convinced, can assist us in this process.

DANGER!
NEW DIRECTIONS IN
CONTEXTUALIZATION*

by Phil Parshall

Recently, I was speaking to a group of young people who are highly-motivated about Muslim evangelism. They excitedly told me of a missionary who had shared a "new" modus operandi for winning the Sons of Ishmael to Christ. This strategy centers around the Christian evangelist declaring himself to be a Muslim. He then participates in the *salat* or official Islamic prayers within the mosque. The missionary illustrated the concept by mentioning two Asian Christians who have recently undergone legal procedures to officially become Muslims. This was done to become a Muslim to Muslims in order to win Muslims to Christ.

Actually taking on a Muslim identity and praying in the mosque is not a new strategy. But legally becoming a Muslim definitely moves the missionary

---

* Reprinted by permission of *Evangelical Missions Quarterly* (Box 794, Wheaton, IL 60189 USA)

enterprise into uncharted territory. I address this issue with a sense of deep concern.

C1 to C6

John Travis,* a long-term missionary among Muslims in Asia, has put us in his debt by formulating a simple categorization for stages of contextualization within Islamic outreach. He defines his six C's as "Cross-Cultural Church-Planting Spectrums." (See page 97.)

Some years ago, a well-known professor of Islam alluded to my belief that Muslim converts could and should remain in the mosque following conversion. Quickly, I corrected him, stating that I have never held that position, either in my speaking or writing. My book *Beyond the Mosque* deals extensively with the issue of why, when, and how a convert must dissociate himself or herself from the mosque (though not from the Muslim community per se).

I do, however, make room for a transitional period wherein the new believer, while maturing in his adopted faith, slowly pulls back from mosque attendance. Too sudden a departure may spark intense antagonism and subsequent alienation. See 2 Kings 5 for an interesting insight on how Elisha responded to the new convert, Naaman, who brought up the subject of his ongoing presence in the heathen temple of Rimmon.

The diagram below helps place in linear perspective the C1 to C5 categories. I submit that C1 starts at low contextualization and works up incrementally to C4 at the high end. All within this sector is legitimate, provided it is constantly cross-referenced and subordinated to biblical truth.

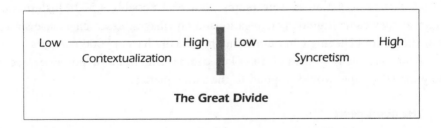

| Low ——————— High | Low ——————— High |
| Contextualization | Syncretism |

The Great Divide

---

* A pseudonym

C5 can be placed anywhere along the syncretism spectrum, depending on how each issue is presented and understood by the Muslim community. Personally, I can only put conversion (or reconversion) to official Islam as high syncretism—regardless of motivation.

When, in 1975, our team of missionaries commenced a C4 strategy in an Asian Muslim country, we faced considerable opposition. One long-term Christian worker in an Islamic land told me basically, "You are on a dangerous slide. Next you will be denying the cross." Well, 23 years later, we are still at C4 and still preaching the cross. And the Lord has greatly honored our efforts in that country.

But now I am the one to protest the "slide," not by our team, but by others who are ministering in various parts of the Muslim world. This slide is incremental and can be insidiously deceptive, especially when led by people of highest motivation. Now, it seems to me, we need to bring these issues before our theologians, missiologists, and administrators. Let us critique them before we suddenly find that we have arrived at a point which is indisputably sub-Christian.

A CASE STUDY

We do have help. In a very limited and remote geographical area in Asia, a C5 experiment has been ongoing since 1983. This ministry provides us with a pretty solid baseline for evaluation, even though it has experienced significant personnel changes over the years.

Twenty-five national couples went to Islampur* to do development ministry. One of the team's goals was to see a C5 type of outreach evolve. In 1995, 72 key people of influence within this movement were interviewed. Researchers suggested that these nationals were representative of possibly 4,500 Muslim converts, as they came from 68 congregations in 66 villages. Researchers also stated that the entire believing community might actually have 45,000 converts.

Below are the responses of these key people. One has to hypothesize about how the lay people would respond to the same queries.

The good news
- 76 percent meet once a week in Christian worship.
- 16 percent meet more than once a week in worship.
- 66 percent read or listen to the Gospels daily.

---

* A pseudonym

- 21 percent read or listen to the Gospels once a week.
- None do so to the Quran. (It is in Arabic and not understood.)
- 55 percent say God is Father, Son, and Holy Spirit.
- 97 percent say Jesus is the only Savior.
- 93 percent say, "Allah loves and forgives because Jesus gave His life for me."
- 100 percent say, "People can be saved from evil spirits by faith in Jesus."
- 100 percent pray to Jesus for forgiveness of sin.
- 97 percent say they are not saved because of Muhammad's prayers.
- 100 percent find peace and closeness to God when reading the New Testament.

The downside
- 50 percent go to the traditional mosque on Friday.
- 31 percent go to the mosque more than once a day. They do standard Arabic prayers which affirm Muhammad as a prophet of God.
- 96 percent say there are four heavenly books, i.e., the Torah (Law), Zabur (Prophets), Injil (Gospels), and Quran.
- 66 percent say the Quran is the greatest of the four books.
- 45 percent do not affirm God as Father, Son, and Holy Spirit.
- 45 percent find peace or closeness to Allah when listening to the reading of the Quran.

What do we have here?

Is this contextualization or syncretism? A few points to emphasize. These are leaders; the work has been ongoing for 15 years; the believers have had access to the New Testament; there have been short-term Bible schools for leadership; and lastly, mosque attendance has been encouraged by the "outside" Bible teachers.

Is this a model to follow or avoid? Certainly, there is an openness and potential here that is expansive and exciting. But whereas a C5 advocate is happy to keep it all within an Islamic religious environment, I am not.

THE MOSQUE

The mosque is pregnant with Islamic theology. There Muhammad is affirmed as a prophet of God and the divinity of Christ is consistently denied. Uniquely

Muslim prayers (*salat*) are ritually performed as in no other religion. These prayers are as sacramental to Muslims as is the partaking of the Lord's supper for Christians. How would we feel if a Muslim attended (or even joined) our evangelical church and partook of communion—all with a view to becoming an "insider"? This accomplished, he then begins to promote Islam and actually win our parishioners over to his religious persuasion.

Even C4 is open to a Muslim charge of deceit. But I disagree and see it as a proper level of indigenization. We have not become a "fifth column" within the mosque, seeking to undermine its precepts and practices. C5 to me seems to do just that and open us to the charge of unethical and sub-Christian activity.

In my former country of ministry, our team had an agreement that none of us would go into a mosque, and engage in the Islamic prayers. One of our group, however, wanted to "experiment" secretly with saying the *salat*. One Friday, he traveled to a remote village and became friendly with the Muslims there. Harry* expressed his desire to learn how to perform the rituals and forms of the prayers.

The Muslim leaders were quite excited to see that a foreigner wanted to learn about Islam. They gave Harry the necessary instruction. At 1 p.m. our missionary was found in the front row of the mosque going through all the bowing and prostrations of the *salat*. No matter that he was silently praying to Jesus. No one knew.

After worship, the Muslim villagers all came up to Harry and congratulated him on becoming a Muslim. Embarrassed, Harry explained that he was a follower of *Isa* (Jesus) and that he just wanted to learn about Islam. Immediately, upon hearing these words, the crowd became very angry.

Harry was accused of destroying the sanctity of the mosque. Someone yelled that he should be killed. A riot was about to break out.

The local *imam* sought to pacify the crowd by admitting that he had mistakenly taught the foreigner how to do the prayers. He asked for forgiveness from his fellow Muslims. It was then decided that Harry should leave that village immediately and never return.

Another experience relates to Bob,* a very intelligent, productive, and spiritually oriented missionary to Muslims. We met together at a conference and exchanged letters and at least one cassette tape over several years. My great concern was that he openly and dogmatically affirmed Muhammad as a prophet of God. To me, Bob had crossed the line into syncretism. Perhaps his motives were

---

* A pseudonym

pure, but this progression of identification with Muslims had gone much too far. Today, Bob is out of the ministry and is divorced from his wife.

Guidelines

In 1979, I wrote the following guidelines to help us avoid syncretism while engaged in Muslim evangelism. Nineteen years later, I reaffirm (and reemphasize) these principles:

1   We must be acquainted with biblical teaching on the subject of syncretism. New Testament passages on the uniqueness of Christ should be carefully observed.

2   Islam as a religion and culture must be studied in depth.

3   An open approach is desired. Careful experimentation in contextualization need not lead to syncretism as long as one is aware of all the dangers.

4   Contextualization needs constant monitoring and analysis. What are the people really thinking? What does the contextualized communication convey? What do specific forms trigger in the mind of the new convert? Is there progress in the grasp of biblical truth? Are the people becoming demonstrably more spiritual?

5   Cross-cultural communicators must beware of presenting a gospel which has been syncretized with Western culture. The accretions to Christianity that have built up over the centuries as a result of the West's being the hub of Christianity should be avoided as far as possible.

Conclusion

No, I am not maligning the motivation of godly missionaries who are practicing and promoting C5 as an appropriate strategy to win Muslims to Christ. Several of these Christian workers are my friends. They long to see a breakthrough in Muslim evangelism. Their personal integrity is unquestioned.

But, yes, I am apprehensive. Where does all this lead us? In that earlier mentioned conference, one young Muslim convert came up to me and said he had followed the lead of the missionary speaker. He went into the local mosque and told the imam that he was a Muslim and wanted to learn more of Islam. His secret goal was to build a relationship with the imam. I asked Abdul* how he felt about what he did. With a look of pain and sadness, he replied that he felt very badly about it and would not do it again.

Before C5 people broadly propagate this strategy to young, impressionable minds who are excited about the "new" and "untried," I urge them to consider more fully both the Islamic charge of deception as well as the long-term consequences of their actions. I am convinced that C5 missionaries are on very shaky theological and missiological grounds.

Let's bring the subject out in the open and dialog together.

---

* A pseudonym

THE C1 TO C6 SPECTRUM*

A practical tool for defining six types of 'Christ-centered communities' ('C') found in the Muslim context

*by John Travis***

The C1-C6 Spectrum compares and contrasts types of "Christ-centered communities" (groups of believers in Christ) found in the Muslim world. The six types in the spectrum are differentiated by language, culture, worship forms, degree of freedom to worship with others, and religious identity. All worship Jesus as Lord, and core elements of the gospel are the same from group to group. The spectrum attempts to address the enormous diversity which exists throughout the Muslim world in terms of ethnicity, history, traditions, language, culture, and in some cases theology.

This diversity means that myriad approaches are needed to share the Gospel successfully, and plant Christ-centered communities among the world's one billion followers of Islam. The purpose of the spectrum is to assist church planters and Muslim background believers to ascertain which type of Christ-centered communities may draw the most people from the target group to Christ and best fit in a given context. All of these six types are presently found in various parts of the Muslim world.

* Reprinted by permission of *Evangelical Missions Quarterly* (Box 794, Wheaton, IL, 60189, USA)
** A pseudonym

C1: Traditional church using outsider* language

May be Orthodox, Catholic, or Protestant. Some predate Islam. Thousands of C1 churches are found in Muslim lands today. Many reflect Western culture. A huge cultural chasm often exists between the church and the surrounding Muslim community. Some Muslim background believers may be found in C1 churches. C1 believers call themselves "Christians."

C2: Traditional church using insider** language

Essentially, the same as C1 except for language. Though insider language is used, religious vocabulary is probably non-Islamic (distinctively "Christian"). The cultural gap between Muslims and C2 is still large. Often more Muslim-background believers are found in C2 than C1. The majority of churches located in the Muslim world today are C1 or C2. C2 believers call themselves "Christians."

C3: Contextualized Christ-centered communities using insider language and religiously neutral insider cultural forms

Religiously neutral forms may include folk music, ethnic dress, artwork, etc. Islamic elements (where present) are "filtered out" so as to use purely "cultural" forms. The aim is to reduce foreignness of the Gospel and the church by contextualizing to biblically permissible cultural forms. May meet in a church building or more religiously neutral location. C3 congregations consist of a majority of Muslim background believers. C3 believers call themselves "Christians."

---

* "Outsider" pertains to the local non-Muslim population
** "Insider" pertains to the local Muslim population

C4: Contextualized Christ-centered communities using insider language and biblically permissible cultural and Islamic forms

Similar to C3, however, biblically permissible Islamic forms and practices are also utilized (*e.g.*, praying with raised hands, keeping the fast, avoiding pork, alcohol, and dogs as pets, using Islamic terms, garb, etc.) C1 and C2 forms avoided. Meetings not held in church buildings. C4 communities comprised almost entirely of Muslim background believers. C4 believers, though highly contextualized, are usually not seen as Muslim by the Muslim community. C4 believers identify themselves as "followers of Isa the Messiah" (or something similar).

C5: Christ-centered communities of "Messianic Muslims" who have accepted Jesus as Lord and Savior

C5 believers remain legally and socially within the community of Islam. Somewhat similar to the Messianic Jewish movement. Aspects of Islamic theology which are incompatible with the Bible are rejected, or reinterpreted, if possible. Participation in corporate Islamic worship varies from person to person and group to group. C5 believers meet regularly with other C5 believers and share their faith with unsaved Muslims. Unsaved Muslims may see C5 believers as theologically deviant and may eventually expel them from the community of Islam. Where entire villages accept Christ, C5 may result in "Messianic mosques." C5 believers are viewed as Muslims by the Muslim community and refer to themselves as Muslims who follow Isa the Messiah.

C6: Small Christ-centered communities of secret underground believers

These are similar to persecuted believers suffering under totalitarian regimes. Due to fear, isolation, or threat of extreme governmental/community legal action or retaliation (including capital punishment), C6 believers worship Christ secretly (individually or perhaps infrequently in small clusters). Many come to Christ through dreams, visions, miracles, radio broadcasts, tracts, Christian witness while abroad, or reading the Bible on their own initiative. C6 (as opposed to C5) believers are usually silent about their faith. C6 is not ideal; God desires his people to witness and have regular fellowship (Hebrews 10:25). Nonetheless, C6 believers are part of our family in Christ. Though God may call some to a life of suffering, imprisonment, or martyrdom, he may be pleased to have some worship him in secret, at least for a time. C6 believers are perceived as Muslims by the Muslim community and identify themselves as Muslims.

TWO RESPONSES

1

MUST ALL MUSLIMS LEAVE "ISLAM" TO FOLLOW JESUS?*

by John Travis**

For the past decade, my family and I have lived in a close-knit Muslim neighborhood in Asia. My daughter, who loves our neighbors dearly, asked one day, "Daddy, can a Muslim go to heaven?" I responded with an Acts 15:11-type "yes": If a Muslim has accepted *Isa* (Jesus), the Messiah as Savior and Lord, he or she is saved, just as we are. We affirmed that people are saved by faith in Christ, not by religious affiliation. Muslim followers of Christ (*i.e.*, "C5 believers") are our brothers and sisters in the Lord, even though they do not "change religions."

Can a Muslim truly accept Jesus as Savior and Lord, thereby reject-ing some elements of normal Islamic theology, and yet (for the sake of the lost) remain in his or her family and religious community? Due to the extreme importance Islam places on community, its nearly universal disdain for those who have become "traitors" by joining Christianity,

---

* Reprinted by permission of *Evangelical Missions Quarterly* (Box 794, Wheaton, IL 60189, USA)
** A pseudonym

and our desire to see precious Muslims come to Christ, finding the answer to this question is essential. I agree with Dr. Parshall; it is time for missiologists, theologians, and others, especially those who work face-to-face with Muslims, to seriously seek God's will over this C5 issue.

The Islampur case study

The "good news" is certainly very good! These statistics indicate that there may be as many as 45,000 C5 believers where, of those interviewed, 97 percent believe Jesus is the only Savior, 100 percent pray to Jesus to forgive sins, 76 percent attend Christ-centered worship once a week, 66 percent read or listen to the Gospels daily, and a full 55 percent understand the Trinity well enough to affirm God is Father, Son, and Holy Spirit! How many American pastors would be delighted to find these same statistics true of their own congregations?

Looking at the "downside" statistics, we should not be surprised that 45 percent feel close to God when hearing the Quran read. Since they don't understand Arabic, it must be the familiar melodious chanting that touches their hearts. (Some C4 and C5 believers with whom I work sing a beautiful worship song which sounds a great deal like Muslim chanting.) It is also not surprising that 50 percent continue to worship in the mosque in addition to attending weekly C5 gatherings. This practice is reminiscent of the early Jewish followers of Christ meeting both in the temple and in homes (with the old community and the new). One village C5 group I know prays at the mosque at noon on Friday, then meets afterwards in a home for Bible study and prayer led by "Achmad" (a pseudonym), a C4 pastor and former Muslim teacher.

In this case these believers actually find mosque gatherings shallow and lifeless, and, for a time, stopped attending. Their absence greatly threatened the mosque leader and he tried to stamp out their Friday afternoon meetings. Achmad suggested they go back to the mosque, meaningless as it was for them. The *imam's* face was saved, and the new believers have continued to meet for over a year. New Muslim inquirers (even two Islamic teachers) have attended.

Concerning the high regard for the Quran among Islampur believers, an apologetic response concerning the Quran must be developed whereby the truth in it can be affirmed (especially for purposes of a bridge for witness), yet it is not put on equal (or superior!) status to the Injil. Fortunately, until such an apologetic is developed, the Islampur believers are regularly reading the Injil rather than the Quran. Returning to the case of my friend Achmad, he holds evening "Holy Book reading sessions" in his home. He often opens by reading a Quranic passage in a respectful manner, then proceeds to the heart of the evening reading from the Torah, Zabur, and Injil (the Bible).

Unsaved Muslims are more likely to attend Bible reading sessions when they also contain some Arabic Quranic reading. Achmad is careful to read Quranic passages which do not conflict with the Bible.

Three final points concerning the Islampur study:

1 These C5 Christ-centered communities are less than 15 years old and consist entirely of new believers from a highly resistant people group. They are very much in process, and their struggles are not unlike what many first century congregations faced. We must hope that the same Holy Spirit whom Paul so relied upon to guide and purify those first groups of believers is active as well in these new Islampur groups.

2 To attain a more accurate perspective, we need to assess the quality of the new believers' lives in Christ and not just their theology. Is the fruit of the Spirit evident and do they now show a deeper love for others? Scripture is clear that by qualities such as these we will recognize true followers of Christ (Matthew 7:20; John 13:35).

3 Were it not for the C5 approach used in this church-planting ministry, would there be these many thousands of new believers to analyze in the first place?

C5 Missionaries (Christians becoming Muslims to reach Muslims)

This perhaps is Dr. Parshall's greatest concern, and overall I agree. Christians becoming Muslims to reach Muslims (*i.e.*, C5 missionaries) is a step beyond simply urging new believers to remain in the religious community of their birth (*i.e.*, C5 believers) for the sake of their unsaved family and friends. In our current situation I have counseled my own Christian-background and workers, especially the expatriates, to take on a C4 expression of faith, and not enter Islam to reach Muslims. Yet I could imagine that in some instances God may call uniquely gifted, well-prepared individuals, whose ministries are firmly backed by prayer, to C5 outreach and religious identity. These C5 missionaries would be Muslims in the literal Arabic sense of the word (*i.e.*, "one submitted to God") and their theology would, of course, differ from standard Muslim theology at a number of key points. They would have to be ready for persecution, and it would be best if these believers were of Muslim background.

If over time they made their beliefs clear, and the surrounding Muslim community chose to allow them to stay, should we not praise God for the opportunity they have to share the Good News in a place few would dare to tread? It would appear that neither "Abdul," the Muslim convert, nor "Harry," the Western missionary, were called and prepared for this kind of work.

Regarding how Muslims would "feel" about such an approach, I think the question is a bit irrelevant. The majority of Muslims that I have talked to object to any activity they perceive as an attempt to attract Muslims to Christianity. However, the C5 approach, which communicates the message of salvation in Christ without the intent to persuade Muslims to "change their religion," might in fact be the one most appreciated by Muslims. By separating the Gospel from the myriad of legal, social, and cultural issues implied in changing religious camps, a more straightforward, less encumbered message can be shared and (we hope) embraced. On the question of how Christians would feel if Muslims entered a church with the purpose of winning converts to Islam, I personally would not be fearful. Indeed, for a variety of reasons, non-Christians often grace the doors of churches, and many in the process come to Christ!

Reinterpreting Muhammad and the Quran

Can individuals be a part of the community in Islam, and not affirm standard Muslim theology? Yes, so long as they remain silent about their unorthodox beliefs. Indeed, there are millions of "cultural Muslims" who have divergent beliefs or know virtually nothing about Islam, yet who, because of birth and the fact they have not formally left the fold, are seen as a part of the community of Islam. However, the goal of C5 believers (unlike C6 believers) is not to remain silent about their faith, but rather to be a witness for Christ. As they share, eventually the issue of the prophethood of Muhammad, the inerrancy of the Quran will arise. A follower of Jesus cannot affirm all that is commonly taught about the Quran and Muhammad.

Certain aspects of the role of Muhammad and the Quran must be reinterpreted. This will perhaps be the most challenging task of C5; not to do so will in time cause these believers to move toward C4 (contextualized, not yet Muslim) or C6 (underground/silent believers). Reinterpretation goes far beyond the scope of this brief article, and would require the input of Muslim leaders who have put their faith in Christ. A tremendous starting point toward reinterpretation is found in Accad's excellent book, *Building Bridges* (1997). As an Arab scholar and pastor, he suggests ways that Muhammad, the Quran, and Quranic verses which seem to deny the crucifixion can be reinterpreted (pp. 34-46; 138-141). He cites, as well, examples of Muslims who have successfully remained in the community of Islam after accepting Christ, some referring to themselves as "Muslims who are truly surrendered to God through the sacrifice of Messiah Isa" (p. 35).

Guidelines for avoiding syncretism in a C5 movement

The idea of Muslim followers of Jesus or messianic mosques has been suggested by a number of key missiologists (see Winter, 1981; Kraft,

1979; Conn, 1979; Woodberry, 1989). We do need guidelines, however, so that a C5 expression of faith does not slip into a harmful syncretism. Those working with new believers should emphasize at least the following in the discipleship process:

1   Jesus is Lord and Savior; there is no salvation outside of Him.

2   New believers are baptized, meet regularly with other believers (this may need to be done with great discretion), and take communion.

3   New believers study the Injil (and Torah plus Zabur if available).

4   New believers renounce and are delivered from occultism and harmful folk Islamic practices (i.e., shamanism, prayers to saints, use of charms, curses, incantations, etc.)

5   Muslim practices and traditions (e.g., fasting, alms, circumcision, attending the mosque, wearing the head covering, refraining from pork and alcohol, etc.) are done as expressions of love for God and/or respect for neighbors, rather than as acts necessary to receive forgiveness of sins.

6   The Quran, Muhammad, and traditional Muslim theology are examined, judged, and reinterpreted (where necessary) in light of biblical truth. Biblically acceptable Muslim beliefs and practices are maintained, others are modified, some must be rejected.

7   New believers show evidence of the new birth and growth in grace (e.g., the fruit of the Spirit, increased love, etc.) and a desire to reach the lost (e.g., verbal witness and intercession).

We must bear in mind that C5 believers, at some point, may be expelled from the community of Islam. C5 may only be transitional, as

Dr. Parshall suggests. Yet, would it not be much better for Muslim followers of Jesus to share the Good News over months or years with fellow Muslims who may eventually expel them, than for these new believers to leave their families and community by their own choice, being seen as traitors by those whom they love?

Conclusion

If perhaps the single greatest hindrance to seeing Muslims come to faith in Christ is not a theologial one (*i.e.*, accepting Jesus as Lord) but rather one of culture and religious identity (*i.e.*, having to leave the community of Islam), it seems that for the sake of God's kingdom much of our missiological energy should be devoted to seeking a path whereby Muslims can remain Muslims, yet live as true followers of the Lord Jesus. The issues involved in such an approach are thorny and complex and require consideration from a number of different disciplines (*e.g.*, church history, Islamics, theology, missiology). A consultation comprised primarily of people involved in sharing Christ with Muslims, which would grapple with the implications of C5, would be beneficial. Any type of ministry undertaken in the Muslim world involves great risk. But for the sake of millions of souls bound for a Christless eternity, and for the glory of God, the risks, efforts, and tensions are worth the price.

2

CONTEXT IS CRITICAL IN "ISLAMPUR" CASE*

by Dean S. Gilliland

I have the report of the "Islampur" project before me. My role was research director. The project was not limited to "Islampur." It was designed to compare and test various models for evangelizing Muslims. The particular report Phil Parshall refers to did not endorse or condemn, but provided three cases for whatever light they might shed on approaches to Muslims in various communities. As far as I know, the use and distribution of the results were left to the discretion of the foundation that provided funds for the project.

Apart from the justified concerns raised in the article, I sense a tone of defensiveness in some of the things Parshall has written.

Since the late '70s Phil has led the way with his books on sensitive thinking about contextualization among Muslims. His writing obviously has raised controversy for some. He has helped us see how cultural innovations can become tools for evangelism among Muslims. Now, in response to a very carefully planned piece of research, he seems to be saying, "Listen, please. I meant this, but not that!" He recalls how an older Christian worker had warned him about being on a "dangerous slide." Now, Parshall feels he is the one who must protest the "slide." If "Islampur" believers have taken the idea of messianic Islam to an unacceptable extreme, Phil wants us to know that neither he nor his team

---

* Reprinted by permission of *Evangelical Missions Quarterly* (Box 794, Wheaton, IL, 60189, USA)

took them there. As one intimately involved in the research project, I would say that, whatever the outcome, perhaps 10 or 20 years from now, it is not Phil's burden to worry about guilt or blame. We don't know everything at this point. Conversion in any mission situation is a process. In this particular case, one of the factors of the process could not be more critical.

Since the article has revealed the "Islampur" case, more needs to be said in fairness to the research. The researcher himself concluded the data presentation with careful words: "Whether in fact a person can be an authentic follower of Jesus, and still remain within the fold of Islam raises strong opinions and emotions on many sides. . . . It is, of course, possible that those who endorse radical contextualization of the Gospel within Islam are wrong." He also wrote, however, that after looking at the entire report, "It does seem that there has been a real work of God among the (name withheld) Muslims."

Little is known from Phil's article about the internal problems caused by leaders who took these followers of Jesus in two directions, causing, finally, a near abandonment of the teaching that should have been continuing. In the background are many painful factors which added to the burden of these simple people who say they believe in and follow Jesus. At one point, the names of key believers in the movement were turned over to the government. Despite internal and external problems, these clusters of followers were able to testify honestly and without coaching, to what Jesus, the Bible, the power of the Gospel, and other Jesus people mean to them.

I must emphasize the critical issue of the context. While the context and contextualization are what this case is all about, too often conclusions about what is right or wrong are generalized without attention to a particular case. A practical and fitting approach in one place will probably not be appropriate somewhere else. For example, the case behind Parshall's example does not fit the research's second case, which was done in Nigeria.

Some 45 million Muslims live in Nigeria. The big difference with "Islampur" is that Nigeria also has 45-50 million people who call themselves Christians. There is no way that Muslims who converted to Jesus

Christ in Nigeria would ever call themselves Muslims.

In fact, it was a rather well-known esoteric model for evangelizing Muslims in northern Nigeria that attracted the research in the first place. The ministry was not integrated with the churches and was supposedly producing believers who were suffering intensely for their faith. Evangelical churches had come to disown the movement because of the secrecy and clandestine style of the leaders. The movement has now collapsed, even though it had received a lot of private publicity and support outside of Nigeria.

Therefore, the Nigeria situation is totally different from the one in "Islampur." In Nigeria the churches are almost apostolic in their boldness before and among Muslims. Form contextualization (except in the far north) is seen as a kind of imitation of the Muslim way and therefore is looked upon as neither necessary nor desirable. Christian-Muslim confrontation saturates the life of the Nigerian people—socially, politically, and religiously.

The Parshall article discusses the appropriateness of an approach in a particular Asian context. The size and strength comparison between Muslims and Christians in "Islampur" is like the elephant to the fly, as it were.

Obviously, this little flock that has turned to follow Jesus—with members who pray to Jesus for forgiveness, who believe that Jesus died for them, and who say he is the only Savior—has to be taken very seriously. Even though they call themselves Muslims, they are not like other Muslims.

The words of Jesus are poignant and sobering:

> "I have other sheep that are not of this fold; I must bring them also and they will heed my voice. So there shall be one flock, one shepherd."
>
> John 10:16

I have mentioned the need for the passage of time because, like any other movement, this one is in process. In the meantime, we should never forget that the Holy Spirit does not abandon his Word or his people. While conversations about the dangers of syncretism are well-intended,

God goes on doing his work through his Holy Spirit, to bless and honor truth and to remove his blessing from error.

I recall discussions I had with African pastors about the implications of the apostle Paul baptizing the Philippian jailer and his family immediately, coming as they did straight out of "paganism." It was an emotional and a highly charged situation, with no church except, perhaps, some women of Lydia's household who had also been baptized quickly and privately. Then, after a confrontation with the police, Paul left them for Thessalonica (Acts 16). How much hope would there seem to have been for isolated converts in a place like Philippi? Still, the church developed there.

I am not saying the situation in "Islampur" is the same as in Philippi, but the Holy Spirit is still at work in poorly informed, sometimes misguided believers. Beyond any human comprehension, the Spirit faithfully guides those who seek the truth. The Good Shepherd said, "I know my own and my own know me" (John 10:14). The church has always been a mystery (Ephesians 3:3,9), but it is God's church, and in the end, God will make the judgment.

$\mathcal{L}$etter to the
EMQ Editor

EMQ has requested me to "respond to the responders" of my October 1998 article, "Danger! New Directions in Contextualization." John Travis, Dean Gilliland, and Joshua Massey are all my highly esteemed friends, two of whom are very involved in Muslim evangelism.

It appears that C1 to C4 are clear and without theological controversy. But what is becoming increasingly obvious is that C5 is diversely interpreted by various practitioners. This has created confusion to the point that I wonder if C5 should be excised from our vocabulary. Consider varying definitions:

- Are believers to be called just "Muslims" or "Muslims, Followers of Isa"? A huge difference.

- Is mosque attendance to be allowed as a transition or to be encouraged as a strategy of permanence?

- Does the convert pray his *salat* in exactly the same way as Muslims?

- Do the converts verbally or by implication recite the *shahadah* affirming Muhammad as the prophet of God?

- Is mosque participation encouraged only for Muslim background believers or is it to be advocated for Christians as well?

- Do Christians legally become Muslims?

- Should Christians go on the *Haj*?

All of the above has been set forth as C5 by varying individuals or groups. Briefly, my apprehensions relate to:

1   Saying one is a "Muslim" without further explanation;

2   Affirming that Muhammad is the prophet of God;

3   Encouraging permanent mosque attendance;

4   Any conversion or reconversion to Islam;

5   A believer going on the *Haj.*

Throughout the above "strategy," I see evidence of purposeful deceit in the name of the higher good of seeing Muslims come to Christ.

Have we unwittingly bought into Fletcher's situation ethics whereby the end justifies the means? It seems to me C4 accomplishes the same stated goal of keeping converts within their community—without the perils of the C5 strategy that pushes open the door to potential syncretism and deceit.

One word about "missiological gossip." It is my view that it is right, proper and even necessary to engage in a forthright discussion of these issues. Such a critique and interaction does not constitute gossip.

My concern is for those who get caught up in the thrill of being "on the cutting edge," and who thereby push "avant garde" missiology to the edge of the cliff. It is only right to post a few warning signs along the perimeters of the abyss.

Yes, God can do "surprising things." BUT never in terms antithetical to His Word. It is in this vein that I share my apprehensions concerning C5. This in no wise diminishes my respect and appreciation for all laborers among the "Sons of Ishmael."

PHIL PARSHALL

CHAPTER 8

THE AMAZING DIVERSITY OF GOD IN DRAWING MUSLIMS TO JESUS*

by Joshua Massey

*When it comes to certain approaches, perhaps
we should wait before passing judgment.*

Scripture shows that God has never been entirely predictable. Who could have foreseen His decision to wipe out most all of humanity and start over with Noah and his family? Who could have guessed that the fulfillment of God's covenant to multiply Abraham's descendants would include polygamous

---

* Reprinted by permission of *Evangelical Missions Quarterly* (Box 794, Wheaton, IL, 60189, USA

marriages? Consider how God asked Isaiah to preach naked for three years, or Ezekiel to roast his food over human excrement (Isaiah 20:2-4; Ezekiel 4:12-15).

As familiar as we may be with the Scriptures, we can't always predict how God will handle a situation. The Pharisees knew the Scriptures extremely well but most utterly failed to recognize Jesus. In God's passion to draw the nations to Jesus, about the only thing we can predict with confidence is that God will do things we don't expect! We must never forget that God is God: His ways are not our ways. He may, therefore, absolutely astonish us sometimes. In fact, God may at times even appear to contradict what He has previously revealed (Acts 10:13), but God never contradicts Himself (Numbers 23:19). Whether He asks us to preach naked or roast our food over human excrement, we need to realize that God is God, and we won't always be able to fit His activity into our limited understanding without some occasional befuddlement and discomfort.

GOD'S UNPREDICTABLE WAYS AMONG MUSLIMS

So has God been doing anything lately in drawing Muslims to Christ that we would not have predicted? Most definitely! One worker, John Travis, has developed what he calls the C1–C6 Spectrum to describe six very different kinds of Christ-centered communities in which we find Muslims worshipping Jesus today.[1] C1–C6 are all realities, not theories. Muslim men and women who at one time only knew Jesus as a prophet of Islam now know him as Savior and Lord in a variety of very different Christ-centered communities.

C1 is a typical transplant of a church from one country to another. Inside a C1 church, everything is almost exactly the same as it would be in its country of origin, including the language.

C2 is basically the same as C1, except C2 uses the local language. C2 doesn't use any Islamic religious vocabulary, but instead has a distinctively "Christian" vocabulary for religious description.

C3 is essentially the same as C2, except C3 uses local music styles, clothing, art, and other native cultural elements. C3 makes a clear distinction between practices that are purely "cultural," and those which are "Islamic." Islamic forms are rejected. C1-C3 believers all identify themselves as "Christians."

---

[1] John Travis, "The C1 to C6 Spectrum: A Practical Tool for Defining Six Types of Christ-centered Communities ('C') Found in the Muslim Context," *Evangelical Missions Quarterly*, October, 1998, pp. 407-408.

C4 is much like C3 but has also adopted biblically permissible Islamic forms and practices (*e.g.*, praying prostrate, perhaps toward Jerusalem; washing before prayer and before touching the Bible; abstaining from pork, alcohol, or from keeping dogs as pets; using some Islamic terms; wearing some clothing popular among Muslims). C4 believers do not call themselves "Christians" but "followers of *Isa* (Jesus)." However, the Muslim community does not generally see C4 believers as fellow Muslims.

C5 is much like C4, with the primary difference being self-identity. Whereas C4 believers identify themselves as "followers of Isa," C5 believers identify themselves as "Muslim followers of Jesus"—much like Messianic Jews call themselves "Jewish followers of Jesus." Islamic theology incompatible with the Bible is rejected. Some C5 believers remain in the Muslim community for as long as they can to "win Muslims as a Muslim" (1Corinthians 9:19-23). In time, however, their deviance from mainstream Islamic theology may lead to their banishment from the Muslim community. But where whole communities of Muslims begin to follow Jesus, the local mosque may be transformed into a Messianic mosque for Jesus. Other C5 believers desire to distance themselves from the mosque and Islam, still preferring to maintain their identity as Muslim followers of Jesus. In contrast to C4, Muslims view C5 believers as Muslim, though perhaps a "strange kind of Muslim." Most Muslims have not met Muslims who follow Jesus, so the curiosity that results from their identification often opens doors to share their faith in Christ.

C6 will be discussed later.

A SURPRISING PROGRESSION

The majority of churches in the Muslim world today are C1-2—which isn't too surprising. But C3-5 represent a surprising progression of God's diversity in drawing Muslims to Jesus.

I use the term "progression" because the surprises didn't start with C5, but with C3. In its day, C3 received plenty of opposition from C1-2 believers, who insisted, for example, that certain musical instruments are inherently evil and inappropriate for any community of Christ-followers. But in time, C3 became more widely accepted, and in turn laid a foundation for C4.

I attribute this "progression" to God (rather than to the contextual experiments of man) based on the firm conviction that no one becomes "Christ-centered" unless God draws him, as Jesus stated so clearly (John 6:44). Phil

Parshall certainly became the vanguard of C4 in the late '70's. Phil endured an extreme amount of opposition from more than a few C1-3 believers. But Phil took the necessary time, and actually wrote a book to build his case for *C4, New Paths in Muslim Evangelism* (Baker Books, 1980). Ironically, less than 20 years after its release, C4 is today probably the most common approach used by new missionaries to Muslims. But who could have predicted 20 years ago that God would raise for Himself still another group of missionaries who believe that God wants to take them beyond C4? C4 surely paved the way for C5, whose major difference is one of identity. Whereas C4 allows any biblically permissible Islamic form or practice, C5 does not claim to go any further, except in the area of self-definition.

C5 practitioners insist that even as Paul argued tirelessly with Judaizers that Gentiles don't have to convert to Judaism to follow Jesus, Muslims don't have to convert to "Christianity" to follow Jesus. C5 believers surely are genuine disciples of Jesus (Acts 15:8,11), but they do not desire to align themselves with what they perceive as that godless Western institution called "Christianity", where (from a Muslim perspective) homosexuals enter the clergy, immodest women worship in scantily-clad summer dresses, and people put their Holy Scriptures on the floor right next to their dirty shoes.

C5 workers point out that Jesus commanded us to make disciples, not converts. If Muslims drawn to Jesus commit to obey all His commands, bearing witness that Jesus is the only mediator between God and man and that only His death on the cross can pay the price for man's sin, what does it matter what they call themselves?

Opponents of C5 will argue, "To call themselves 'Muslim' means they adhere to certain Islamic beliefs that flatly contradict Scripture!"

C5 practitioners respond, "That sounds like the same argument Judaizers used against Paul, since Gentiles were well known by all Jews to be unclean, uncircumcised, and mostly sexually immoral idolaters. 'How is it possible,' Judaizers must have asked Paul, 'to be both Gentile and a follower of Jesus? The two terms are mutually exclusive!' And yet we find this phrase, 'Gentile believers' twice in the Book of Acts—which must have been quite disturbing to the Judaizers, many of whom no doubt loved the Lord Jesus deeply."

"But," opponents of C5 contend, "to remain a Gentile follower of Jesus is different from remaining a Muslim follower of Jesus, since being Gentile is an issue of ethnicity, not adherence to a false religion." C5 practitioners respond, "Tell that to Peter, who, though he may not have been able to point at a religious body of literature claiming to describe 'Gentileism,' nor an order of priests claiming to represent the offices of 'Gentileism,' believed he'd be polluted from entering a God-fearing Gentile's home. So while 'Gentileism' may not have been a cohesive religious institution per se, being Gentile surely carried implications of religious consequence, deeply ingrained in the psyche of every Jew and Judaizer who objected to their inclusion in the church without first converting to Judaism."

CHRISTIAN BACKGROUND VS. MUSLIM BACKGROUND

Every C5 worker I know sees a huge difference between someone from a Christian background taking a C5 identity and someone from a Muslim background becoming a C5 believer. In fact, one pro-C5 team I know has a countrywide policy disallowing anyone from a Christian background from becoming C5; their identity can go no further than C4. If someone from a Christian background goes around calling himself a Muslim, all they'll do (according to popular C5 opinion) is either look like a total phony, or mislead Muslims into thinking they had converted to Islam. So when I use the term "C5 believer," I am always referring to those who were raised Muslim by a Muslim family. This distinction becomes even more significant when considering the question of deceit in a C5 approach.

HONESTY IN C5 IDENTITY

While C1–4 workers may assert that following Jesus requires one to cease identifying himself as a "Muslim" in name, C5 workers believe identity is not solely based on one's theological position. For example, C5 believers, or "Muslim followers of Jesus," see themselves as far more "Muslim" than "Christian," even though they disagree with the common Muslim belief that the Bible has been corrupted and Jesus was not crucified. How can they possibly see themselves as more Muslim than Christian in spite of these theological differences?

To answer this question, we must first ask, "Whom do they see as 'Christian'?" In parts of the world where significant numbers of C5 believers exist, they are mostly looking at C1–2 believers. When C5 believers compare themselves to C1–2 "Christians," they say, "I don't pray like a Christian, unwashed in a pew with my shoes on; I pray like a Muslim. I don't dress like a Christian, with Western pants and collared shirts; I dress like a Muslim. I don't talk like a Christian, with all their strange terms to describe God and His prophets; I talk like a Muslim.

I don't eat like a Christian, pork chops and *haram* meats (*i.e.*, from animals not butchered in the *kosher* way); I prefer *halal* meats, like a Muslim. I don't have a Christian name, like John, Tom, or Paul; I have a Muslim name." Thus, C5 believers are being entirely honest when they identify themselves as "Muslim" followers of Jesus.

C6 INDICATES FAITH NOT YET MADE PUBLIC

While C6 accurately describes a certain Christ-centered community of believers, it doesn't fit well in this spectrum in other respects, particularly, in the area of contextualization and self-definition. For throughout C1–5, we can see a progression in contextual "friendliness" with a Muslim's culture, Islamic forms, and even Muslim identity. But any sense of contextual progression ends at C5, for the defining factor of C6 is whether or not a believer's faith in Jesus is made public. C6 believers surely practice a wide range of self-definition, and if we ask them how they think their countrymen would best be reached with the Gospel, we would surely hear a variety of replies all along the C1–5 spectrum.

CHRISTIAN RESPONSE TO GOD'S DIVERSITY

I see two common responses to God's unpredictable diversity in drawing Muslims to Christ.

1 Accuse brothers up the spectrum of compromise, syncretism, and heresy

We should never gloss over the genuine concerns of our brothers who sense significant dangers in a C4–C5 approach. But some, instead of praying for the protection and fruitful labors of those involved in C4–C5, judge them as having crossed from contextualization into syncretism. Some in turn spread their opinions of heresy to others and engage in what we could call "missiological gossip." To be fair, they don't see it as gossip at all, but as alerting God's people to the sloppy doctrine of compromising saints.

I am not referring here to differences on the non-negotiables of the Gospel (2 Peter 2:1). Missiological gossip occurs when we elevate disputable matters to such an extent as to condemn our brothers of wrongdoing in areas where Christ has given us freedom. Satan's ancient strategy to divide and conquer is ever-present among missionaries to Muslims who accuse their Christ-centered brothers of watering down the requirements of the Gospel to make it more palatable for Muslim acceptance. They assume they know full well how God draws Muslims to Jesus, and it doesn't include a C4 or C5 approach. They have forgotten that God is not always completely predictable, and in His passion to reach the nations may actually surprise us sometimes.

2 Accuse brothers down the spectrum of obstructing the flow of the Gospel with a culturally insensitive, extractionist approach

Pride can easily develop in those who are early adopters of God's unpredictable ways, as if they are on the cutting edge of a movement of God due to some, personal ability of their own. Many fall into a trap believing the approach God has called them to is the approach for everyone to use among Muslims. Paul offers some incredibly specific instruction on such issues in Romans 14:22: "So whatever you believe about these things keep between yourself and God." One wonders if Paul's seasoned advice throughout Romans 14 isn't rooted in some pretty hard lessons he himself learned when dealing with the Judaizers (Galatians 5:12).

I believe both responses fall far short of Christ's command to love one another as He has loved us. Both responses also seem to ignore Paul's instruction not to pass judgment on one another in disputable matters, nor to judge another man's servant, for "to his own master he stands or falls; and he will stand, for the Lord is able to make him stand" (Romans 14:4).

There is a better way, a third response to God's amazing diversity in drawing Muslims to Christ, which I believe Peter and James modeled for us at the Jerusalem council.

3 Accept God's diversity in drawing Muslims to Jesus, blessing and praying for those who do not share our philosophy of ministry

The words of James no doubt have inspired every believer called to contextualize: "It is my judgment, therefore, that we should not make it difficult for the Gentiles who are turning to God" (Acts 15:19). You see, with all the accusations of compromise and syncretism on one side, and "making it hard for Muslims to enter the kingdom" on the other, we need to remember that not all Muslims are the same.

MANY KINDS OF MUSLIMS

There are many kinds of Muslims, each positioned in their own spectrum of how near and dear Islam is to their hearts. Many Muslim countries may easily contain all of the groups listed below, and many Muslim groups may also have individual members who share a greater sense of affinity and belonging to some of these groups than they do to their own ethnolinguistic people.

NOMINAL MUSLIMS	Muslims in name only, who only go to the mosque on *eid* (a major Islamic holiday) once or twice a year.
FRINGE MUSLIMS	These Muslims, often urban youth, are infatuated with Western culture and MTV. Some are disappointed with their religious leaders, who, they believe, are living in the past and not taking advantage of all that modernity offers.
LIBERAL LEFT-WING MUSLIMS	These are open-minded Muslims who aren't intimidated by conservative Islamic fundamentalists. They are often well-educated and financially well off.
CONSERVATIVE RIGHT-WING MUSLIMS	This term needs no explanation.
ULTRA-ORTHODOX MUSLIMS	Islamic reformist movements, like the *Wahhabis* (called "The Protestants of Islam"), frown on what has become of Islam throughout the world today: a mix of Quranic observance with superstitions, sacred shrines, richly ornamented tombs, divination, omens, and excessive reverence of Muhammad.
MODERN MUSLIMS	These have successfully integrated Western technology with Islamic devotion and are

proud to be part of a global Islamic community.

MYSTICAL MUSLIMS

Sufis and folk Muslims who, according to *Wahhabis* and conservative right-wing Muslims, are desperately in need of serious reform.

COMMUNISTIC MUSLIMS

In some parts of Central Asia and other former communist lands, Islamic identity has been almost completely stripped away.

"RICE" MUSLIMS

Some poor animistic tribes of sub-Saharan Africa or low Hindu castes of South Asia convert to Islam for material benefit or economic convenience.

This list is by no means exhaustive, but no matter how many kinds of Muslims we list, I believe they will all fit into one of three categories in their attitude toward Islam.

**MUSLIMS DISILLUSIONED
WITH ISLAM**

Iranian Muslims are a great example. So many saw what Khomeini did to their country under the banner of Islam and said, "If this is Islam, we want nothing to do it."

**MUSLIMS AMBIVALENT
ABOUT ISLAM**

They are ignorant and apathetic about Islam. They don't know and they don't care.

MUSLIMS CONTENT WITH ISLAM

These Muslims love their Islam and believe with all their heart that Islam is the only true path to God. When they look at Christianity, they see countries with the highest divorce rate in the world, where selfish ambition and materialism are at their zenith, where sexual immorality and homosexuality are accepted, and whose economic appetites led to the colonization and exploitation of Muslim nations and their national resources. Even when they meet born-again Christians, they are often repulsed by "Christian culture." They are impressed with the person of Jesus, but totally unimpressed with Christianity.

Each of the three attitudes has a high and low end on its spectrum. High contentment could represent devout Muslims as well as propagators of Islam. Low contentment could represent liberal left-wing Muslims who may not be too impressed with (perhaps even embarrassed by) the dogmatism of many Islamic leaders but are nonetheless very proud to be Muslim. Most communistic and rice Muslims would probably fall somewhere on the ambivalence spectrum, while fringe Muslims can be found anywhere from low ambivalence to low contentment.

DIFFERENT STROKES FOR DIFFERENT MUSLIMS

I believe C5 offers great promise. C4 is also excellent, but it isn't hard to understand why many Muslims would much prefer to learn about Jesus from a "fellow Muslim" rather than from a non-Muslim (i.e., C1–C4). For a Muslim to enter the home of a "Christian" to learn about religious matters is akin to treason. But entering a fellow Muslim's home—even though a Muslim following Jesus may be rather unusual—is much less likely to worry watchful neighbors. In fact, they may even go to see what this study of the Taurat, Zabur, and Injil (i.e., the Bible) is all about!

And when the Muslim seeker after God comes home with some literature about Jesus, it is C5 literature, often printed by well-respected Muslim publishers, not by suspicious-looking Christian organizations. Therefore, such literature doesn't need to be hidden under a mattress. Instead, it can be freely shared with family and friends.

And because the C5 believer was raised as a Muslim in a Muslim family, he's worlds apart from the peculiar foreigner claiming to be "Muslim." In contrast,

MUSLIM ATTITUDES TOWARD ISLAM

HIGH DIS.	LOW DIS.	HIGH AMB.	LOW AMB.	LOW CONTENTMENT	HIGH CONTENTMENT
	Iranians	Kazakhs		Arabs, South and Southeast Asians	

Muslims Disillusioned with Islam

Muslims Ambivalent about Islam

Muslims Content with Islam

124

he really talks like a Muslim, observes proper respect for holy books like a Muslim, washes before prayer, and eats food like a Muslim. The dietary habits of C5 believers allow Muslim guests to be at ease during meal times.

The door God can open for C5 workers was certainly seen by one North American brother in Asia who fasted and prayed for six months that God would lead him to a Muslim-background believer gifted in sharing the Injil (Good News). After finding Rashid in a C3 work and training him in C5, John sent Rashid out to reach Muslims as a Muslim. In less than two years, Rashid started ten "congregations!" (They aren't called "churches.")

Which approach do you think will be most effective with Muslims who are totally disillusioned with Islam?

Not C4 or C5! Muslims disillusioned with Islam want out! They are ripe for conversion to "Christianity." C1–3 should, therefore, be most suitable—depending on their preferred language and cultural setting. Ask any Persian Muslim background believer at an Iranian Christian Fellowship what he or she thinks about C4 contextualization to reach Muslims, and you'll probably get a confused look followed by the question, "Why in the world would anyone want to do that?"

Which approach might be most effective with Muslims who are ambivalent about Islam?

I don't know. It could be C1–5! Let's see whom God raises to be His witnesses among them. Then, let's pray for their work to bear much fruit.

THE COST OF DENYING GOD'S DIVERSITY

Denying God's matchless diversity in drawing Muslims to Jesus damages the cause of Christ in far greater ways than merely wounding our brothers with accusations discrediting their missiological methods or theological scruples. Denial can damage trust between brothers called to reach the same people. Those who don't trust each other don't generally pray together. Like a cancer, distrust can be quite contagious among co-workers. Rather than rejoice at what God is doing in so many different ways and learning from one another, we avoid sharing valuable information with those who might disapprove—to save ourselves from tiresome controversy.

I know brothers who don't feel free to share some thrilling developments in their C5 work with C3 brothers laboring among the very same people group. Because these C3 brothers have judged the C5 work as having "gone too far," they cannot rejoice that these Muslims are being reached with the Gospel and in turn spreading the Good News of His life and teaching far and wide.

Ground-breaking works like this can be seriously jeopardized by dogmatic C3 brothers who feel it is their duty to alert the saints to what they perceive as heresy or syncretism. Add to this the issue of physical danger such news could cause responsive Muslim participants and their families, and one can begin to see the escalating cost of denying God's diversity in drawing Muslims to Jesus. Surely, not all C3 believers are so dogmatic. Numerous C3–4 workers rejoice with great pleasure over how God is blessing this C5 work, but the vigilance in security that must be taken to keep this news from our more dogmatic brothers can be uncomfortably challenging.

Conclusion

When you hear a brother engaging in missiological gossip, discrediting another for his approach either up or down the C1–5 spectrum, kindly stop him, and help him see that not all Muslims are the same. God therefore does not call all of His messengers to reach them in the same way. As dangerous or outdated as an approach may seem, God will use a variety of Christ-centered approaches to reach a variety of Muslims.

And be on your guard! For if God is anything like He has been throughout history, He will surprise you occasionally. Let us heed Paul's instruction not to judge our brothers on disputable matters. Instead, "rejoice with those who rejoice" (Romans 12:15) and "make every effort to do what leads to peace and to mutual edification" (Romans 14:19).

When you meet workers who have been called to different points on the C1–5 spectrum than you have, encourage them. Pray for God's protection and blessing upon them, acknowledging that God will use them to reach Muslims that you won't likely reach, "for God is not willing that any should perish" (2 Peter 3:9).

Contextualization among Muslims: Reusing Common Pillars

by J. Dudley Woodberry

Recently, I stood in the great mosque in Qairawan in present-day Tunisia and looked at the collection of pillars from various sources that had been assembled together into one harmonious whole. As was also done elsewhere in the Empire, the early Muslim builders of Qairawan had freely incorporated pillars from previous Christian churches—and modified and whitewashed them—to make them blend into their new "home."

These pillars illustrate what also took place in early Muslim religious observance, for what have come to be known as the "pillars" of Islam are all adaptations of previous Jewish and Christian forms. If this fact were better understood, some of the current Muslim and Christian reaction to contextualization would be alleviated, for then it would no longer seem artificial.

The present study notes some current plans that have been drawn up for reusing these pillars of faith, and the reaction that these have elicited from Muslims and Christians. Then, an attempt is made to add to this material in two ways. First, we look more closely at the previous use of these pillars by Jews and Christians, to see the extent to which we can reutilize what was originally our own. Second, we evaluate a contemporary people movement to Christ among Muslims where the believers are adapting the pillars of their previous faith to bear the weight of their new faith in Christ.

Various Perspectives on Reusing the Pillars

The need for contextualization has been expressed by Muslim converts and inquirers. Once I received a letter from a West African country which described some new believers who objected to attending the local church for the following reasons:

> "Their customs are too different from ours. They keep their shoes on, sit on benches (and close to women at that), and they beat drums in church. We are used to worshipping God by taking our shoes off, sitting and kneeling on mats, and chanting prayers in the Arabic and _____ languages. Also we teach our women at home. If we go to the _____ church, we will feel very uncomfortable. What's more, our other Muslim friends will not join us. If we worship God the way we are used to, other Muslims will be interested. But we will pray in the name of Jesus and teach from the Arabic and _____ Bibles."

Not only have the worship forms been irrelevant or offensive to the person of Muslim background, but the Bibles used have often shrouded the Gospel in foreign terms. The traditional Bengali Bible, for example, often used a Hindu rather than a Muslim vocabulary. Even the most commonly used Arabic translation of the Bible by Eli Smith and Cornelius Van Dyck (first published in 1865), adopted some Syriac religious and ecclesiastical terms not seen in Muslim Arabic. Likewise, it utilized some Syriac names of Bible characters that are different from those adopted by the Quran (Koran)—for example, *Yuhanna* rather than *Yahya* for John and *Yasu'* rather than *Isa* for Jesus. The translators consciously avoided using the wording and style of the Quran. An Omani sheikh lamented:

> I have the Gospel, too. One of your missionaries gave me a copy twenty years ago. I frequently get it down and try to read it but its Arabic is so strange that I understand nothing.

Such problems have led to a number of recent studies applying contextualization theory to Muslims, monographs on specific topics, and contextualized materials for Muslims.

Despite the need for contextualization, Christian communities in the Muslim world have often opposed it. The opposition echoes a comparable tension in the early church between the Hebrew Christians who used Jewish forms, and the new Gentile Christians who felt free to use other forms. Gabriel Habib, the Greek Orthodox director of the Middle East Christian Council, in a letter to many evangelical leaders in North America, asserted:

> Unfortunately, we have all too frequently attempted to "contextualize" our sharing of the gospel—at the risk of diminishing the value of the churches' spiritual heritage. The loss of such a precious spiritual heritage in our efforts to communicate the message of Christ diminishes the real potential of accumulated spiritual experience.

In a questionnaire for Arab Christians in Jordan and Bahrain, Bruce Heckman asked, "How do you feel about Muslim believers using Islamic styles of worship when they meet together?" The negative answers included, "The use of Islamic styles of worship is wrong. We cannot accept expressions of worship that relate to idolatry or strange rituals." Another affirmed, "I personally believe Islamic worship is devised by the devil. The worship structure of Muslim believers should therefore be different and not attached to the past."

Heckman then asked, "What could be the effects of using Islamic styles of worship?" The negative answers included, "Those using Islamic style of worship would deviate from true Christianity." Another believed, "Using old forms of worship would take them back to the life from which they were delivered." Still another affirmed, "Continuity with the past will tie the Muslim believer to darkness."

Not only resident Christians but Muslims too have objected to Christian contextualization. Ata'ullah Siddiqi in *Arabia: Islamic World Review* (July, 1987) charged:

> Christian missionaries are now adopting a new, underhanded style in their outreach to Muslims. Known as the *Contextualized Approach*, it means they now speak in the context of the people and the culture of the country where they are operating, and are less honest in their dealings with simple, often illiterate, peasants. They no longer call

themselves openly Christians in a Muslim area, but "Followers of Isa."
The church is no longer a "church," but a "*Masjid Isa.*" Missionaries
assiduously avoid calling Jesus the "Son of God" to Muslims, who no
matter how ignorant will be alarmed by the term. He is called to them
"*Ruhullah*" (the Spirit of God).

The Malaysian *New Straits Times* (Kuala Lumpur, March 24, 1988) reported on a government white paper on Christian attempts at contextualization in which the church "would emulate the Muslim practice of reading the Quran when reading the Bible, sitting on the floor, using the *rehal* (wooden stand) to prop up the Bible," and wearing clothing traditionally worn by Muslims. Such practices are seen as deceptive, confusing, and causing "suspicion between Malays and Christians."

Considerable debate was caused in Malaysia when *The Star* (Kuala Lumpur April 5 1988) reported on a bill passed by the Selangor state government forbidding non-Islamic religions from using the following words: *Allah* (God), *Rasul* (Apostle), *Fatwa* (legal opinion), *Wahyu* (from *Wahy*—revelation, *Iman*—faith), *Imam* (leader of mosque prayer or the Muslim community), *Ulama* (religious scholars), *Dakwah* (from *Da'wa*—lit. "call," mission), *Nabi* (prophet), *Hadith* (prophetic tradition), *Syariah* (from *Shari'a*—religious law), *Injil* (Gospel), *Ibadah* (religious duties such as prayer), *Qiblat* (from *Qibla*, direction of prayer), *Salat* (ritual prayer), *Kaabah* (cubical building in the Meccan mosque), *Haj* (from *Hajj*—pilgrimage), *Kadi* (religious judge), and *Mufti* (giver of legal opinions; today, sometimes the religious leader).

To these prohibited words were added such exclamations as *Subhanallah* (Praise be to God!), *Alhamdulillah* (Praise be to God!), *Lailahaillallah* (There is no God but God!), and *Allahu Akbar* (God is greater!). A similar bill was passed in Malacca (*The Star*, April 7, 1988) as had previously been done in Kelantan, Trengganu, Negri, Sembilan, and Penang.

Whatever the final outcome, it is significant that the Muslim community felt these words and exclamations were exclusively their own. Their opposition to such contextualization as well as the similar opposition of many Christians might be alleviated if it were shown how many of the religious terms and worship forms are the common heritage of both communities.

PREVIOUS USE OF THE PILLARS BY JEWS AND CHRISTIANS

Islam may be viewed as originally a contextualization for the Arabs of the monotheism inherited directly from Jews and Christians, or indirectly through Arab monotheists. This interpretation of the earlier preaching would be supported by references to the Quran as an Arabic book, confirming the earlier revelation (e.g. *sura* [chapter] 46:12, Egyptian ed./11, Fluegel, ed.). Ultimately, of course, the message was seen to be for all humans (*sura* 34:28/27). All that is necessary for our purposes, however, is to show that the pillars of faith along with associated vocabulary were largely the previous possessions of Jews and Christians. Any reusing of them then is but the repossession of what originally belonged to these communities.

The earliest Muslim exegetes showed no hesitation in recognizing the Jewish and Christian origin of many religious terms in the Quran. Later, the orthodox doctrine was elaborated that the Quran was a unique production of the Arabic language. But Arthur Jeffrey argued that Syriac was the major source of borrowed vocabulary. This borrowing is of special interest because a number of the words banned to non-Muslims in parts of Malaysia can be shown to have been used by Jews or Christians before the advent of Muhammad (A.D. 570-632). They are treated here because of the relevance of a number of them to the "pillars" of Muslim faith and practice.

Since our purpose here is limited to showing the origin of these "Islamic" terms, we shall not do the detailed "componential analysis" that a Bible translator would to see the use and meaning of these terms in Muslim sources as compared to the use and meaning of these and other terms in Christian sources. Nor shall we consider the emotions their use by Christians may arouse nor the primary associations they may now have with one religious community and the new meanings it may have given to the terms. Again, our purpose here is only to show that Jews and Christians were already using many of these terms when Muhammad began his preaching; so they have been held in common. Subsequently, when we look at the pillars of religious observance themselves, we will investigate their meaning and function as well as their source.

The terms banned in Malaysia include the following:

- *Allah* is of Christian Syriac origin and was in use long before Muhammad's time.

- *Wahy* (revelation) is at least etymologically related to Jewish-Aramaic and Christian Ethiopic words and is used by the pre-Islamic poets.

- *Nabi* ((prophet) is probably from Jewish Aramaic rather than Syriac and was apparently known to the Arabs long before Muhammad.

- *Injil* (Gospel) is based on the Greek *euaggelion*, and probably came through the Ethiopic branch of Christian Abyssinia.

- The *Qiblat* (direction of prayer) obviously predates Muhammad. We find allusion to it in 1 Kings 8:44 and clear references to it in Daniel 6:10. Syriac Christians faced the east; and Jews faced Jerusalem—the direction from which it was changed in *sura* 2:142/136-152/147. One tradition, reported by al-Tabari, even ascribes the change to remarks by Jews concerning Muhammad's dependence on Judaism.

- *Salat* (ritual prayer) may be from Jewish Aramaic but is more probably from Syriac and was familiar in pre-Islamic times.

- *Haj* (pilgrimage) is from the Hebrew *hag*, meaning "festival" in Exodus 23:18 and Psalm 81:3.

Similar Jewish or Christian pre-Islamic usage can also be found for exclamations banned in parts of Malaysia—for example, *Subhanallah* (Praise be to God!). *Allah* has already been traced to the Syriac before Muhammad, as can *subhan*. Likewise, the Semitic scholar Eugen Mittwoch finds *Allahu Akbar* (God is greater!) similar to the benedictions of the Jewish *tefillah* prayers performed three times a day. There were, of course, alterations of meaning as words and practices moved from Jewish and Christian systems of thought to a Muslim one; but, as will be seen, the systems were similar enough that the core meanings remained.

Pillar 1: Confession of Faith (*shahada*)

The first part of the Muslim confession of faith (*shahada*—"I bear witness that there is no god but God") is based on verses like *suras* 37:35/34 ("There is no god but God") and 112:1-2 ("Say, 'He [is] God, One *[ahad]*. God the Alone'"). The wording, as Hartwig Herschfeld indicates, is apparently based on the *shema* in Deuteronomy 6:4 ("Hear O Israel, the Lord our God is One *[ehad]* Lord").

Both emphasize the same word *ahad*. The Talmud of Jerusalem cites certain rabbis as counseling the faithful to put emphasis on this word.

Not only is the form of the *shahada* similar to the *shema* and apparently is based on it; the functions of the two are the same. They not only introduce every formal service of worship but are the basic confessions for both faiths. Those confessions separate the Hebrews and the Muslims from the surrounding polytheists. Both also linked the affirmation of who God is with the obligations due Him. The *shema*, especially in its longer form in Numbers 15:37-41, introduces commandments. The relationship is pointed out in Mishna *Berakoth* 2:213 where it says that one takes on "the yoke of the kingdom of heaven" by reciting the first sentence and "the yoke of the commandments" by reciting the subsequent part. Furthermore, that which is affirmed in the first sentence of the *shema*—the unity of God—forms the basis for the first commandment of the Decalogue: "Thou shalt have no other gods before me." The same relationship between confession and obligation is seen in the *shahada*, for this first pillar affirming what God is is followed by four pillars concerning obligations to him. The same linkage is found in the Quran 20:14: "In truth, I am God. There is no god but I; therefore serve me, and perform the prayer of my remembrance."

That which has been said about the *shema'* in the Old Testament can also be said about it in the New, for Jesus gives it as the most important commandment in Mark 12:29-30.

In looking for the meaning of these confessions to the devotees, we must note their simplicity and clarity. Further, both *shahada* and *shema* require more than intellectual assent. The *shahada* is prefaced by "I bear witness" and the *shema* is introduced by "Hear O Israel": both require confession. This is more than James speaks of in 2:19: "You believe that God is one; you do well. Even the demons believe—and shudder."

As it involves rejection of polytheism, it also involves the rejection of intermediaries and associates with God in popular beliefs. In Sufi mysticism it involves the rejection of all earthly gods like wealth. It means seeing his signs in all things. "Wherever you turn, there is the face of God' (*sura* 2:115/109).

Many traditions mention only the uniqueness or unity of God as the essential article of belief. The traditional confession goes on, however, to declare, "Muhammad is the apostle of God" based on the quranic passage like *sura* 4:134/135. We shall not deal with this part here because it is obviously an addition to Jewish and Christian faith.

When Christians look for a substitute affirmation, it is noteworthy that Islam's most celebrated theologian Abu Hamid al-Ghazali (d. 1111) twice gives a confession that Muslims as well as Christians should be able to accept the *shahada* with the name of Jesus substituted for Muhammad: "There is no god but God and Jesus is the Apostle of God." Alternatively the Christian might substitute one of the early Christian confessions reflected in the New Testament, such as "Jesus is Lord" (Romans 10:9).

Pillar 2: Ritual prayer (*salat*)

In the Asian case study we shall be analyzing below, Muslims watched Christian relief workers come and selflessly serve them. They said that they should be called angels because they were so good, kind, and honest, "but they do not say their prayers." It was not until they were seen praying publicly at regular times that they were finally accepted as godly.

One of the first definitions of a Muslim was one who "pronounces the name of the Lord and prays" (*sura* 87:15). Yet the term chosen (verb *salla*—"to bow"; noun *salat*) had long been used for institutionalized prayer in synagogues and churches. *'Aqama 'l-salat* (to perform the prayer) was apparently borrowed from the Syrian church while Muhammad was still in Mecca, but the roots of the prayer service are also seen in Judaism as will be shown in the terminology, postures, and content.

Although the Old Testament mentions morning and evening prayer (Exodus 29:39; Numbers 28:4), Judaism developed three prayers a day on the pattern of Psalm 55:17 (cf. Daniel 6:10) as is seen in the Talmud of Jeru-salem. Christian monks prayed seven times a day on the pattern of Psalm 119:164. The Quran does not mention the five prayers but gives a variety of prayer times (*suras* 2:238/239; 17:78/80; 20:130; 24:58/57). The traditions, however, clearly list five; so Islam took a middle position. Of significance for Muslim converts is the fact that the early Jewish Christians maintained their former institutionalized prayer times and places (Acts 3:1; 10:9; 16:13).

PREPARATIONS

The removal of sandals in places of prayer (*sura* 20:12) follows the Hebrew pattern (Exodus 3:5) also practiced by many Eastern churches. The ablutions also reflect the earlier faiths. The minor ritual ablution (*wudu'*) is used to get rid of "minor" ritual impurity (*hadath*). The Jewish influence here is evident in the latter part of Muhammad's life: "You, who believe, when you prepare for the prayer, wash your faces and your hands up to the elbows and rub your heads and your feet up to the ankles" (5:6/8; cf. 4:43/46). The Old Testament Tabernacle had a basin for washing the hands and feet of the priests before they entered the presence of the Lord (Exodus 30:17-21; 40:30-32), and others also were to consecrate themselves when coming into his presence (1 Samuel 16:5). Muslims follow the same order in their ablutions as the Jews do—the face, then the hands, then the feet. The name of God is pronounced, and the right side is done before the left. Each part is washed three times.

"Major" ritual impurity (*janaba* or major *hadath*) requires washing of the total body (*ghusl*) before prayer. This is necessitated by such occurrences as seminal discharge or menstruation. It is also common practice before Friday noon prayers and the two major annual feast days (*Id al-Fitr* and *Id al-Adha*). The quranic distinction is based on *sura* 5:6/8-9 which adds to a prior description of the minor ablutions "if you are in a state of pollution, purify yourself."

Again, similar details are found in Judaism where occurrences such as seminal discharge and menstruation require bathing the body (Leviticus 12:1-5; 14:8; 15; 17:15; Numbers 19:19). The Friday bath in Islam corresponds with the sabbath bath in Judaism. Likewise, the bathing of the convert to Islam corresponds with proselyte baptism in Judaism, which, of course, was the precursor of Christian baptism. In light of the fact that both Christian baptism and Muslim proselyte *ghusl* are reinterpretations of Jewish proselyte baptism, it might be possible to interpret Christian baptism as proselyte *ghusl* without causing as much furor as arose earlier when a Christian author temporarily raised the question of a possible alternative initiation rite for baptism.

Another parallel is rubbing the hands and face with sand (*tayammum*) if water cannot be found, which is permitted by both the Quran (*suras* 4:43/46 and 5:6/9-9) and the Talmud. Christian baptism too has been performed in the desert with sand.

The function of the absolutions is purity from defilement (4:43/46; 5:6/8-9; 87:14-15), and water from heaven is also "to put away . . . the defilement of Satan" (8:11). The intention is inward purity which is seen as both an act of God (5:6/9; 24:21) and of the worshipers themselves (9:108/109) resulting in Paradise (20:76/78). Therefore, the purification obviously involves the forgiveness of sin.

The Bible likewise associated ablutions with purity of heart (Psalm 24:3-4; Isaiah 1:16-18; Ezekiel 36:25-26; John 3:4-5; Hebrews 10:22). Jesus went further in shifting the emphasis from the ablutions to purity of heart (Matthew 15:1-20; Mark 7:1-23). The writer of the Epistle to the Hebrews makes ablutions merely a foreshadowing of inner purity provided through Christ (Hebrews 6:1-2;

9:10-14). Church fathers like Tertullian and Chrysostom emphasized that such rituals were deprived of value unless accompanied by purity of heart.

Christ and the church, however, made the ablution of proselyte baptism more prominent than the other two faiths did and emphasized the symbolism of being dead to sin and buried with Christ and being resurrected with him to newness of life. The other two faiths, as has been seen, practiced a proselyte baptism; but circumcision has been a more central confession of faith for Judaism, as has the *shahada* for Islam.

Along with ablutions, another preliminary essential in Muslim prayer is the proper orientation (*qibla*). It comes from *'aqbala 'ala* (direction toward a point) and, as has been noted, has ancient roots. The Garden of Eden was toward the east (Genesis 2:8), as was the door of the tabernacle (Exodus 27:13), and the temple entrance in Ezekiel's vision (47:1). It was the direction from which the glory of God came.

Zechariah compared Christ to the rising sun (Luke 1:78), thereby associating him with Malachi's prophecy of the sun of righteousness that would come with healing (Malachi 4:2). Thus, Christians in the early centuries prayed toward the east, even though Jesus had made plain to the woman of Samaria that places and orientation were not important in the worship of God (John 4:19-24).

The Jews prayed toward Jerusalem (1 Kings 8:33; Daniel 6:10), a practice regulated in the Talmud. Muslims for a time prayed toward Jerusalem (sixteen or seventeen months according to al-Bukhari): It remained a center of devotion because of the temple area (now the Dome of the Rock and the Aqsa Mosque) where Muhammad is reported to have gone in his night journey (*sura* 17). The direction of prayer, however, was changed to Mecca in *sura* 2:142/136-152/147 As Jerusalem had been the center of the world for Jews (Ezekiel 5:5), Mecca became the center of the world for Muslims. Mosques came to include a *mihrab* (a niche indicating the direction of Mecca) as some synagogues had a *mizrah* (indicating the direction of Jerusalem).

In noting the prescribed direction of prayer, the Quran (*sura* 2:115/109), like the Talmud, recognizes that God is everywhere. The Quran, however, notes that true piety consists not in the direction you face; it teaches that piety consists of belief in God, the Last Day, the angels, the Book, and the Prophets, and to give of one's substance to the needy, to perform the prayer and pay alms, to fulfill one's covenant, and endure adversity (2:177/172).

The worshipers also must pronounce their intention (*niya*) to perform the *salat*, specifying the number of times they plan to repeat the ritual. Although the term does not appear in the Quran, it probably developed under Jewish influence to become analogous to the Hebrew *kawwana* and the Latin Christian *intentio*. The value of any religious duty depends on the intention of the devotee. As thus developed, the meaning gets somewhat closer to that of Jesus in the Sermon on the Mount where he moves the focus from the external act to the heart condition (Matthew 5:17-28).

PRAYING

The Muslim postures of prayers also replicate those of Jews and Christians. First, there is the posture of standing (*sura* 22:26/27). In the Old and New Testaments, worshipers stood to pray (1 Kings 8:14,22; Nehemiah 9:2; Mark 11:25). The Jewish *tefilla* prayers were called *'amida* (standing), indicating the posture when they were performed. The second posture is bowing (*sura* 22:26/27, 77/76), which has an equivalent in Jewish piety and communicates the sense of humble servitude that the genuflection does in the Roman Catholic mass.

The third posture is prostration with the forehead on the ground (*sura* 22:26/27,77/76). Again, this form is found in both the Old and New Testaments (Numbers 16:22; 1 Samuel 24:8; Nehemiah 8:6; Matthew 26:39). It is the equivalent of the Jewish *hishtahawah* and a similar Eastern Christian form. On Yom Kippur rabbis and cantors still prostrate themselves in this way, and I have observed Coptic Orthodox monks and worshipers do this in worship. Prostration with the body fully extended is practiced in Roman Catholic ordination and consecration and on Friday and Saturday of Holy Week.

The fourth posture is half kneeling and half sitting. Kneeling is a biblical form; sometimes the hands are lifted up as in biblical times (Psalm 28:2; 134:2; 1 Timothy 2:8).

The content of the prayers also have stylistic agreement with Jewish and Christian prayers. The repetition of "God is greater" (*Allahu akbar*) corresponds with benedictions like "God is blessed" in the Jewish *tefilla*. The recitation of the *Fatiha*, the first chapter of the Quran, includes materials that would be common in Jewish and Christian prayers. In fact, the missionary statesman Samuel Zwemer recited it in a public gathering in Calcutta in 1928 and then concluded with the words "in Jesus' name, Amen." The use of "Praise be to God" in the beginning of the *Fatiha* corresponds to a similar blessing in Syriac liturgy.

Blessings upon Muhammad come after the basic prayer ritual (*rak'a*) and are, of course, an addition to Jewish and Christian worship. The prayer concludes with the worshiper turning to the left and the right and saying, "Peace be upon you." This form also concludes the main Jewish prayer as the "passing of the peace" is often included in the celebration of the Christian Eucharist.

The Friday prayer is mentioned in *sura* 62:9 where the day is called "the day of Assembly" (*yawn al-Jum'a*), the same meaning as the Hebrew name *yom hakkenisa* for the sabbath. The development of these prayers during the Umayyad Period (A.D. 661-750) may have been under Christian influence. The choice of a day each week was a result of Jewish and Christian contacts according to a Tradition:

> The Jews have every seventh day a day when they get together [for prayer], and so do the Christians; therefore, let us do the same.

Goitein argues that Friday was chosen because it was a market day in Medina when people could more readily come to prayer. Unlike the Jewish sabbath, and the Christian Sunday, it was not a day of rest. *Sura* 62:9 suggests they leave their trafficking to come to prayers. Unlike the biblical account of creation where God rested on the seventh day, and the children of Israel were to do likewise (Genesis 2:2-3; Exodus 20:8), the Quran makes a point of noting that God was not tired after the six days of creation (*sura* 50:38-37)—a topic also noted by Jewish scholars.

The supererogatory night vigil (*salat al-lail; tahajjud* meaning "waking" in 17:79/81) reflects the Syriac Christian ascetic practice of keeping awake (*shahra*). Its function included merit (especially during Ramadan, the month of fasting, and before the two major annual festivals), and it loosens one of the knots that Satan ties in the hair of a sleeper.

The *imam* who leads the prayers corresponds to the *sheliah hassibbur* of Jewish worship. Both can be done by any qualified person in the community.

MEANING AND FUNCTION

When we turn to the meaning and function of prayer in Islam to see how adaptable aspects of it are for Christian worship, we encounter formidable misunderstandings between the two communities. Constance E. Padwick, who has done so much to lead us into the heart of Muslim prayer, said of several excellent books on Christian prayer in Arabic:

> When put into the hands of Moslems (unless those educated in Christian schools) these books have proved to be nearly unintelligible. Not only are the fundamental thoughts of Moslem readers about God and

> about prayer very different from those of the Christian writers, but through the centuries the Church has developed her own Arabic Christian vocabulary, and even when she uses the same word as the Moslem, she may read into it a Christian meaning of which he knows nothing. The first and most obvious example of this is the very word "salat," which for the Moslem means the prescribed prayers of the five hours, and for the Christian is full of many rich and delicate meanings.

We have, however, seen sufficient overlapping of forms and shall see an overlapping of meanings and functions, so that understanding and adaptation of prayers between the two communities is possible.

First, it is necessary to make the distinction between corporate liturgical worship (*salat*) and personal invocation (*du'a*)—a distinction found in both traditions (e.g., *sura* 14:40/42; Matthew 6:6-13; Acts 4:24-31). Islam and liturgical Christians focus on the former and nonliturgical Protestants emphasize the latter. Here we shall direct our attention to orthodox/orthoprax meanings and functions rather than those of the mystical Sufis and folk Muslims.

The concept of acquiring merit through prayer is strong in Islamic thought—both in the traditions and in contemporary practice. Recently, a nine-month pregnant Syrian woman explained, "In my condition the merit is multiplied 70 times."

Judaism developed a strong legalism (e.g., Tobit 12:9) as did the postapostolic church, which led to Alexander of Hales (d. 1245) advancing the doctrine of the Treasury of Merit. Protestants, however, although seeing the rewards of prayer (Matthew 6:5-6) and that good can lead to life and divine acceptance (Romans 2:6-7; Acts 10:35), do not see it as merit but the fruit of faith. Salvation is not seen as a result of merit (Titus 3:5); therefore, Protestants would want to eliminate this function of prayer.

Muslims have viewed the *salat* as a duty; yet it is more. Muhammad is reported to have said, "the *salat* is the comfort of my eyes." Likewise he is quoted as saying, "If one of you performs the *salat*, he is in confidential conversation with God." It functions to intensify belief: "between man and polytheism and unbelief lies the neglect of *salat*."

The prayer has been described as providing cleansing: "the *salat* is like a stream of sweet water which flows past the door of each one of you; into it he plunges five times a day; do you think that anything remains of his uncleanness after that?" Likewise we read, "an obligatory *salat* is a cleansing for the sins which are committed between it and the following one." Since the *salat* proper does not include penitence, the anticipated forgiveness is apparently based on human merit and divine mercy. However, it is common practice to insert before the final pronouncement of peace: "O God, forgive me my former and my latter [sins], my open and my secret [sins] and my extravagances and what Thou dost know." Furthermore, as has been seen, the ablutions include a sense of inner cleansing.

The ritual prayer includes many themes that Christians share:

1 WITNESS ("I bear witness that there is no god but God" in the call to prayer which, however, also witnesses to Muhammad's apostleship; cf. Deuteronomy 6:4).

2 GOD'S MERCY ("In the name of God, the Compassionate, the Merciful" in the Fatiha; cf. Psalm 86:5 and pre-Islamic use of these introductory words in south and central Arabia in early Arabic manuscripts of the Bible after Muhammad).

3 PRAISE TO GOD ("Praise be to God" in the Fatiha; cf. Hebrews *Haleliu Yah* and Latin Christian *Alleluia*).

4 GOD'S SOVEREIGNTY ("Lord of the worlds" in the Fatiha; cf. Talmudic *Melek ha 'olam*—king of the universe).

5 JUDGMENT ("King of the Day of Reckoning" in the Fatiha; cf. Romans 2;2-3; John 5:22; Matthew 25:34; 1 Corinthians 15:24).

6 WORSHIP ("Thee do we worship" in the Fatiha; cf. Exodus 24:1. The Hebrew *hishtahawah* and Greek *proskyneo* indicate prostration).

7 REFUGE ("To Thee we cry for help," in the Fatiha; cf. Psalm 46:1).

8 GUIDANCE ("Guide us in the right path" in the Fatiha; cf. Psalm 31:3; 119:1).

9 GOD'S GLORY ("Glory to my Lord" in the *ruku*; the nominal form of *sabbaha* is used, borrowed from the Hebrew and Aramaic *shabeah* of Jewish worship).

10 GOD'S GREATNESS ("the Great" in the *ruku*; cf. Psalm 48:1).

11 GOD'S EXALTATION ("the Most High" in the *sujud*; cf. Psalm 83:18).

12 PETITION AND INTERCESSION (possible in the *du'a*; cf. 1 Timothy 2:1).

Obviously there is considerable overlapping of the themes of Muslim and Christian prayer. Christian prayer can include most of Muslim prayer except the references to Muhammad and, for Protestants, prayer for the dead. This has been evident in the study of the *salat* with its inclusion of the Fatiha.

Muslim prayer cannot include quite as much of Christian prayer because of the references to God as Father, Jesus as Lord, the Trinity, and the crucifixion of Christ. Although Muslims may misunderstand parts of the Lord's Prayer, its themes resonate in Muslim devotion; and a tradition even says that Muhammad proposed a prayer which is obviously a free rendering of the Lord's Prayer without the initial words "Our Father."

THE MOSQUE

Some Muslim followers of Christ stay for at least a time in the mosque as the early Jewish followers of Christ remained in the temple and synagogue. Where whole villages have turned to Christ, they have reutilized the mosque for a church. Others have continued mosque-like worship. To evaluate the appropriateness of these approaches, we shall seek to determine the extent to which the mosque has been influenced by synagogues and churches and what its meanings and functions are.

The word for a mosque, *masjid*, is from the Aramaic, and has the root meaning "to worship" or "prostrate oneself," found also in the Ethiopic *mesgad*, used for a temple or church. In the Quran, it is a general word that is used not only of Muslim sanctuaries, but also of the Christian sanctuary associated with the Seven Sleepers of Ephesus (*sura* 18:21/20) and the Jewish temple in Jerusalem (if we adopt the traditional interpretation of *sura* 17:1). Ibn Khaldun (d. 1406) still used the word in a general sense to include the temple of Solomon. The underlying meaning of "synagogue" and "church" (*ekklesia*) is "gathering" as is *jami'*, a word that increasingly came to be used for mosques.

Muhammad certainly knew about synagogues and churches or chapels, for they are mentioned in the Quran (*sura* 10:40/41). As Islam spread, various arrangements with Christian and Jewish sanctuaries developed. In Damascus, tradition says that the church of St. John was divided, half for Muslims and half for Christians. In any event, the two centers of worship were beside each other until the mosque incorporated the church.

In Hims in Syria and Dabil in Armenia, Muslims and Christians shared the same buildings. Umar, the second caliph, built a mosque on the site of the temple in Jerusalem where later the Dome of the Rock was built. Many churches and synagogues were transformed into mosques. Muslims were told, "Perform your *salat* in them [churches and synagogues]; it will not harm you." The transfer of buildings was further facilitated whenever they were associated with biblical people who were also recognized by Islam. On the other hand, the second caliph, Umar is reported to have declined to perform the *salat* in the Church of the Holy Sepulcher to guard against its being made into a mosque.

The mosque performed many functions. Primarily for worship, it also was a place for public political assembly or even for strangers who needed a place to sleep and eat. Worship included not only prayer but might include the repetition of the names and praises of God, a practice cultivated by the Sufis.

Mosque worship also included the recitation of the Quran. Here the influence of the previous monotheistic faiths is evident. *Quran* is from the Syriac *qeryana*, used to denote the "reading" or "reciting" of the Scripture lesson by Christians, as the Muslim *qira'a* (the recitation itself) is the equivalent of *Qeri'a* of the synagogue. Sermons too were included, especially at Friday noon. Evidence of Jewish and Christian influence would seem to include the requirement of two sermons, with the preacher standing but pausing to sit down in between. This would correspond with the practice of the rabbi sitting while the law was rolled up, between the reading of the Torah and the prophets.

The earliest mosques were open spaces with arbors or booths, but they soon developed under Christian influence. Pillars and other materials were taken from churches and the booths were replaced with pillared hills. The caliph Abd al-Malik (646-705) had Byzantine builders erect the Dome of the Rock in Jerusalem, consciously copying the dome of the Church of the Holy Sepulcher. His son al-Walid (d. 715) not only had Byzantine architects transform the basilica of St. John the Baptist in Damascus into the Umayyad Mosque, but used Christian architects to direct the building of the mosques of Mecca and Medina. When he was inspecting the work in Medina, an old man said, "We used to build in the style of mosques; you build in the style of churches."

The minaret may have been influenced in a number of ways. It was not part of the earliest mosques, but was included when churches such as the basilica of

St. John in Damascus became mosques. The church had a watchtower—the meaning of *manara*, its common Muslim name. It may also have been influenced by the dwelling-towers of Christian ascetics in North Africa where it had the name *sawma'a* (a saint's cell) and was used as such in Egypt and Syria.

The *mihrab* (a niche indicating the direction of prayer) was not in the earliest mosques. In churches it was a principal niche that might contain the bishop's throne or an image or picture of a saint. Muslim literature attests that it was taken over from churches. It was even opposed because it was inherited from churches and was compared with altars as the holiest place. It is the place where the *imam* stands. Churches that became mosques, such as the Hagia Sophia in Istanbul, often had to alter the inside to indicate the *mihrab*. A Roman Catholic orphanage in Kabul, Afghanistan, supervised by the Islamicist S. de Beaurecueil, had two orientations so that Christians and Muslims could worship in the same room.

The *minbar* is probably a loan word from Ethiopic and means "seat, chair." Traditions indicate that the original maker was a Byzantine or Coptic Christian. 'Amr, the companion of Muhammad who conquered Egypt, had one made in his mosque, and it was said to be of Christian origin. Obviously, it was analogous to a Christian pulpit.

A platform (*dakka*) from which the *mu'adhdhin* gives the call to prayer is found in larger mosques. There is also a *kursi* (a wooden stand with a seat and a desk to hold a Quran). The seat is for the reader (*qari*, *qass*). Water for ablutions is often provided in a basin (*fisqiya* or *piscina*, which in the Mishna and Syriac is *piskin*). Unlike churches, in mosques, pictures and images are banned. The use of carpets is traced back to Muhammad, who used a mat woven of palm leaves.

Of interest here is that Rabbi Abraham, who inherited the position of "leader of the Jews" upon the death of his father Maimonides in 1237, demanded that pillows be removed from synagogues, and carpets and prayer mats be used. He believed that Islam (and especially the Sufis) had preserved many practices of the former Jewish sages, such as the use of these along with prostration and kneeling, ritual immersions, and nightly prayers.

Since Islam expresses a total way of life, and traditionally "religion" and "politics" were not separated, the functions of the mosque were, and to a lesser extent still are, broader than most churches today. Originally, the caliph was appointed the leader of the *salat* and the preacher (*khatib*) for the community and was installed on the *minbar*. In the provinces governors served a similarly broad function, administering "justice among the people" and the *salat*. The mosque also served as a court of justice. Some early judges sat in judgment beside the *minbar* or in the square beside the mosque—practices that were also associated with churches.

To determine the extent to which Muslim followers of Christ may still worship in a mosque or mosque-like context, we need to determine the function of both mosques and churches. Contemporary mosques are more like Christian chapels (where people only worship) than local churches (where people are also members), although many mosques in the United States have also assumed the latter function. The early Christian community applied themselves to teaching, fellowship, breaking of bread, prayer, performing signs and miracles, sharing, and praising God. They continued to go regularly to the temple, but broke bread in their homes (Acts 2:42-47). Here we at least have a precedent for continuing the previous incomplete worship even as the new believers remembered Christ's death (the completion of the worship) in their homes. Paul continued to go to the synagogue and temple until put out (*e.g.*, Acts 19:8-9; 21:26-30). James, too, still worshipped in the synagogue, or a place called a synagogue (James 2:2).

Pillar 3: Almsgiving (*zakat*)

Zakat is obligatory almsgiving of a prescribed percentage of different kinds of property (2½ percent for most) and distributed to the needy. The Quran specifies the recipients of various kinds of alms as parents, relatives, orphans, the poor, the needy, travelers, those who work on [collecting] them, those whose hearts are to be conciliated, slaves, debtors, and for God's purposes (2:115/211; 9:60). *Zakat* is an Aramaic loan word which originally was a general term for virtue but came to be used by the rabbis for charitable gifts, an understandable shift when almsgiving was considered as particularly virtuous. The same shift in meaning can also be traced in the Quran from virtue in general (*suras* 87:14; 92:18) to almsgiving (*sura* 7:156/155; 21:73).

Sadaqa is another quranic word for almsgiving. It too is a loan word from the Hebrew *sedaqa* or *sedeq*, meaning "honesty" or "righteousness," but was used by the rabbis for "almsgiving." The relationship between upright actions (*sedeq*) and caring for the poor is already seen in Daniel 4:27). The word *sadaqa* is used in two ways in the Quran and the traditions. First, it is a synonym for *zakat* (obligatory alms) in the Quran (*sura* 9:58-60, 103/104-104/105) and the traditions (where al-Bukhari talks about *sadaqa* in sections on *zakat*). Secondly, *sadaqa* is used for voluntary almsgiving (e.g., 2:263/265-264/266), sometimes called *sadaqat al-tatawwu'* (alms of spontaneity).

'Ushr is a tithe on produce levied for public assistance. It was similar to the tithes on the land of the Mosaic law (Leviticus 27:30-33; Numbers 18:21-26). In places, half went to the poor and half went to the ruler.

Almsgiving had great importance in all three monotheistic faiths. The Quran makes a clear distinction between believers, who give alms (*suras* 8:2-4; 23:1-4), and disbelievers, who do not (*sura* 41:7/6). There is considerable concern that alms be given to the poor (*sura* 9:60)—a concern shared with the Old Testament (Deuteronomy 15:11; Proverbs 19:17) and the New Testament (Matthew 6:1-4; 25:35-46).

There are numbers of parallels between the Quran and the Bible. One has to do with not giving to be seen by people. The Quran indicates that God does not love those who dispense their goods ostensibly to be seen by people (*sura* 4:38/42) in a context that suggests almsgiving. Likewise, Jesus said, "When you give alms sound no trumpet before you as the hypocrites do . . . that they may be praised by men" (Matthew 6:1-4). In the Quran, however, public giving is all right: "Say to my servants who believe, that they . . . expend of that we have provided them, secretly and in public" (*sura* 14:31/36). It says, "If you publish your freewill offering, it is good but, if you conceal them and give to the poor, that is better" (*sura* 2:271/273). Islam's most celebrated theologian, Abu Hamid al Ghazali (d. 111) even argued in the *Ihya* that much can be said for both open and secret alms, depending on the circumstances and the motive.

Another parallel between the Quran and the Bible has to do with the attitude and conduct that accompanies almsgiving. *Sura* 2:262/263 says, "Those who expend their wealth in the way of God then follow not up what they have expended with reproach and injury, their wage is with their Lord." Paul speaks of the importance of attitude in 2 Corinthians 9:7: "Each man should give . . . not reluctantly or under compulsion, for God loves a cheerful giver" (NIV).

Still another parallel between the two Scriptures has to do with God's recompense. Although the Quran warns not to give in order to gain more (74:6), rewards are promised: "What you give in alms desiring God's face . . . they receive recompense manifold" (*sura* 30:39/38). The reward is compared to the multiplication of corn when it is planted (*sura* 2:261/263).

Proverbs 19:17 likewise promises, "He who is kind to the poor lends to the Lord, and he will repay him for his deeds." Jesus also said, "Give and it will given to you" (Luke 6:38). The rich young ruler whose focus on wealth kept him from following Jesus was told, "Go, sell your possessions and give to the poor, and you will have treasure in heaven. Then come, follow me" (Matthew 19:21 NIV). Jesus knew "wherever your treasure is, there will your heart be also" (Matthew 6:21).

There is an area in which alms accomplish a function on which Protestants would take issue. The Quran affirms:

> whosoever forgoes it [legal retribution] as a freewill offering (*sadaqa*), that shall be to him an expiation (*kaffara*) [for his own sins] . . . the expiation [for breaking oaths] is to feed ten poor persons . . . or to clothe them, or to set free a slave . . . expiation [for slaying game during pilgrimage is] food for poor persons (*Sura* 5:45/49,89/91,95/96).

The Roman Catholic canon in the Apocrypha has a similar teaching: "almsgiving atones for sin" (Ecclus 3:30), and "almsgiving delivers from death and saves people from passing down to darkness" (Tobit 4:7).

Some of the church fathers also associated almsgiving with the forgiveness of sins. The second epistle attributed to Clement of Rome claims: "Almsgiving is excellent as penitence for sin; fasting is better than prayer, but almsgiving is better than either. . . . almsgiving alleviates sin" (16:4). Cyprian, Athanasius, Jerome, and Augustine also associated almsgiving with the forgiveness of sins.

Much more could be said on the function of *zakat* in contemporary Muslim economics. But, from a Christian perspective, we need to note that Jesus expected it to be a regular part of the believer's practice (Matthew 6:3); and James classified attention to orphans and widows in their affliction to be part of religion that is pure and undefiled before God (1:27). Yet underlying all Christian giving should be the response of gratitude for God's "inexpressible gift" (2 Corinthians 9:11-15).

Pillar 4: Fasting (*sawm*)

Fasting is listed as a characteristic of those who submit to God—that is, true Muslims (*sura* 33:35). Many Christians, however, believe it is wrong, or at least unwise, to keep the fast of Ramadan. To evaluate this, as with the other pillars, we need to look at the roots, meaning, and function of Muslim and Christian fasting.

The words which Muslims use, *sawm* and *siyam*, originally had a different meaning in Arabic, "to be at rest." In Judeo-Aramaic usage, however, they already meant "fasting," which suggests this was the source of Muslim use. This connection is supported by the Quran which makes the prescription to fast a

continuation of the prescription to previous recipients of revelation (*sura* 2:183/
179). The traditions are even more specific:

> The Prophet came to Medina and saw the Jews fasting on the day of 'Ashura.
> He asked them, "What is this?" They told him, "This . . . is the day on which
> God rescued the children of Israel from their enemy. So Moses fasted this
> day." The Prophet said, "We have more claim to Moses than you." So the
> Prophet fasted on that day and ordered Muslims to fast on it."

The first year in Medina, the fast was "a few days," apparently the ten days
of penance leading up to the Jewish Day of Atonement—'Ashura (the "tenth" in
Hebrew-Aramaic), the word Muslims use. It was also a time of seclusion for the
pious in the place of worship—a practice that later was incorporated by Muslims
into the last ten days of Ramadan and called i'tikaf, when that month was made
the required fast.

Other practices are also similar to Judaism. Abstaining from eating and drinking in the day but not at night was Jewish. Even in biblical times this was sometimes practiced (Judges 20:26; 2 Samuel 1:12; 3:35). Likewise, the Quran says,
"Eat and drink until the white thread becomes distinct to you from the black
thread at dawn" (*sura* 2:187/183). The source is the Jewish *Mishnah*.

Fasting has played a significant role in Judaism and Christianity—including
those of extended periods like the month of Ramadan. Moses, Elijah, and Jesus
all fasted forty days and nights (Deuteronomy 9:9,18: 1 Kings 19:8; Luke 4:1-2).
Jesus expected people to fast (Matthew 6:16-18), and Paul fasted frequently (Acts
13:2; 2 Corinthians 6:5; 11:27). Fasting was emphasized by the church fathers,
and the forty-day fast or self-denial at Lent is even mentioned at the Council of
Nicea in 325.

When we look at the meanings and functions of Muslim and Christian fasting, we see many parallels and some differences. For the Muslim, fasting is above
all an act of obedience, for it is prescribed by them (*sura* 2:183/179). Secondly, it
is an act of commemoration of the "descent" of the first verses of the Quran on
the twenty-seventh of Ramadan (*sura* 44:1-5/4). Thirdly, in the traditions it has
developed the meaning of contrition and forgiveness that is more prominent in
the Judeo-Christian tradition. One says, "All sins are forgiven to one who keeps
Ramadan out of sincere faith and hoping for a reward from God." Another
affirms, "When the month of Ramadan starts, the gates of heaven are open and
the gates of hell closed." The reference to the gates of heaven being open seems

to be based on the old Jewish practice of praying when the temple gates were open since that was a propitious time. This same sense of pardon is found in the fasts for expiation (*suras* 2:196/192; 15:89/90, 95/96). The concept is very prominent in the biblical examples (Deuteronomy 9:25-29; Exodus 32:30; Nehemiah 1:4-6; 9:1-2; Matthew 12:41), as it is in the Torah. Likewise, the Roman Catholic Church has used the fast as penitence and preparation before the Mass and leading into Holy Week.

The nights of Ramadan are times of joy and celebration, and decorations are often put in the streets during the month. Although fasting was used to express sorrow in biblical times (e.g., 2 Samuel 1:11-12), it could also be a time of joy (Zechariah 8:19).

Christians are given warnings against the misuse of fasting (Matthew 6:16-18; Luke 18:10-14), but Jesus expected his disciples to fast (Mark 2:18-20). It is interesting that Paul includes his going hungry as one of the deprivations he endured so that he would "put no obstacle in any one's way" (2 Corinthians 6:3). Lack of fasting is seen by Muslims as being irreligious. God asked the Israelites, "Was it really for me that you fasted?" (Zechariah 7:5 NIV). We need to ask ourselves the same question.

Pillar 4: Pilgrimage (*Hajj*)

Not too much attention will be given to the pilgrimage, since it was an adoption and reinterpretation of pagan rituals. The traditions make this clear. Muhammad's wife Aisha, for example, told how the pagans used to enter a consecrated state (*ihram*) in the name of the idol Manat. Out of honor for that idol, they did not perform the pilgrimage ritual between the hills of alSafa and al-Marwa at the Kaaba until the Quran explained that they were now symbols of God (*sura* 2:158/153).

Despite its pagan origin, many of its elements were those that God adopted for use in the schoolhouse of his children Israel. The word *hajj* is the Hebrew *hag* used in Psalm 81:4 (v. 3 in English) for a sacrifice when the Israelites were gathered in Jerusalem. Likewise, the word *qurban*, frequently used to describe the festival of sacrifice during the pilgrimage, is used for "offering" or "consecrated" in Leviticus and Numbers.

Muslims are required to perform the pilgrimage once in their lifetime if possible, as the Israelites were to go to Jerusalem three times a year. One of these, the feast of tabernacles, has a number of similarities to the *Hajj*—for example, going around the sanctuary (Psalm 26:6) as Muslims do around the Kaaba, and standing before God as an act of worship.

The concept of the mosque of Mecca being *haram* (a sacred place restricted to Muslims—*sura* 9:28) has its counterpart in the court of the Gentiles for Gentiles, who could not enter the temple. Mecca is seen as the place of the Last Judgment, as Jerusalem is. Abraham is associated with the Kaaba, as Jews associate him with Mount Moria under the temple area. The Kaaba has a covering (*kiswa*) which is replaced every year like that of the tabernacle. The direction of prayer for Muslims and Jews has been toward their respective sanctuaries. As the temple had a place for ablutions, the Meccan mosque has *zam zam* water, later supplemented. As Muslim pilgrims put on white clothing when in a consecrated state, so the high priest put on holy garments (Leviticus 16:4). Likewise, the hair is not cut when one is in a consecrated state as was the case with the biblical Nazarite vow (Numbers 6:5).

If all these elements were used by God in his schoolhouse for his people, can they not serve again for lessons as he gathers a new people for himself? The lessons will no longer be in Mecca. As Jesus told the woman of Samaria, worship will not be restricted to specific locations (John 4:20-24). God, however, used pilgrimages to teach the people lessons concerning his holiness and their unity as a people. We shall need to find ways to do the same.

CURRENT REUSING OF THE PILLARS

The case study we are considering is in a Muslim country that has had missionaries and churches for many years. Very few conversions have come from the Muslim community; almost all the Christians were from another religious group.

Five years ago the church responded to a natural catastrophe by sending twenty Christian couples to serve there, only one of whom was from a Muslim background. Their work was appreciated, but their Muslim neighbors would not eat the food they gave them. It was assumed that the Christians were "unclean" when they prepared it because they did not bathe (*ghusl*) in the morning when they may have had sexual relations the night before. When they changed their bathing habits, their Muslim neighbors ate their food. The Christians were called angels because of their service, but were still considered "irreligious" because they did not perform ritual prayers (*salat*). Even when God answered their prayers miraculously, their neighbors did not follow Christ until the Christians were seen to perform ritual prayers.

Less than three years ago a more contextual approach was adopted with help from some who had studied with Fuller School of World Mission personnel. Only Muslim converts were employed in the villages, and many thousands have since responded. God used a number of factors along with the contextualization. The New Testament had been translated, using Muslim vocabulary rather than words from the other religion, and copies had been sold throughout the villages. Natural catastrophes had occurred which were interpreted as divine judgment, and the Christian couples had responded with a wholistic ministry. These Christians had prayed for the sick, the natural catastrophes, and for personal relationships, and God had answered with amazing power. Muslims who opposed the conversions were even stricken with ailments.

An important factor was that some of the Christian leaders knew the Quran well. The Muslims believed that Muhammad would be an intercessor on the Last Day. The Christians challenged this, asking if they could show him mentioned by name in the Quran in this role. The Christians showed that only one whom God approves may intercede (*suras* 19:87/90; 20:109/108; 53:26/27). The *Injil* (Gospel), which the Quran affirms, says that God approved of Jesus (Matthew 3:17; Mark 1:11; Luke 2:22), and states that he is the only mediator between God and humanity (1 Timothy 2:5). This would fit in with the common Muslim belief that Jesus will return as a sign of the Hour of Judgment—a belief they base on *sura* 43:61.

When asked about their attitude toward the Quran, the Christians answered that it was meant for the people of Mecca and neighboring villages according to *sura* 6:92: "This is the Book that we have revealed, a blessing and a confirmation to those who were before it, and that the Mother of Cities [Mecca] may be warned and those who are around her." Sometimes other verses were used to show that the Quran was for Mecca and the Arabs. When they were asked about their attitude toward Muhammad, they said that he was a prophet to the Arabs according to the same verse and others. Historically, this is a valid interpretation of part of the Quran; although ultimately Muhammad saw his mission as universal (*sura* 34:28/27).

Although the old practice of debating is normally viewed as counterproductive today, in at least one union of villages the chairman called on the followers of Jesus to defend their position against four religious scholars. A Muslim spokesperson started, "We, the people of this area, are Muslims. . . . We heard that you came here to make us Christians, which is a foreign religion, a religion of infidels." Here "Christian" is being described as "foreign" and "disbelief"; so the convert refused to be called one and said that he had nothing to do with the

Christians in the country (who originally were from a different religious community).

The follower of Jesus claimed to be a "Muslim." This led to a discussion between "brothers" of what a Muslim was. The follower of Jesus said that according to the Quran a "Muslim" is one "who has completely surrendered himself to the will of Allah." He could point to this meaning of the term in the Quran (2:112/106; 3:64/57) where it is also used to describe Jesus' disciples (5:111,112). Thus, he was technically right in the sense that he had completed his submission to God through Christ, though historically, of course, the word has come to be restricted to those who follow the message delivered by Muhammad. The followers of Jesus have come to be called "believers"—a term more in keeping with the original followers of "the Way" before they were called "Christians" in Antioch.

After being assured that the follower of Jesus believed in the final judgment, the Muslim spokesperson asked, "Do you believe that Muhammad is the mediator on the day of final judgment?" The follower of Jesus responded, "Does the Quran say so?" When the four scholars could not show a verse that clearly did, the news spread, and many decided to follow Jesus.

Decisions are normally made in groups. The chairman announced that another meeting would be held the following month. If the scholars won, the followers of Jesus should return to Islam. On the other hand, if they lost, he and his relatives would follow Jesus. In another situation, a Sufi mystic leader learned in a Good Friday message that the veil of the Holy of Holies was torn from top to bottom. He cried, "Why should I bother with the law any more if Jesus has opened up the Holy of Holies?" He is now leading his disciples to follow Jesus. Attempts are made to keep social units together by baptizing people only if the head of the family is also being baptized.

Conversions are following the web pattern along family, friendship and occupational lines. When whole villages come, the mosque remains the center of worship. Teachers of their new faith are supported locally in the pattern of the *imams* of the mosque.

Muslim convert couples developed a prayer ritual which follows the Muslim pattern but expresses their new allegiance to God through Jesus. Morning prayer starts with the normal "intention" (*niya*) to pray but adds "in the name of my Lord and Savior Jesus Christ" before the traditional exclamation "God is greater" (*Allahu akbar*). In the first *rak'a* (the basic ritual which is repeated), Psalm 23 or any other biblical passage is recited. The rest of the *rak'a* follows the traditional postures and praises to God, although "All praise to Jesus Christ" may be substituted for the first.

The Lord's Prayer is recited in the second *rak'a* plus another passage if desired. After two *rak'as*, the worshiper adds to the thanksgiving, "Please give me favor to worship you this way until your [Christ's] second coming." Then the regular greeting and blessing are given to the ones on the right and left of the worshiper. A time for *du'a* (spontaneous prayer) is suggested for intercession and petition. The *iqama* (which normally includes an affirmation of Muhammad's apostleship) is altered to:

> God is love. God is love.
> And all praises belong to God.
> Present. Present before God.
> Present. Present in the name of Jesus Christ.

The remaining four daily prayers, plus any additional *rak'as* at these times, follow the same pattern with different Scripture passages indicated for each. After the night prayer a special prayer of three *rak'as* is suggested. In the first, John 1:12 is recited followed by:

> O Almighty God, the experience that you have given me to be your child through placing my faith in Jesus Christ and accepting him as my personal Savior, give the same experience to the lives of the ___ million Muslims of _____.

In the second *rak'a* John 3:16 is recited with the prayer:

> O God, the experience that you have given to me to have eternal life through your gift of grace in the Lord Jesus Christ, I claim the same experience in the name of Jesus Christ for the lives of _____ million Muslims of _____. Please acknowledge this.

Psalm 117:1-2 is recited in the final *rak'a*. At the conclusion, time is spent in intercession for the country, government officials, believers and their leaders, neighbors, relatives and oneself.

*   *   *

We have seen that the so-called "pillars of Islam" have for the most part been used before by Jews and Christians and, with some adjustments, are being used again. Their forms, meanings, and functions have been sufficiently similar to allow this to happen. Yet, many factors could weaken or topple them and what they support. One is the problem of training leadership for such a creative and rapidly growing movement. A second is how to build bridges to other segments of the church without inhibiting growth. The demise of the Nestorian Church gives mute witness to the results of being isolated.

A third problem is how to reuse Muslim forms without retaining Muslim meanings, such as merit. A fourth is how to avoid an ossified contextualization that inhibits maturity—an apparent problem of the Jewish believers to whom the Epistle to the Hebrews are written. Despite the dangers, we are seeing God blessing the refurbishing of these pillars in our day as they bear the weight of new allegiances to God in Christ.

What is happening can be visualized in the Hagia Sophia, a fourth-century church that was close to its Jewish and Eastern foundations. Its pillars held up a dome on which was painted the face of Christ. Muslims made the church into a mosque—altering the direction of prayer, adding the names of Muslim heroes, and painting over some of the Christian mosaics. Over the face of Christ in the dome they painted the quranic words "God is the Light of the heavens and earth" (*sura* 24:35). The same pillars continued to hold up this witness. Should the artisans painstakingly remove its paint as they have from some of the other Christian pictures, they could once again see "the light of the knowledge of the glory of God in the face of Christ" (2 Corinthians 4:6). And the same pillars would continue to hold it up.

POINTING THE WAY: THE TRANSLATOR'S ROLE IN CONTEXTUALIZATION

by Bill and Jane

W hen we landed at Citex (City X) airport in 1983 something else also landed with us. As we descended from the night sky into that new world, a world dominated by the religion of Islam, our notions concerning identification and contextualization also descended from the realm of theory to practice, from the realm of speculation to application.

Our preparation for that moment had included the standard introductions to Cultural Anthropology at Bible college and linguistics school. There we were taught to view 'culture' in its broadest sense as 'the integrated system of learned behavior patterns which are characteristic of the members of a society and which are not the result of biological inheritance.'

Our teachers also challenged us to develop a biblical perspective on the subject. What is God's attitude toward culture and what, therefore, should our attitude be? All cultures, like all individuals, reflect both the image of God and the depravity of man. Nevertheless God, the originator of human culture, views it 'primarily as a vehicle to be used by Him and His people for Christian purposes, rather than as an enemy to be combatted or shunned.' God is 'above' or outside of culture but chooses 'to work through and in terms of the cultural matrix in which human beings are immersed.'

In preparation for our future role as cross-cultural communicators of the Good News, we were also taught to draw a distinction between the 'essence' of Christianity and its cultural 'expression.' Christianity is not linguistically or culturally monolithic (as, for example, Islam would like to be) but is kaleidoscopic. God, the God of infinite variety, is delighted when people from around the world worship Him in their own culture. Just as God does not want to destroy sinful individuals but to transform them, He also does not want to destroy or negate culture but to transform it into some thing beautiful for Himself. The 'essence' of Christianity, a personal, faith-allegiance relationship with God through Christ, should be expressed in ways which are appropriate within its cultural context. In other words, it should be 'contextualized.'

We came to view contextualization as the cultural correlate of our organization's approach to translation. We were taught that the goal of translation is not to find equivalent forms but to express equivalent meaning. A great diversity of linguistic forms can express the meaning of a passage of Scripture. In the same way, a great diversity of cultural forms can express Christianity's 'meaning' or 'essence.' Contextualization is to culture what idiomatic translation is to language.

During this period of training, the Lord also gave us a keen interest in Muslim people. Friendships with Lebanese neighbors in our home city prompted us to peruse much of the literature which is currently available on witnessing to Muslims and Christian missions to Islam. As we studied this material, we were reminded of and disturbed by the fact that the vast majority of Muslims remain indifferent, resistant, and antagonistic to the Gospel. "Why is this so?" we asked. From our theological perspective it is no more difficult for God to save a Muslim than it is for Him to save, for example, a North American hedonist. The human heart, all human hearts, are equally in bondage to sin and equally in need of God's Spirit to set them free. Why, then, has the Gospel made such little impact on the world of Islam?

As we pondered on this question and particularly as we read Phil Parshall's book *New Paths in Muslim Evangelism*, we came to the conclusion that, from a human perspective at least, unChristian, Christian attitudes are a major problem. Traditionally, missionaries have demanded that Muslims accept both Christ and their culture (and, of course, reject and be rejected by their own culture in turn). Their spiritual conversion and their cultural conversion are inseparably and necessarily linked in our minds. We will not accept the one without the other.

Christians and Muslims are still locked in a Crusade mentality. The armies are assembled. The battle lines are drawn. And, to make sure that there is no confusion in the field, each army requires that its soldiers wear distinctive uniforms. Muslims must look like Muslims and Christians must look like Christians. Each man must wear his community's emblems prominently and proudly (e.g., names, salutations, dress, grooming, manner of prayer, fasting practices, architecture, day of worship). These distinctions must be maintained so that friends and foes can be clearly identified, and so that defections and betrayals can be cheered and jeered appropriately. And, of course, when crossovers do occur, the convert is required to divest himself of his old garb and put on the uniform of his new comrades-in-arms. We may be willing to practice the principles of identification and contextualization among those who are no threat to us (animists, for example), but when it comes to Islam, our great archrival, we are prepared to concede nothing. No quarter is asked, no quarter is given.

Convinced that this state of confrontation and cultural competition is sinful we determined that, during our stay in Islamex (Islamex Country X), we would do nothing to perpetuate it. In fact, we felt that we should try to identify as closely as possible with the Muslim community; to participate in their culture and to adopt and adapt for our own use those elements of their culture which are not in conflict with biblical principles. We felt that it was our responsibility to demonstrate by our lives that it is possible for a person to be loyal to Jesus Christ, and to express that faith in ways which are appropriate in a Muslim context. We felt that it was our responsibility to model (albeit imperfectly) a new way whereby a Muslim can love and follow the Lord without divorcing himself from his community and cultural heritage.

But when the rubber hit the runway in 1983 these perceptions and plans had to be applied and tested in real-life situations. And the landing, as might be expected, was not entirely smooth. The following is a brief report on our attempts to identify with the Muslim community in Islamex and, in particular, with the Ethnex (Ethnic Group X) among whom we worked.

IDENTIFICATION

1 Muslim names

Soon after we arrived we asked a young friend to suggest good Muslim names for our sons. He wrote down their names. While we learned how to pronounce these, he went home to consult with his friends and came back with the verdict. And our sons have been known by the names he suggested ever since. Another friend gave Jane her new name and Bill had already selected his before he came.

We received many positive comments about the fact that we had adopted Muslim names. Of course, some people assumed that we had become Muslim because, as one friend put it, a change in name usually indicates a change in ideology. But our explanation that we had chosen the names to make things easier for our friends was accepted. Our friends do use our Muslim names, and always seem pleased to draw attention to these names when introducing us to others.

2 Religious affiliation

At first we were reluctant to be pigeonholed as either Muslim or Christian. When we were asked about our religious affiliation we would reply evasively using the quranic expression, 'Ahle Kitab' (People of the Book). After a moment of hesitation, the person would often reply, "Ah, so then you are Christian."

For awhile we also experimented with 'Isa Muslims' (Jesus Muslim), but got into some fruitless discussions with Muslim friends who wanted us to change it to 'Isa Musulman' (Muslims in Islamex commonly refer to themselves as 'Musulman'). And again people would often reply, "So, you are Christians then!"

Finally, realizing that people were determined to pigeonhole us anyway and wanting to avoid any charges of duplicity, we adopted the term 'Isayi' which is how our Ethnex friends commonly refer to Christians. It translated roughly as 'the Jesus one' or 'the one who follows Jesus.' And since we wanted everyone to be aware of our loyalty to Jesus, it seemed like an appropriate title.

3 Salutations and other standard expressions

We always used the standard Muslim greeting "Assalamu alaikum" and the response "Alaikum salam." (We understand that Islamex Christians generally use the abbreviation "Salam" among themselves.) We also occasionally used the expression "Bismillah-ur-Rahman-ur-Rahim" ('In the name of God, Most Gracious, Most Merciful') when beginning a meal or a journey or a task. But there are many other expressions used in a wide variety of situations which we have not mastered.

4 Dress

While in Islamex we wore the national dress, an outfit consisting of wide, baggy pants and a long-tailed shirt. We frequently received positive comments from people who were pleased that we found their national dress both comfortable and attractive. (Many Westerners do not wear it.)

But this clothing is not just a 'national' dress. It is the Muslim dress. Some of our conservative Muslim friends would not be caught dead in Western pants and shirt—not just because they find them uncomfortable but because they are considered un-Islamic. People occasionally assumed we were Muslim simply because we were wearing the Muslim dress.

5 Grooming

Conservative Muslim women wear their hair long (down to the lower back). Short hair is considered unfeminine and un-Islamic. One of Jane's friends opined that any woman who cut her hair short would go to hell. One of our Western friends who has short hair was once subjected to a body search by some ladies to ascertain her gender. Needless to say, Jane wore her hair long—but not quite as long as Muslim friends who apparently were not concerned about split-ends.

A woman's hair must also be braided and covered. A woman with hair uncovered is considered immodest. A woman with long hair blowing in the breeze is considered wild and wanton and seductive. Jane kept hers braided and covered in the presence of Muslims.

For Muslim men, wearing a beard is a requirement. Religious leaders and teachers of all ranks, seminary students, *Hajis* (those who have made the pilgrimage to Mecca), and 'evangelists' and missionaries wear beards almost without exception. Laymen who want to make a statement concerning their piety and good character also wear beards.

However, most men in Islamex (at least in our area) do not wear beards but prefer the moustache. Even the President whose love for Islam is well publicized wears only a moustache, and has been commented on this inconsistency publicly. But the moustache seems to be the minimum requirement. One sees very few barefaced men.

When Bill arrived in Islamex he was sporting a big, bushy beard. He was occasionally asked if he was a Muslim simply because of his beard and clothing. Prior to our first visit to Ethnex District he asked an Ethnex friend if he should shave it off (thinking, perhaps, that the Ethnex people might not approve of a beard). The friend responded, "Oh no, they will respect you!"

However, during our first summer in Islamex Bill got an infection on his chin and had to shave the beard off to facilitate healing. He did not regrow it afterwards and now has a moustache. Some of his friends were a little puzzled, perhaps thinking that he was backsliding from his religious commitments. The medical explanation seemed to satisfy them, however, and Bill was happy to be free of the beard not only because it is much cooler without it but because he sees Muslim religious leaders as modern-day Pharisees and does not want to be identified with them. He would rather identify with the average male who considers himself a good Muslim but who doesn't wear his religion on his sleeve— or on his face!

6 Purdah

Purdah, the system whereby sexually mature females are kept hidden ('curtained off' or 'veiled') from the view of men who are not related to them (and the standards of modesty which are inherent in that system place many more demands on women than on men). However, the *purdah* system is not practiced uniformly throughout Islamex. The manner and degree to which it is applied varies from region to region, from village to city, from class to class, from sect to sect and even from house to house. It was, therefore, difficult for us to figure out how or with whom to identify.

However, we decided that it would be better to start at the conservative end of the scale and 'loosen up,' if possible, than to start at the liberal end and have to 'tighten up.' So, within a few weeks Jane purchased her first *burqah* and wore it whenever she left the house. [*Burqahs* come in several different styles. The old-fashioned kind looks like a badminton shuttlecock with cloth mesh on peepholes for the woman to look through. The more modern type consists of a coat or cape (usually black) with a veil. Jane's first *burqah* was the old-fashioned type.

The response of Muslim men to Jane's *burqah* was quite positive. Conservative Muslims are concerned with the erosion of traditional values that has taken place under Western influence and they were happy that a Western woman was upholding the old standards of modesty. When our Ethnex male friends introduced us to other people and gave a little background explanation about us to them, they almost always mentioned the fact that Jane wore a *burqah* (Jane, of course, would not be present on such occasions).

Jane received, however, a few negative comments from some young, female schoolteachers who were more liberal in their outlook. They felt that Jane's wearing of the *burqah* was a very retrogressive step. They were happy to be free of it. They felt that Jane should wear a *chaddor* (a large sheet wrapped around the body) like they themselves wore.

After awhile we began to notice that some of our conservative, upper-class Ethnex lady friends who lived in Citex had developed a flexible approach. In Ethnex territory, they wore a modern-style *burqah* but in Citex wore a *chaddor*. Following their example, Jane evolved the following "system": in some of the more liberal areas of the country (*i.e.*, in the national capital and some of the larger cities) she would wear only a light scarf thrown over the shoulders. In Citex, the provincial capital where we lived (a more conservative area), she would wear a *chaddor* to the Old City or to the cantonment or around the University area. To visit her friends in the village nearby, she would wear a modern-style *burqah*. She would also wear this *burqah* when flying to or walking around in Ethnex town, the administrative center of the district in which Ethnex people live. When traveling in outlying areas of Ethnex District (i.e. when on the road) she would wear a full-length *chaddor*, but when staying in an Ethnex home she would wear a half-size *chaddor* as is the custom of the women there. The old, village-style *burqah* was allowed to languish in the closet.

Concerning who was allowed to see whom, we observed the customs of the house we were visiting. Bill would let Jane and the boys approach the door and knock first, and make the initial contact. He would stand back and wait for the host to usher him into the guest room when the way was clear. If the ladies in the house were keeping strict *purdah*, then Bill would not see them and would not even refer to them, although he would make the standard, general inquiry, "How is everything in the house?"

If the women presented themselves, he would greet them politely and would inquire about their health, etc. but would avoid being familiar and would converse primarily with the men. He would never go into the family area of the house, unless invited to do so by the host and only when he was present.

7 Dietary restrictions

While in Islamex we did not eat pork or drink wine (with the exception of two occasions when we were offered a glass by Christian friends in their homes). We did not keep any forbidden (*ha'ram*) substances in our house. We felt that it was important that our Muslim friends know that our pots and dishes and cutlery had not been contaminated, and that we could satisfy them on that point if asked.

8 Standard of living

We tried to maintain a modest standard of living so as not to distance ourselves from our friends, most of whom were not wealthy. We lived in a small rented quarter with three rooms, a closet-sized kitchen, a bathroom and a courtyard. We did not have servants. Our friends seemed to feel comfortable in our home and often commented how nice it was and how adequate it was for the four of us (even though we often felt cramped for space).

Our single, major departure from a modest standard of living was the purchase of a Jeep in our third year to facilitate travel to and within Ethnex District. In retrospect, it was not a wise move. Apart from the economics of it, it placed us on the level of high-ranking government officers in the district—not a good way to develop rapport with the common man. We sold the vehicle prior to our recent departure from Islamex and in the future plan to rely on public transport.

9 Worship

Within the first few months of our arrival, Bill asked a friend to teach him how to pray in Muslim fashion and how to do the preliminary ablutions. With this information and the assistance of a booklet on the subject entitled *Elementary Teachings of Islam*, we proceeded to write a Christian version of the prayer routine (which is more accurately thought of as a liturgy or worship service). We followed the basic format of body postures; substituted quotes from the Bible for the Arabic words; and eliminated the repetition that is involved in Muslim prayer by organizing the quotes around the themes of God's holiness, God's justice, and God's love. We then memorized the prayers and used them ourselves, being careful to do the necessary ablutions first, and to pray with the head covered and feet unshod on a clean surface, and to face in the direction of the Ka'aba in Mecca.

Bill occasionally prayed in this fashion in the homes of our Ethnex friends when we visited them. They know we are followers of Jesus, but never raised any objections and would always render any assistance required with courtesy and respect (*e.g.*, to provide a prayer mat or to point out the 'Qibla,' the direction of prayer in that vicinity). On one occasion a friend asked Bill what he was saying in his prayers. Bill replied that he was speaking in English using words from the Bible. His friend chuckled and said that perhaps it would be better to use the Arabic words.

10 Going to the mosque

On two occasions Bill went to a mosque to participate in congregational worship, once in Citex and once in Ethnex District. On the first occasion he went with non-Ethnex friends who had jumped to the conclusion that he was becoming or had become a Muslim. On the second occasion, he went with an Ethnex friend to a small mosque in his friend's village. His friend knew that he was a Christian. There was no untoward incident on either occasion.

However, Bill did not make a practice of attending the mosque during the stated prayer times. He does not believe that it is wrong to do so but chose not to make a habit of it for several reasons. First, he did not find it particularly edifying. He would try to pray his prayers (silently and in English) but was distracted by the others. The language barrier also made the proceedings of little interest. He also did not want to create a stir, or to fire false rumors, or to cause any problems by his presence. He feels, however, that he should participate in congregational worship from time to time if for no other reason than to learn what is done on those occasions.

While in Ethnex District, however, Bill did make it a practice to go to the local mosque early in the morning or in the afternoon (not during the stated prayers) to have his Quiet Time. He would pray in Muslim fashion and then read the Bible. Mosques are very peaceful and clean and very conducive to worship. Sometimes other worshippers would wander over to see what Bill was doing, and occasionally would ask him what he was reading. Bill would respond that he was reading the 'Taurat' or 'Zabur,' or 'Injil' (Torah, Psalms, or New Testament). Once a young man muttered something in disgust and walked away but that was the only negative response he received.

11 Fasting

We participated in the month-long Fast of Ramadan every year while in Islamex. Whether alone in our own home or with Muslim friends in their homes we would get up in the middle of the night to have 'breakfast,' and then would refrain from eating or drinking until the fourth *Azan* (Call to Prayer) in the evening. If we missed any days during the month for some reason, we would make them up afterward.

Our Muslim friends were amazed that we would participate in the Fast voluntarily. (They participate under compulsion from their community.) We explained that, for Christians, fasting is not a requirement but is recommended for certain special purposes (*e.g.*, to spend more time in prayer and study of God's Word, to bring before God some very urgent and important requests). We said, therefore, that we were very happy to participate with them in their fast. They were very pleased with this. In fact, this shared suffering did more to establish empathy and friendship with them than anything else.

12 Festivals

There are two major religious festivals ('*Eids*') in the Muslim year. *Eid-ul-Feir* (Festival of Breaking) is celebrated at the end of the month of Ramadan when the Fast is over (broken). It is celebrated with great joy, not to mention relief! *Eid-ul-Azha* (Festival of the Sacrifice) is celebrated two months and ten days later at the time of the pilgrimage. Muslim families who can afford it will sacrifice a sheep, goat, or cow at this time to commemorate Abraham's sacrifice of Ishmael (sic) and then will distribute some of the meat to relatives, friends, and neighbors. During *Eid* celebrations it is customary for Muslims in Islamex to wear new clothes, and to go to the homes of their relatives and friends to offer congratulations. There they are served cold drinks, or tea, and sweets. And, of course, they receive visitors in return and show the same hospitality. We always participated in these festivals. We were not always in a position to buy new clothes nor were we able to sacrifice an animal but we always put on our Friday best and made the rounds to congratulate our friends. We also made preparations to entertain those who might visit us. During the big *Eid* we also accepted and ate any of the sacrificed meat that came our way.

On the first day of both *Eids* at about eight o'clock in the morning, Muslim men gather at a specially designated and prepared *Eid* ground to offer prayers. Bill did not participate in those prayers but was present on one occasion to observe.

13 Day of Worship

In Islamex we observed Fridays as our day of rest and worship in keeping with Muslim practice. The other six days of the week were working days. National and expatriate Christians generally worship on Sunday. Some also take Friday off either by choice or by necessity.

14 Death customs

When a death occurs, it is expected that friends and relatives will visit the house of the deceased to console the bereaved, to pay their respects, and to offer prayers for the departed soul. These prayers are fairly standard it seems and are in Arabic.

We do not believe it is a Christian practice to pray for the dead, but we did go to pay our respects if we knew the family fairly well and on one occasion, Bill offered a 'Prayer for the Bereaved' in English.

It is also customary for neighbors to bring prepared food to the house of the deceased. (The bereaved are in mourning, of course, and cannot prepare food for themselves.) This goes on for three days. We were able to do this on several occasions and it was much appreciated.

15 Handling the Holy Books

Muslims handle the Quran with great respect and care. They keep it wrapped in a thick, clean cloth and place it on a high shelf above all other literature. They carry it cradled in their arms or on their head, and would not dream of placing it on the floor or under their chair. Before and after reading the Quran, they may kiss it.

We had to leave behind our North American sloppiness in this area when we went to Islamex. We took copies of the Bible and the Quran with us protected by good quality leather covers that zipper shut. We placed these books side by side on a special shelf in our house, and when reading the Bible in the presence of a Muslim, we would kiss it. When we gave copies of the Bible or New Testament to our friends we would wrap them in cloth especially purchased for that purpose.

OBJECTIONS

The decision to follow the course of action described above was not taken lightly. In fact, we approached the subject of identification with Muslims with considerable trepidation, recognizing the controversial nature of it. However, we read as much as we could, prayed about it, talked about it and attacked the issue from every conceivable angle. We raised as many objections as we could think of and tried to deal with them one by one. Some of the objections pertain to identification in general; some pertain to identification with Muslims in particular. The following is a brief list:

1 Total identification is impossible

> Total identification is impossible. No matter how hard you try to dress like them, eat like them, live like them, talk like them, act like them, etc., you will never be accepted as an insider because you can never divorce yourself from your own identity and culture. You can't fool anybody. Therefore, you need not and should not try.

This objection states an obvious truth, but the goal of identification is not to achieve the impossible or to deceive anyone, nor is it to deny or reject one's own culture and identity (which would be psychologically unhealthy).

One's identity is a composite of two perceptions: who you think you are and who others think you are. The goal of identification with people of another culture is to acquire a second identity, to move towards biculturalism in the same way that language learning moves one toward bilingualism. It is to feel less and less like an outsider and more and more like an insider and to be regarded in that same way by the members of the other group. It is to reduce to the fullest extent possible the cultural distance that initially separates the outsider and the insider. We believe that physical identification or participation in the culture is an essential element in this process and, in the context of Christian missions, the onus is on the outsider to move culturally toward the insider just as God took the initiative to identify with man.

Take, for example, the (trivial?) matter of clothes. When we first arrived in Citex we were struck by how strangely everyone was dressed. And when first put on, their baggy pants and long shirt felt very odd. Now, however, wearing them seems perfectly natural. We are at home in them. We like how they look and feel.

And we feel quite comfortable in the bazaar among other people who are dressed 'normally' like us. And our friends who might have been surprised initially now think nothing of it. In short, our wearing of their national dress has reduced the cultural distance between us and them, and has helped establish rapport.

Another important goal of identification is to develop empathy for people of another culture, to begin to see and experience life as they do. This can only be done by participating in their culture, just as the Lord participated in our joys and sufferings here on earth. One could be, for example, the world's leading expert on the Fast of Ramadan having read widely and interviewed Muslims and observed them during the Fast. But without participating in the Fast one could not know how it feels to be a Muslim during that month. One's knowledge would be theoretical, not experiential (and one would also, we expect, be more inclined to be critical of the practice).

2 Total identification is unnecessary

> The essential element in identification is love. If you love people and accept them and respect them, they will know it. Identifying with them physically (i.e., dressing and eating and living like them) is unnecessary.

True. At least partially true. Physical identification without love is mimicry at best, or mockery at worst. But if one of the goals of identification is to demonstrate love and respect for, and acceptance of a people and their culture (the two cannot be separated), then how will this love, respect, and acceptance be demonstrated?

To use the example of clothes again—we could praise the traditional dress of our Islamex friends. We could comment favorably on its appearance and on how comfortable and cool it must be, and on how suitable it is for sitting on the floor. But if we refuse to wear it, our friends would conclude rightly that our praise was superficial or insincere, and that down in our hearts, we still felt that our Western pants and shirts and dresses were superior. Love, respect, and acceptance must be demonstrated in tangible ways.

The same is true when it comes to more weighty matters. We could tell our Muslim friends that we find many aspects of their public and private worship acceptable, and even commendable. However, when we pray *their* way—this is indisputable and dramatic proof that we mean what we say. It is a clear demonstration of respect for, and acceptance of that custom.

(We have been interested to note that these objections against physical identification or excessive participation in the culture are usually raised by missionaries in Third World countries who want to maintain a Western standard of living and lifestyle.)

3 Islam must be totally rejected

> The religion of Islam is inspired by the devil, and Satan is using it as a
> powerful weapon to wage war against the Lord Jesus Christ. Islam is
> also a total way of life. In it there is no distinction between religion and
> culture. The good (if there is any) and the bad are inextricably linked.
> Therefore, Islam must be rejected *en toto* and the convert from Islam
> must completely divorce himself from it.

Islam, as a religion and a culture, is 'inspired' by the devil and is being used by him to keep hundreds of millions of people in bondage to himself. But Islam is not unique in this. The same can be said about every religion and culture in the world, including 'Christianity' and Western culture. The Bible teaches (we believe) that every human being is infected by sin in every part and faculty. The same is, therefore, true of every culture. But God's approach to sinful human beings and sinful cultures is not rejectionist and destructive but redemptive and transformative. Of course, some elements of all cultures (occult practices or prostitution, for example) are so demonic, or contrary to the explicitly stated laws of God that they must be rejected outright. However, many other practices can be reinterpreted, reoriented, and cleansed by the Spirit of God and brought into God's service. And this also applies to Islam.

(If one took the rejectionist argument to its logical conclusion, one would have to utterly reject all cultures, and try to create somewhere a society with an absolutely unique 'Christian' culture. Such attempts have been made but have always failed because sin can't be left behind, nor can culture itself. The product of such attempts is always a sinful variation of an already existing culture.)

On the subject of spiritual warfare, it is true that a fight to the death is taking place between Islam and Christianity. We are not among those who believe that dialogue will eventually iron out the major differences between the two faiths. Between Islam and Christianity there is a gulf fixed, an ideological gulf that cannot be bridged. When everything else is stripped away, the fundamental point of contention remains: loyalty to Mohammed and the Quran or to Jesus and the Bible.

167

But down through the centuries, this basic spiritual conflict has often been obscured by conflict at the military, political, economic, and cultural levels. The underlying spiritual battle has been amplified into a competition between civilizations. We are convinced that our way of life is superior to theirs and they are convinced that their way of life is superior to ours. And neither side is willing to compromise. There isn't much middle ground.

However, it is the middle ground we are looking for and hoping to find, with God's help. By demonstrating respect for Muslim culture we are attempting to deflect attention away from culture to Christ, away from trivial, inconsequential matters to the One who demands the loyalty of all men. This is our message to them,

> "We are followers of the Lord Jesus Christ. We love Him very much and will never abandon Him. However, as loyal followers of Christ, we are free and happy to pray in your way or in our way, to fast in your way or our way, to dress in your way or our way, to relate male to female in your way or our way, etc. These things don't matter."

Culture is not the issue. Christ is the issue!

To follow this approach, however, we have had to deal first with our own negative feelings and then with the negative feelings of fellow believers. The conflict spoken of above has embedded a strong aversion to Islam deep within the Christian psyche. Islam made its initial dramatic gains at the expense of the Christian church. Europe almost fell to Muslim armies on several occasions. The Crusades did nothing to improve relations, and since that time European colonialism, the Palestinian issue, OPEC, international terrorism, and the Ayatollah have kept the pot on the boil. Islam is the only major world religion to have arisen after Christianity, and it poses a direct challenge to Christ, and stubbornly resists Christian missionary efforts. We feel threatened by it. We are on the defensive. We are reluctant to concede that there might be anything good or redeemable in it. Rejec-tionist sentiment springs, we believe, from this deep reserve or hatred of Islam and, therefore, must itself be rejected for that very reason. If the principles of identification and contextualization are valid and applicable to other cultures, then they are also applicable to Islam, our traditional prejudices notwithstanding.

4 This approach creates confusion

When Muslims observe your behavior they will naturally conclude that you have become a Muslim. This approach is therefore a betrayal of the Lord Jesus Christ. A clear witness must be maintained at all times. There must be no confusion.

Muslims who casually observe our behavior from a distance often do conclude that we have become Muslim. And rumors have circulated in Ethnex District to this effect. But the sky has not come crashing down. We don't believe that God is in heaven chewing his nails or gnashing his teeth because a few Muslims have jumped to an erroneous conclusion.

What God is concerned about, and what are concerned about, is that our Muslim friends know where our loyalties lie. And this is not a complicated matter. When we are introduced to someone for the first time, we are often asked if we are Muslim (because of our names or clothing or way of praying, etc.). We simply respond that we are 'Isayi,' followers of Jesus, and that clears up the matter. Our response may, of course, raise other questions in their minds but that is good. We want them to ask questions.

If we took it as an operating principle that under no circumstances must any confusion ever be created, then we could not even use Muslim greetings or wear Muslim dress. We would have to present Christ and the Good News and ourselves as something completely foreign to them. This principle, of course, would also be applicable in other situations. In every culture, in every context, Christianity would have to be presented as culturally 'other,' so as to avoid confusion. We don't believe there is any biblical basis for such an anti-culture approach to Christian missions. The apostle Paul, while maintaining a clear witness for Christ, became 'all things to all men' in order to win some. We are trying to follow his example.

5 This approach condones error

When you condone or accept part of Islam, you are condoning or accepting all of it. Muslims will assume that you also accept the prophethood of Muhammad and the inspiration of the Quran. You must not allow such assumptions to be made.

This is really another way of stating the confusion argument and our answer is the same. We are not concerned about the premature conclusions of casual observers. We are concerned that our Muslim friends know that we are loyal to Jesus Christ and the Bible. And they do know. Once a good friend of ours was introducing Bill to a group of men. He mentioned that we had adopted Muslim names and that Jane was observing *purdah* and that we were keeping the Fast. One of the men asked if we had become Muslim. Our friend replied, "No, they have accepted our culture but not our ideology. (Turning to Bill) Isn't that correct?" Bill replied, "Yes."

6 This approach is a denial of Christian freedom

> Islam is a legalistic and ritualistic religion. It is, in essence, a return to Old Testament legalism. But Christ died to save us from all that. Your approach is, therefore, retrogressive. You are steering the Muslim convert back into the slavery from which Christ wants us to free him.

First, a word about legalism. Obedience to a code of law is not legalism. Legalism (in the theological sense) is obedience to a code of law in order to win divine favor. It is a question of improper motives.

(Incidentally, the Old Testament is not legalistic. It contains many rules and regulations, to be sure, but those laws were not given as a means of salvation. Believers in the Old Testament were saved by grace through faith just as we are.)

Next, a word about ritual. Performance of ritual is not ritualism. Ritualism (as we understand it) is performance of ritual in order to win divine favor. It is, again, a question of improper motives. Performance of ritual is not wrong in itself. All human behavior is highly ritualized. Whether we are tying our shoe-laces, or greeting someone on the street, or going to church, we follow 'scripts' or 'routines' which we have learned (often without conscious effort). Very little of what we do is completely random or spontaneous.

Concerning corporate worship, Protestants have generally reacted against Roman Catholic and high church ritualism. We abhor cold, lifeless liturgies and printed prayer books. We want our worship to be warm and spontaneous. Some have taken this to the nth degree, and do not plan worship services at all, but wait patiently for the Spirit to move one of the assembled to lead in prayer, song, etc. But it does not take a keen observer very long to detect the 'routines' that underlie even the most 'spontaneous' Christian worship.

There is no question, however, that Muslims obey their laws and perform their rituals with improper motives. Their teachers instruct them to expect rewards from God for their piety. And the more they do (they are told), the more they can expect. Religion is viewed as a system of rewards and punishments. A Muslim is justified by his works. And he must do it all on his own. There is no one to help him.

However, when a Muslim comes to Christ, all this changes. He realizes that his obedience and performance has accomplished nothing, and that he must rely, instead, on what Christ has accomplished for him. His piety, henceforth, will be an expression of thanksgiving for salvation, not a futile attempt to attain salvation.

However, when a Muslim's motives undergo this radical transformation, will his methods also necessarily change? Will he have to jettison everything that was part of his former religious experience? We think not. We believe that there are many elements of Islamic culture and religion which can be reinterpreted and reworked by the convert with the guidance of the Holy Spirit and that, properly motivated, he is free to practice them.

And that brings us back to the question of freedom. The Muslim convert's freedom in Christ is at stake here and must be defended at all costs because the religion of Islam does not grant linguistic or cultural freedom to its adherents. In theory every Muslim in the world should be a carbon copy of Muhammad (who was an Arab). Linguistically, the Quran is only the Quran in Arabic. Translations are only 'interpretations' of the Quran and are not regarded as authoritative. From Day One the convert to Islam is required to read the Quran and to pray in Arabic and even to use the Arabic greetings when addressing other Muslims. Culturally, the ideal is that every Muslim in the world should follow the Arab pattern and dress, pray and fast, etc., like every other Muslim. (This is not the case in reality, of course, because Muslims are just as factious as Christians and culture is a very powerful and resilient force.)

In contrast, Christianity not only permits but encourages linguistic and cultural diversity. We attach great importance to the original Scriptures written in Hebrew and Greek (we refer to them to check our understanding) but we believe that good translations in English or Swahili, for example, are equally authoritative and beneficial. Christians are not required to master Hebrew and Greek, but are encouraged to study the Scriptures in their own language. Similarly, converts are not required to adopt someone else's culture in order to come to Christ, but are allowed to come to Christ in terms of their own culture. This is the issue that was settled at the Council of Jerusalem in the first century (Acts 15). It was acknowledged that Jews were free to come to Christ as Jews, and that Gentiles were free to come to Christ as Gentiles (without becoming Jews first). A cultural conversion was not required to validate a spiritual conversion. We believe that the Lord also wants Muslim people to come to Him, and to express their newfound faith in ways which are culturally appropriate to them. If He grants them this freedom, can we do otherwise? No, this approach is not a denial of Christian freedom. It is an affirmation of it.

7 This approach is cowardly

> This approach will encourage timid, cowardly converts (if they are real converts!) to come tiptoeing to Christ through the back door. This is not right. Muslim converts must be encouraged to maintain a strong and vigorous witness for Christ right from the start and to face the inevitable persecution courageously.

Genuine converts will witness for the Lord (their love for Him can not be contained), and persecution will follow (it can not be avoided). But it is up to them to decide when and where and how and to whom to witness.

It would certainly take courage for a Muslim convert to stand up in the mosque on Friday and proclaim loudly that Jesus Christ is the Son of God, or to take a long, cool drink of water in the bazaar at noon during Ramadan, or to return sacrificed meat that had been sent to him as a gift by relatives and friends during *Eid,* or to refuse to pay the tithe (*zakat*). But what would such a 'witness' accomplish? Nothing, apart from his own death or expulsion from his community.

The Muslim convert needs time to get to know the Lord better, to study the Scriptures, to assess his culture and former way of life in light of his new allegiance to Christ, to develop the good character which is the fruit of the Spirit, and to witness to his closest friends and relatives. This whole process would be immediately aborted, however if, under pressure from some well-intentioned but wrong-headed missionary, he was encouraged to 'take a stand' on these inconsequential cultural matters. When persecution comes (and it will), it should be on an issue that matters and is clearly understood by all, and the only issue that matters is loyalty to the person of Jesus Christ.

8 Outsiders are not qualified to contextualize

Culture is a very complex thing. Outsiders, such as yourselves, can never understand the hidden meanings that are attached to the various elements of Islamic culture or the ways in which those elements inter-relate. You are, therefore, not qualified to contextualize. You will make serious mistakes. Your job, as translators, is to give them the Word of God. Let the Muslim converts themselves do any contextualizing that needs to be done.

It is true that we outsiders can never comprehend Islamic culture, or even a particular Islamic culture, the way an insider can. We can't even come close. It is also true that it should be the responsibility of the Muslim converts themselves to decide what elements of their culture must be rejected outright, retained unchanged or reinterpreted for continued use.

However, this does not mean that translators or missionaries have no role to play in contextualization. On the contrary, they have a key role to play as models or signposts, pointing to a new way which Muslims have never considered before.

As things presently stand, a Muslim who is considering conversion to Christianity assumes that he will have to change his name, reject his religion and culture in its entirety, and be rejected by his family, friends, and community in turn. He also assumes that he will have to openly associate with the low-class Christian community who eat pork, let their women wander around 'out of control,' and who collect garbage, sweep the streets and clean toilets for a living. (And we wonder why there are so few conversions!)

It is hard for Westerners to comprehend what conversion to Christianity means in an Islamic society. In our society we can accept Christ or reject Christ, and still be regarded as solid members of our community. But consider what happens, for example, when a red-blooded American boy, a professing Christian and a member of a fine upstanding family, goes off and joins the Hare Krishna. His conversion is regarded as a slap in the face for his family and friends and everything for which they stand. He has rejected his own culture and opted for some inferior, freaky, foreign religion. Those who love him feel betrayed, and hurt, and angry, and even in our tolerant society he may be disowned.

This is what we are trying to avoid. We are trying to show our Muslim friends, by our example, that there is an alternative, that there is a way for them to love the Lord Jesus and still remain solid citizens of their community, in fact, exemplary citizens of their community. We may have made mistakes. We may make others. (We trust that the Lord will prevent us from making serious mistakes.) But our example is not meant to be negative. It is suggestive. We are only pointing out the path to our Muslim friends. They are the ones who will have to walk down it.

Missionaries to Muslims do not have the luxury of neutrality on these issues of identification and contextualization. If they do nothing, if they insist on retaining their own cultural expression of Christianity, or if they try to shift responsibility onto the shoulders of colleagues or some future hypothetical Muslim converts, then their long years of association with Muslims will only serve to reinforce the notion in Muslim minds that Christianity is foreign, that it is the religion of some other community. Response to the Gospel will remain minimal. The status quo will not change.

9 Problematic practices

a) FACING MECCA

> Facing Mecca while praying is an open endorsement of Muhammad and his religion. There is no way this practice can be retained in Christian worship.

Muslims pray in the direction of the Ka'ba, the small shrine located in the central courtyard of the Sacred Mosque in Mecca. Concerning the Ka'ba, the Quran states that 'Abraham and Ismael raised the foundations of the House' (*sura* 1:127). The meaning of this is not clear, but 'Muslim legend has interpreted the phrase to mean that they rebuilt a shrine first erected by Adam of which only the foundations still existed' (*Encyclopaedia Britannica*, 1966, Vol. 13, p. 178). Abraham and Ishmael then dedicated that building to the worship of the one true God.

Muslims believe that they are following the religion of Abraham (Quran, *surah* 2:130). They look to him as the father of their faith, just as we look to him as the father of ours. And there is a sense in which, through Ishmael, they can be regarded as estranged or misguided children of the covenant. In fact, they still bear the mark of the covenant, circumcision. We are, therefore, happy to face the Ka'ba when we pray, and in so doing identify with them as they identify with the patriarch. Of course, our prayer for them is that they may soon become Abraham's spiritual children in reality.

Concerning the direction of prayer, there are also some practical matters to consider. All mosques are constructed in such a way that when the worshippers face the front of the mosque they are also facing the Ka'ba. Many Muslim homes also have areas set aside for prayer which are oriented in that direction. Should we recommend to the Muslim convert that he stop using those facilities? Or should we recommend that he face in any direction **but** the Ka'ba? (He would immediately incur the wrath of everyone around him if he did.) No. As a Christian, he is free to pray in any direction he chooses, including the traditional direction. In doing so, he will be identifying with Abraham whose real faith he has now discovered and made his own.

b) ABLUTIONS

> The Muslim practice of doing ablutions before prayer is based on the pagan belief that physical and moral defilement can be washed away with water. This, of course, is wrong. Christ said that moral defilement is in the heart where water can't touch it and we believe that it is Christ's death on the cross which has taken away our sin and made us fit to come into the presence of God. This practice must be dropped.

Christians customarily take a shower, brush their teeth, comb their hair and put on clean clothes before going to church. They do this out of reverence for God. God is a very important person (the most important person!) and we should not 'come into His presence' dirty and unkempt.

Many Muslims are farmers or laborers or tradesmen. Would we really want to recommend that they stop washing up before prayer when they become Christians? Would we want the new community of Muslim converts to gain a reputation for being dirty? We think not. Washing up before prayer is a good practice, as long as it is understood that it is meant as a way of communicating respect for God and, of course, staying clean (and it does have merit even from the point of view of personal hygiene and health).

c) THE SACRIFICE

> The sacrifice of an animal during *Eid-ul-Azha* commemorates the ransom of Ishmael with a ram, which, of course, is historically

> inaccurate. Muslims also regard it as a way of gaining favor with
> God. Christians, of course, do not offer blood sacrifices because
> Christ has offered himself as our sacrifice once and for all. Chris-
> tians, therefore, should not participate in this festival.

First of all, it needs to be clarified that there are no idols or altars involved in the Muslim 'sacrifice.' The animals are slaughtered in the customary manner by pronouncing the name of God over them (*Allahu akbar,* 'God is Great') and slitting their throats. They are then butchered and some of the meat is distributed as charity to the poor, and some to relatives and friends.

The Muslim convert will certainly want to evaluate this practice of sacrifice in light of the Scriptures. First, he will want to get the facts straight, that it was Isaac, not Ishmael, who was involved in the incident, and why it had to be Isaac. He will also need to be taught the significance of that event— that it pointed forward to the sacrifice of Christ, and that Christ's sacrifice has taken care of our sin once and for all.

If it is clearly understood, however, that the sacrifice is commemorative, not propitiative or meritorious, we see no reason why the practice should be discontinued. [It appears that Jewish Christians in the early church still participated in the Old Testament sacrificial system (Acts 21:20-24).] In fact, for a community of Muslim converts, the Sacrifice Festival could serve as a functional substitute for our Good Friday celebrations.

d) PURDAH

> *Purdah,* the segregation and seclusion of women, is an archaic
> institution built on male chauvinism and bigotry. It denies women
> their God-giver. rights in society and subjects them to many abuses.
> Christ came to set men and women free from bondage. Christians,
> therefore, must not condone or parti-cipate in the *purdah* system
> in any way, shape or form.

Human behavior can be divided into the good, the bad and the sub-ideal. Sub-ideal behavior is not explicitly condemned by God (it is not immoral), but neither does it measure up to His ideals concerning how human beings ought to live. An example is the institution of slavery. Nowhere in Scriptures is there even a hint that slavery should be abolished. However, laws were given to curb its abuses and the Holy Spirit has worked steadily over a long period of time to eradicate the practice in societies where there has been a strong Christian influence.

We believe that the *purdah* system is not the ideal way of relating male to female in society, or of preventing illicit sexual activity (which is its aim). Ideally, male and female should be governed by an internal commitment to high moral standards. In the absence of the indwelling Holy Spirit, however, Muslims have opted for a system of external constraints designed to enforce moral behavior.

The *purdah* system also seems to be built on some strong prejudices against women. Their spiritual and intellectual capacity is thought to be inferior to that of men and (most dangerous of all) their morals are suspect. If some immoral activity is discovered, the presumption of guilt often rests on the female. She seduced the male and how could he have resisted? The burden of maintaining moral purity, therefore, rests on the female, and since she cannot be trusted, she must be kept under control.

How to 'handle' women and human sexuality is probably the great cultural issue that divides Muslims and Christians. They are appalled by our lewdness and licentiousness and advocacy of sexual abandon. They have seen Western films and magazines, and believe that Christian women, in general, are promiscuous. They may be enticed by it, to be sure, but they wouldn't dream of letting their wives and sisters and daughters behave that way, and they would disown them or kill them if they did!

We, on the other hand, can't understand how they can keep their women as virtual prisoners in their homes, and deny them the right to go out and get an education or a job—or even to buy their own underwear! Our society values individual freedom above sexual morality; they see things the other way around. On balance, it is hard to say who is right.

In any case, we do not think that a frontal attack on the *purdah* system is advisable. The modification or eradication of that system is not (we believe) the first item on God's agenda. First, they need the Word of God; then they need the Holy Spirit to apply that Word to their hearts, and to build a system of internal constraints, and to change their views concerning the nature, status, and role of women. In the meantime, it is the duty of female missionaries to bend over backwards (setting aside their hard-won rights, if necessary) to demonstrate that Christian women are morally beyond reproach, and that they can be trusted. If this means wearing a *burqah*, so be it.

10 This approach does not work

> You were in Islamex for over three years with no success. You won
> some friends, but did not win any converts. And your Ethnex friends
> did not even show much interest in the Gospel. The approach does
> not work and therefore should be abandoned.

We never expected that this approach alone would bring about a significant turning
to Christ among the Ethnex people. For that to happen three things are required:

First, they must have the Word of God readily available in their own
language in a form that will facilitate and encourage its use (and, so far, not one
word has been translated).

Second, there must be a powerful work of the Holy Spirit among them to
bring them face to face with the Risen Lord and to give them the desire to follow
Him no matter what the cost. It will take a miracle, no doubt many miracles, to
break them free from Satan's grasp.

Third, there must be a powerful work of the Holy Spirit in the worldwide
and national church to change Christian attitudes toward Muslims and to change
the missionary's approach to Islam. The old, adversarial, competitive, imperial-
istic, chauvinistic, extractionist, intolerant approach does not work. That has
been proven beyond a shadow of a doubt. If the status quo is to change, a new
way must be found whereby Muslims can come to Christ in the context of their
own culture and community. Cross-cultural workers are responsible to point the
way by word and deed and must be prepared to do so.

CONCLUSION

Several years ago an Ethnex friend confided to Jane that he thought that Bill
would become a good Muslim eventually.

We found his statement encouraging for several reasons. First, we had obviously succeeded in communicating to him our respect for his culture. He could
see that we were happy to be with them and were comfortable with many of their
customs. Second, we had succeeded in communicating our interest in spiritual
things and our commitment to clean living. He had noted our respect for God,
and our honesty and our lack of interest in the common vices. And third, we had
succeeded in communicating that we were not Muslim, although we had
accepted many aspects of Islamic culture.

However, as the years go by and his predictions concerning Bill's conversion to Islam is not fulfilled, we hope that he will begin to ask the question why. "Why do Bill and Jane refuse to become complete Muslims? It would be so easy for them. They obviously respect our culture, and are God-fearing people. All they would have to do is accept the prophethood of Muhammad (PBUH) and the Quran and that would be it. Then, they would be one with us, fully accepted. And they would receive great honor and respect. And we would do favors for them, and provide accommodation for them, and even help them arrange suitable marriages for their sons. But they refuse. They stubbornly remain loyal to Jesus Christ and the Bible. What is so special about that Book? What is so special about that Person?"

Of course, as he weighs that decision, a flood of other questions will come into his mind. Will I have to change my name? Will I be cut off from my people? How will I pray? When and where will I pray? Will I no longer be able to go to the mosque? What will happen when the Fast of Ramadan comes? Will I offer a sacrifice during *Eid* or not? Should I pay the welfare tithe (*zakat*)? And if my family should follow me in this decision; how will it affect the women in my household? As he contemplates these things, we hope that he will think about us and realize that he can become a loyal disciple of Jesus Christ and remain a respected, functioning member of his community.

RAMADAN:
SHOULD MISSIONARIES
KEEP THE MUSLIM FAST?*

Yes, because it may be the best time to make new friends, or to develop deeper levels of spiritual relationships.

by John Speers

The shift from a fruitful ministry among nominal Catholics (our first term) to Muslim evangelism (our second term) had not been easy. Our transfer to a poor, urban Muslim community had coincided with Ramadan, the month of fasting. Strict prohibition applies to food, drink, cigarettes, and lovemaking during the 14 daylight hours throughout the 30-day period.

The nights had been noisy as people feasted, while the days found those same people more religiously-minded than normal, and very suspicious at our

* Reprinted by permission of *Evangelical Missions Quarterly* (Box 794, Wheaton, IL 60189 USA)

arrival. It had not been a good time for us. We decided Ramadan was perhaps the best time to go away for a vacation.

A year later, with nothing to show for our efforts at making some inroads into this resistant community, Ramadan came around again. Perhaps with some desperation, and certainly with some apprehension, we decided that I would try to keep the fast, while my wife Brenda would support and encourage me.

COMPROMISE OR CONTEXTUALIZATION

When my missionary friends and some of our supporters heard about it, a lot of questions popped up. Generally, Evangelicals are indifferent—if not hostile—toward missionaries who observe Ramadan. The team leader of one Muslim ministry told me that only four of his 20 members were keeping the fast. That ratio is probably a fair representation of missionaries' attitudes. To keep Ramadan or not has serious theological repercussions. Does participation equal compromise?

Two conclusions freed me to keep the fast. First, was the realization that equally devoted missionaries differ. A number of missionaries in evangelical agencies advocate a contextual approach to the fast. They withstand their critics with scriptural evidence, chiefly Paul's argument in 1 Corinthians 9:22: "To the weak I became weak, that I might win the weak. I have become all things to all men, that I might by all means save some."

Who would not keep the fast, if it were known that by so doing some people would come to faith in Christ? To me, emanating from Paul's argument, is my second reason for keeping the fast: ". . . that by all means I might save some." How can we know if identification with Muslims at this level will produce fruit, unless we try?

BENEFITS

It would be gratifying if I could say that some have been saved as a direct result of my contextualized Ramadan fast. Regardless, the following benefits—perhaps neither conclusive nor spectacular—have convinced me of the potential of continuing to observe the fast.

1 Interpretation of presence

After looking at several potential homes to rent in our Muslim community, we stopped for a Coke at a local eatery. Soon a curious crowd gathered and the inevitable question arose, "Who are you, and why do you want to move into our community?" We cringed as we sought an inoffensive yet ethical response.

"Missionary." is an acceptable title in many parts of the world. It is well understood and interpreted by the people in a way that gives both respect and an open door for telling the Gospel. Among Muslims, however, many missionaries continue to seek a different term to explain their presence. Linguist, teacher, student, and language learner, among others, have been tried and often found lacking.

Without any point of reference, Muslims often stereotype missionaries first as Americans and then as Christians. Both are derogatory terms. They see missionaries through the lens of American mass media and conclude that we represent the antithesis to their own values. The missionary begins lower than "square one" in establishing a viable witness.

Ramadan offers the chance for a very different interpretation of the strange visitors. Because Ramadan is the essence of Muslim piety, anyone who observes it is recognized as a devoted seeker of God. In some languages a special word is used to mark those who have completed the entire 30 days without fault.

I have found that as a direct result of my participation in Ramadan, I am being seen much differently by our community. This is most noticeable in people's introductions: "This is John, a follower of the Prophet Jesus. He doesn't eat pork, and he kept the whole fast." Spiritual conversations born of mutual respect, rather than the customary debate, repeatedly followed this introduction.

2 Initiation of friendships

In some Islamic nations shopkeepers report sales increases of up to 50 percent during Ramadan. The days of fasting are offset by evenings of feasting. Food, fellowship, and Quranic readings are the order of the night. The bond of the Islamic community grows deeper at Ramadan, as rich and poor alike share in the fast and the feast.

It is not surprising, then, that many missionaries find it difficult to maintain or initiate new friendships during this time. When the total focus for 30 days is piety and fellowship within the community, the Muslims easily forget their

Christian friends. Missionaries are especially frustrated.

. Participation in the fast offers a different perspective. Near the end of our first week, we ventured into the unknown, and invited a family to break the fast in our home at sunset. The meal was so positive that Brenda's supporting role became primary. During the next three weeks we entertained another 50 people, many previously unknown to us, and sent food to an additional 100. Their response was remarkable.

Actually, Ramadan may be the best time to initiate new friendships, or to cultivate old ones to deeper spiritual levels. The natural tendency toward feasting offers ample opportunities for initiating new relationships. The prevailing spirit of piety opens the door for discussions about spiritual matters.

3 Instruction in culture

Without an appropriate understanding of our presence in their community, it's hard to start friendships. Without friendships, it's hard to learn language and culture. By participating in the fast, we entered into the heart of both language and culture. We learned more about social structures, the Muslim faith, and felt needs during those 30 than days in the previous eight months.

4 Identification

From the outset we sought an incarnational ministry. Our location, home, and lifestyle (including going without a car) were part of our identification with the people. But we were still considered to be the wealthiest residents.

The fast gave us the chance for a truer assimilation into their society. I shared in their thirst, hunger, and the feast. I identified with them at the core of their lives. For the first time, I felt more on the inside of their society than on the outside.

5 Intercession

Christians are instructed to fast in secret. Ramadan is a public display of perceived righteousness. It wasn't easy to find the balance.

Before beginning the fast, I decided that Ramadan would simply be a method of identification, an experiment in empathy. However, Brenda and I agreed to cover the entire month in prayer. As the fast progressed, two things happened.

183

More time for prayer, physical weakness, and a focus on the Lord deepened our intercessory burden. Our new friendships and freshly acquired knowledge of the culture in turn fueled our intercession.

6 Inspiration to persevere

Building deeper friendships is a slow process in the Muslim community. Our results are so negligible for so long that our supporters at home don't understand what we are doing. Discouragement sets in.

However, we found that Ramadan gave us our first ministry encouragement in more than a year. Not only budding friendships, but the community's new respect for our spirituality brightened our outlook and gave us new outlets for ministry. We were inspired to press on, both in our mundane daily tasks, and also in creative experiments to find other bridges to our Muslim friends.

CONCLUSION

Gaining benefits from keeping the fast does not come without risks. Misunderstandings arise, not just among fellow missionaries, but also among Muslims. Some of the latter thought I had converted. I had to make long explanations. However, not once did I get a negative response from a Muslim for keeping Ramadan.

Ramadan regresses 14 days each year on the Gregorian calendar. The next 10 years will be the easier in a physical sense to keep the fast in the Muslim world, as it progressively falls in the cooler season with shorter days.

I suggest that an experimental approach, coupled with sensitive education of our supporters, mission colleagues, and Muslim friends can clear the way to a profitable Ramadan experience. Can we continue to neglect the Ramadan fast with such potential benefits?

CHAPTER 12

THE VALLEY
OF DECISION

*by Lyndi Parshall**

It was a beautiful tropical, sunny day. A chicken scurried across the road. Akbar Khan watched it as he walked toward the village market. He turned down the dusty street and there stood the talk of the town. A large, bright yellow building stood majestically before him, practically shining in the blazing morning sun. He stood on the corner watching what was going on. People were walking through the gate, dressed in their best clothes.

Just yesterday, his father had laughed at the person everyone called a missionary. Akbar wasn't too sure what he thought about the man. He had observed him when the building they called a "church" was being built. The missionary always wore clean suits, and he seemed to have plenty of them. Of course, if he supplied the money to build the building, he must have a lot of money left over.

Just then, he saw Mohammed, the silversmith, go in the gate of the church. Akbar watched with curiosity. There was word going around that Mohammed had come to believe what the missionary was preaching. People said his attitude

---

* The author, a missionary kid (MK) from Bangladesh, wrote this paper while a high school student at Faith Academy in Manila.

had changed and that he was a much nicer man now with more patience.

Akbar's curiosity grew. What did this missionary have to say? Most of the people in his village spoke contemptuously of the white man. They were jealous of his money and wondered why he couldn't use it to help them instead of spending it on a silly building.

A young boy chasing a stray cow ran into Akbar jolting him into remembering that he was supposed to be canvassing for the prices of lamps. The month of fasting would be coming up soon and he wanted to have a good lamp by which to see when he ate in the early hours of the morning.

Akbar was tempted to go inside this foreign church, and see for himself what was going on. His wife would probably get mad at him if he did. Slowly, he walked towards the gate, noticing the barbed wire running along the top of the high walls which was put there to keep out the beggar kids. Then he looked up at the cross standing tall on the top of the building. How awful! The cross! What a symbol of hatred *that* represented to Akbar. It reminded him of the grotesque stories he had learned in school about the Crusades—how his Muslim ancestors had been killed by cross-carrying Crusaders.

Akbar decided not to think about it, but to go on in. He felt strange going to a place of worship on Sunday. Normally, he would have gone on a Friday. He followed the little brick walkway past the small cement house where the national evangelist lived with his family. He looked in and saw a fan hanging from the ceiling. What luxury! Electricity! Why, even the Muslim holy man doesn't have a cement house. Only the banker and other high class people have electricity. He then made his way to the front door of the church.

Akbar reached down to unbuckle his sandals. But he noticed that there were hardly any shoes outside compared to the number of people inside. How repulsive! In a mosque no one is allowed to wear shoes. He pulled off his sandals, added them to the small pile, and then walked in the door. He looked up towards the front of the room and saw an elevated stand that held some books on it. Then he saw another cross behind the pulpit.

His eyes swept the room. It was full of chairs—new ones. Where did the white man get all his money? How different from the mosque where you sit on the floor. He noticed that men were on one side and women on the other. That was good, but even that was unique because women usually would not go to a mosque.

On the front row, sitting all together was the missionary's family—the husband, wife, and two daughters. Akbar was amazed to see them all together on the women's side. He hoped no one else would be offended like he was.

His eyes fell on a picture on the wall. It was of a man who looked nice enough, with long hair and a beard, but then, slowly he read the words under the picture—"Jesus Christ." He couldn't believe it! No Muslim would have a picture of a prophet hanging on a wall! It was totally forbidden. His thoughts were interrupted when a little boy ran by him. He turned around and looked for a place to wash his face, hands, and feet. Surely, they would have a washing place like the mosque does. But, no, there was none. He walked down the center aisle looking for someone he knew. He saw a few familiar faces, but decided to sit by himself so he could silently analyze the service. He found a seat and sat down. Picking up one of the books, he saw that it was thick and nicely bound. He opened it and tried to read it, but he couldn't really understand the words. One word he saw was the "Bible." This was the Christian's holy book. Did they just let it lay around where it could get messed up? Didn't they care if someone dropped it or touched it with dirty hands?

He looked up and saw the missionary's children running around. In a mosque, children wouldn't be allowed to be a nuisance. The children were playing with the same type of book he had in his hands—the Bible. Didn't the missionaries care if their children showed disrespect to a holy book?

Akbar saw flowers by the pump organ and wondered if they were for decoration, or if they were an offering to the Jesus man. He caught sight of a paper lying on the floor that a child had dropped. There was a picture on the paper of a small fenced area with some animals in it. He saw a cow, a horse, a pig. A PIG!! How terrible. Oh, that's right. The missionary didn't think pork was bad. Now, that he thought about it, Akbar remembered that someone had told him the missionaries bought pork from the Christian butcher. They actually eat the vile meat!

He looked up towards the white man and his family again. What beautiful clothes they wore. How that watch shone in the sun. Looking at the missionary's wife, he saw that she wore a sleeveless long dress. Even the high class women in the town didn't wear sleeveless blouses with their saris. It was indecent! He noticed she didn't have any way to cover her head when she prayed.

Just then, the evangelist stood up in the front and began to talk. He welcomed everyone, then gave some announcements. Then he told them to turn to page 30 in a song book. Were they going to sing? Sure enough, a man got up and went to the pump organ and began to play. It was very strange to him as Muslims only chant their songs.

Akbar reached for the only other book he saw and found the page. He couldn't read well enough to follow along too well, so he just listened. The tunes were totally foreign. He could tell everyone was having trouble singing the song. He liked chanting much better.

The foreigner then stood up and read a passage out of the Bible. My, what an accent! After ten years in this country, couldn't he speak more like we do? Akbar noticed that most of the national women covered their heads, but the white woman did not. When the foreigner was finished reading, he sat down and the service went on. They then said they would take an offering. Some men got up and passed around a plate so that people could drop their money into it. In a mosque this would not be done in this manner. The church system seemed like begging to him. He wondered what the money was for. Surely, the white man had plenty!

Again, the missionary got up and began to speak. Akbar listened for awhile, but at the word "Jesus," he could no longer listen. As a Muslim, he only saw Jesus as a good prophet that lived long ago—not as the "Son of God." How repulsive to think of God having relations with Mary and having a son whom they named Jesus.

The missionary stopped talking and began to pray. Akbar noticed the people all closed their eyes, but they didn't change positions. None prostrated themselves. They just sat in their chairs. How different was this religion!

The service ended and people began to file out. Akbar got up and, as he walked out the door, the missionary shook his hand and mumbled something he couldn't understand.

He put on his sandals and went out into the road. He heard someone call out to remind everyone to come again that night. Akbar went out the gate and toward the lamp shop thinking of what he had seen and heard.

That night, he went out to stand in front of the well-lit church. Akbar watched the people going in. He stood and pondered the events of the morning. Looking to his right, he saw his mosque in the distance lit with small flickering candles. He looked back at the church once—then turned and began to slowly walk down the dusty road towards the mosque.

CHAPTER 13

BRIDGE THE GAP: AN ALTERNATE WORSHIP STYLE

(A response to Lyndi Parshall's story)

by Ashkenaz Asif*

After dumping fodder for the cow, Akbar Khan went inside the house to get the empty can in which he was to bring some kerosene oil for the lamp. His wife was still in bed. She reminded him that he should ask the new doctor how much it would cost for her medicine as well as for the children's. As he picked up the can and a bag for groceries, he looked down the steep twisting pathway. At the very bottom, along the valley floor, a river wound around the mountain. Today, there wouldn't be many people in town because it was Friday. He started off briskly so he would have time to say his *Nimbus* (prayers) in the mosque.

After some time he left the mountain path and walked along the road. Walking faster caused him pain in his right foot. His foot had been crushed weeks ago

---

* The author, a Pakistani, pastors a church in his country. He believes that a worship service can serve as a bridge in evangelism in a Muslim community. He was inspired to write this story after reading "The Valley of Decision," a short story written by Lyndi Parshall, to whom he is grateful.

by his cow's hoof and though the wound had healed, it still frequently pained him.

When he came to his friend Akram's shop, he bought the needed items. Together they headed towards the mosque for their *Nimaz*. While on the way, Akbar asked his friend about the new doctor and his clinic, recently started in town. Akram said he had heard that the treatment was good and the charges low, but that there was one drawback: the people were Christians.

"Christians!" Akbar exclaimed in surprise. Some people from Akbar Khan's village had gone to a hospital in another area where *Angrez* (English) people had treated them. When they returned they had some Christian books. One book had a picture of the prophet Moses. Later, these were handed over to the *maulvi* (Muslim priest). These people had also mentioned that the Christians had preached before they gave any treatment.

"I wonder what kind of people these Christians are," Akbar thought to himself. But he rid himself of all thoughts of Christians when he found himself in front of the mosque. He began to prepare for *Wuzooh* (ablutions). After prayers they came out and put on their shoes. Akbar decided he would go and see this doctor. Akram responded that if his employee at the shop was not off for the day, he would have liked to join him. Instead, he gave him directions to the clinic and then returned to his shop.

Akbar soon found the clinic. It was on the outskirts of the town. He saw a sign which stated that it was a non-profit clinic, run by donations. He had not yet finished reading the information on the sign when a man appeared from inside. Akbar turned to him as the man greeted him cordially. Akbar couldn't tell whether the man was a Christian or a Muslim because he spoke to him in his own language and wore clothes as he himself wore.

"I want to see the doctor," said Akbar Khan.

"But the clinic is closed today," the man told him. "Are you ill?"

"No, not I, but my wife and children. I want to know how much it would cost for a checkup and some medicine. May I see the doctor?" he asked hopefully.

"Come with me. I am going in that direction," the man replied.

As they walked together for a few minutes Akbar became certain that the man was a Pakistani. Presently, they came to a house.

"I think the Doctor Sahib has gone inside," the man said as he stopped outside the door.

"Where?" Akbar Khan asked impatiently.

"Inside the worship house," he replied as he pointed to a room attached to the house. Akbar looked and saw an ordinary room where a few people were placing their shoes in a row on the verandah.

"I think you could talk to him after the worship time," the fellow replied.

"That's all right. I'll wait outside," Akbar said, while starting to move away.

"No, no. It wouldn't look right. Come along with me," the fellow insisted and began to take the things from Akbar's hands.

"Me in a worship service! I'm a Muslim and perhaps . . . well . . . this is a Christian worship service," he said hesitantly.

"Yes, I know that you are a Muslim. But we would not have any objections if you would like to come and join us," the man said with a smile.

"Well, . . . all right, I'll come."

Both of them took off their shoes. Akbar followed his companion and stepped slowly into the room. It was a small room with people sitting on a rug spread on the floor. One man sat in the front and read something out loud. Akbar sat down with his friend in one of the rows. He was not sure if the man on his left was Pakistani or not. Looking up, he saw something written in Urdu with beautiful calligraphy. It was enclosed in a glass frame and was hanging on the wall. On his left was a large curtain and when a momentary breath of wind pushed it aside, he noticed, to his surprise, some women sitting in the room as well. Meanwhile, his companion picked up something from the shelf on the wall. He unwrapped it. It was a book which he placed on a wooden holder.

"That must be an *Injil*," he thought to himself.

After completing his observations of the room he turned his attention to the man in front. He had finished reading now, and was addressing the people. He wore a white *shalwar* and *kameez* and had a beard. There could be no doubt that this man was a Pakistani. In fact, he looked like his *maulvi*, though, unlike him, he spoke very politely.

"Do we have any guests today?" he asked as he glanced over the worshipers.

"Yes, I have a guest with me—Akbar," his companion replied. Akbar's heart quickened.

"We welcome you, sir," the leader of the worship said. Then he mentioned some sick people and several other needs.

"Let us pray," he said as he raised his hands. Akbar listened carefully as he prayed. The leader thanked God for many things. He asked for guidance and help. He prayed for the sick and as he did Akbar also prayed silently that his wife would be healed soon.

They finished praying and everyone said, "Amen."

After the prayer the leader asked someone to read a passage from the Holy *Injil*. It was the account of *Isa al Masih* (Jesus the Messiah) healing a person who could not walk. It reminded Akbar of the beggar to whom he had given 25 *paisa* (a pittance) earlier that day in front of the gate of the mosque. The leader continued to talk though Akbar had difficulty understanding all he said. What he could understand, however, was that there were two kinds of sickness—one physical and one spiritual, and that *Isa al Masih* could heal both of them just as he had done for the sick man. The leader closed the book again and the people began to chant some *hamd* (a chant in honor of God). Akbar had always enjoyed listening to *hamds* on his radio at home. He liked this kind of chanting. They chanted another *hamd* that was even nicer than the first, and Akbar felt calm and peaceful inside his heart. The leader prayed again, and he noticed that one of the men had his eyes closed. He wondered if perhaps he was in deep meditation. The prayer ended and this time Akbar uttered an "Amen" as well.

The leader stood up, wrapped up the book again, and placed it behind the curtain in a cupboard. Then he walked out. People stood up and started out one by one. He noticed they were putting money in a big box beside the door. "Oh, this must be the *hadya* (offering)," he thought.

As he went out, many people greeted him. His companion told him that he could talk to the doctor now. He was told that it would not cost much and inwardly he sighed with relief. At least he would not have to sell his goat. He was about to leave when his companion reminded him that he had forgotten his bag and kerosene on the verandah. He picked them up and was saying good-bye to his friend when the man who led the worship service came and greeted him, thanking him for being present. Akbar asked if there would be a worship service next Friday as well, and the man assured him that they were held every Friday. They shook hands and Akbar started back to his village.

He walked down the road, the chanting still echoing in his mind. He noticed that the pain in his foot was gone. He thought he would ask his friend Akram to go to the worship service with him next Friday. He paused and looked up the mountain toward his village. It was a comforting sight to see smoke rising from the chimneys on the ridge of the mountain. He would be home before dark, he thought, smiling to himself, as he set off again at a faster pace.

Contextualized Medical Ministry Among Muslims

by Phil Parshall

Staff

2 foreign doctors
2 foreign nurses
2 foreign men trained in public health, preventive medicine, and theology
A small national staff of dedicated, sensitive Christians

- All staff should have training in a contextualized methodology of evangelism among Muslims.
- Language proficiency

Ministry

- Small hospital of 10 beds. Every effort would be made to keep it simple and small.
- Emphasis in the hospital on outpatients and referrals from field workers.
- No Gospel propagation on a formal basis. Only personal witness and verbal offers of special contextualized literature. There would be no literature or other type of Christian expression overtly displayed. The name of the facility would be something like "Haven of Hope" or "Refuge of Peace." The word "Christian" would be totally avoided. Staff would conform to the social expectations of the Muslim community.
- Field workers would gear their work toward educating villagers on how to avoid illness. Evening classes which focus on preventive medicine would

be held in villages. Gospel witness by these workers would be only on a personal basis and thus very low key.

- Difficult medical cases and surgery would be referred to the nearest government facility.
- Patients would pay at least something toward their treatment.
- The facility would be located in a totally Muslim area.

Lifestyle

- All property would be rented.
- Staff would seek not to cluster in housing. Houses would be simple. An effort would be made to avoid having vehicles. Perhaps motorcycles could facilitate travel within the villages and yet be low profile.
- The small hospital would be in a building similar to others in the town.
- Maximum interaction with nationals would be encouraged, professionally as well as socially. This would lead to a natural, yet unstructured sharing of one's faith.

Strategy

- This would be determined by the *mission* before recruitment of staff begins. Only staff agreeable with this *modus operandi* would be accepted.

Toward Developing a Mission's Position on the Use of Contextualization in Ministry among Muslims

by Phil Parshall

WHEREAS the Word of God commands evangelism among all peoples of the world

We therefore affirm our commitment to utilize all divine and human resources in the fulfillment of this evangelistic imperative.

WHEREAS one billion living Muslims have been largely ignored as an evangelistic priority

We therefore affirm our desire to employ spirit-directed strategies to present Christ to these children of Ishmael.

WHEREAS the rights of many Muslims have been violated and exploited through colonial domination

We therefore affirm the advisability of approaching Muslims with utmost sincerity, humility, and graciousness.

WHEREAS the term "contextualization" in some circles has been interpreted as a synonym for syncretism

We therefore affirm our commitment to a "contextualized missiology" which is strictly limited to only those means and methods of Muslim evangelism which are under the authority of the Word of God, and which are in harmony with an orthodox view of Evangelical theology.

WHEREAS Muslims are living in a great variety of cultural settings and socio-economic conditions.

We therefore affirm our need to adapt creatively to various modes of dress, eating styles, and living standards with a view toward maximum integration within Muslim communities.

WHEREAS Islam places great emphasis on following a worship ritual of profession, prayer, scripture reading, fasting and almsgiving

We therefore affirm that Muslim inquirers and converts should be taught biblical worship in a manner maximally equivalent to the forms and procedures to which they have been accustomed. This will need to be done with constant reference to theological grace, as well as freedom of ritual that Christians experience as opposed to the meritorious and legalistic nature of Islamic worship.

WHEREAS a majority of Muslims live in the financially needy Two-Thirds world

We therefore affirm our commitment to holistic ministry among Muslims seeking, in Christ's name, to assist in sensitive development projects which will not be, in fact or perception, merely an inducement toward their conversion to Christianity. This process should not detract from our goal of establishing a financially indigenous church of Muslim converts.

WHEREAS Muslims often do not adequately understand the Gospel as framed in Western thought and linguistic forms

We therefore affirm the priority of production of new literature which will communicate more effectively within the Muslim's own particular world view. Christian radio and television programming will also be evaluated by these criteria.

WHEREAS a majority of Muslims are directly affected by folk religious practices.

We therefore affirm our openness to involvement in spiritual warfare and power encounter against demonic forces in areas of healing, exorcism, and intercessory prayer.

WHEREAS gathering together large numbers of new believers may not be practical or wise

We therefore affirm the appropriateness of small gathered clusters of Muslim converts meeting informally for worship and discipleship. Where possible, this should be done in conjunction with a local evangelical church. If this proves unfeasible, the converts should be encouraged to meet on their own.

FINALLY, we affirm our commitment to long-term involvement in Muslim evangelism. We recognize there will be discouragements and casualties in the outworking of this process of engagement with the forces of darkness. But, by God's grace, we will persevere and see precious fruit from the household of Ishmael gathered into the Kingdom of God.

PART THREE

PROCLAMATION:

THE NEED FOR RELEVANCE

AND THEOLOGICAL BALANCE

CHAPTER

14

THE CONFLICT OF DOGMATISM WITHIN A PLURALISTIC WORLD

by Phil Parshall

Having graduated from a very conservative Christian liberal arts college, I felt I was more than adequately prepared to confront the challenge of heathen Islam. Arriving in Bangladesh (then East Pakistan) in 1962, my wife of nine months and I were quickly sent off to a remote village which was bereft of such "modern" conveniences as electricity, running water or paved roads. We settled into a nineteenth century lifestyle and began observing the "heathen" who were entrusted to us—a couple of raw, 23 year-old youngsters—by the God of all the universe with the privilege and responsibility of presenting ultimate, dogmatic TRUTH to them. I was cocky and confident. The onlooking Bengali Muslims referred to me as a *kutcha butcha, i.e.,* an unlearned baby! But, no matter, my armor of dogmatic assurance was unpierced. I was right, they were wrong. Simple!

But—not so simple. Each afternoon 50-year old Abdul walked by our front yard. His total composure was exemplary. Always friendly and respectful to me, he seemed to possess a deep abiding peace that indicted me as I struggled with my own restless surging temperament. Abdul's long white robe and prayer hat indicated he was a very religious Muslim.

After a few months of Bengali study, I decided to visit Abdul in his small watch shop which was just down the street from our home. My *modus operandi* of witness had been carefully thought through and rehearsed. I would ask him what Allah, Prophet Muhammad, and the Quran had done personally and spiritually for him. He would then be at a loss for words. Immediately, I would take the Sword of the Spirit (as mediated through my personal testimony) and pierce him with Absolute Truth. He would be stricken mute and, thus, begin his quest for salvation as found only through Jesus Christ.

Abdul warmly greeted me, and offered me a rickety chair which was made even more precarious by an uneven mud floor and my 180-pound frame. My Muslim friend possessed nothing of this world's goods. His six foot by six foot shop and all its contents would be worth less than $100.

We chatted generally for a few minutes and then I requested Abdul to share his spiritual testimony with me. Immediately, his face lit up as that of an angel, and he enthusiastically began to tell me of the abundance of joy and peace that he had received as a result of being a devout Muslim. This layman shared the reality of Allah that he experienced as he arose at daybreak to begin the five-times-a-day Muslim prayer ritual. The Quran was his guide on the pathway of life. With a spontaneous gesture of enthusiasm, Abdul leaned forward close to my face, and blurted out, "Oh, it is so wonderful to be a Muslim!"

I slowly arose, shook my friend's hand and walked out the door.

I felt betrayed:

- Betrayed by my Christian college. Why hadn't they told me that the "heathen" can be so devoted to one God, and be so totally content in their "heathenism?"

- Betrayed by my mission. Why wasn't I compelled to become more aware of Islamic theology and reality before walking onto Muslim turf?

- Betrayed by my Lord. In my youthful naiveté I had possessed a devastating spiritual pride. I was totally right, and they were totally wrong. Now, how could God allow a Muslim to deliver such a heartfelt testimony of warmth, graciousness and reality to me?

The years have come and gone since 1962. Struggles have not ceased, but perhaps a few insights have increased in the crucial area of the interactions that take place when there is a definitive clash of two conflicting views of Truth. These reflections are an attempt to address this issue, with a purposeful emphasis on its outworking from a grassroots perspective.

CONFLICT

Holding firmly to an evangelical theological position on the uniqueness of Christ sets the stage for conflict. Consider the view of the renowned professor of religion, Wilfred Cantwell Smith:

> May I take for illustration a phrase, not unrepresentative, which was under discussion recently by the United Church of Canada's commission on faith, and which ran as follows: "Without the particular knowledge of God in Jesus Christ, men do not really know God at all." Let us leave aside for the moment any question of whether or not this is true. . . . My point here is simply that, in any case, it is arrogant. At least, it becomes arrogant when one carries it out to the non-Western world. In the quiet study, it may be possible for the speculative mind to produce this kind of doctrine, provided that one keep it purely bookish. But except at the cost of insensitivity or delinquence, it is morally not possible actually to go out into the world and say to devout, intelligent, fellow human beings: "We are saved and you are damned," or, "We believe that we know God, and we are right; you believe that you know God, and you are totally wrong."
>
> This is intolerable from merely human standards. It is doubly so from Christian ones. Any position that antagonizes and alienates rather than reconciles, that is arrogant rather than humble, that promotes segregation rather than brotherhood, that is unlovely, is *ipso facto* un-Christian (Smith 1982:13-14).

It would be easy to simply relegate Smith and his writings to the liberal Christian camp and thus not give weight to his ponderings. My wife, Julie, and I had the privilege of being invited to dine with the Smiths at the Harvard Faculty Club in 1983. As we interacted, I could only conclude Smith's views have evolved from the interaction of a tender conscience with a world full of diverse views of conceptual truth. This Harvard professor grew up in an evangelical home and spent some years in Muslim Pakistan teaching in Forman Christian College. His charge of arrogance against our evangelical position may be unacceptable to us, but perhaps a sensitive hearing of Smith can assist us in a better understanding of how we should adhere to and present to others our specific belief in the uniqueness of the person of Jesus Christ.

Some time back, I was driving through a Muslim area of Manila with a missionary friend. As we passed Muslim homes built with slanted roofs of Islamic architecture, we observed scores of Muslims dressed in their colorful malongs. This was a world apart from the rest of the ten million residents of westernized Manila. I said reflectively, "You know, John, the rightness of our view' of Truth depends on every man, woman, and teenager in this community spending an eternity in Hell. That is, of course, assuming they do not become Christians—as has been the case up to now." It is a solemn thought that, according to our evangelical theology, it is an impossibility for both Muslims and Christians to coexist in a blissful heaven. How sobering and also conflictual this is to the Christian.

Lesslie Newbigin, in *The Open Secret* contributes his thoughts,

> Can it really be believed that God, who is creator of heaven and earth, by whom and for whom all things exist, has concentrated his purpose of salvation on these minuscule communities in the little world of the eastern Mediterranean, leaving the millions in China and India and Africa, who at the same moment are living, praying, suffering, and dying, outside of the realm of salvation until they are "discovered," many centuries too late, by the explorers and missionaries of these chosen people? If this doctrine of the election of a chosen people appointed to be the bearers of salvation for all mankind seems intolerable to many sincere Christians in the twentieth century, has it not really been intolerable from the beginning?

My emotional struggle with the traditional evangelical position on the uniqueness of Christ took a quantum leap when I assisted survivors of the 1970 cyclone tragedy in Bangladesh. Within an eight-hour period 500,000 God-created Muslim and Hindu Bangladeshis were drowned in the world's greatest natural calamity of the twentieth century. As I worked with Southern Baptist missionaries overseeing the digging of fresh water wells, I was at times overcome with a sense of spiritual despair. Not one of the 500,000 was a Christian. Not one. Half a million people were swept into eternity without Christ by God-controlled "nature." Incidentally, I cannot, like others, somehow speak of nature and natural calamities as if they are a force apart from God's control and direction. If that is so, I have to dilute my view of God's sovereignty, authority, and power.

I have never been the same since 1970.

Then there is the theological hermeneutical conflict. I was speaking in Nigeria on the subject of contextualization and sensitivity in witness to Muslims. A missionary in African dress came up to me at the conclusion of the meeting and enthusiastically told me of Neal Punt's book, *Unconditional Good News*. This book advocates biblical universalism, and has caused Punt to be a target of intense criticism within his Reformed denominational circles.

Punt particularly highlights the story of Cornelius the God-seeker in Acts 10 along with 1 Timothy 4:10 which indicates God is the Savior of all men; and then Titus 2:11 that states, "The grace of God that brings salvation has appeared to all men." These Scriptures have been explained in a variety of ways, but there remains some measure of theological fog. Otherwise, there would not be so many scholars maintaining such hermeneutical diversity on the issue.

What about the conflict of Scriptures of varied religions? In the Quran (Pickthall translation) sura 112, verses two and three say, "Allah, the eternally Besought of all! He begetteth not nor was begotten." I would like to ask you to take a moment to ponder these Quranic verses and then make a mental statement as to whether you agree with it or not. Does God beget or was God at any point begotten?

I have asked seminary students this question in a number of countries. Always there is consternation. The normal vote is a tie. Half of the students affirm and half deny. Can we be comfortable with saying God was begotten at a point in time and space? Is the womb of Mary a "begotten" experience for God? What about John 3:16 in its reference to begotten? We are brought inextricably into a dilemma. Islam particularly brings confusion to us as the Quran seems bent on denying anything remotely connected with the incarnation.

Other religions bring their share of perplexity to us by affirming so much that is true and good. Morality is uplifted. Sin is denounced. And in Hinduism, a comfortable pluralistic acceptance of all religions is set forth.

The critic of evangelicalism asks with pungency, "How can you be so bigoted and so narrow?" Under the barrage of stinging criticism many begin to look for a way out. Martin Goldsmith documents Norman Anderson's postulate.

> In his writings Professor Norman Anderson, the Christian theologian and Islamicist, suggests the possibility that God may save some on the grounds of their humble repentance and faith in God. In this he denies the possibility that they should be saved because of their religious piety, for the Bible clearly rejects any idea of salvation through good works or merit. He is therefore not suggesting at all that anyone is saved on the basis of their religious sincerity. But perhaps God may apply the saving work of Jesus Christ to those who have a humble and repentant faith which looks to God for his gift of eternal life by grace. They may never have heard of Jesus but God still may apply the shed blood of Christ to such people. We realize of course that such ideas remain in the realm of speculation and cannot be proved by Scripture. But again we have to remind ourselves that God is the judge; we are not (Goldsmith 1989:137).

C. S. Lewis and contemporary missiologist Charles Kraft have leaned toward this position in their writings. Other mission leaders have generally been uncomfortable with a move in this theological direction.

Currents and cross-currents. The task of unravelling all the claims and counter-claims to religious truth can leave one totally bewildered and perplexed. I am reminded of how Wilfred Cantwell Smith teasingly looked out to those of us sitting in his class and said, "The study of comparative religions makes one comparatively religious." Perhaps Smith stands as exhibit A to his own statement.

In the midst of such conflict, can the evangelical stand up with a clear and ringing confession of belief in and adherence to the doctrine of the uniqueness of Christ as the way to God?

CONFESSION

What are we Evangelicals confessing and why are we confessing it? Let us return to W. C. Smith's comments on evangelical belief. Smith deplores our "intolerance, insensitivity, delinquency, antagonism, alienation, arrogance, unloveliness, and bias toward segregation." These are pejorative words. He goes on to say evangelical exclusivism can more easily be promoted in a book-lined study than in the real world. At least on that point I can agree with Smith. My 36 years in Asia have made me leery of scholars resident in the West who deliver sweeping pontifications that affect the world of missions and theology. Perhaps more sensitivity could be incorporated into their deliberations if they would take up residence in the third world, and write from the perspective of an intensive inter-action with poverty, anti-westernism, and pluralistic religious expressions.

My basic problem with Smith is not with his humanistic emphasis. Chris-tians are to love and to walk humbly with all of God's created beings. But Smith seems to read his Bible with an overwhelmingly presuppositional bias, leaning almost totally toward God's love and man's love. Where is a theological balance that allows for the hundreds of biblical passages that deal with God's wrath? Do we emasculate the Bible by undercutting the natural antithesis that runs as a continuing thread from Genesis to Revelation? Light and darkness; saved and lost; righteous and wicked; eternal life and eternal death; grace and judgment; heaven and hell; sheep and goats—all point to a distinct differentiation between groups of people who walk divergent paths and follow variant religious tradi-tions. Because we are heralds of a total biblical message, are we to become guilt-ridden by Smith's emotive and denunciatory words?

Bishop Stephen Neill, in his excellent book, *Crises of Belief*, addresses the issue.

> Christian faith claims for itself that it is the only form of faith for men. By its own claim to truth, it·casts the shadow of imperfect truth on every other system. This Christian claim is naturally offensive to the adher-ents of every other religious system. It is almost as offensive to modern man, brought up in the atmosphere of relativism, in which tolerance is regarded almost as the highest of the virtues. But we must not suppose that this claim to universal validity is something that can quietly be removed from the Gospel without changing it into some-thing entirely different from what it is (Neill 1984:30).

In another of his books, *Christian Faith and Other Faiths*, Neill raises a pro-phetic warning that "the danger of the approach of 'congenial understanding' is that we may all get lost in a fog of geniality" (Neill 1961:233).

Evangelicals are a very Scripture-oriented people. A high commitment to the Bible as God's Word is perhaps our primary identification as a community. It seems to us that the uniqueness of Christ is set forth, in the Bible, as an un-equivocal theological premise. John 14:6 presents Christ as the only way to God; Acts 4:12 states, "Salvation is found in no one else, for there is no other name under heaven given to men by which we must be saved;" and 1 Timothy 2:5 tells us that Christ is the one mediator between God and man. Terry Muck, writing in

Christianity Today, states, "The uniqueness of Christ has been a cornerstone of orthodoxy for nearly 2,000 years. No major theologian has ever denied it. Most have championed it vigorously. But incredible as it may seem, this may well be the key theological issue of the new decade" (Muck 1990:14).

This assertion of uniqueness is the whole motivation and thrust behind the missionary enterprise. If Christ is but an optional way, then let every man be content according to his own religious persuasion. In such a case, the dynamic thrust of propagation in the New Testament comes out looking misguided at best, and harmful at worst.

The apostle Peter was definitely a dogmatic propagator of a unique message. In Acts 4:19-20, he states to his persecutors, "Judge for yourselves whether it is right in God's sight to obey you rather than God. For we cannot help speaking about what we have seen and heard." Paul, in 1 Corinthians 9:16 says, "I am compelled to preach. Woe to me if I do not preach the Gospel." His whole life was a case study in being totally consumed in propagating a compelling message. One searches in vain to find passages in Scripture that indicate Paul was of the opinion that Christianity was just another religious option for mankind to consider.

Douglas Webster, in his *Yes To Mission*, proposes that we all relax with the word dogmatic.

> The Gospel is dogmatic and cannot be anything else if it is to remain Gospel. It is as dogmatic as any news-item which may affect us, for good or ill, any day. Unless the Church and its theologians can return soon to a much more positive and ringing declaration of the eternal Gospel, we shall not be in a position to play a very significant part in the next—and probably unusually difficult—phase of the Christian mission (Webster 1966:17).

As statistics prove, the conciliar movement did not heed Webster's warning given in 1966. A generally inclusivistic view of religious faith undercut their involvement in the missionary enterprise. Their shift toward an emphasis on social concern in its many ramifications has pretty well smothered out evangelistic concerns. Not completely—but enough to represent what can be termed a paradigm shift. Certainly, Wesley would create a measure of controversy if he were alive today preaching his messages of old throughout the Methodist churches of the world.

Evangelicals, on the other hand, have held quite tenaciously to dogmatism. Herein one finds the dynamics for church growth we have enjoyed in recent decades, particularly in the third world.

Confession may well lead to persecution. One can only read the closing verses of Hebrews chapter 11 and thoughtfully ponder. But, confess we must. So, how can we best confess a dogmatic message which, if accepted, can potentially lead our hearers toward a path of alienation and pain? This thought brings us to our next section.

EMPATHY

Mohandas Gandhi reflects back on an experience he had while listening to an evangelical missionary in South Africa:

> I listened to his discourse on the efficacy of prayer with unbiased attention, and assured him that nothing could prevent me from embracing Christianity, should I feel the call. I had no hesitation in giving him this assurance, as I had long since taught myself to follow the inner voice. I delighted in submitting to it. To act against it would be difficult and painful to me. . . .
>
> This Convention was an assemblage of devout Christians. I was delighted at their faith. I met the Rev. (Andrew) Murray. I saw that many were praying for me. I liked some of their hymns, they were very sweet.
>
> The Convention lasted for three days. I could understand and appreciate the devoutness of those who attended it. But I saw no reason for changing my belief—my religion. It was impossible for me to believe that I could go to heaven or attain salvation only by becoming a Christian. When I frankly said so to some of the good Christian friends, they were shocked. But there was no help for it.
>
> My difficulties lay deeper. It was more than I could believe that Jesus was the only incarnate son of God, and that only he who believed in him would have everlasting life. If God could have sons, all of us were His sons. If Jesus was like God, or God Himself, then all men were like God and could be God Himself. My reason was not ready to believe literally that Jesus by his death and by his blood redeemed the sins of the world. Metaphorically, there might be some truth in it. Again, according to Christianity only human beings had souls, and not other

living beings for whom death meant complete extinction; while I held a contrary belief. I could accept Jesus as a martyr, an embodiment of sacrifice, and a divine teacher, but not as the most perfect man ever born. His death on the Cross was a great example to the world, but that there was anything like a mysterious or miraculous virtue in it my heart could not accept. The pious lives of Christians did not give me anything that the lives of men of other faiths had failed to give. I had seen in other lives just the same reformation that I had heard of among Christians. Philosophically there was nothing extraordinary in Christian principles. From the point of view of sacrifice, it seemed to me that the Hindus greatly surpassed the Christians. It was impossible for me to regard Christianity as a perfect religion or the greatest of all religions.

I shared this mental churning with my Christian friends whenever there was an opportunity, but their answers could not satisfy me: . . .

Though I took a path my Christian friends had not intended for me, I have remained forever indebted to them for the religious quest that they awakened in me. I shall always cherish the memory of their contact. The years that followed had more, not less, of such sweet and sacred contacts in store for me (Gandhi 1957:135-138).

Gandhi, a Hindu, was in my opinion one of the greatest men who ever lived on this earth. I have read nine biographies and autobiographies of Gandhi. The film Gandhi captivated me so much I have watched it four times.

What do we do with his musings on Christianity? He listened carefully for three days to the message and understood at least some of the basics of biblical teaching. Overall, he was fairly impressed with Christians. He enjoyed the hymns of the church. He committed himself to "embracing Christianity" should he hear an inner voice telling him to do so.

Gandhi died a Hindu uttering these words, "O Ram." What do we conclude as we contemplate the present abode of Gandhi's soul? He heard and he rejected. He rejected not out of meanness or a refusal to thoroughly consider; but rather, out of measured conviction.

This very real dilemma does not dilute my convictions given in the last section, but it does highlight a struggle any sincere Christian engages in as he interacts with the real world. Dogmatism in belief does not negate the obligation we have to walk in another man's sandals. This process is what we call empathy. Neill has defined empathy as "the attempt to enter as far as is possible into the thoughts and experiences of others without losing the integrity of one's own independence" (Neill 1984:18).

Professor Ninian Smart was teaching a course on *Worldview* at Harvard. One day he asked all of us to meet for eight hours and discuss the subject of empathy. What an interesting day it was! In the class was a Hindu, a Moonie, many Christians of liberal persuasion, and one evangelical—me. But, I did appreciate anew the sincerity with which people held differing views. We sought to listen to each other, and then weigh carefully the conflicting claims. For the first time I really understood why an intellectual Ph.D. student could be an avid disciple of Rev. Moon, even to the point of allowing himself to be married to an unknown girl as arranged by Rev. Moon. This was done in a mass marriage ceremony conducted in Madison Square Garden. This student was extremely gracious and appeared most devout.

There were four of us Merrill Fellows at Harvard Divinity School in 1983. The other three were: a liberal Christian lady who was head of a Boston group of churches; a middle-aged Ph.D. pastor of the second largest Seventh Day Adventist church in America; and the third was Jane, who is a non-theistic, Universalist-Unitarian church pastor. She was my great challenge. Within a short time, she told me of her research project in seminary when she took video clips of Hitler, Mussolini, and Billy Graham and made a close study of crowd manipulation techniques each had employed. Her enthusiastic and utterly dogmatic conclusion was that all three had used the same psychological means to achieve their desired ends. What a way to begin a relationship!

For whatever reason, Jane hated Evangelicals. She would taunt me by telling of her friend who would rather have her son watch an X-rated movie than tune in to an evangelist on television. My goal for the next four months was to become her first ever evangelical friend. Julie and I worked hard to break down her prejudices. How exciting it was at the very end of our time together to have Jane come to us and say, "As you know, I have no love for evangelical Christianity. But for the first time I have come to see Evangelicals in a new light. Thanks for coming into my life." It was empathy that pushed us into Jane's world.

Empathy is not particularly easy to implement, especially for those of us committed to an absolute view of Truth. Theologian Hans Kung has stated, "Absolute truth becomes tolerant only when people no longer believe in the absoluteness of truth." Interesting statement.

Evangelical Christians and dedicated Muslims know this tension. Martin Goldsmith, in his book *What About Other Faiths?* tells of a rude letter he received from a Muslim.

> One day I received a letter from a Muslim objecting to a book I had written entitled *Islam and Christian Witness*. The writer detailed the horrors of hell towards which I was heading. He knew the exact number of scorpion and snake bites to which I would be subjected. The long list of other tortures filled several pages (Goldsmith 1989:130).

It is a misconception to place all Muslims into a common mold. They are "red-eyed fanatics wielding M-16's in their quest for political gains." They are "sex crazed males enjoying four wives each." They are all "religious, praying five times each day." Their leaders "cut off the hands of all thieves." Such generalizations are as true as beginning a statement with "All Christians . . ." and then filling in whatever you like, based on what you have seen some Christians do. Stereotypes based on some sensational event are totally inadequate. I have met many Muslims who totally deplore violence, and those who are committed to a monogamous marital relationship. There are devout Muslims and there are nominal Muslims, just as is so in our Christian community. Empathy takes us beyond stereotypes.

For 20 years in Bangladesh, we lived within hearing range of the Muslim call to prayer. I like to hear it. I enjoy the melodious chant of a Muslim at 4:45 a.m. exhorting people, "Arise, come to prayer. It is better to pray than sleep." How many Christians, dedicated as they are to their view of absolute truth, are willing to outwork their faith by going to church to pray at 5 a.m. each morning?

Some of our missionary friends in Bangladesh used to declare fervently their relief in getting out of "Satan's stronghold," and being able to go to Hindu India for a nice relaxing vacation once a year. Without undermining the joys of a vacation, it always seemed to us that India was more of Satan's stronghold than was Bangladesh. Hinduism, with its idolatry, sensuality, and its grotesque ceremonies, appeared to have much more of the demonic in it than a religion committed to one God, prayer, and fasting.

In one Muslim country, empathy led a team of missionaries to move in close to Islam. This was done after a great deal of group discussion. The purpose was to construct a "form" of Christian expression that was biblically true as well as culturally relevant to Muslim norms. Dress, worship styles, linguistic forms, and social relationships were all appropriately adapted. The result has been very exciting. Many Muslims have come to accept Christ as Lord and Savior of their lives. The offense of western packaging of the Gospel was minimized. The only offense, then, that Muslims had to deal with related to content. That, of course, is still a major stumbling block to the majority of Muslims in that land.

Empathy for social structures led the team to reject what has been termed "extraction evangelism." Converts remain in the context of their pre-conversion homes and employment. Flight, for protection, to the nearest church or mission compound has not been encouraged. This new sensitivity to parents, friends, and employers is appreciated, though in some cases it has also been problematic where local opposition has been great.

Empathy made the team look anew at social and health projects. Many Muslims regard such activities as highly unethical means of inducing simple, poor villagers to convert to the "white man's religion." Being forced to sit in a hospital waiting room surrounded by Gospel propagation creates tremendous antagonism in some sectors of Muslim society. The team is still working through credible options that will allow them to demonstrate Christian love and care without these ministries being used or perceived simply as a lever to generate conversions.

My writings often mention Dr. Ali, a very dedicated and devout Bangladeshi Muslim who is one of my closest friends in life. We have integrated our families. My life has been tremendously enriched by this deep friendship. Neither of us has in any way compromised our religious convictions. As one can imagine, religion has been a very frequent topic of our conversation.

In 1982, following major surgery in Bangladesh, my wife was told she had a very serious type of cancer. Life became a swirl of activity as we packed to return to the States. Each day the Ali family was at our home bringing food and saying prayers for Julie. At the moment of our departure, Ali and I acknowledged that we may never again meet on this earth. It was emotionally wrenching to realize there was an eternity separating us. We were both confident of our view of truth, and only one of us could be correct.

Mutual empathy led us to state that we would continue to study each other's religion. If we ever felt truth was in the other's position, then we would convert. To me it is only proper to make myself as vulnerable as I am asking my Muslim friend to be.

Wonderfully, we found out that Julie never had cancer, and that the scare was a result of poor lab work. The Alis and we continue a relationship fostered by visits, long distance phone calls and letters.

Empathy which does not involve a compromise of belief and action should know no boundaries. Perhaps we Evangelicals should be known more widely as "empathizers"—as well as "evangelizers."

Conclusion

Problems remain. I still struggle theologically, emotionally, intellectually, and spiritually with the issues raised in this paper. However, I must confess to an uneasiness concerning a trend observed among Evangelicals which downplays issues relating to the uniqueness of Christ. Hell is now "eternal separation from Christ." God's wrath is seldom referred to. Jonathan Edward's sermon, "Sinners in the Hands of an Angry God," would not play well in contemporary, more sophisticated Boston. A recent survey of 16 evangelical colleges and seminaries in the USA revealed that 30% of the students affirmed that those who never had an opportunity to hear of Jesus Christ could nevertheless go to heaven.

I can "empathize" with the dilemma of those students. However we try to reconcile the problem of those who have never heard, we still feel vulnerable, either biblically or pragmatically. In the end we must leave this with the Just God in whom is our ultimate confidence. He alone knows the hearts of all, and will most assuredly judge righteously.

In the meantime, our compelling commission is to fervently preach the Good News to every creature. This should be more than enough to occupy our mental and physical energies. May we discharge this obligation with Christian conviction impregnated with empathetic love. Hopefully, then our dogmatism that outworks in a pluralistic context will have the guiding power of light and the attractive qualities of salt.

Bibliography

Gandhi, Mohandas K. *An Autobiography: The Story of My Experiments With Truth.* Boston: Beacon Press, 1957.

Goldsmith, Martin. *What About Other Faiths?* London: Hodder & Stoughton, 1989.

Muck, Terry. "Many Mansions?" in *Christianity Today*, May 14, 1990, p. 14.

Neill, Stephen. *Christian Faith and Other Faiths.* London, Oxford University Press, 1961 (second edition, 1970).

_____. *Crises of Belief.* London: Hodder and Stoughton, 1984.

Newbigin, Lesslie. *The Open Secret*. London: SPCK, 1978.

Parshall, Phil. *New Paths in Muslim Evangelism*. Grand Rapids: Baker, 1980.

_____. *The Cross and the Crescent*. Wheaton: Tyndale House, 1989.

Pickthall, Mohammed Marmaduke. *The Meaning of the Glorious Koran*. New York: Mentor, nd.

Punt, Neal. *Unconditional Good News*. Grand Rapids: Eerdmans, 1980.

Smith, Wilfred Cantwell. *Religious Diversity*. New York: Crossroad, 1982.

Webster, Douglas. *Yes to Mission*. New York: Seabury Press, 1966.

THE SEVEN GREAT MYSTERIES OF GOD

(Written for Bangladeshi Mystical Muslims)

by Phil Parshall

The aged *pir sahib* watched solemnly as the long piece of cloth was passed among his disciples. Each of the 100 men who were being initiated eagerly grasped one section of the cloth. The *pir* then took the end of the cloth, and stood and prayed for the forgiveness of sins of each of his devotees.

Following this, a large pitcher of lemonade was brought to the pir. He touched his finger to his tongue and then put his finger in the lemonade. This was done three times. Assistants of the *pir* took the juice and gave a small glass to each of the disciples.

This brief ceremony depicts a search for a meaningful and mysterious encounter with God through the intermediary efforts of the pir. The disciples were sincerely reaching out in pursuit of a real and vital relationship with the one true God.

Life is full of mysteries. The most intellectual scientist has not yet begun to probe the depths of the universe. Likewise, who can understand the marvel of the human brain? And what can be said of a little seed that grows into a towering, strong banyan tree? Man is inadequate to comprehend the tremendous truths of life.

And . . . then there is God! He is so great, so powerful, so mighty, so awesome. Can mere man ever come to comprehend a God who is so full of mystery? There is an exciting verse in the Injil Sharif which says, "*The mystery which has been hid from the past ages and generations is now made manifest to his people*" (Injil Sharif, Colossians 2:6).

Yes, now, in this age, we can unlock the deep mysteries of God. Let us look at the following seven mysteries of God:

1 The Mystery of Creation
2 The Mystery of Evil
3 The Mystery of the Law
4 The Mystery of Mercy
5 The Mystery of Hazrat Jesus
6 The Mystery of Salvation
7 The Mystery of Assurance

1 The Mystery of Creation

In the Al-Torat, Genesis 1:1,2, we read,

> "In the beginning God created the heavens and the earth. and the earth was formless and void and darkness was over the surface of the deep; and the Spirit of God was moving over the surface of the waters."

There are men who deny that there is a God. These are learned men who believe that somehow the earth, moon, sun, and stars just happened. The Al-Torat deals with the mystery of the beginning of the world, and refutes the ideas of such unbelievers.

When was the "beginning"? Our small minds cannot begin to think in terms of eternity! We think about "Ayub's presidency," or the year of the great cyclone, or 1971 as the year Bangladesh became a free nation. But, we can't do much better than remember back to our great-grandfather. What must it be like to think of thousands and perhaps millions of years ago when God wonderfully created all those beautiful stars that we see on a clear night?

And then, most amazing of all, God formed the earth and made it possess all that was necessary for the habitation of man. The Al-Torat tells how Hazrat Adam and Eve were created in perfection. They were told to go and subdue the earth. All of the animal kingdom was to be in subjection to them.

How lovely must have been the Garden of Eden! Perhaps it was full of the fragrance of gardenias and roses. There may have been an abundance of luscious mangoes, oranges, and pineapples. Surely, there was a mighty river flowing nearby which most likely overflowed its banks in the rainy season. What a delightful picture of peace and happiness. How contented Hazrat Adam and Eve must have been!

But then . . . .

2 The Mystery of Evil

As we all know, Satan came into the Garden and introduced sin and evil into the world. But, where did Satan come from? The Injil Sharif gives a very clear answer to this great mystery.

> "And there was war in heaven, Michael and his angels waging war with the dragon. And the dragon and his angels waged war, and they were not strong enough, and there was no longer a place found for them in heaven. And the great dragon was thrown down, the serpent of old who is called the devil and Satan, who deceives the whole world; he was thrown down to the earth, and his angels were thrown down with him."
>
> Revelation 12:7-9

So there was a mighty rebellion in heaven. But Satan was not strong enough to be victorious over God and his angels. His punishment was to be cast out of perfect heaven. Satan and his helpers took up residence on earth where he went about as a roaring tiger seeking whom he could devour (Injil Sharif ,1 Peter 5:8). We can all imagine the danger of facing a ferocious Bengal tiger in the Sunderbans. Such is the danger of the power of Satan's working among the people of this earth.

The first two created people, Hazrat Adam and Eve, had a choice set before them in the Garden of Eden. They could obey God and eat freely of all the trees with the exception of one. Or they could listen to the advice of Satan and take of the fruit of the forbidden tree. How sad it is that Hazrat Adam and Eve clearly disobeyed God and became the world's first sinners. Their sin has a direct effect on you and me. In the Injil Sharif, Romans 5:12, we read, *"Therefore, just as through one man sin entered into the world, and death through sin, and so death spread to all men, because all sinned."*

Many people do not like to admit they are sinners. In pre-liberation days, I remember talking once to a high Pakistani government official. He was kind and gracious. However, when I began to talk about how all of us as humans are guilty of sin, my friend became angry and declared, "What! You are saying I am a sinner? That is not true. I have not done anything against God."

The Injil Sharif, in 1 John 1:8, declares, *"If we say that we have no sin, we are deceiving ourselves and the truth is not in us."* Is there anyone who can say he has never told a lie, never had an evil thought or never received or given bribery? A little child may be clearly instructed not to touch the packet of biscuits on the table. But, as soon as mother leaves the room, the child grabs the biscuits and eats them as quickly and as secretly as possible.

Yes, sin is a universal disease. It creates divisions within families. Societies are torn apart by hatred. Nations go to war causing horrible loss of life. The human race has gone far from the path of God.

Injil Sharif 2 Thessalonians 2:7 says, *"For the mystery of lawlessness is already at work."* What is the way out for sincere people who desire to follow God? Has God made a plan to enable sinners to return to Himself?

3 The Mystery of the Law

Hazrat Moses was a man of God. We are told he was willing to forsake a life of great ease in the king's palace in order that he might serve God. In a miraculous way, Hazrat Moses was used to deliver the people of God from a wicked pharaoh.

During the time of wandering in the hot Sinai desert, Hazrat Moses had a very special meeting with God. We read about it in the Al-Torat, Exodus 19:16,17.

> "So it came about on the third day, when it was morning, that there were thunder and lightning flashes and a thick cloud upon the mountain and a very loud trumpet sound, so that all the people who were in the camp trembled. And Hazrat Moses brought the people out of the camp to meet God, and they stood at the foot of the mountain."

What a day of mystery and excitement! God was about to reveal the Law through His devoted servant, Hazrat Moses. Consider the privilege of being selected by God to receive a revelation which would be known to all people of all ages as The Law.

God gave many laws which should be followed by mankind. A few of these were: everyone should love God with all their heart; it is sin to curse God; no one should worship idols; anyone who committed adultery would be guilty of a grave sin, both against mankind and against God; stealing is a sin; lying and coveting is against the will of God.

All of these laws were given to man for a specific purpose. Al-Torat Exodus 20:20 tells us that this reason was so that man *"would not sin."*

How good it would be to say that, after receiving the Law, everyone loved God and obeyed all His commands. But is that what happened?

No, indeed, it seemed like mankind became even greater sinners. They knew the truth of God's path, but they rejected it. They chose to disregard God, His Law, His will, and His peace.

The Law is something like a doctor diagnosing an illness. It is the first step toward a cure. The Law reveals the illness of mankind which is called sin. All can understand God's standard of holiness through the Law. Then they can see how they fail to meet God's standard of righteousness.

But, is it enough to just diagnose a disease? Would anyone be happy to be told by a doctor that he has a stomach ulcer, but not be given the proper medicine to cure the problem? No! It is extremely important not only to be diagnosed, but also cured.

The Law is important and helpful—but not totally adequate. We must go on to see God's further provision of a remedy to the great problem of man's alienation from all that is holy and righteous. This leads us to consider the miracle of God's mercy.

4   The Mystery of Mercy

The Al-Jabur, Psalm 103:10-12,17 has some beautiful words concerning the mercy of God.

> "God has not dealt with us after our sins; nor rewarded us according to our iniquities. For as the heaven is high above the earth, so great is his mercy toward them that fear him! As far as the east is from the west, so far has he removed our sins from us .... The mercy of the Lord is from everlasting to everlasting upon them that hear him."

Isn't this an encouraging word from God's Holy Word? If God gave us what we deserve, we would all spend eternity in hell. But—there is hope for sinful man. Satan's work does not have to end in victory.

Here is a great mysterious word. How far is the east from the west? How far is heaven above the earth? The Al-Jabur does not give us the answer. Rather, it points us to the vast distance God has put between us and our sins. Who can measure the breadth and depth of God's mercy? It is from everlasting to everlasting.

Another descriptive passage concerning God's mercy is found in Al-Torat Exodus 34:6,7.

> "The Lord, the Lord God, merciful and gracious, slow to anger, and abounding in loving kindness and truth; who keeps mercy for thousands, who forgives iniquity, transgression and sin."

No man can stand before God and declare his own righteousness. No person is good enough to be able to demand entrance into heaven. Yes, we may have fasted and prayed with great regularity; we may have given many alms to the poor—but God declares clearly in Injil Sharif Titus 3:5, "Not by works of righteousness which we have done but according to God's mercy He saved us."

Our righteousness is often only external. We give money to beggars on the train or bus so that other fellow passengers will see us and praise us as religious persons. But God looks on the heart. Man judges by external appearances, but God searches the innermost part of our being.

Our sin separates us from God. But God joins us to holiness and righteousness through His unfathomable mercy. Let us see how God has chosen to do this wonderful and mysterious work.

5   The Mystery of Hazrat Jesus

In Injil Sharif 1 Timothy 3:16, we find a very famous passage in which Hazrat Jesus is linked to the great mystery of godliness.

> "And by common confession great is the mystery of godliness: He (Hazrat Jesus) who was revealed in the flesh, was vindicated in the Spirit, beheld by angels, proclaimed among the nations, believed on in the world, taken up in glory."

How amazed Mary was to be told by an angel that she was to have a baby even before she had a physical relationship with a man. Such a thing would be totally impossible! Yet, this is exactly what happened. Hazrat Jesus Christ was born without a human father. God Himself miraculously placed the seed of life within the womb of Mary.

Here we see the unique relationship of Hazrat Jesus to God. Over and over in the Injil we read that Hazrat Jesus was the "Son of God". This has caused a problem to many people. How can God who is Spirit be the father of a son? Such a thought is blasphemous.

Surely, this is so. God is wholly spirit and has no form. It is impossible to think of God having a physical relationship with a woman. What, then, does the term "Son of God" really mean?

These words are to be interpreted in a spiritual sense. There is nothing physical in them at all. "Son of God" is a term which simply points to the close and mystical relationship between God and Hazrat Jesus. It is a union of a spiritual nature. This is why the Injil Sharif speaks of the "great mystery of godliness." This truth of God takes us beyond our normal intellect into the realm of the spirit and into the deep mysteries of God.

Hazrat Jesus often refers to Himself as "Son of Man." Yes, the Messiah became totally man in order that he might identify with God's created beings. Have you ever tried to talk to an ant? You could shout or even whisper ever so lightly. Still the ant can never comprehend your human words. The only way you can communicate with an ant is to actually become one. Surely, you have watched ants as they put their heads together and talk one to another.

In a similar way, sinful man refused to listen to the God who is so much more great and powerful than he is. So the Injil Sharif declares that God sent Hazrat Jesus as a man to planet earth in order to declare God's path of mercy and forgiveness of sin. Hazrat Jesus was totally man and yet in Injil Sharif John 10:30, Hazrat Jesus could declare that "I and the Father are one."

The Injil Sharif clearly also states that Hazrat Jesus was without sin. He never told a lie, never lusted after women or gave bribery. His main work during the last three years of His life was to preach the Kingdom of God, heal the diseases of the afflicted, and teach His disciples the deep things of the Spirit.

How sad that the people of Palestine hated the Light and rejected the One who said in Injil Sharif John 14:6, "I am the way, the truth and the life." Hazrat Jesus was and is today the Way to God. A beautiful summary of who Hazrat Jesus is and what He has done is found in Injil Sharif Hebrews 1:1-4.

> "God, after He spoke long ago to the fathers in the prophets in many
> portions and in many ways, in these last days has spoken to us in His

Son, whom He appointed heir of all things, through whom also He made the world. And He is the radiance of His glory and the exact representation of His nature and upholds all things by the word of His power. When He had made purification of sins, He sat down at the right hand of the Majesty on high; having become as much better than the angels, as He has inherited a more excellent name than they."

6   The Mystery of Salvation

How can man know God? Is it possible to be assured of spending eternal life in heaven with our Creator? Where does one go to obtain freedom from one's heavy burden of sin? Can peace with God be a reality in this life?

All mankind is in desperate need of salvation. The Injil Sharif gives us guidance in this area of great mystery. Let us see both what salvation is and what it is not.

SALVATION IS NOT OBTAINED BY KEEPING THE LAW

Injil Sharif Galatians 3:11 states, *"No one is justified by the law before God."* Injil Sharif Ephesians 2:9 declares that salvation is *"not as a result of works."* No matter how hard we try, we are totally unable to keep all of the Law. Injil Sharif James 2:10 reveals the high standard of God, *"For whoever keeps the whole law and yet stumbles in one point, he has become guilty of all."* A person may not be guilty of murder or adultery—but is there a person who can say he has never told a lie or had an evil thought? No, we are deeply condemned and the Law is inadequate to free us from the shackles of sin.

SALVATION IS RECEIVED THROUGH FAITH IN HAZRAT JESUS CHRIST

Injil Sharif Galatians 3:24 indicates the relationship of the Law to Hazrat Jesus. *"Therefore the Law has become our tutor to lead us to Christ, that we may be justified by faith."* The Law was preparation for salvation; the fulfillment is faith in Hazrat Jesus. What would you think of a person who needed a tutor all of his life? Yes, at an early stage of life man requires assistance and enlightenment. But later, it is time to move on to a more mature stage. The Law is necessary to point out vividly our corrupt condition before God. But, then, we find that release from sin and bondage comes through our faith in Hazrat Jesus. *"If righteousness comes through the Law, then Christ died needlessly"* (Injil Sharif Galatians 2:21).

SALVATION IS NOT GAINED BY THE BLOOD SACRIFICE OF ANIMALS

It has been the habit of men through all ages to seek to appease God by the offering of the blood of chickens, goats, cows, or camels. These offerings have been given as a substitution for the sin of man. But what is God's evaluation of such acts?

> "For it is impossible for the blood of bulls and goats to take away sins.
> . . . In whole burnt offerings and sacrifices for sin God hast taken no
> pleasure. . . . And every priest stands daily ministering and offering
> time after time the same sacrifices, which can never take away sins"
> (Injil Sharif Hebrews 10:4,6,11).

SALVATION IS IMPARTED THROUGH THE SACRIFICE OF HAZRAT JESUS

How exciting to realize that Hazrat Jesus has become the perfect sacrifice for the sins of all people of all ages!

> "For it was fitting that we should have such a high priest, holy, inno-
> cent, undefiled, separated from sinners and exalted above the
> heavens; who does not need daily, like those high priests, to offer up
> sacrifices, first for His own sins, and then for the sins of the people,
> because this He did once for all when He offered up Himself. . . . But
> He, having offered one sacrifice for sins for all time, sat down at the
> right hand of God. . . . In Him we have redemption through His blood,
> the forgiveness of our trespasses, according to the riches of His grace"
> (Injil Sharif Hebrews 7:26,27; 10:12; Ephesians 1:7).

Hazrat Jesus came into the world for the express purpose of becoming the sacrifice of God. Now men and women, rich and poor, and people of all races—all have access to God. There is no barrier to the wonderful salvation so freely offered through the blood of Hazrat Jesus Christ.

SALVATION IS NOT PROVIDED BY RELIGIOUS TEACHERS

Thousands of people flock to huge meetings of renowned religious teachers. Great sums of money are donated in the hope of securing release from sin.

Other people visit gravesites and pray that a departed religious leader will somehow intercede to God on their behalf. God's plan has never been for one sinful person to be enabled to provide salvation for another sinner. Only a righteous and perfect individual can be the Savior of mankind.

SALVATION IS PROVIDED BY THE MEDIATOR, HAZRAT JESUS CHRIST

> "For there is one God and one mediator also between God and men, the man Jesus Christ" (Injil Sharif 1 Timothy 2:5).

In one of the greatest of all mysteries of all ages, we find that God sent Hazrat Jesus from the perfection of heaven to take up residence on this corrupted earth. Hazrat Jesus took his position between sinful man and a holy God. He became a mediator. There is no further need of sacrificed animals. Nothing now stands between man and God. The Savior Hazrat Jesus Christ, Who is alive today in heaven, has removed all barriers.

These are the wonderful truths about God's plan of saving men from their sins.

7 The Mystery of Assurance

Assurance is a wonderful thing. We like to be assured of the permanence of our employment. It is also important to be assured of the love of our family. Assurance gives peace; whereas doubt causes unrest.

Most people in the world have no assurance of where they will spend eternity after they have died. It is commonly agreed that there will be an after-life and that man's soul will live forever. Almost everyone believes in the existence of heaven and hell. But few have the assurance that their spiritual being will live on eternally in the presence of God.

One of the greatest revealed mysteries is that a provision has been made for each man to know whether or not he will spend eternity with God. And this wonderful knowledge and assurance can be obtained right now—in this present life!

Hazrat Jesus Christ's own words in Injil Sharif John 5:24 help us to understand this truth.

> "Truly, truly, I say to you, he who hears My word, and believes Him who sent Me, has eternal life and does not come into judgment, but has passed out of death into life."

This verse points to the importance of believing in the living Hazrat Jesus. This act of faith is the key which opens the door to eternal life. Hazrat Jesus, through His death, has accepted the sting of judgment. We are now free to experience life and light in place of death and darkness.

Injil Sharif 1 John 5:13 tells us that *"These things I have written to you who believe . . . in order that you may know that you have eternal life."*

This is one of the great verses of assurance in the Injil Sharif. We are told that by believing in Hazrat Jesus, there is a sure knowledge that we will be privileged to live forever in the presence of God. There is no doubt in this verse.

One final word

Injil Sharif Revelation 10:7 states, *"But in the days of the voice of the seventh angel . . . the mystery of God is finished."* The concluding mystery of life will be completed in the last days. Are you ready to meet God in the great concluding point of all history? You can be, if you put your faith in Hazrat Jesus Christ Who not only died, but rose from the dead and is alive in heaven today. He is the **Great Key** who unlocks all the great mysteries of life and death.

*   *   *

This booklet can be freely revised and translated into any Muslim language. If this is done, please send a copy of the completed work to:

Phil Parshall
Box 3104, Makati City
1271 Philippines

Note: *Sahib* – A respected person; *Sharif* – Holy or Sacred; *Hazrat* – A title of respect; *Pir* – A Sufi holy man of mystical bent

Pharisee and Publican

by Martin Goldsmith

There were once two Muslim men who went to the mosque to pray. The first man was a devout Muslim who had been to Mecca on pilgrimage, prayed regularly five times a day, and was known in the community for his piety. He went to the mosque that day with total confidence, for he knew all the prescribed rituals of how to wash himself before entering the mosque, as well as the set movements and words of the prayers. He entered the mosque, went straight to a prominent place in the center towards the front and performed his prayers with absolute perfection. But while praying, his thoughts wandered away to the pretty girl who lived next door and he pictured to himself her shapely figure.

The second man to come to the mosque had lived a thoroughly rotten life of moral degradation. Having not prayed for many years he had forgotten the details of the outward rituals of washings, prayer movements, and even the words one recited in prayer. But he was deeply aware of the evil of his behaviour, and longed to get right with God again, start a new life, and make amends for all he had done until then. Shyly, he approached the mosque, dipped his hands in the pool of water to wash his hands and face, left his sandals outside the mosque and slipped quietly in. Feeling a bit out of place, he went behind a pillar in the hope that no one would see him. Deeply moved with a spirit of repentance he abandoned any attempt to remember the set words and movements of prayers; so he turned to God with simple words of his own.

Which man was righteous in the sight of God?

The Prodigal Son

There was once a *hanif* (one who has the true religion)
who had two sons.
The younger said to his father,
"Father, according to the will (*wasiya*), let me have
the fixed share (*fara'id*) of the inheritance (*mirath*)
that is coming to me."
And the father divided his means and his property
between the younger and the elder son.

Now the elder son was a devout Muslim who prayed
regularly five times a day
and had gone to Mecca on as many pilgrimages.
No one was respected more among the townspeople
for his religious devotion than this elder son.
He was a man who performed his prayers in the mosque
with absolute perfection
and could read the Quran so well
that he would hold the audience spellbound.

It wasn't long, however, until the younger son
got everything he owned together,
and left for a far country
where he squandered his money
in a dissolute life of sinfulness (*fisq*)
and moral depravity.

And when he had spent his entire inheritance,
and had not one thing left

to remind him of his wonderful father,
there arose a terrible famine in that land;
and the younger son began to feel his loss.

So he hired himself out to one of the local infidels
who put him on his farm to feed the pigs.

The younger son would willingly have filled his empty belly
with the husks the pigs were eating,
but he was treated worse than the swine
for no one offered him even that to eat.

He finally came to himself
and started thinking like a rational (*'aqli*) being,
like a true son having the disposition of his father.

He said, "How many hired servants of my father's household
abound in food and I perish with hunger!
I will arise and stop straying from the right course (*fasaqa*)
and go to my father,
and I will say to him,
"Father, I have sinned against heaven
and in the presence of you.
And I no longer think I am worthy to be called your son:
make me not like my elder brother who thinks himself worthy,
but make me like one of your hired servants."

Then he arose and came to his father.

Now it was the tenth day
of the month of Pilgrimage (*Hajj*) to Mecca,
and the elder son, being somewhat bored,
decided to stay home for a change.

But when the younger son was yet a great way off,
his father saw him

and was moved with love and compassion,
and his father ran to the younger son
and clasped him in his arms
and kissed him with tenderness.

And the son said to him,
"Father, I have sinned against heaven
and in your sight,
and I am no longer worthy
to be called your son."

But the father said to his hired servants,
"Bring forth the best robe
and put it on him;
and put a ring on his hand
and shoes on his feet;
and bring the calf we have been fattening
and kill it;
we are going to have a *Qurbani Id* celebration
such as has not been since the time Ibrahim
celebrated the redemption of his son.
Because this son of mine was dead
and has come back to life;
he was lost
and now he has been found."

And the great feast began.

It was almost night when the elder brother
returned from the mosque,
and, on his way back,
as he drew near the house,
he could hear the sounds of the communion (*wisal*)
of the father and his son.
Calling one of the hired servants,
the elder brother asked what all this was about.

And the hired servant said to the elder son,
"Your brother has returned safe and sound (*salim*),
and your father has personally sent word
for the *Qurbani Id* sacrifice and the festivities to begin.
Did you not know that he is calling for you?"

Now the elder brother was furious and refused to go in.
He would have nothing to do
with this sort of religious practice (*din*).
Would Allah act like his father?
Would Allah bestow a reward (*matwaba*) on a son
with an innate disposition (*qariha*) that was rebellious (*'asin*)?˙
And not only that, one who had no merit (*tawab*)
because he had done absolutely no good deeds
or right conduct (*ihsan*)
—would Allah act like this sort of father?
The elder brother resolved never to be like such a one
and he sat and brooded in the outer darkness.

Presently, the elder brother
thought he saw another servant approaching
but it was his father coming to give him a personal word
in order that the elder son could start thinking like a rational (*'aqli*)
    being
and enter into the spirit of the whole house (*jam'a'a*).

So his father pleaded with him.

Finally, the elder son answered his father:
"Look, all these years I have submitted
to you as a slave (*abd*),
and I can boast without shame that I have religiously obeyed
all of your laws (*shari'a*).
Yet I return from the mosque
and I hear the sounds of the communion (*wisal*)

between you and this prodigal (*mufarrit*).
Am I now to humble myself
and enter into a house
with this sort of fellowship (*zamala*)?"

Then the father looked at him with anguished love
and said,
"You know the costly death a testator (*murith*)
must somehow undergo in order that
through the word (*kalima*) of his testament (*'ahd*)
his heirs may receive all that he has."
And yet you seem to love me
more like a self-justifying slave
than a trusting and humble son."

The father put his arm around his son and said,
"Are you so far away from knowing me
that you cannot rejoice that the one
who strayed from the right course (*fasaqa*)
has found renewal (*tajaddud*),
and has been rightly guided (*rashid*)
to the salvation (*marashid*) of Allah?
For like you
your brother had a natural disposition (*sajiya*)
that is dead,
but now he has been restored (*jadda*)
to the abundant life of communion (*wisal*)
as an heir of his father's house.

PART FOUR

POWER

ENCOUNTER

What Kind of Encounters Do We Need in Our Christian Witness?*

(Power encounter must be biblically balanced with truth and commitment encounters, if we are to succeed in our world mission.)

by Charles H. Kraft

We're hearing more about power encounter these days among non-charismatics. We are more open and less afraid of spiritual power than we used to be. Several missionary training institutions now include courses on power encounter. But there are extremes we want to avoid. My task in this article is to offer an approach to power encounter that is biblically balanced with two other encounters that Evangelicals have always emphasized.

---

* Reprinted by permission of *Evangelical Missions Quarterly* (Box 794, Wheaton, IL 60189, USA)

THE BASIC CONCEPT

The term "power encounter" comes from missionary anthropologist Alan Tippett. In his 1971 book, *People Movements in Southern Polynesia*, Tippett observed that in the South Pacific the early acceptance of the Gospel usually occurred when there was an "encounter" demonstrating that the power of God is greater than that of the local pagan deity. This was usually accompanied by a desecration of the symbol(s) of the traditional deity by its priest or priestess, who then declared that he or she rejected the deity's power, pledged allegiance to the true God, and vowed to depend on God alone for protection and spiritual power.

At such a moment, the priest or priestess would eat the totem animal (*e.g.*, a sacred turtle) and claim Jesus' protection. Seeing that the priest or priestess suffered no ill effects, the people opened themselves to the Gospel.[1] These confrontations, along with those classic biblical power encounters (*e.g.*, Moses vs. Pharaoh, Exodus 7-12, and Elijah vs. the prophets of Baal, 1 Kings 18) formed Tippett's view of power encounter.

More recently, the term has been used more broadly to include healings, deliverances, or any other "visible, practical demonstration that Jesus Christ is more powerful than the spirits, powers, or false gods worshiped or feared by the members of a given people group."[2] The concept of "taking territory" from the enemy for God's kingdom is seen as basic to such encounters.

According to this view, Jesus' entire ministry was a massive power confrontation between God and the enemy. The ministry of the apostles and the church in succeeding generations is seen as the continuing exercise of the "authority and power over all demons and all diseases" given by Jesus to his followers (Luke 9:1). Contemporary stories about such encounters come from China, Argentina, Europe, the Muslim world, and nearly everywhere else where the church is growing rapidly.

Tippett observed that most of the world's power are power-oriented and respond to Christ most readily through power demonstrations.[3] Gospel messages about faith, love, forgiveness, and the other facts of Christianity are not likely to have nearly the impact on such people as the demonstrations of spiritual power. My own experience confirms Tippett's thesis. Therefore, cross-cultural workers

---

[1] Alan Tippett, *People Movements in Southern Polynesia* (Chicago: Moody Press, 1971), p. 206.

[2] C. Peter Wagner, *How to Have a Healing Ministry* (Ventura, Calif.: Regal Books, 1988), p. 150. See also John Wimber, *Power Evangelism* (New York: Harper & Row, 1985), pp. 29-32, and Charles Kraft, *Christianity with Power* (Ann Arbor: Servant, 1989).

[3] Tippett, *op. cit.*, p. 81.

ought to learn as much as possible about the place of power encounter in Jesus' ministry and ours.

ADDITIONAL ENCOUNTERS

Of course, missionaries face several questions about power encounter. One of the basic ones is how to relate power concerns and approaches to our traditional emphases on truth and salvation. Let me suggest that we need to use a three-pronged approach to our witness.

Jesus battled Satan on a broader front than simply power encounters. If we are to be biblically fair and balanced, we must give two other encounters equal attention—commitment encounters and truth encounters. We need to focus on the close relationship in the New Testament between these three encounters. Here's an outline that will help:

Jesus Christ confronts Satan

1   **CONCERNING POWER** This results in power encounters to release people from satanic captivity and bring them into freedom in Jesus Christ.

2   **CONCERNING COMMITMENT** This results in commitment encounters to rescue people from wrong commitments and bring them to a relationship with Jesus Christ.

3   **CONCERNING TRUTH** This results in truth encounters to counter error and to bring people to correct understanding about Jesus Christ.

Throughout the world many Christians who have committed themselves to Jesus Christ, and who have embraced much Christian truth, have not given up their pre-Christian commitment to and practice of what we call spiritual power. The powers of darkness which they formerly followed have not been confronted and defeated by the power of Jesus. So they live with a "dual allegiance" and a syncretistic understanding of truth.

Therefore, some mistakenly assume that if they confront people with healing and deliverance campaigns to show them Christ's power, they will turn to him in droves. They assume that those who experience God's healing power will automatically commit themselves to the source of that power.

However, I know of several such campaigns that have produced few, if any, lasting conversions. Why not? Because little attention was paid to leading the people from an experience of Jesus' power to a commitment to him. These people are accustomed to accepting power from any source. Therefore, they see no greater compulsion to commit themselves to Jesus than to any of the other sources of power they regularly consult.

I believe Jesus expects power demonstrations to be as crucial to our ministries as they were to his (Luke 9:1,2). However, any approach that advocates power encounter without giving adequate attention to the other two encounters—commitment and truth—is not biblically balanced. Many people who saw or experienced power events during Jesus' ministry did not turn to him in faith. This should alert us to the inadequacy of power demonstrations alone as a total evangelistic strategy.

A BALANCE OF ENCOUNTERS

We can see the three kinds of encounters outlined above in Jesus' ministry. Typically, he started by teaching, followed by a power demonstration, then a return to teaching, at least for the disciples (e.g., Luke 4:31ff.; 5:1ff.; 17ff.; 6:6ff.; 17ff., etc.). Appeals for commitment to the Father or to himself appear both implicitly and explicitly throughout his teaching. Jesus seems to have used power demonstrations more when interacting with people who had not yet become his followers, focusing more on the teaching of truth with those already committed to him.

His appeal for commitment to at least the first five apostles (Peter, Andrew, James, John in Luke 5:1-11, and Levi in Luke 5:27-28) occurred after significant power demonstrations. Once his followers had successfully negotiated their commitment encounter, their subsequent growth was primarily a matter of learning and practicing more truth.

First century Jews, like most people today, were very concerned about spiritual power. Paul said they sought power signs (1 Corinthians 1:22). Jesus' usual practice of healing and deliverance from demons soon after entering a new area (e.g. Luke 4:33-35,39: 5:13-13; 6:6-10,18-19, etc.) may be seen as his way of approaching them at the point of their concern. When he sent out his followers to the surrounding towns to prepare the way for him, he commanded them to use the same approach (Luke 9:1-6; 10:1-9).

Jesus' reluctance to do miraculous works merely to satisfy those who wanted him to prove himself (Matthew 12:38-42; 16:1-4) would, however, seem to indicate His power demonstrations were intended to point to something beyond the mere demonstration of God's power. I believe that he had at least two more important goals. First, Jesus sought to demonstrate God's nature by showing his love. As he said to Philip, "If you have seen me, you have seen the Father" (John 14:9). He freely healed, delivered, and blessed those who came to him and did not retract what he had given, even if they did not return to thank him (Luke 17:11-19). He used God's power to demonstrate his love.

Second, Jesus sought to lead people into the most important encounter, the commitment encounter. This is clear from his challenge to the Pharisees when they demanded a miracle, that the people of Nineveh who repented would accuse the people of Jesus' day who did not do likewise (Matthew 12:41). Experiencing God's power may be both pleasant and impressive, but only a commitment to God through Christ really saves.

THE NATURE AND AIMS OF THE ENCOUNTERS

The three encounters—power, commitment, and truth—are not the same, but they are each intended to initiate a process crucial to the Christian experience aimed at a specific goal.

1   The concern of the **truth encounter** is understanding. The vehicle of that encounter is teaching.

2   The concern of the **commitment encounter** is relationship. The vehicle of that encounter is witness.

3   The concern of the **power encounter** is freedom. Its vehicle is spiritual warfare.

Truth and understanding have a lot to do with the mind; commitment and relationship rest primarily in the will; and freedom is largely experienced emotionally.

1   Truth encounters

Truth encounters in which the mind is exercised and the will is challenged seem to provide the context within which the other encounters take place and can be interpreted. Jesus constantly taught truth to bring his hearers to ever greater understanding about the person and plan of God. To teach truth, he increased their knowledge. However, in Scripture, knowledge is grounded in relationship and experience; it is not simply philosophical and academic. The truth encounter, like the other two, is personal and experiential, not merely a matter of words and head knowledge.

When we focus on knowledge and truth, we enable people to gain enough understanding to be able to interpret accurately the other two encounters. For example, a power demonstration has little, or wrong significance unless it is related to truth. Knowledge of the source of, and the reason for the power are essential for proper interpretation of a power event. The need for such knowledge is probably why Jesus used his power demonstrations in the context of teaching his disciples.

A diagram of what I have been saying about the nature and aim of truth encounters looks like this:

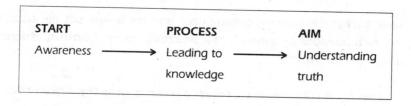

START   **PROCESS**   **AIM**

Awareness   ⟶   Leading to   ⟶   Understanding
                   knowledge   truth

2 Commitment encounters

Commitment encounters, involving the exercise of the will in commitment and obedience to the Lord, are the most important of the encounters. For without commitment and obedience to Jesus, there is no spiritual life.

The initial commitment encounter leads a person into a relationship with God. Through successive encounters between our will and God's, we grow in intimacy with and likeness to him, as we submit to his will and practice intimate association with him. Initial commitment and the relationship that proceeds from it are tightly linked to truth, both because they are developed within the truth encounter and because a relationship with God is the true reason for human existence.

Implied in the commitment encounter is the cultivation of the fruits of the Holy Spirit, especially love toward God and man. We are to turn from love of (or, commitment to) the world that is under the control of the the evil one (1 John 5:19) to God who loved the world and gave himself for it. As we grow in our relationship with him, we become more like him, conforming to the image of Christ (Romans 8:29).

The commitment encounter looks like this:

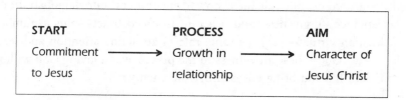

START   **PROCESS**   **AIM**

Commitment   ⟶   Growth in   ⟶   Character of

to Jesus   relationship   Jesus Christ

3 Power encounters

Power encounters contribute a different dimension to Christian experience. They focus on freedom from the enemy's captivity. Satan is the blinder (2 Corinthians 4:4), restricter, hinderer, crippler—the enemy who attempts to keep people from commitment to God and truth. Though he works on all human faculties, the enemy seems particularly interested in crippling people emotionally. If people are to move into commitment to Christ, they need emotional freedom.

The power encounter process may be diagrammed as follows:

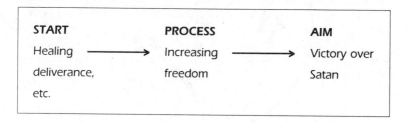

START   **PROCESS**   **AIM**

Healing   ⟶   Increasing   ⟶   Victory over

deliverance,   freedom   Satan

etc.

For the one who is healed, delivered, blessed, or otherwise freed from the enemy's grip, the major payoff is freedom. However, for an observer, the impact is likely to be quite different. If properly interpreted, the encounter communicates basic truths about God's power and love. The observer sees that God is worthy of his trust because he is willing and able to free people from Satan's destructive hold, as we see in the this diagram:

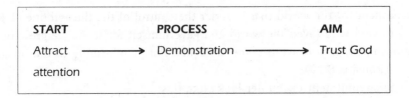

START	PROCESS	AIM
Attract attention	⟶ Demonstration ⟶	Trust God

Although we do not call them power encounters, our demonstrations of love, acceptance, forgiveness, and peace in troubled times—plus a number of other Christian virtues—play the same role of attracting attention and leading people to trust God. These all witness to the presence of a loving God willing to give abundant life and bring release from the enemy.

THE ENCOUNTERS WORK TOGETHER

Our missionary witness needs to use all three encounters together, not separately, as we can see in this three-part circle:

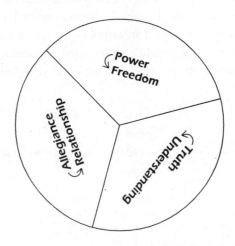

People need freedom from the enemy to (1) open their minds to receive and understand truth (2 Corinthians 4:4), and (2) to release their wills so they can commit themselves to God. However, they can't understand and apply Christian truth, nor can they exercise power, without a continuing commitment to God. Nor can they maintain the truth and their commitment without freedom from the enemy won through continual power encounters. We constantly need each of these dimensions in our lives.

The diagram on page 254 shows the inter-workings of these three aspects of Christian life and witness in more detail.

There are three stages in the process, the third of which results in witness to those at the start of Stage 1. At the start (Stage 1), people are under Satanic captivity in ignorance and error and are committed to some non-Christian allegiance. Through power encounters, they gain freedom from that captivity, moving from the blindness and will-weakening of the enemy into openness to the truth. Through truth and commitment encounters, they receive enough understanding to act on, plus enough challenge to induce them to commit themselves to Christ.

In the second stage, having made their commitment to Jesus, people need continued spiritual warfare to attain greater freedom from the enemy's continued efforts to harass and cripple them. They also need continued teaching and challenges to greater commitment and obedience. They grow in their relationship to God and his people through continued encounters in all three areas.

In the third stage, this growing relationship results in power encounters through prayer to break the enemy's power to delude, harass, cause illness, demonize, and the like. These encounters are accompanied by truth and commitment encounters, so that believers are challenged to greater commitment and bedience, especially in witness to those in the first stage.

Beyond our own Christian growth lies our witness. At the end of his ministry, Jesus taught much about his relationship to his followers and theirs to each other (e.g., John 14-16), as well as about the authority and power he would give them (Acts 1:8). He carefully related power and authority to witness (e.g., Matthew 28:19,20; Mark 16:15-18; Acts 1:8).

He told the disciples to wait for spiritual power before they embarked on witness (Luke 24:49; Acts 1:4), just as Jesus himself had waited to be empowered at his own baptism (Luke 3:21,22). We are not fully equipped to witness without the freedom-bringing, truth-revealing power of the Holy Spirit (Acts 1:8).

SOME GUIDELINES FOR EVANGELICALS

Because Satan is a master at deceit and counterfeiting, we must encounter or confront him, rather than simply ignore him. And we know as we confront him that greater is he who is in us than he who is in the world (1 John 4:4), and we thank God that Jesus has "stripped the spiritual rulers and authorities of their

STAGE	START	NEED	PROCESS	RESULT
STAGE 1	Satanic captivity	Freedom to understanding	Power encounter	
	Ignorance/error	Enough understanding	Truth encounter	Commitment to Jesus Christ
	Non-Christian commitment	Challenge to commit to Christ	Commitment encounter	
STAGE 2	Commitment to Jesus Christ	Spiritual warfare to provide protection, healing, blessing, deliverance	Power encounter	
		Teaching	Truth encounter	Growing relationship to God and his people
		Challenges to greater commitment and obedience	Commitment encounter	
STAGE 3	Growing relationship to God and his people	Authoritative prayer	Power encounter	
		Teaching	Truth encounter	Witness to those at the beginning of Stage 1
		Challenges to commitment	Commitment encounter	

power" (Colossians 2:15). But we are still at war and we are commanded to put on armor and fight against the "wicked spiritual forces in the heavenly world" (Ephesians 6:11-12). So, although we know how this war will end, many battles remain and we need to know our enemy and how to fight him.

As we survey the world's mission fields, we find many places where Christians still have dual allegiances. Many believers, including pastors, still go to shamans, priests, and other spirit mediums. At the same time, charismatic and Pentecostal churches specializing in power encounter evangelism and witness are growing rapidly in most parts of the world.

Many of us Evangelicals grew up with a knowledge-truth brand of Christianity, that pays little if any attention to power encounters. But we go out to witness and evangelize among people who have grown up in spirit-oriented cultures and often find that solid, lasting conversions to Christ are hard to achieve with our knowledge-truth approach alone.

Satan counterfeits truth, instills damning allegiances, and provides power. He has, as it were, three arrows in his quiver. However, generally, evangelical missionaries have only two, so their work often founders on the rocks of dual allegiance and nominalism.

We encounter commitment to other gods and spirits with the challenge to commitment to Jesus Christ. But when the people need healing, or seek fertility, or when there isn't enough rain, or there are floods, too often our answer is the hospital, the school, and modern agriculture. We provide secular answers to what to them (and the Bible) are basically spiritual issues.

We have encountered Satan's counterfeit "truths" with the exciting truths of Christianity, but often in such an abstract way that our hearers have seen little verification of that truth in our lives. In most cases, both missionaries and the local Christians are more impressed with scientific than with biblical truth.

The missing element for them and for us is the "third arrow," genuine New Testament power, the continual experience of the presence of God, who every day does things the world calls miracles. We must encounter Satan's counterfeit power with God's effective power. Truth and commitment alone won't do. We need all three kinds of biblical encounters, if we are to succeed in our world missions.

THE RELEVANCE OF POWER MINISTRIES FOR FOLK MUSLIMS

by J. Dudley Woodberry

All morning we had watched the people trickle into the city from the surrounding villages waving flags. Like fallen rain pouring out of little crevices
into ever larger gullies, they combined with similar streams of people until they
poured into a hollow by some shrines of Muslim holy men.

We had joined the resultant flood and were now waiting in line to file through
the tomb of a saint. As we passed by the grave, people pressed their hands or
bodies against the sides to draw power or blessing (*baraka*) from the spirit of the
deceased saint. Some wore amulets to protect them from the evil eye or the spirits. Cloth, hair, and replicas of cradles were hung on a tree as people prayed for
healing or made vows. Then we climbed a hill to a shrine where a holy man (a
pir) surrounded by Hindu-type pictures dispensed his power or blessing to the
needy who clustered around him.

I sat down to reflect. Here we were in the outskirts of Islamabad (lit., the place of Islam) the capital of Pakistan (lit., the pure land), a nation created so Muslims could live according to the Law of God as they understood it. Yet the felt need of at least those who had gathered for religious purposes was power (which may be generally defined as a capacity to produce results). They had come at a **time** of power (a *mawlid*—a birthday or holy day of one or more saints), wearing **objects** of power (*tawizes*—amulets), to visit a **place** of power (a *mazar* or *ziarat*—a shrine), or a **person** of power (a *pir* or *wali*—a holy man) to offer a **prayer** for power or receive a power **incantation** to ward off the power of the **spirits**.

How different all this was from the Islam I was prepared to meet. I had just finished a dissertation on contemporary creeds in Islam at the suggestion of Sir Hamilton Gibb, who felt I would profit from research on the system of doctrine in Islam. Here the focus was **truth** rather than power. Prior to that I had studied the most celebrated Muslim theological treatise, the *Ihya* of al-Ghazali. Here he dealt with the concepts of theology and the experience of God in worship—**truth** and **mystery**. I had written a thesis on the quranic vocabulary for sin—a focus on **sin** and **righteousness**, which I had perceived to be a major felt need. I had also wandered through Palestinian refugee camps, even arrested and questioned as a spy, and experienced the concern for **justice**.

In all these cases I had studied and experienced ideal or formal Islam. Today, I was experiencing folk Islam with its mixture of animism. Yet most of these people participated in both forms of faith. They went to the mosque on Friday with its focus on **truth**, **righteousness**, and **mystery**; and they went to the pir during the week if their child was sick to get **power** to ward off harm. Obviously if the presentation of the Gospel was to meet them where they were, more attention had to be paid to power along with the other religious concerns—hence the following study.

FORMAL AND FOLK ISLAM

Formal in contrast to folk Islam may be called "high" as opposed to "low," "ideal" instead of "popular," or "orthodox/orthoprax" versus "animistic." The high form centers on the obedience and the worship of God. The word *islam* means "submission." Conversely, the low form seeks to manipulate what is divine for human purposes. While the orthoprax Muslims may meditate on the names of God in worship, the folk Muslims will try to use those names to accomplish their own ends. One book, *Ninety-nine Names of Allah* by Shems Friedlander, published in a number of languages in Nigeria (1978) and Pakistan (n.d.), tells how many times and in what context to repeat each name to get, for example, power, health, and protection from harm, hunger, bad habits, disaster, sickness, fear, danger, miscarriage, enemies, childlessness, and sin.

Folk Muslims may feel a certain uneasiness about associating traditional beliefs and practices with God, but they see in them a source of power so they try to integrate the two systems. In a rice ritual of the Maranaos of the Philippines, the leader enjoins: "Praise to Allah! Pray that we will not sin in inviting the *tonong* (spirits). He created the *tonong*." The devotees then ask the *tonong* to be intermediaries, and "Pray to Allah that all farmers will have a bountiful harvest." Finally, the leader again admonishes the farmers to pray to God that they might not sin in inviting the *tonong*, but God created them and, the leader adds, "gave them power." This need for power leads them to risk an offense against God.

In high Islam, the mosque is the place for submission; while in low Islam, the shrine is the place of power or blessing (*baraka*). In ideal Islam the Quran and Traditions of Muhammad are the primary sources of authority; whereas in popular Islam, the Quran itself, or selected portions of it, serve as power objects to ward off harm, and books on magic serve as guides.

In high Islam, the practitioners are *imams* or *ulama*, recognized for their formal training or intellectual knowledge; but in low Islam, the practitioner is a *pir* or *wali* who has prepared by such means as 40 days and nights of fasting, and is recognized for his or her power or *baraka*.

HISTORICAL INTERACTION BETWEEN HIGH AND LOW ISLAM

The Interaction of the ideal and popular has taken place since the rise of Islam. The new faith both reacted against and was colored by the animism that existed in Arabia. Stone fetishes, sacred trees, and sacred wells were rejected as power objects, but Muslims treated the Black Stone and the Zam Zam water in the sanctuary of Mecca as sources of *baraka* or power.

Power people like sorcerers and soothsayers were rejected (*Mishkat*, Bk 22, chap. 3, para. 1); yet some of the first utterances of Muhammad took the form of soothsaying and, by demanding obedience to God and His Prophet, the Arabian Prophet laid a foundation from which Muhammad veneration, and then saint veneration would rise. Likewise the spirits (*jinn*) and personal spirits (*qarina*) were incorporated into the quran.

Finally, the power ritual of the pilgrimage was included in the orthoprax cult. Even though its pagan origins were radically reinterpreted, it still included the Black Stone and the Zam Zam water, which continued to be treated as sources of *baraka* or power.

The Quran condemned sorcery, and the authoritative traditions of Muhammad condemned such magical practices as divination but allowed certain forms of it (*Mishkat,* Bk. 22, chap. 3, para. 1). Thus, what we see repeatedly is the camel's nose in the tent.

The spread of Islam was frequently carried on by mystics (*Sufis*), who already were syncretistic in beliefs and practices. This further facilitated the incorporation of local animistic beliefs and practices into local manifestations of Islam. Fundamentalists decried this as the major sin of associating other power or administration with that which is God's alone (*ishrak fi'l-tasarruf*), but the fusion of animistic with the formal faith became widespread, and with it the concern for power. The more the mix included folk elements, the greater the focus on power.

High Islam, of course, also includes a concern for power, though the source of that power shifts more to God. For example, tribal West Africans pray to the ancestors as sources of power. As they became more Islamized, they may pray through the ancestors to God. As they become still more fully Islamized, they pray to God for the ancestors who need *baraka*.

POWER IN THE FOLK-ISLAMIC WORLD VIEW

The felt need for power is so great among folk Muslims that their entire world view is seen through the spectacles of power—one lens being "powers" (power through living beings) and the other lens being "power" (forces). These two categories can in turn be divided into those that are helpful, and those that are harmful. The two dimensional limitations of a page restrict us to listing these helpful and harmful beings and forces in four columns.

We might better visualize them on four different pages of a book, all connected through the common spine. This might better express: 1) that many of the beings and forces can slip back and forth between being helpful and harmful; 2) the helpful beings and forces are in conflict with their harmful counterparts; 3) the beings interact with forces. The dotted horizontal lines indicate that these are not rigid divisions. Angels, for example, may pass from the other world to this world.

POWER CONFRONTATION IN
FOLK-ISLAMIC WORLD VIEW

	POWERS (BEINGS)	POWER (FORCES)	POWER (FORCES)	POWERS (BEINGS)
Other-worldly	God Angels good spirits (jinn)	*qadr* (divine decree) Heavenly Tablet	bad fate	Shaytan (Iblis)
This-worldly	fairies	*Baraka* (power, blessing) vows	evil eye cursing	*shaytans* (jinn) *qarina* (personal spirit)
(extra-ordinary)		*dhikr* (reciting divine names)	omens	
	apostles	*haram* (sacred locations)	*haram* (taboo)	*dews* (powerful spirits) *als* (spirit witches)
	prophets dead saints	good magic amulets	evil magic	Zar (divining spirit) *balbalang* (spirit with human trunk and wings)
	ancestors	sacred objects		
	recently dead	magic numbers designs		
	walis, pirs (saints) *Secret Societies* *"bush devils"*		Secret Societies "bush devils" visions	
(ordinary)		visions dreams	dreams disbelievers	
	pious Muslims other Muslims	herbs, drugs, alchemy natural forces		

From the array of helpful and harmful beings and forces pitted against each other, it is evident that the folk Muslim wants to acquire the aid of helpful beings and forces and avoid those that are harmful. The confrontation is evident in the rites of passage.

ATTEMPTS TO ACQUIRE HELPFUL POWER

At birth, helpful power is acquired by reciting the call to prayer in the infant's right ear, and the confession of faith in God and Muhammad (the *shahada*) in the left ear. An amulet is attached to the body to guard against the evil eye and incense burned to drive away the *jinn*. Among the Tausug of the Philippines, noise will be made to frighten away the *balbalan* spirits who are believed to have trunks of men and wings. Also, anyone suspected of having an evil eye is kept away. The placenta is buried or put in an amulet in Mindanao to guard the relationship between the child and his or her spirit twin. The mother in turn is protected from various spiritual beings in Iran by an onion over her head, and by quenching red-hot iron in her drinking water.

Naming is done on an auspicious day such as the birthday (*mawlid*) of Muhammad or one determined by astrology. A derogatory name may be chosen so as not to attract the *jinn*, and any compliment is accompanied by the exclamation *mashalla* ("what God wills") to show there is no jealousy that might attract the evil eye. A substitutionary *aqiqa* sacrifice of a lamb may be made so that the child will be preserved.

Circumcisions likewise would be performed on similar auspicious days by a person with *baraka* at a place such as a shrine oriented toward Mecca. The Samal of the Philippines likewise will not walk over a rice pestle at such times.

Marriages similarly will be held on auspicious days as places of power. Also the couples' birth dates will be checked by astrology and their names by alchemy to make sure that the two will be compatible. When the wife is pregnant she may tie amulets or strings above and below the fetus to ward off *jinn* and the evil eye, and those believed to have an evil eye or to be jealous will be kept away.

Finally, at death, people are made to face Mecca in their final moments as later in burial. Those ritually unclean are kept away. Messages to the archangels may be buried too. Friends and relatives acquire merit by sewing the shroud, carrying the bier, and digging the grave. On the fortieth day after death, when the spirit is believed to leave the body, the merit is transferred to the deceased.

These rites of passage demonstrate the constant power confrontation in their world view and the resultant fear in which they live. Since much of their faith and practice expresses the kingdom of darkness, there is still another confrontation with which the Christian is concerned and that is with the kingdom of light.

CHRISTIAN POWER MINISTRIES AMONG FOLK MUSLIMS

In the light of folk Muslims' felt need for power, it is noteworthy that the rise of Christianity in southwestern Arabia is attributed to power ministries by the oldest extant biography of Muhammad (d. 632), Ibn Hisham's recension of a work by Ibn Ishaq (d. 767). It tells of a Christian construction worker who cursed a snake which died, prayed for a blind boy who was healed, and then in God's name cursed the local sacred palm tree which was uprooted by a wind (*Ibn Hisham*). The last account fits the original restricted definition of a "power encounter."

Today, the major movements to Christ in the Muslim world are among folk Muslims. With their felt need for power, it is not surprising that all of them are associated with power ministries—exorcisms, healings, and even reports of the dead being raised. These accounts range from such widely separated countries as Burkina Faso in Africa, Bangladesh in South Asia, and Indonesia in Southeast Asia.

Because of the relevance of power ministries to folk Muslims and the fact that God is using them, we need biblical models. Therefore we might ask how Jesus and Paul would encounter power in folk Islam. Illustrations will be drawn from contemporary experiences.

HOW JESUS WOULD ENCOUNTER POWER IN FOLK ISLAM

Jesus lived in a world concerned with power similar to the world of folk Islam that we have observed. There were **spirit** powers which he exorcised (*e.g.*, Luke 9:37-43). The woman with an issue of blood treated the hem of his garment as a power **object** (Luke 8:41-56). The Pool of Bethesda was a power **place**, and when the water was stirred it was a power **time** (John 5:1-47). Anointing the sick with oil (Mark 6:13) or exorcising by believing prayer and command (Mark 9:14-29) might be seen as power **rituals**. Our Lord himself was a power **person** (*e.g.*, Luke 5:17-26).

Jesus' sending out of the disciples in a power ministry in Luke 10 suggests what he would do with similar folk Muslims. We read that "the Lord . . . sent them . . . two by two" (vs. 1). The first principle we see is that **he would go in partnership**. Although he originally faced his Adversary alone, he developed an approach of partnership. The powers are real, and discernment is needed. The most significant work among folk Muslims in South Asia has placed a couple in each village.

The passage goes on: "The Lord . . . sent them ahead of him . . . into every . . . place where he . . . was about to come" (vs. 1). **Secondly, he would have the way prepared for himself.** Every major advance of the Church has had a period of preparation, of preevangelism. A man named Inayat, who has an effective power ministry in Pakistan, finds that healing and salvation usually come gradually after preparation in teaching.

Jesus continues, "Pray . . . the Lord of the harvest to send out laborers" vs. 2). **Thirdly, he would pray for reinforcement as he entered the spiritual warfare.** The most effective power ministries among folk Muslims in South Asia are team ministries. One team is made up of 15 believers from Brethren, Roman Catholic, Pentecostal, and Episcopal backgrounds. This is spiritual warfare so prayer is essential. In another country in which there was flooding and erosion of the river bank, a naked madman called for five Christian couples to pray that the erosion would stop. They waded into the river and prayed from 8:30 a.m. until noon with villagers watching and jeering. Then the wind changed, the water calmed, and the erosion stopped. Two villagers accepted Christ, and others still point to the place on the bank where the erosion stopped.

"I send you out as lambs in the midst of wolves," Christ said (vs. 4). **Fourthly, he would enter the encounter with a power that is expressed by vulnerability, by the cross.** Our Lord conquered the cosmic powers by the cross (Colossians 2:15), and we can expect to be "partakers of Christ's sufferings" (1 Peter 4:13). This year in a South Asian country, a Muslim leader became a follower of Christ. A mob gathered to kill him. He prayed and someone shouted that someone else had been critically injured. The mob disbanded and ran to the other man's house.

Christ's instructions included, "Carry no purse" (vs. 4). Yet elsewhere the disciples are told to take one and even to get a sword (Luke 22:35, 36). This suggests **fifthly that he would alter his approach according to the timing of the context.** We note historical cycles in the more extraordinary signs and wonders, with the greatest concentrations being when there are major expansions of the Church.

Jesus goes on to tell the disciples, "Whenever you enter a town and they receive you, . . . heal . . . and say, . . .' The kingdom of God has come near to you.'" Conversely, they are told to leave any place that does not receive them while they announce that "the kingdom of God has come near" (vs. 8, 10-11). **Sixthly, he would focus on the receptive but still leave a witness with those who are not.** Currently, folk Muslims are more receptive than the orthodox, suggesting that we should focus on the former while we still give a witness to the others.

The disciples' instructions were to "heal the sick" and proclaim the nearness of the kingdom (vs. 9), and they reported that the demons were subject to them (vs. 17). **Seventhly, He would engage in a holistic ministry of healing and announcing God's rule, of demonstration and proclamation in which healing is a sign of the kingdom.** In a South Asian country, doctors declared a three-year-old girl to be within hours of death. A Christian couple prayed for her and she was healed. Four followed Jesus. The villagers were given instruction during the next few months and nine more believed. With the subsequent combination of demonstration and proclamation in the area, the numbers have mushroomed.

The unresponsive are told, "Woe to you . . . for if the mighty works done in you had been done in Tyre and Sidon, they would have repented" (vs. 13). **Eighthly, He would note that power ministries lead to opposition as well as faith.** As in our Lord's day both responses are found. Where hundreds became Christians in a South Asian locality a mob estimated at 10,000 came with petrol to kill a convert. They got sidetracked on learning of an *imam* in the area who had also become a follower of Jesus. The latter was able to calm all but two who then began rolling on the ground in pain and had to be hospitalized. The news led about 200 more to follow Christ.

The disciples returned and reported that "even the demons are subject to us in your name." Jesus responded, "I saw Satan fall like lightning from heaven" (vs. 17-18). **Ninthly, He would show that world views need to be expanded to include the spirit world and the cosmic battle there.** This lack in most Western world views is what Paul Hiebert has called "the flow of the excluded middle."

Jesus gave the disciples authority over "serpents and scorpions and over all the power of the enemy" (vs. 19). **Tenthly, he has given and gives authority in both the physical and the spiritual realm.** The story above, of Christians praying for the flooding and erosion to stop, illustrated how God responded to prayer concerning the physical elements. One of the lessons that Christians who are oppressed by spirits need to learn is that they have authority to command them to leave.

The disciples are warned, "Do not rejoice in this, that the spirits are subject to you; but rejoice that your names are written in heaven" (vs. 20). **Eleventhly, he would prioritize evangelism over exorcism.** Some involved in a ministry of exorcism have found it monopolizing so much of their time that other areas of ministry like evangelism have suffered.

Then Jesus addressed God as "Father, Lord of heaven and earth" (vs. 21). **Twelfthly, he would demonstrate that instead of being a place of fear of potentially harmful beings and forces, the universe is under the control of a personal, loving Father.** The previous analysis of folk Islam has demonstrated that the folk Muslim lives in fear.

Christ's prayer then recognizes that God has "hidden these things from the wise and understanding and revealed them to babes" (vs. 21). Finally, he would observe that, for understanding such spiritual realities, simple faith and teachableness are more important then erudition. Most of us in academia or in foreign missionary service have had to learn about the spirit world and spiritual warfare from the common people we serve. Richard De Ridder observed how unprepared his formal training in traditional Reformed Theology left him for dealing with the spirit world in which his people lived. He concluded, "This is a chapter of Reformed Theology that still has not been written, and which perhaps cannot be written by the West."

HOW PAUL WOULD ENCOUNTER POWER IN FOLK ISLAM

Ephesus in Paul's day, as described in Acts 19, contained the major elements found in folk Islam. It had **spirit** powers (vss. 11-20) and power **objects** in the silver shrines of Artemis (vs. 24) and the sacred stone that fell from heaven (vs. 35)—a meteorite like the Black Stone in the Ka'ba in Mecca. It had a power **place**, the temple of Artemis (vs. 27), and power **times** when there were celebrations in honor of the goddess. There were power **rituals**, the Jewish exorcists who tried to use the name of Jesus as a power word (vs. 13). Other rituals would have been used by those who practiced the magic arts (vss. 18-19). We can infer from what Paul said and did in this context what he would say and do among folk Muslims.

In Ephesus "he entered the synagogue and for three months spoke about the kingdom of God. Then he "argued daily in the hall of Tyrannus. This continued for two years, so that all . . . heard the word of the Lord" (vss. 8-10). The **first** principle is that **he would engage in power ministries in the context of teaching.** The spiritual effectiveness of Inayat's power ministry in Pakistan, to which we have referred, is that it is always carried on in the context of teaching. Healings and exorcisms that are not in the context of extended teaching seldom make much permanent impact on the Church. Such teaching was necessary in an African country when a folk-Muslim sorcerer followed Christ. Deception had become such a way of life for him that it was a difficult habit to break, a task needing all the spiritual reinforcement possible.

We read that "when some were stubborn and disbelieved, speaking evil of the way before the congregation (of the synagogue), he withdrew" (vs. 9). The **second** principle has already been seen in Luke 10: **he would focus on the receptive.**

The account continues, "God did extraordinary (lit., not the ordinary) miracles (lit., powerful deeds) by the hands of Paul" (vs. 11). **Thirdly, God would use him in the miracles but God would be the One accomplishing the task.** Conversely, folk Muslims tend to focus on the human instrument as the power person. **Fourthly,** the word "extraordinary" reminds us that there is also an ordinary way that God works; so we may note **God would also use him in ordinary ways.** We need to remember that the God who does extraordinary things is also the One who established and works through the laws of nature such as healing through medicine. Even the gift of grace to endure unchanged suffering is a work of God.

The extraordinary works are described: "handkerchiefs and aprons were carried away from his body to the sick, and diseases left and the evil spirits came out of them" (vs. 12). **Fifthly, he might let objects convey the power, but the power would be God's, not the objects'.** As Jesus used saliva in enabling eyes to see, a Coptic Orthodox priest in Egypt used to send some of his saliva in a bottle to the sick who could not come to him, and God would sometimes heal them.

"Itinerant Jewish exorcists," we read, "undertook to pronounce the name of the Lord Jesus over those who had evil spirits" (vs. 13). Here and elsewhere where the activities of those other than Paul are described, the principles are stated without reference to Paul. **Sixthly, real evidences of the power of God are often accompanied by counterfeits.** Folk Muslims have fabrications of the works of the Spirit. Some exorcise spirits in the *Zar* cult, speak in tongues, prophesy concerning the future, or collapse in unconsciousness in a state like being "slain in the Spirit." Thus, discernment is needed to decide between: (1) what is real and what is an illusion; (2) what is of God and what is of the Devil; and (3) what has a physical or psychological or a spiritual cause, or any combination of these.

The evil spirit answered the exorcists, "Jesus I know, Paul I know, but who are you?" (vs. 15). **Seventhly, spirits recognize the authority of Jesus and those in whom he resides.** Folk Muslims try to appease or threaten spirits, but the Christian can speak with authority because Christ is over all such powers (Ephesians 1:20-21). God's superior power was evident in an African country where a Muslim tried to put a curse on a Christian convert. It backfired, and he got deathly sick. No medicine man could help him; so he had to contact the Christians who prayed for him. He was healed and became a Christian.

The passage continues, "the man in whom the evil spirit was leaped on them, mastered all of them, and overpowered them" (vs. 16). **Eighthly, spirits have real power, using the bodies they inhabit.** In the same African country just described a sorcerer put a curse on three people who became insane though they were later restored to mental health through Christian prayer.

The result in Ephesus was that "fear fell upon them all" (vs. 17). **Ninthly, evidences of power elicit fear which can only be balanced when God is seen as a loving Father.** As has been demonstrated previously, the mood of folk Muslims is that of fear.

The verse continues, "and the name of the Lord was extolled" (vs. 17). **Tenthly, signs of the power of the kingdom should lead to the exalting of the king.** This is often not the case since folk Muslims just want healing and usually do not care from where it comes. In Mindanao, the sick may go to the Muslim shaman, the Catholic priest, the government hospital, and the Protestant missionary.

In Ephesus, many new believers confessed their practices of magic and burned their books on magic (vss. 18-19). **Eleventhly, Christian converts often continue magical practices.** In Faisalabad (formerly Lyalpur) in Pakistan, people cast off their Muslim amulets at an evangelistic meeting, and then outside bought St. Christopher's medals for stronger Christian amulets. A Christian holy woman in the capital city of Islamabad wrote Bible verses, rather than quranic verses, for amulets.

Twelfthly, magic seeks mechanistically to manipulate rather than submit to the will of God. This is a temptation to Christians as well as Muslims. **Thirteenthly, materials associated with magic need to be destroyed.** If a former Muslim sorcerer in an African country had not burned his paraphernalia, he said, he probably would have used it to discover and curse those who stole his boat and fishing net, his only means of support for himself and other converts who had lost their jobs and homes.

The result in Ephesus was that "the word of the Lord grew mightily" (vs. 20). **Fourteenthly, the demonstration of God's power should lead to the increase of** the message rather than be an end in itself. This is why significant church growth has only resulted when power ministries have been combined with teaching.

Finally, the story concludes with the silversmiths, because of their economic interests, stirring up the populace by appealing to their religious concerns and civic pride. Then the legal and governmental institutions are identified as means of expressing complaints or redressing wrongs (vss. 24-39). **Lastly, the "powers" with which the Christian must contend with are not only spirits but human institutions, be they commercial, religious, legal, or governmental.** These are included in the biblical definition of the "powers."

Current converts in the countries described have lost their jobs, their families, and some cases, their lives. They have been called disbelievers and faced court cases to deprive them of their property. In such situations those Christians with a means of livelihood have provided for others. In another case, they have tried to form a cooperative. Though the New Testament leads Christians to expect suffering with no guarantee of escape in this life, God did avenge such treatment in one African town where Muslims have been persecuting Christians. A friend, whose judgment I trust, personally saw and reported that, for five months this year in daylight, balls of fire struck the fences and later the homes of Muslims who persecuted the Christians. God's power comes in judgment as well as mercy.

Last year my wife, my youngest son, and I visited Ephesus. The Temple of Artemis, one of the seven wonders of the ancient world, had all sunk into the marsh except one pillar which bore witness to the glory that had been. Nearby stands the Isa (Jesus) Mosque representing the orthodox faith that has replaced the old paganism. Yet the mosque is surrounded by homes in which are hung glass replicas of blue eyes (*nazars*) to ward off the evil eye—reminders of the folk beliefs and practices that are mixed with the orthodox. Yet, like the temple before, these too will pass away. All that will be left is the name on the mosque —Jesus—since, as the previous residents were told, He sits "far above all . . . power" (Ephesians 1:21).

NOTE: Many categories have been adapted from Paul Hiebert, "Power Encounter and Folk Islam," *Muslims and Christians on the Emmaus Road*, ed. J. Dudley Woodberry (Monrovia, CA: MARC, 1988), pp. 52-54, and Bill Musk, "Popular Islam: An Investigation into the Phenomenology and Ethnotheological Bases of Popular Islamic Belief and Practice" (Doctoral Diss.; Pretoria: University of South Africa, 1984), p. 164.

TOWARD AN SIM POSITION ON POWER ENCOUNTER

Like many other mission societies, SIM has been raised up by God as a religious order to plant the church of Jesus Christ throughout the world. By the very nature of our ministry, we are called upon to enter enemy territory and engage in spiritual warfare. In this war zone, we often find ourselves challenged by the spiritual forces of darkness. How we deal with spiritual power encounter is of vital importance to us individually and corporately.

C. S. Lewis, author of *Screwtape Letters*, commented that there are two common mistakes that one can make in dealing with the enemy. The first is in giving him too much emphasis; the other, in not giving him enough.

The dilemma which faces the evangelical world in general and conservative evangelical missions like SIM, in particular, is precisely that of which C. S. Lewis warned. For on the one side, if we ignore our enemy, we cannot wage war effectively. But on the other, if we become unduly preoccupied with these issues, we will find ourselves detracted from our ultimate purpose, or embroiled in paralyzing controversies.

The related subject of the miraculous in Christian ministry is currently receiving unusual attention. Contemporary Bible colleges and seminaries are rapidly adding courses in spiritual warfare, power encounter, and signs and wonders to their curricula. Current Christian books and magazines of both popular and scholarly variety are flooded with discussions on this topic. Popular lecturers crisscross the continents to expound the issue. A new denomination, VINEYARD CHRISTIAN FELLOWSHIP, focusing on signs and wonders, is growing rapidly. Indeed, a movement identified as "The Third Wave" calls upon the evangelical world to accept that signs, wonders, and miracles, as seen in the miracles of Jesus and the apostles, are to be expected in today's church.

It is the intent of this paper to spell out SIM's position in these areas. To this end, we have studied the Scriptures and sought input from a study group composed of SIM missionaries and SIM-related national church leaders. Our findings were carefully scrutinized by a group of SIM theologians as well as by several prominent pastor-teachers who are deeply involved with SIM. This paper was then approved by SIM's International Council and noted by the Board of Governors. What is represented in this paper is an attempt to clarify SIM's position on this important topic.

Part I

SPIRITUAL WARFARE

In SIM, we do recognize the reality of the spirit world. One article in our doctrinal statement states that we believe in "the personality of Satan, who is called the devil." No one can be a member of SIM without accepting that reality.

Further, SIM missionaries and related national church leaders are not strangers to spiritual encounters with the demonic world. National church leaders report incidents of spiritual attacks on national Christian workers. Our missionaries relate case studies in which they have seen those once bound by Satan delivered from demonization through the powerful name of Jesus.

1 Dealing with the demonic

From our collective experience and study of Scripture, several important principles emerge:

- The ability to expel demons is not related to any spiritual gift, but has to do with the believer's position in Christ and His authority over the principalities and powers (Ephesians 1:19-21; 2:4-6). We deny anyone's claim of being especially gifted as an exorcist.

- We do not actively seek out opportunities to exorcise demons, but when confronted in ministry, we should not hesitate to respond (Acts 16:16-18).

- Because Jesus "disarmed the powers and authorities" at the cross, and because we are granted a position over them in Christ, we believe that ultimately they must obey direct commands given in the powerful name of Jesus (Colossians 2:15; Acts 16:18).

- We recognize that there may be incidents when an individual may have to deal with such encounters alone. We strongly advise, however, that this should be a group ministry (Matthew 17:21).

- Sometimes the demonized have more than one evil spirit troubling them. For this reason, it may be helpful to discern the name of the dominant spirit and deal with it first (Luke 8:30).

- Great care must be given to those who have been delivered. They must be urged to confess Christ as their personal Savior. They should be taught how to pray in the name and authority of Jesus. They should be surrounded by loving Christians who are aware of their spiritual authority (Luke 11:24-26).

- Those involved in this ministry should do so realizing that all ministry is through the grace of God. They should examine their own hearts to see if there is unconfessed sin, any desire for self-exaltation, or any gap in their spiritual armor through which they can be attacked (Ephesians 6:10-19). They must beware lest they be lifted up with pride and thus fall into the temptation of the devil himself (1 Timothy 3:6; 1 Corinthians 12:7).

- If such incidents are recounted publicly, great care must be taken to give all the credit and glory to Christ, at whose name the demonic world trembles (Acts 14:15; 15:12).

2 Influence, control, possession

Within this consensus there are areas where we have honest questions among ourselves. For instance, not all of us are agreed as to the degree to which evil spirits can affect believers, particularly those in a backslidden condition who knowingly, or unknowingly, dabble in the occult.

We all agree wholeheartedly that every believer receives the Holy Spirit at conversion and is indwelt by Him (Romans 8:9). But we also note that Paul and John encouraged church leaders to "test the spirits and see if they be from God" (1 Corinthians 12:3; 1 John 4:1). Is it possible that some believers, while claiming that they had spiritual gifts from God, were unwittingly manifesting the influence or control of evil spirits?

One of our number related that when he applied such a test to a person claiming spiritual utterance an evil spirit manifested itself and was cast out in the name of Jesus. Do we then question the salvation of the person so afflicted?

Several members of our study group have witnessed incidents in which evil spirits spoke through professing believers and openly confessed that these backsliders belong to Jesus, and that the spirits had come back to trouble them because they had become involved again with worshiping Satan. When such persons repented and confessed their sin, they were immediately released.

From a practical point of view, if one is confronted by such a situation, it must be dealt with even if all the theological implications are not understood. But in theological terms it is difficult to determine the exact degree to which an evil spirit can influence, control, or possess a believer. On this continuum, some would draw the line between influence and control. Others would draw it between control and possession.

Note the three words which we have used: possess, influence, control. We resolutely deny that Satan or any evil spirit can possess a believer in the sense of ownership. Believers belong to God. Jesus knows His own (John 10:14). No one can take them out of His hand (John 10:28,29). But no one would doubt that Satan and his demons do have power to influence believers, at least to the degree of serious temptation (Acts 5:3ff). Where believers are not walking in fellowship with the Lord, where they are not filled with all the fullness of God, where they have given place to the devil, we know that the demonic can gain a strategic foothold (Ephesians 4:27). Whether this can include outright control is an area of question.

As in other issues where controversy could threaten our unity, those who entertain such questions must agree not to make them a point of division.

One further word of clarification: When we speak of someone being demonized, we are speaking of an evil spirit taking control of someone in such a way that the evil spirit speaks through or otherwise affects the faculties or person of that individual.

We know of those who see demonic manifestation in all sorts of sins and shortcomings of the flesh. But we see no biblical precedent for casting out demons of anger, lust, hatred of one's mother-in-law, etc. We know of deep crippling damage which has been done to Christians who have been dealt with in this way. We believe that the biblical method for dealing with such sins is to repent and confess them to God. Any other teaching relieves sinners of their personal responsibility to confess their own sins to God (1 John 1:9).

3 Spiritual warfare at a deeper level

Even though many within SIM have had experiences and theological insights of the type discussed, this was not an area of major emphasis or concern. In fact, dealing with the demonized is not where most of our missionaries feel the heat of spiritual battle.

For in dealing with the demonized, we are usually dealing with isolated incidents. Dramatic as exorcism may be, our missionaries and church leaders are involved essentially in turning the hearts of whole ethnic groups from "darkness to light and from the power of Satan to God" (cf. Acts 26:16-18). Indeed, exorcism as described above may be seen only as one visible expression of the much larger cosmic battle.

Far more serious are the pervasive powers of darkness which have blinded whole people groups to the light of God. We are concerned about those "powers and authorities," about those world forces of darkness, those spiritual forces of wickedness which stand opposed to the advance of the Gospel and the spreading of God's kingdom on earth (Ephesians 6:12).

We want our missionaries, our related churches, and all Christians everywhere, to recognize that there are dark spiritual forces which have enormous power over entire clans, villages, towns, ethnic groups, and even over nations (Daniel 10:11-13). It is as we learn to take up the weapons of our warfare, and attack these strongholds of wickedness that God's Spirit will be released to turn men and women to himself, bring salvation to the lost, and revive His church.

Biblically, spiritual warfare includes both resisting the devil as well as standing firm in our faith (1 Peter 5:8,9). Often our struggle is not so much a deliberate focusing on evil powers in conscious resistance as in living a life of disciplined responsiveness to the Lord, who has power over them. In Ephesians chapter 6, the Christian's resistance to evil powers is effected by the disciplines of truth, a life of righteousness, readiness to witness, faith, giving attention to the Word, and intercessory prayer.

We are called to take up the weapons of our warfare, which are really God's weapons of warfare (cf. 2 Corinthians 10:4; Ephesians 6:11). We should be greatly encouraged as we see that these weapons are the same ones with which our blessed Lord did battle while upon the earth. (Note Isaiah 11:5; 49:2; 52:7; 59:17). It should encourage us to know that He used these weapons when sharing our humanity so that ". . . he might destroy him who holds the power of death" (Hebrews 2:14).

At the cross, Jesus "disarmed the powers and authorities" (Colossians 2:15). We are challenged to get into the battle, to take up God's full armor against a naked and defenseless foe, and wield the offensive weapons of praise, the sword of the Spirit, and intercessory prayer. Through faith, mighty faith, and by prevailing prayer, we shall be numbered among the overcomers (Ephesians 6:16; 1 John 2:13,14).

Part II

SIGNS, WONDERS, AND MIRACLES

"Power encounter" is a general term which includes "spiritual warfare" as well as "signs, wonders, and miracles." Spiritual warfare refers to the confrontation which takes place between a believer, as God's agent on earth, and the forces of demonic darkness. In signs, wonders, and miracles (works of power), the focus is not so much on direct confrontation with the demonic as on supernatural displays of God's power over the natural elements of our fallen world. In either case, God's power is visibly displayed.

1 The purpose of signs and wonders

God's purpose in signs, wonders, and miracles (the miraculous) appear to be many:

- In the days of Moses, God displayed His power in signs and wonders in order to convince Pharaoh of His sovereign reality, as well as to draw attention to Moses as His servant (Acts 7:36).

- In the days of Elijah, God demonstrated himself by fire to show himself as superior over all the prophets of Baal (1 Kings 18).

- God used Naaman's healing through the word of Elisha to prove that no god in all the world is equal to the God of Israel (2 Kings 5:15).

- In the days of Daniel, God spared the three Hebrew children to cause Nebuchadnezzar to recognize His sovereign power (Daniel 4:2). Daniel was spared from the lions so that Darius might know that the Lord reigns in heaven (Daniel 6:27).

- On the day of Pentecost, Peter reminded the multitude that the ministry and message of Jesus was attested to by signs, wonders, and miracles (Acts 2:22). In the same chapter, it is stated that many signs and wonders were performed by the apostles immediately after the day of Pentecost (Acts 2:43).

- In the early church, the people prayed: "Sovereign Lord . . . enable your servants to speak your word with great boldness. Stretch out your hand to heal and perform miraculous signs and wonders through the name of your holy servant Jesus" (Acts 4:24-30).

- Stephen, the deacon and Philip the evangelist both performed signs and wonders (Acts 6:8; 8:6). We learn from the latter account that, whatever the purpose of signs may be, it certainly is not something to be purchased with money for personal gain. Peter sternly rebuked Simon the sorcerer, who sought such power with money and warned him, "You have no part or share in this ministry, because your heart is not right before God" (Acts 8:21).

- Signs of power were present as Paul, Barnabas, and Silas went about their missionary journeys. They were used to silence the opposition of Elymas the sorcerer and so amazed Sergius Paulus that he believed, "for he was amazed at the teaching about the Lord" (Acts 13:12). Later, when Paul and Barnabas addressed the Jerusalem Council, they told how God had used signs and wonders in their ministry among the Gentiles. It would seem that they used this argument to prove that the Gentiles were just as much a part of the church as were the Jews (see Acts 15:12).

- Similarly, when Paul's authority as a true apostle was challenged, he went to great lengths to explain how he had preached the Gospel freely, suffered for the Gospel intensely, and had performed signs and wonders among them, as any true apostle would have done (2 Corinthians chapters 11 and 12, especially 12:12).

- From 1 Corinthians 12:9 and Galatians 3:5 it would appear that miracles were not uncommon in the early church; and not necessarily at the hands of the apostles only, but rather as part of the spiritual gifts which God gave sovereignly to believers.

- Finally, God will use signs and wonders in the future. Joel prophesied about "wonders in the heavens and on the earth" (Joel 2:30; cf. Acts 2). Many of these are yet to be fulfilled. Further, we are warned that when the "lawless one will be revealed," he will come displaying counterfeit miracles, signs, and wonders (2 Thessalonians 2:9).

It would appear that God uses the miraculous in many ways. Signs and wonders validate His message and His messengers. They can create a sense of awe in believers and foster faith in unbelievers. They can also be used to chasten those who attempt to obstruct His purposes. They come at particular times and seasons when God, for whatever reasons, chooses to make himself manifest.

Some have attempted to give precise definitions to the use of signs and wonders, and then go about showing why God must or cannot do such things today. But any attempt to confine or limit their use would require a full understanding of all that God is doing. In this regard, Paul exclaimed: "Oh, the depth of the riches of the wisdom and knowledge of God! How unsearchable his judgments, and his paths beyond tracing out! Who has known the mind of the Lord? Or who has been his counselor?" (Romans 11:33,34).

Perhaps, the most we should say is that God performs the miraculous when it suits His purposes and when He chooses to reveal His own glory. We do need to make the point, however, that the miraculous is not always overt. There are periods in sacred history when the waters of the miraculous go underground only to spring up again at some other time and in another place as God sovereignly directs the flow of His eternal plans (cf. 1 Samuel 3:1).

2 The spiritual and natural worlds

If we believe that Christians are positioned in Christ with authority over the demonic world, what about authority to heal, work miracles, and demonstrate

God's power through signs and wonders in the natural or fallen world about us?

The point of departure for some modern practitioners is not through "gift" theology, or through "healing in the atonement" theology, or in the popular "prosperity" theology. Rather, it is through "kingdom of God" theology and more particularly through the issue of "spiritual authority."

With regard to God's kingdom, some assume that because Jesus came to set up the kingdom of God, and since we believers are part of that kingdom, we already have all the rights and privileges of that kingdom. This has led to confusion over what some theologians refer to as "already" in God's kingdom and what is "not yet."

We need to recognize that our world is still under the Adamic curse. Though Christ came to inaugurate His kingdom, that kingdom is yet to be fully implemented. Jesus acknowledged this when He taught us to pray, "your kingdom come."

The apostle Paul teaches that all fallen creation is presently "groaning as in the pains of childbirth right up to the present time" (Romans 8:22). Though our world is subjected to frustration, it is subjected in hope (Romans 8:20). We eagerly await the day when all sorrow, suffering, pain, and death will be done away as God establishes His eternal kingdom. But it is not until the new Jerusalem comes down out of heaven that the loud voice from the throne cries, "There will be no more death or mourning or crying or pain, for the old order of things has passed away" (Revelation 21:4).

The claim of this new movement is that today's disciples have the same authority to heal, cast out demons, and work other miracles as did the early disciples in the days of Jesus. They argue that as Jesus gave authority to those disciples to heal the sick, raise the dead, cleanse the leper, and cast out demons in His pre-resurrection commission, (cf. Matthew 10:8) that same authority is to be passed on to all believers today as part of their birthright. They point out that the same disciples who received authority in Matthew chapter 10 were later instructed to teach their disciples all that the Lord had commanded them (cf. Matthew 10:8; 28:19,20). Thus, we, who are Christ's disciples today should expect the miraculous in ministry.

This teaching, however, ignores the fact that those pre-resurrection commands to the early disciples are very specific as to their time and situation. In Matthew chapter 10, those early disciples were also instructed to take no money with them, to take no change of clothes, to stay in one place only and not to move from house to house. Moreover, they were commanded not to go to the nations (*ethnos*) but only to the "lost sheep of Israel" (Matthew 10:5). No honest interpretation of these passages could assume that all these commands would apply to the missionaries (apostles are "sent ones") of our day. Rather, they were given for a "specific mission with limited objective" (Smedes 1987: 20:30).

3 Suffering in our fallen world

Another error we need to avoid is believing that all pain, sorrow, and calamity can be directly attributed to the evil one. The division between the demonic and the fallen aspects of our world is not always clear. We know, for instance, that sickness is part of our fallen world. Some sicknesses, as in the case of Job, can be inflicted by Satan. Even there, permission had to be obtained from God himself. It certainly does not follow that all sickness is demonically induced. Paul encouraged Timothy to take medicinal wine for his stomach's sake. He did not prescribe exorcism. The man born blind in John chapter 9 was afflicted, "that the work of God might be displayed in his life." At the burning bush God said to Moses, "Who makes [man] deaf or dumb? Who gives him sight or makes him blind? Is it not I the Lord?" (Exodus 4:11).

Suffering is a fact of our fallen world. Indeed, God's incredible wisdom is displayed when He uses suffering as a tool to refine character, teach us truths about himself, and, as in the case of Paul, make us weak so that His grace and power may be all the more evident in us. We must not forget that it pleased God to bruise His own Son on the cross: "It was the Lord's will to crush him and cause him to suffer" (Isaiah 53:10). From His suffering has come our salvation. Our theology is often colored with the desire to escape the disciplines of the cross, and reach too quickly for the crown. Paul, however, reminds us that we shall rule with Him, if we suffer with Him (2 Timothy 2:12). Any theology which fails to recognize God's purpose in suffering is sub-biblical.

4 The spiritual dimension in various world views

Much of the current literature on this topic points out that our Western worldview tends to be highly rationalistic. Conversely, in the non-Western world people are much more aware of the spiritual dimensions of life and are more open to accepting supernatural phenomena. This is certainly true, but as we consider this we need to beware lest we fall into the trap of becoming animists ourselves, that is, of adopting the animistic worldview which sees everything as related to the spirit world.

Animists try to manipulate their world through placation of the evil spirits. Western rationalism tries to control its world through the application of certain laws of science. Both systems overlap in their attempts to control their world. Animistic spiritualism and Western rationalism both need to come under the judgment of Scripture.

If we are not careful, we can become like the animist who sees spirits behind everything. The copy machine doesn't work; so you need to cast out the demon. The car won't start; and there's another demon. You run the red light because the devil made you do it. And worse, you are ticketed by a policeman—a messenger of Satan to buffet you! This kind of thinking gives altogether too much emphasis to the demonic. It causes one to treat every natural phenomenon as if it were of diabolic origin.

We Christians, and missionaries in particular, will pave the way for syncretism if we teach that we can manipulate God's Spirit to do our bidding (Prior 1987:38-40). All we would be doing would be substituting the manipulation of evil spirits for manipulation of the Holy Spirit. God forbid! The harmful effects of such doctrine could be enormous, especially in animistic societies.

5 A key theological distinction

We believe that believers do, indeed, have authority over demonic principalities and powers because of their position in Christ (Ephesians chapters 1 and 2).

But does that same authority extend into our natural world into areas such as healing and performing miracles in the same ways as the pre-resurrection disciples to whom Jesus gave such authority?

We think not. All authority in heaven and earth now belongs to Jesus (Matthew 28:19). We move at His command. We do not command Him. Jesus taught us to pray, "your will be done on earth as it is in heaven" (Matthew 6:10). Too many people today want to change that prayer to read, "My will be done in heaven as I want it on earth." We must never become confused over who is master. God will not be manipulated into doing our will. Even the Lord Jesus, prayed "Yet not as I will, but as you will" (Matthew 26:39).

How is it then, that a believer may have authority to expel evil spirits, but not have authority to heal and perform other miracles? The distinction is that in Christ we have been granted a position above the principalities and powers (Ephesians chapter 1 and 2). We have authority over them and command them in the name of Jesus. But we are not placed in a position of authority over God to command *Him*. The prophet Isaiah declared:

"This is what the Lord says—the Holy One of Israel, and its Maker:
Concerning things to come, do you question me about my children,
or give me orders about the work of my hands?"

Isaiah 45:11

The obvious answer is, "You'd better not, for I am God."

When we desire to see God intervene miraculously in the affairs of men or nature, we come to our sovereign Lord and present our requests, not our commands, before Him. We are not demanding our *rights*, but rather exerting the *privilege* which He has given us to come before Him confidently in our time of need (Hebrews 4:16).

Part III

THREE TIMELY PRINCIPLES

Seventy years ago, SIM founder and first General Director, Rowland Bingham, took issue with the teaching of his day that divine healings was in the atonement, and therefore "every true Christian had a right to take healing in the same way as they accepted salvation." According to this teaching, if true Christians were sick, they were living "below their privilege." Thus healing was taught as the right of the believer.

In his book, *The Bible and the Body*, Bingham argued that though the motive of wanting to see healing for a suffering world was commendable, this doctrine simply was not supported in Scripture or in true experience of ministry. Indeed, Bingham argued, such teaching was really a deterrent to the Gospel because it held out false hope. He cited numerous incidents where such teaching left behind a wake of disillusioned people whose faith was crushed when God chose not to provide the miraculous.

This does not in any way imply that Bingham or we in SIM deny God's power or willingness to heal and perform miracles. Bingham's point was that God can and does heal, but on the basis of His sovereignty, not on the basis of our authority.

With regard to the question of the place of the miraculous in our ministry, SIM bases its position on three timely principles of Scripture: the sovereignty of God; the primacy of the Gospel; and the unity of the body.

1   The sovereignty of God

The principle of God's sovereignty is absolutely fundamental to our understanding of all signs and wonders, and distributions of the gifts of the Holy Spirit. In 1 Corinthians 12:4-11, Paul listed nine spiritual gifts, including "gifts of healing" and "working of miraculous powers," *i.e.*, miracles, and then concluded by saying,

> "All these are the work of one and the same spirit, and he gives them to each man, *just as he determines.*"
>
> 1 Corinthians 12:11

In Hebrews 2:1-4, the writer speaks about our "great salvation," and then proceeds to explain how this salvation came down to us:

> "This salvation, which was first announced by the Lord, was confirmed to us by those who heard him. God also testified to it by signs, wonders and various miracles, and gifts of the Holy Spirit distributed *according to his will.*"

In our discussion of signs and wonders we must avoid extreme positions on both sides. On the one side there are those who say that such phenomena have no place in ministry today. On the other side there are those who give them such emphasis that they are in danger of neglecting other important truths of Scripture.

We do well here to recall that heresy is not so much the acceptance of error as it is taking of a doctrinal truth to an extreme position. With regard to the topic at hand, it is a dangerous thing to tell God what He *must* do. By the same token, it may be equally as dangerous to predetermine what He *cannot* do.

For our part, SIM has chosen a position "between the shoals of denying the possibility of miracles in our day, and the rocks of presumption that demand miracles according to our need and schedule" (Smedes 1987:17). We acknowledge that God can and will do whatever pleases Him in any given situation.

Our stand is with the three Hebrew children who told Nebuchadnezzar:

> "If we are thrown into the blazing furnace, the God we serve is able to save us from it, and he will rescue us from your hand, O king. But

*even if he does not, we want you to know, O king, that we will not
serve your gods or worship the image of gold you have set up."*

Daniel 3:17,18

Some argue that signs and wonders and miracles were authenticating signs and limited to those through whom God was granting "normative revelation," *i.e.*, the Scriptures. They say, such signs and wonders terminated with the inscripturation of God's special revelation in the New Testament.

Some who take this position hold that these were certain enablement given to certain believers for the purpose of authenticating or confirming God's word when it was proclaimed in the early church before the Scriptures were penned. They believe that these sign gifts were temporary. Once the Word of God was inscriptured, the sign gifts were no longer needed and they ceased.

This position, however, has come under increasing attack from both exegetical and historical perspective. For instance, some take 1 Corinthians 13:8-10 to show that gifts such as prophecy, tongues, and knowledge would "cease" and "pass away" "when perfection comes." They argue that "perfection" must refer to the completion of revelation and thus think they have proof that certain gifts have ceased.

The problem, however, is that equally competent Bible scholars have argued that "perfection" does not refer to inscripturation at all, but rather to the second coming of Christ. If that position is correct, it would argue strongly that such gifts are indeed valid throughout the whole church age and prove exactly the opposite of the naysayer's position.

Others point to Hebrews 2:4 to make the case that it was only at the first, *i.e.*, at the beginning of the church age, that God used signs, wonders, miracles (works of power) and distributions of His Holy Spirit to confirm the word.

The problem here also is an exegetical one, for there is no certain proof that the word "first" applies to the signs and wonders. Many would interpret it as applying only to the fact that our great salvation was "first announced" by the Lord Jesus himself.

It is argument and rebuttal like this which have caused some to take strong issue about the assumption that all such demonstrations were limited to the authentication of Scripture. In fact, some current writers declare that there is nothing in Scripture that indicates that signs and wonders were meant to stop after the early days of Christianity. They contend that theories about the termination of certain spiritual gifts all come from human interpreters under the influence of Western world views and not from God's Word.

Others make the same point by suggesting that theories of cessation are theological judgments rather than historic observations.

The historical evidence would seem to indicate that signs, wonders, and miracles of all kinds did not end with the death of the apostles or with inscripturation. Some writers press this point by quoting extensively from Irenaeus who, about 180 A.D. wrote:

> "In Christ's name the Christians are driving out devils. . . . Others have foreknowledge of things to come; they see visions, and utter prophetic expressions. Others still heal the sick by laying their hands upon them, and they are made whole. Yea, moreover, as I have said, the dead even have been raised up, and remain among us for many years."
>
> (*Against Heresies* by Irenaeus as quoted in Williams 1989:134)

It is well-known that Tertullian, Cyprian, and Origen, all of whom lived in the third century, long after the canonization of Scripture, testify to the miraculous in the early church. Origen (200-258 A.D.) wrote that he personally witnessed "many delivered from serious ailments, and from mental distraction and madness, and countless other diseases, which neither man nor demons had cured." (Quoted in Smedes 1987:36)

Some of the greatest revivals of history have had displays of signs and wonders very similar to those being claimed today, especially the revivals of Wesley, Whitefield, the Great Awakening of the 18th century and the Welsh revival (*cf.* John White, *When the Spirit Comes with Power*, especially chapters 2-6).

SIM founder and first General Director, Rowland Bingham, had much to say about the role of signs, wonders, and miracles in his book, *The Bible and the Body*. He wrote:

> ". . . miracles of healing, however much they may have decreased after the Apostolic age, never entirely ceased, and that in the records of the Church, and the memoirs of her saints, accounts of supernatural healing are by no means uncommon." (Bingham 1921:13)

Bingham also readily affirmed that signs are present in our world today:

> "In most of the foreign fields there have been such displays of His power for a sign. Missionaries could duplicate almost every scene in the Acts of the Apostles during the past hundred years of their activities. Where,

for the glory of the Christ, for the establishment of His Word, for the furtherance of the Gospel, signs are necessary or expedient, there He gives the signs, *according to His own will."* [Emphasis mine.] (Bingham 1921:66)

Note that Bingham saw no cessation of signs when God saw it would be useful for His purposes. The bottom line with Bingham, and with us, is the sovereignty of God.

We would like to make it clear that although there may be some who feel that such signs have no place in our present day, SIM has never taken any official position that signs, wonders, miracles, or any specific gifts have ceased. Today, seven decades after Bingham took this stand, we affirm his words as our position:

"Where, for the glory of the Christ, for the establishment of His Word, for the furtherance of the Gospel, signs are necessary or expedient, there He gives the signs, according to His own will."

2 The primacy of the Gospel

The first danger to be avoided in this issue is faulty theology. Equally dangerous is a faulty emphasis. Many proponents give such emphasis to signs and wonders that they overlook the real purpose to which Christ's followers are called. (Recall C. S. Lewis's concern, lest we give the enemy too much emphasis.)

Each record of the Great Commission as given in the four Gospels and the Book of Acts carries a slightly different emphasis. In Matthew, it relates to the authority which the Lord Jesus has in heaven and on earth with the particular task of making and teaching disciples in every nation. In Mark, the focus is on preaching the Gospel throughout the whole world. In Luke, the emphasis is on preaching forgiveness and the coming of the Holy Spirit. In John, the emphasis is on going into the world in the same way that Jesus was sent into the world. In Acts, the emphasis is on the progression of witness from Jerusalem to the ends of the earth in the power of the Holy Spirit.

In all of the above, there is only one comment regarding the place of signs and wonders in evangelism. That is the disputed passage in Mark 16:17 where we read, "And these signs will accompany those who believe. . . ." Though the textual debate is beyond the scope of this study, we make the point that whether or not this passage was penned by Mark, and not added later as some suggest, the thrust of the text is not that signs and wonders are necessary to bring people to faith, but that the life and ministry of the new community of believers will be confirmed ("demonstrated to be standing") by supernatural signs.

This phenomenon is not uncommon in the mission fields of the world today. Many times, when the Gospel comes into a stronghold of Satan, those who first accept it are held suspect by the unbelieving majority. Sometimes, God allows the miraculous to take place so the rest of the community can see that the new teaching about Christ is indeed something of divine origin. As time passes, the life and testimony of the believers becomes its own authentication. SIM can point to numerous places where large numbers of people have believed after they have had time to watch the first converts and see the power of God in their transformed lives. The Gospel's greatest attestation is a transformed life.

While it is true that some have ignored the possibility of the miraculous, others argue that evangelism should be preceded and undergirded by supernatural demonstrations of God's presence, so that resistance to the Gospel is overcome by the demonstration of God's power.

Though no one should deny that God is able to bring spectacular displays of His power to bear at the time of preaching of the Gospel, we should not fall into the trap of thinking that displays of power will automatically accompany the Gospel. They may or they may not. If we follow our first principle that signs are given sovereignly, it must follow that God alone decides if and when signs are useful to encourage faith.

Signs, wonders, and miracles can be used as a temporary means to enhance faith. But that which is lasting and builds faith is the preaching of God's Holy Word. "Faith comes from hearing the message, and the message is heard through the word of Christ" (Romans 10:17). It would be a huge mistake to assume that God must work miracles to cause receptivity and foster faith. On one occasion, Jesus said, "They will not be convinced even if someone rises from the dead" (Luke 16:31). On another occasion He said it was a "wicked and adulterous generation" that was always looking for a miraculous sign (Matthew 16:4). Paul said, "Jews demand miraculous signs and Greeks look for wisdom, but we preach Christ crucified: a stumbling block to Jews and foolishness to Gentiles, but to those whom God has called, both Jews and Greeks, Christ the power of God and the wisdom of God" (1 Corinthians 1:22-24).

We need to concentrate on and emphasize what God has given us to do. It is given to us to preach the Gospel. That must be done whether or not there are signs and wonders. If God sovereignly chooses to perform signs and wonders, that is wonderful and we will thank Him. If He chooses not to perform signs, we will also thank Him, for the Gospel itself is the power of God through faith unto salvation. Whichever way He chooses, we will concentrate on what He has told us to do: preach the Gospel, disciple believers, and teach His Word.

If evangelists go into a town or village thinking, "If only a miracle would occur here, the whole town would come to Christ," their emphasis is on the miraculous. Rather, they should go saying, "Christ has commanded us to preach the Gospel. We will do that with all the energy and enabling which He gives us. And if He should grant some miracles of power, all the better. We will thank Him for that."

In northern Ghana a visiting evangelist proclaimed the Gospel with truth and clarity. At the end of his message he said, "If there is anyone sick here today, Jesus has promised to heal you. Come forward and receive your healing." People came forward, but no one was healed. The next year, when the same evangelist came to town, people were overheard saying, "Don't listen to this fellow. Last year he promised that everyone would be healed, and nobody was."

If only he had emphasized the Gospel and called people to faith and repentance he could have reaped an eternal harvest. Instead, he had confused the issue and created a stumbling block to faith.

3 The unity of the Body

What then shall SIM do as a mission body? Should we encourage the use of signs and wonders in ministry? Should we forbid it? We can gain some perspective from Paul's instruction to the Corinthian church in the use of spiritual gifts, for there were people who considered themselves "spiritual" and yet were abusing the gifts (cf. Hemphill 1988:43ff).

Paul avoided what may have seemed the easy road: outlawing the use of specific gifts in the church altogether. Under the guidance of the Spirit, he chose the delicate balance of not quenching the Spirit by forbidding the use of genuine gifts, and by giving clear teaching that would correct errors and direct the proper use of gifts in the church. Here is what he laid down for the Corinthians in his first epistle to them:

1   Recognize that God gives all His gifts sovereignly (12:11,18).

2   Gifts in public must be for the edification of all (14:3-5).

3　All should be done in peace and without confusion; properly and in an orderly manner (14:33,40).

4　Those who are acting outside scriptural guidelines should be ignored (14:37,38).

5　All gifts, miracles, or signs should be open to the examination of others (14:29-32).

6　Genuine gifts and ministry should not be forbidden (14:39).

7　Everything should be done undergirded with selfless *agape* love which never fails (chapter 13).

For our purposes, it is of interest that Paul made distinction between what was done privately and what was done in public or in the church. As a Mission we have no desire to make rules which preclude the possibility that God may indeed work in miraculous ways. Rather, we must make sure that what happens within our Mission family or in the church body at a public level conforms to our common understanding of that which pleases God.

As SIM missionaries we are all volunteers who have set aside our particular doctrinal distinctives to work in an interdenominational mission. We have rallied around the common goal of preaching the Gospel and planting the church throughout the world. The diverse nature of our organization means that its members must agree to allow one another liberty in expression and experience.

By the same token, being a member of such a mission means agreeing to work within a broad consensus. If a person's conviction or overemphasis threatens to break our consensus, the Mission's unity is threatened, and becomes dangerous to its existence. We must never allow that to happen.

SUMMARY

This is the SIM position on Power Encounter:

- We encourage our missionaries and all true saints of God to put on the armor of God, and to take up the weapons of spiritual warfare, and get into the battle for the souls of lost men and women.

- We believe that God is sovereign over all. When it serves His purposes and brings glory to His name, He has performed and can perform signs, wonders, and miracles according to His will. We do not believe, however, that we have the right or the authority to demand such miracles.

- We believe that God has clearly commanded us to preach the Gospel, disciple the nations, and teach His Word. We will continue to make this our emphasis. If God in His sovereignty allows the miraculous to take place, we will praise Him. If not, we will still praise Him, for the Gospel itself is the power of God through faith unto salvation.

- We believe that God has called us to disciple believers into churches equipped to fulfill Christ's Commission. As an interdenominational mission, we cannot allow any one to over-emphasize secondary or tertiary distinctives of doctrine or practice in such a way as to threaten our unity or bring division to our Mission. We do welcome, however, all who can work within our consensus.

- In short, we accept the miraculous in ministry where:

  1 It is in harmony with the Word of God.

  2 It brings glory to the Lord Jesus and not to an individual.

  3 It calls attention to the Gospel and not to a person.

  4 It does not impinge on the sovereignty of God.

  5 It is subject to the judgment of others.

  6 It does not pursue or overemphasize in a manner which could threaten the unity of our Mission.

CONCLUSION

We believe with all our hearts in a God who is powerful and willing to show himself mighty in His good time. We will preach the Gospel with fervor for it is the "power of God for the salvation of everyone who believes: first for the Jew, then for the Gentile" (Romans 1:16). We will pray, as did the early church, that He would enable His servants to speak the Word "with great boldness." Nor will we fear to include the request that God would stretch out His hand "to heal and perform miraculous signs and wonders" through the name of His holy servant Jesus (Acts 4:29,30).

In so doing, we will also make every effort "to keep the unity of the Spirit through the bond of peace" (Ephesians 4:3).

BIBLIOGRAPHY

Bingham, Rowland V. *The Bible and the Body*. Toronto: Evangelical Publishers, (originally published in 1921) fourth ed. 1952.

Bridge, Donald. *Signs and Wonders Today*. Leicester, England: InterVarsity Press, 1985.

Coggins, James R. and Paul G. Hiebert, eds. *Wonders and the Word*. Winnipeg, MB: Kindred Press, 1989.

Flynn, Leslie B. *19 Gifts of the Spirit*. Wheaton, IL: Victor Books, 1974.

Hay, Ian M. *Unity and Purity: Keeping the Balance*. Toronto: SIM Canada, 1983.

Hemphill, Kenneth S. *Spiritual Gifts: Empowering the New Testament Church*. Nashville, TN: Broadman Press, 1988.

Houston, Graham. *Prophecy: A Gift for Today?* Downers Grove, IL: InterVarsity Press, 1989.

Kraft, Charles H. *Christianity with Power*. Ann Harbor, MI: Servant Publications, 1989.

MacArthur, John. *The Charismatics*. Grand Rapids: Zondervan, 1978.

Prior, David. *Jesus and Power*. Downers Grove, IL: InterVarsity Press, 1987.

Rahner, Karl. *Spiritual Experiences*. London: Herder and Herder, 1962.

Smedes, Lewis B. (ed). *Ministry and the Miraculous*. Pasadena, Fuller Theological Seminary, 1987.

Sproul, R. C. *Surprised by Suffering*. Wheaton, IL: Tyndale House Publishers, Inc. 1989.

Steyne, Philip M. *Gods of Power: A Study of the Beliefs and Practices of Animists*. Houston: Touch Publications, Inc. 1989.

Torrey, R. A. *What the Bible Teaches*. Old Tappan, NJ: Revel, 1984.

Wagner, C. Peter. *On the Crest of the Wave: Becoming a World Christian*. Ventura, CA: Regal Books, 1983.

_____. *The Third Wave of the Holy Spirit*. Ann Harbor, MI: Servant Publications, 1988.

Walker, Andrew. *Restoring the Kingdom*. London: Hodder and Stoughton, 1988.

White, John. *When the Spirit Comes with Power: Signs and Wonders among God's People*. Downers Grove, IL: InterVarsity Press, 1988.

Williams, Don. *Signs, Wonders and the Kingdom of God: A Biblical Guide for the Reluctant Skeptic*. Ann Harbor, MI: Servant Publications, 1989.

Wimber, John. *Power Evangelism*. San Francisco: Harper and Row, 1986.

Articles

Bingham, Rowland V. "Why Work Internationally?" in *The Evangelical Christian*, January 1913.

Searles, Ken. "All Power & Signs" in *Kindred Spirit*, Summer 1989.

Tippet, Alan R. "Possessing the Philosophy of Animism for Christ" in Donald A. McGavran, *Crucial Issues in Missions Tomorrow*. Chicago: Moody Press, 1972.

Unpublished Papers

Baker, Ken. "A Case for Power Encounter as a Part of Church Planting Strategy." Trinity Evangelical Divinity School, 1988 (Available: SIM International Resource Center).

Corwin, Gary R. "Power Encounter: The SIM Experience." Trinity Evangelical Divinity School, 1989 (Available: SIM International Resource Center).

Parshall, Phil. "Power Theology and Practice." n.d. (Available: SIM International Resource Center).

PART FIVE

INTEGRITY

IN MINISTRY

MISSIONARIES AND MORALITY

by Phil Parshall

Rather distractedly, I glanced through the orientation packet that had been given to me and to the other 400 missionaries who had gathered together for a special school of missions. I had been invited to give lectures to this gathering of God's choice servants who are known to prioritize biblical teaching on spiritual reality.

Suddenly, my eyes became riveted to a photocopy of a Moody Monthly article which told a graphic story of a pastor who succumbed to the temptation of renting and covertly watching an X-rated video. Later in the day, I sought out the person responsible for the inclusion of the reprint in the packet. "Jack," I asked, "out of the thousands of choices for articles to be given to your missionaries, why did you choose one that dealt with sexual failure?"

With a slight tinge of embarrassment the reply came, "Phil, in this day of sexual promiscuity, I am concerned that some of our missionaries, in a moment of despair or overwhelming temptation, may yield and go the same route as that pastor did. Most of them own video machines and a wide selection of films are available to them just about anywhere they live in the world."

Kudos to a mission which is willing to forthrightly confront an issue which has too long been ignored in our ranks. In the name of discretion, we have only been willing to deal with moral failures on a curative basis and have not backed up to a pre-fall point with strong advice on prevention. I personally have never read an article or heard a lecture on the missionary and sexuality in my 29 years on the mission field apart from a few lectures I have given on the subject—though I realize this may have been done unbeknown to me.

Leadership magazine made a bold step in its Fall, 1982, issue when it printed an anonymously written article entitled, "The War Within: An Anatomy of Lust." This overwhelmingly pungent autobiographical account by an evangelical pastor chronicled his gradual descent into a voyeuristic world of reading pornography, watching X-rated movies, and attendance at nude bars.

Christianity Today conducted a survey in 1987 that asked its readers, "Since you have been over 21, have you ever done anything with someone (not your spouse) that you feel was sexually inappropriate?" Responses were:

	YES	NO
Laypersons	45 percent	55 percent
Pastors	23 percent	77 percent

(Stafford 1987:36)

There has been a great deal of publicity recently concerning immoral acts among Roman Catholic clergy. "A. W. Richard Sipe, a former Benedictine monk, estimates that half the 53,000 Roman Catholic priests in the U.S. are breaking their vow of celibacy . . . about 28% of the priests are engaged in relationships, many of them enduring, with women. An additional 10% to 13% indulge in intimacy with adult men, and 6% pursue adolescents or children, usually boys" (Toufexis 1990:45). These figures, however, are disputed as being too high by U.S. Catholic church officials.

More to the point would be completed questionnaires I received from 390 evangelical missionaries who serve with 37 mission societies in 32 countries. Ten stated they had not remained sexually moral since becoming a missionary, while eight chose not to answer the question. Twelve have attended X-rated movies, and 62 have "infrequently" watched R-rated films. Sexual fantasies of lust are a problem to 272 missionaries. One-third responded that they read, on occasion, sexually stimulating literature.

Add to the above the actual experiences of moral failure on the mission field, of which the following are but a few true accounts:

- Jim found language acquisition to be totally impossible. Life in his small village was basic and boring. As a coping mechanism he began to fill his mind with soft-core pornography found in the local market. One late night, he became so disoriented that he went into the bedroom, put his hands around his wife's neck, and began to choke her to death. Her screams jolted him back to reality—and to sobbing repentance.

- There had been suspicion for years. But most of his colleagues felt that the problem was one of mild indiscretion. But then proof emerged that this renowned and gifted missionary was repeatedly sexually immoral. His downfall has jolted thousands.

- Bill was an accomplished theologian-missionary. Over the years he had become cold and aloof with his wife. The maid in the home began to look extremely attractive. One day, in the absence of his wife, Bill had a "symbolic marriage" to the national girl followed by sexual relations which led to a scandalous divorce, and subsequent marriage to the maid.

- The two couples were closest of friends, sharing together the joys and trials of first-term missionary experience on the field. Slowly, an unhealthy attraction began to emerge which resulted in both couples divorcing, and one of the husbands marrying the other wife.

- Life was hectic and lonely for Sue. She was vulnerable when a married man offered to befriend her. Soon friendship with this non-Christian national became sexual. Sue reluctantly agreed to leave the field under the insistence of the mission society.

- Jane and Barbara so enjoyed each other's presence. They considered it a privilege to be together in the ministry. What started out as an affectionate hug between friends soon commenced a metamorphosis toward full sexual expression. Today, they are still seeking to pull their lives together in moral purity.

Are these accounts typical or atypical among our evangelical missionary community? Without hesitation, I affirm them as exceptions rather than the rule. Yet, as we pilgrimage and minister (often within sex-saturated societies) we would be remiss not to frankly admit the potential of moral lapses in our ranks. Admission should lead to specific steps toward prevention.

Let me make a few concrete proposals, some of which apply to mission structures, and others which are more personal in nature. First, for mission boards:

1   Every pre-field orientation should include two sessions on sexual issues. One should be plenary and the other divided into male and female groups. All individual interviews should probe for disfunctionality in sexual experience or attitudes.

2   New missionaries should be required to read a few specially chosen books on the subject of sexuality.

3   On the field, orientation classes can include a lecture on the particular physical temptations the missionary will face in his/her new setting. There was resistance in 1974 when I sought to implement this with our newly-arrived 14 missionaries. These "closet attitudes" should be set aside in the interest of our corporate moral well-being.

4   Accountability should include sexuality. Leadership must be aware of the danger signs of misplaced affection or other physical aberrations.

5   Encourage the husband and wife to travel together in ministry, even to the point of the mission giving financial subsidy. Vulnerability is at the highest point when one is lonely and anonymous. In 1970, I traveled alone from Dhaka, Bangladesh, to Singapore. I was accommodated overnight by the airline in a hotel in a respectable section of Bangkok, Thailand. While taking a short walk, I was pro-positioned by three taxi loads of beautiful Thai girls. Returning to my room, I was met by the bellboy who offered to send a girl to my room for five dollars. I knelt by my bed wet with sweat, and thanked God for delivering me from that which in actuality, for me at least, would have been worse than death. Not one person in Bangkok knew me. At that early point in my missionary career I could have been easily destroyed. Presently, it is my goal and

desire to have my wife, Julie, accompany me in all my travels. When this is impractical because of children in school, etc, effort should be made to have stopovers with acquaintances. Once, I was uneasy about a two-day travel delay in Amsterdam, so I arranged to stay with YWAM folk in that city which is so full of temptations.

And now to the individual:

1   Beware of lust. Men, particularly will struggle with this mental sin, probably until death. Calvin Miller has stated that "Lust is a cannibal slowly nibbling himself to death." Lust is progressive. We start with impersonal mental lust which slides into lingering lust with a specific person which then becomes expressed lust in an act of sexual deviation. There must be a disciplined resolve not to feed our minds on magazines, videos, or any other media which gives birth to lust. If television or a video machine contributes to sexual temptation, then it is best to remove these from one's home and life.

2   Set perimeters of that which is acceptable and unacceptable in your life. For instance, it is important to me to be able to say that, following marriage, I have never touched another woman in lust; I have never removed my wedding ring; and I have never arranged a meeting with another woman for my emotional or physical fulfillment.

3   Accountability with one's spouse is all important. But often a husband hesitates to discuss sexual temptation with his wife because of (a) embarrassment; (b) fear of rejection; (c) potential nagging; or (d) possible destruction of marital trust. A climate of openness should prevail that will assist each marriage partner in maintaining sexual purity. Above all, allow the Bible to be central in guiding one's marital relationship.

4   Accountability with a person of the same sex. Often men find it easier to share their struggles with another male who knows firsthand the intensity of sexual temptation. In addition to openness with Julie, I have a missionary friend with whom I have a reciprocal relationship of accountability. We are "shockproof friends" ready to listen, empathize, and counsel one another.

5   It is imperative to keep romance strong in marriage. There must be on-going tangible affirmations of such devotion. This can best be accomplished by small acts that may be "unnatural" to one's lifestyle. Continuing to open the car door for the wife, serving coffee in bed on Sunday morning, a kiss after morning devotions, holding hands as you give grace for food, etc., can all be small but meaningful facilitators toward keeping romance alive and well in the marital union. I once talked with a missionary who had committed adultery. My piercing question of "Why?" was met with, "Phil, Barbara made me feel so alive, so totally and dynamically alive!" Perhaps I am unusual (though I think not), but that is exactly how I feel with my wife of 30 years. But this does not happen automatically. It requires a constant vigilance and discipline.

6   The maintenance of physical neatness and attractiveness is extremely important for both husband and wife.

All of the above is suggestive rather than exhaustive. Much more could be explored. But the purpose of this article is simply to open up this important subject and trust that it can be addressed in appropriate forums to a greater degree.

BIBLIOGRAPHY

Stafford, Tim. "Great Sex: Reclaiming a Christian Sexual Ethic." *Christianity Today*, 2 October 1987.

Toufexis, Anastasia. "What to Do When Priests Stray." *Time*, 24 September 1990.

Note: Names have been changed in this article so as to avoid embarrassment to involved persons.

THE TIGER OF LUST

by Phil Parshall

One terribly bleak day in Bangladesh where my wife, Julie, and I were serving as missionaries, we received word of the spiritual defeat of the man who led me to Christ, ordained me, and pastored a church which generously supported us. This outstanding soulwinner and president of a very large Bible college divorced his wife and married one of his students who was 30 years his junior.

Not long after that, my wife's spiritual mentor commenced a sexual affair with a married mother of two young children. The church where he was an associate pastor became suspicious and hired a detective to put him under surveillance. Within a short time he was confronted with indisputable proof of his promiscuity. He then resigned his church position, divorced his wife, and later married a woman who was not the same person as was the object of his initial adulterous affair.

Such is the "spiritual heritage" of my wife and myself. These two occurrences have been the most traumatic spiritual experiences in our 38 years while on the mission field. But by no means are these isolated incidents. I have known evangelical missionaries who were adulterous, homosexual, or addicted to pornography. In reflection, I can only conclude that God's chosen servants are very special targets of sexual temptation. In recent years, our cloistered existence has been bombarded with a level of fleshly enticement that has been overwhelming.

Easy access to pornography, immoral movies, and the Internet have dented the armor of the pulpit as well as the pew. Battle-fatigued men of God have begun the insidious slide downward without even being overtly aware of how, when, and where it all began.

This slide is described in James 1:14 and 15, "But each one is tempted when he is carried away and enticed by his own lust. Then when lust has conceived, it gives birth to sin; and when sin is accomplished, it brings forth death." The process of temptation becoming lust, which births sin and results in spiritual death, is well known to thousands of Christian leaders. I have sought to describe this fleshly syndrome in terms of a graph which can assist married Christian men to identify clearly the stages of sexual enticement. It is obvious that the sequence will vary in many instances. But, in a general way, the downward path to moral ruin can be illustrated as seen in this graph.

LEVEL	DESCRIPTION
1	Enjoyment of another woman's personality.
2	Appreciation of her body.
3	Thoughts of physical lust.
4	Emotional desire.
5	Initiation of casual encounters.
6	Mutual arrangement for frequent meetings.
7	The first lustful touch.
8	Total deceit with one's wife.
9	Intimacy without full sex.
10	The physical act of adultery.

Level one is a normal bilateral sociological function. Men are placed in close proximity to women in every sector of society. It is only natural to find another person's personality pleasing and enjoyable. But it is at this point the Tiger of Lust begins lurking in the shadows.

The next two levels, unfortunately, are closely interlinked. To look appreciatively upon God's unique creation is not only natural but universal. But this *look* so easily becomes perverted and undergoes a metamorphosis into lust. The Christian is beginning to confront an all-out attack on the very core of his spirituality. Victorious Christians are the ones who wage the most serious and successful battles for holy thoughts at levels two and three.

Level four becomes personal. Lust can be more easily shaken off if it is only directed toward a body and not a mind. Emotional desire sets the stage for a compromise of marital exclusiveness. Something internal seems to be wildly raging out of control. Misery as well as excitement vie for center stage. A lifetime of stable moral values cries out for reinforcement. Yet the flesh tantalizes and prods one to move closer and closer toward the precipice. Rationalization sets in. It becomes ever so difficult to turn back.

Levels five and six are outworkings of a premeditated decision to move forward. The die is cast. Promiscuity is reinforced by physical presence, casual at first, and then by mutual arrangement. This is followed by the first touch of lust. The body pulsates with new life and thrilling sensations. Sensuality is all-embracing. Not only the body, the brain also has been seduced. In the euphoric glow of the flesh, Jesus Christ has been thrust aside into the darkness of a total eclipse.

The eighth level of ongoing and total deceit with one's wife is one of the saddest aspects of moral failure. Self-destruction is a premeditated choice of personal anarchy. But to reject the love and beauty of a wife once loved is cruelty in its rawest form. It digs a furrow deep into the soul.

Level nine. The Tiger has come out of the shadows and now boldly stalks its prey. It is moving in for the final assault. The sought one is tired and confused. Capitulation, without due consideration to consequence seems the only way of release. The pace of flight slackens and the Tiger draws nearer . . . and nearer . . . and nearer. . . .

Level ten. The strong, gnashing teeth of the devourer closes tightly around the conquered one. At first, a feeble attempt at resistance . . . then quiet acquiescence. All that is seen is a barren, God-forsaken wasteland with a majestic Tiger standing regally astride the fallen warrior. All that is heard is the roar of Satan's victory amidst the deafening silence of the cosmos.

How does the Christian avoid such a terrible scenario of spiritual suicide? The secret lies in recognizing two realities. The first is how horrible the end result of sexual sin inevitably will be. The second is the urgency of stopping the process of defeat at the earliest instance. Level two should be a red flag to the sensitive Christian. Anything further can be self-perpetuating, and is fraught with disastrous consequence. A popular contemporary teaching is restoration theology. Christ forgives and forgets. Without denying the broad perimeters of the restoring grace of our Lord, I personally would prefer to emphasize God's **protective** mercy which will keep me from a sin so powerful that it can destroy not only me but also those whom I love most.

Prevention is always to be preferred over treatment. The two greatest deterrents to immorality are a warm, vital, ongoing relationship with Jesus Christ and a sparkling, joyful, sustained love affair with one's wife. With this focus in life, there can be assurance that the Tiger of Lust will yet be tamed.

IS YOUR MARRIAGE PASSIONATE . . . OR PASSIONLESS?

(An article written for SIM missionaries)

by Phil Parshall

Em Griffin is a professor at Wheaton College who wrote in his excellent book, *The Mind Changers,*

> "There came a night in Jeanie's and my marriage when all this came to a head. It started out typically enough. I had been away at a three-day conference and had taken a plane back early so I could speak to a church group. Then I came home thoroughly exhausted and plopped into bed. In a despairing voice Jeanie said, 'Em, I know you still love me, but I don't feel it any more, and it's hard to feel love for you anymore either.' And all of a sudden my world came crashing in."

Perhaps few SIM spouses would feel free to articulate such a powerful statement, but to one degree or another has the heat of our passion cooled since those intoxicating days of early marital bliss?

Then, passion ruled the roost. Not just physical compulsion, but emotional as well. What a delight to bask in one another's presence. Hours of mutual communication were as refreshing as a cooling shower after a day with the Tauregs in the sand dunes of the Sahara. Oh, the bliss of hands held together in a warm clasp of commitment. And, yes, frequent articulated affirmations of the magic, mystical words, "I so love you" with the anticipated response, "Oh, but I love you more!"

And now the years have moved us on in the unrelenting aging process. About that we can do nothing. But is the marriage relationship doomed to orbit from Spring to Winter—or even to metamorphose into a dull, gray late Autumn?

My friend, David Pickard, General Director of OMF has mentioned to me several times his concern for the multiplicity of "passionless marriages" that he has observed within the missionary community. It would be my considered opinion that David is on the mark. No, not divorce or adultery. There are sad instances of moral failures, but they are still rare enough to shock.

But the incremental cooling of passion is much more insidious. Over a period of years its effect is hardly recognized. It becomes a "Well-that-is just-the-way-we-are" type of thing. Sadly, it is more easily detected by others, nationals included, than by ourselves!

So what has happened along the way? Let's try a few expressive words: BABIES, COMPULSIVE MINISTRY, THE TERRIBLE TWOS, FINANCIAL PRESSURES, ADOLESCENT KIDS, HOME ASSIGNMENTS, DIFFICULT CO-WORKERS, FRUITLESSNESS, FRUSTRATING LIVING CONDITIONS, HADES VISITING OUR STATION EACH APRIL AND MAY, TENACIOUS TIREDNESS, THE EMPTY NEST SYNDROME, A MIRROR THAT REFLECTS REALITY—all this along with a SPOUSE WHO IS NOT ALWAYS AS CONSIDERATE AS A CHRISTIAN SHOULD BE! With an accumulation of the above—and much more—A PASSIONATE MARRIAGE? You gotta be kidding!

No, no, I'm not kidding. This is serious stuff. It makes or breaks. It brings reinforcement, or it causes disintegration. Out of this reality emerges either a life of togetherness and joy and sparkle—OR an endurance race sprinkled with pain and hurtful falls.

Is there a way forward? I am utterly convinced the passion can remain—and be fostered, and be enhanced—as we pilgrimage on through life. Please understand, I'm not postulating perfection. There will be dips along the road. We are temperamental and fallen creatures. We can't always "feel" and "act" lovingly. Selfishness constantly asserts itself. But I am talking about a lifestyle of a couple being utterly committed to the path of passion—physical, spiritual, and emotional passion—together.

So first comes this commitment, and then follows the discipline. In dialogue, speak frankly with your spouse about reigniting your first love. What turns you on, and what turns you off? What hurts, and what gives joy and reassurance? Work through specific issues. Come up with a game plan designed to mutually satisfy and edify.

For me this exercise suggests a few simple disciplines. For years I always opened the car door for my lover. For many subsequent years, I ceased to open the car door for my lover. I now again open the car door for my lover. We used to hold hands for grace, then not so, now so. Serving her coffee (and a newspaper) in bed at 6:30 A.M. on Sundays isn't backbreaking, but it is appreciated—as is my doing the dishes when our househelper is off duty. Things I didn't do, now I do. These, plus other specifics are registering a message—"Hey, I really do love and respect you—and I want to show it!"

One of the really biggies in all this is what our kids are seeing as we model the marriage institution. Be assured of deja vu, "What goes around, comes around." They are our 24-hour-a-day (more or less) disciples. You can expect to see in their marriage what they have absorbed from Mom and Dad for 18 formative years. One of our greatest satisfactions in life, after 38 years of marriage, is to see our one and only child enfolded into blissful marital union for the past seven years. Heaven on earth!

Howie Brant and I took a most memorable ministry tour together in 1994. One country we visited was his home turf in the 9,000 foot high mountain plateaus of Ethiopia. On an unforgettably cold night we slept (?) in a huge round house or hut. Animals were making their various noises (and smells) in their allotted half of the house. Howie and the elders were gathered closely around the fire in the middle of the hut chatting non-stop in Amharic while sipping the world's most obnoxious coffee (a mixture of coffee, salt and butter). I was hunkered down as far as I could get on the floor in my bedroll seeking to find breathable air in the enclosed hut—praying that I could quickly get to sleep, and in the process not be asphyxiated.

Every ten minutes or so, I would glance at the fire. An Ethiopian lady was constantly feeding the flames. Without her vigilance and commitment to add wood to the fire, there would soon be nothing but cold ash.

Is that a marital parable? Passion needs reinforcement and discipline without which the fire slowly dies down to nothingness. May we couples in SIM all be committed to stoke the fires of passion in our marriage so that we might be flames of reality, example, and joyful reinforcement to one another, and to our children.

MISSIONARIES:
SAFE OR EXPENDABLE?*

by Phil Parshall

This subject became more relevant to me this afternoon. As I drove up to my Reading Center which is adjacent to a Manila inner-city squatter area of Muslims, I noticed large scribbled words spread across the front, "All of you are infidel for us! You Americans." Soon, with the aid of a knife, I had scratched out three words and set forth a more benign message, "All of you are for us!"

The contemporary scene in our world reverberates with both political and religious crises. Missionaries, especially Americans, find themselves caught in the crossfire of competing ideologies. Afghanistan, Sudan, Liberia, Peru, and Colombia are just a few of the hot spots.

Within the last two years in Mindanao, Philippines, an Italian priest was murdered, two Operation Mobilization young people were killed and 35 injured in a bombing, John Speers was shot in the head, a single lady missionary underwent the humiliation of rape, an American Catholic worker was held captive for 68 days, and two Filipinos affiliated with the Far East Broadcasting Corporation

* Reprinted by permission of *Evangelical Missions Quarterly* (Box 794, Wheaton, IL 60189, USA)

were brutally killed while on the air. In another Asian country a police guard has been posted outside the bedroom window of a renowned missionary surgeon who has received death threats. Violence against expat Christian workers is perhaps at a level higher than that of any time in this century.

Our response is of critical importance. It appears to me that the tilt is toward a strategy for maximum safety and a minimum of risk-taking. We missionaries are being bombarded with seminars and advice on how to avoid danger. The multiple scenarios of potential disaster are enough to make a well-adjusted missionary cross the line into paranoia. At that point, fear kicks in as the dominant emotional response. This then can lead to a curtailment of ministry, and even to withdrawal.

PRECEDENTS

What really is a proper position of balance? More to the point, is balance the biblical response to danger? As we survey the New Testament do we not find vulnerability more common than concern for personal safety? John the Baptist, James, and Stephen all paid the high price of martyrdom for Kingdom concerns. Stephen particularly walked to the precipice with considered resolve. It would appear from the Acts record that he could have closed shop at any moment and escaped the wrath of his assassins. But with uncanny conviction he pressed on to his last breath testifying to the sufficiency of the grace of God.

And what about the Apostle Paul? The book of Second Corinthians is missionary autobiography at its apex. Paul, in this moving epistle, chronicles a life of frequent risk and deprivation. The only complaint the Apostle seems to register for us to ponder is the lack of other Christians willing to join him in his exploits for Christ. The stonings, floggings, imprisonments, shipwrecks, hunger and lack of clothes were all regarded as "light and momentary troubles." A present-day supporting church receiving such a written chronicle of trials from their missionary would most likely counsel immediate withdrawal to a safety zone. Fortunately for all of us, the Antioch church was more visionary in their dealing with this pioneer of the faith who would blaze a path of Gospel propagation across Europe. We today stand in debt to this one who by contemporary mission standards would likely be referred to as a reckless eccentric. I simply regard him as one who saw himself as expendable in the affairs of the God of the universe.

Many have followed in the train of these anointed men. Rowland Bingham and two colleagues landed in Africa exactly one hundred years ago. Within one year two of the young missionaries had died. With a heavy heart, Bingham returned to North America, recruited more "expendables," and sailed once again toward the dark continent. Today the mission he founded, Society for International Ministries (SIM), has close to 2,000 personnel within its ranks and four million affiliated nationals in its centenary year. It is humbling to acknowledge the debt we in SIM owe to one man who counted his physical life of so little consequence to himself.

PRACTICAL CONSIDERATIONS

If, by definition, expendability equals volunteer martyrdom, then I could accomplish this with one swift act. Tomorrow I would go into the Muslim Center here in Manila and loudly proclaim a message of Christ and of denunciation of Islam. Within moments I would be in the presence of the Lord.

We as missionaries are to be spirit-led pragmatists. This posture allows us to combine the spiritual with being street smart. It is not proper to court death in our ministry. On the other hand, neither is it right to so value our lives that every new advance is negated by an overemphasis on risk potential.

The following are a few specific considerations which can be mooted by mission societies and individual missionaries.

- In the October, 1977 issue of *Evangelical Missions Quarterly*, I wrote an article entitled, "A Small Family is a Happy Family," (a birth control slogan in Bangladesh). It is my most infamous writing. In it I postulated practical reasons for limiting missionary families to two children. Understandably, it generated controversy—most forcefully from missionaries with four children!

  At the risk of being called obstinate and insensitive, I reiterate the value of small families, particularly for ministry in areas of volatility. In every serious assessment of danger, we in leadership first of all give major consideration to the dependents' safety. We find the advisability of withdrawal usually increases with the number of children in a given family. When my wife and I declared our intent to work in Bangladesh, we decided to limit our family to one child. I have no regrets, but I can certainly see strong reasons for two children. In any event, this mobility has allowed us to forego several missionary evacuations in our career.

  There, likewise, are points in favor of sending our well-adjusted single men and women into areas of conflict. If these individuals are so called, they should be supported and encouraged. Many are the illustrations of our best missionary pioneers who have come from these ranks. There, of course, will be culture and other issues to be considered.

- Missions should have general evacuation policies. It is, however, important for leadership far from the place of crisis to allow field personnel to be fully decisive in emergency situations. There must be a bond of trust with local missionaries.

    Even down to the level of the individual missionary, I support maximum autonomous decisions. In 1965, my wife Julie, our six-month-old daughter, and I were in India on vacation when the Pakistan-India war broke out. During the next few months our missionary colleagues in East Pakistan (now Bangladesh) pulled out. Communications between India and Pakistan were virtually non-existent. After the war ended, we felt very strongly we were to return to the "unknown," even though embassies were advising against foreign presence. I am forever grateful that our mission graciously allowed us to travel a circuitous route back to the land of our calling. They did require us to write a letter absolving them of responsibility, which I was more than glad to do. If they had decided not to risk our future into the hands of the Lord at that crucial moment, that may well have closed our mission's ministry in that land and the subsequent fruit that has evolved since 1965.

- There must be accommodation for those who do not feel they can enter a violent area. Likewise, no pressure, direct or indirect, is to be placed on missionaries who decide a withdrawal is mandated. All humans are uniquely created with a variety of emotional response. The body's nervous system is overwhelmingly complex. There are people, Christian and non-Christian alike, who simply do not experience fear. I tend to think Winston Churchill was one of those men. Then there are the timid who, perhaps like Timothy, will struggle with fear all of their lives. It is not up to one group to judge the other. For sure, the Scriptures and prayer can help alleviate and temper fear. But for many, total release remains an elusive quest.

    In recent upheavals in southern Philippines, we have seen a variety of responses. Some have felt a strategic retreat was necessary. In one case a pastor received a death threat which led him to take down his church sign. But he stayed on. A large group of Christian workers, having been the recipients of threats, have declared that if they are in the will of God then that is all that matters. One said he could as easily be killed in the States as in the Philippines. He felt safe in God's place for him wherever that might be.

Even the Apostle Paul showed flexibility. In Lystra, he was stoned and left for dead. A miraculous recovery occurred followed by withdrawal. It is interesting to note that within a short time Paul is back in Lystra exhorting his disciples with these words, "We must go through many hardships to enter the Kingdom of God."

- One of the important components in making decisions about risk-taking relates to the opinions of nationals in the country where we serve. Foreigners may be a great encouragement to them in moments of adversity. Conversely, such a presence may endanger their lives. We, as expat missionaries, have come to serve. Our decisions therefore must be made in tandem with those whose lives we may most affect.

In 1971 a civil war broke out between East and West Pakistan. The Bengali people of the East desperately wanted a foreign presence to remain so their sufferings could be documented to the world. It is with some measure of sadness that I have to say, a very large majority of missionaries were on the first evacuation planes that flew out of the airport. Yes, it was a time of overwhelming turmoil and chaos. Rumors of rape were so widespread that after a few weeks I, too, sent my wife and daughter over to West Pakistan for two months. Those ensuing nine months of war were hell on earth.

But my point is the national Christians simply could not believe their spiritual leaders would so quickly leave them to face the crucible alone. Yes, the embassies had advised evacuation, but seldom if ever do they demand withdrawal. We had our own choice to make.

Without judging individual situations, it does seem more than a handful of missionaries could have remained to shepherd the flock through their dark night of pain. Perhaps a missiology of expendability was lacking.

CONCLUSION

In December, 1989, John Speers excitedly called me from the States to say that he and his wife Brenda and two small children would soon be joining us in Manila in Muslim outreach. After a very successful term of church planting among Roman Catholics they were ready for the "harder challenge" of Muslims. What a sheer delight to work with John for the next 18 months.

On June 11, 1991, I received one of the saddest phone calls of my life. John Speers, missionary *extraordinaire*, a Jim Elliot in the making, had just been catapulted into eternity as a result of a Muslim bullet exploding in his brain. His beautiful, talented wife became an instant widow. Three-year-old Shannah and one-year-old Josiah no longer had a precious daddy. The ultimate outworking of expendability became final, at least in this life.

Should John have taken such a risk? What about those in the south of the Philippines today? In Liberia? In Columbia? In Peru?

Scripture and mission history seem to lead us to ponder anew the fuller implications of the term "missionary expendability."

CHAPTER 23

WHY SOME PEOPLE ARE UNPRODUCTIVE*

by Phil Parshall

Feeling both pain and perplexity, my missionary friend dropped his bomb on me: "Phil, as I have worked with and traveled among missionaries I have been shocked to meet many who seem so unmotivated and slothful. Large numbers of them seem to be spinning their wheels. Is this a common phenomenon?"

His piercing observation jarred me to write this article, but I hesitated because missionaries are supposed to be among the most sacrificial and highly motivated people in the world. How could I question their performance? How could I even suggest that many of them are lazy and unproductive, when over the nearly three decades of my own work I have known many who are overworked and some who have suffered burnout because of their zealousness for Christ?

Nevertheless, to be honest, I had to admit that there was and is another side to the stereotype of the unflagging missionary. I have not kept notes, so what

---

* Reprinted by permission of *Evangelical Missions Quarterly* (Box 794, Wheaton, IL 60189, USA

follows is an impression based on my travels and observations over the years. I estimate that 30 percent of missionaries are hyperactive, 20 percent are balanced, and 50 percent are underactive relative to their potential.

Hyperactive missionaries usually work in institutions, where they have to report to superiors. Their 8-hour schedules are regulated and they often have to finish their work in the evenings. Their lives generally are orderly and fulfilling. However, hyperactive missionaries tend to overdo it and they suffer for this.

The rest of this article will deal with the underachievers, who mostly do not work in regulated, supervised activities. We find them among church workers, evangelists, researchers, and language students. Church planters among Muslims and Hindus frequently fit this category.

Why should this be so? For two reasons, generally. First, their own attitudes, and second, the proliferation of high tech distractions. Something useful can easily become frivolous and eat up your time.

ATTITUDES

Volunteerism

Most Western job structures are all-pervasive, with expectations clearly set forth. Salaries usually fit the responsibilities. Not so in missions, however. Missionaries can easily slacken their pace when they feel unappreciated, unrecognized, and underpaid. Even their spiritual zeal can be quenched when they feel like they are giving out so much and receiving so little in return. Easily, a "who-cares?" attitude leads to a work slowdown.

Nearly two decades ago, Robert Evans, founder of Greater Europe Mission, propounded what seemed to many to be a revolutionary idea. He suggested that mission agencies should recognize accomplishments by their people—things like advanced degrees and published books and articles—and reward them accordingly with salary increases. To my knowledge, not many agencies do this, even though I think it would help to remedy a major cause of underactivity.

Such recognition is not unspiritual. Sometimes we forget that Jesus promised rewards for faithfulness. Professionalism, in the good sense, can be enhanced by downplaying volunteerism. Whether we like it or not, a person who feels professional and is treated with the dignity due a professional is much more likely to perform well than is someone who simply regarded as a volunteer.

Accountability

Missionaries jealously guard their autonomy. Many, if not most, dread submitting work reports. They want freedom to decide how to use their time and effort. Result: conflicts with their supervisors.

I know of a case where, when forced to account for his time in ministry, a missionary had to admit that it came to 12 hours a week. What is his supervisor supposed to do? In this incident, he sought to convince the worker of the total inadequacy of his performance. Supervisors need to do this, while recognizing that too much pressure could force the missionary to resign.

Accountability must be given not only to the administrator, but also to the team's spiritual counselor. Underactive missionaries may need more than lectures and books on productive time management, however. They may face intense spiritual battles, which leads to the third element in attitude, discouragement.

Discouragement

Never in my ministry have I met so many discouraged missionaries as I have in the past five years. Why? Is it because we fail to reach our Western "instant success" expectations? Is it because the methods we learned in school don't work in the real world? Are we simply overcome by our spiritual impotency in the face of evil and unbelief? Are we falling short of our deepest spiritual aspirations? Are we incapable of handling both emotionally and intellectually, the deep questions of evil, suffering, and poverty?

Whatever the answer, discouragement incapacitates many of us. Gloom settles over many missionaries like an early morning fog. Ritual without zeal takes over. Their unspoken goal is to put in their time and survive until furlough or retirement.

Mission leaders need to face this condition. How can we revive and energize these people? Perhaps with things like seminars, achievement recognition, and counseling.

Fear

One day my wife Julie and I were standing in front of our Reading Center in the Muslim area of inner-city Manila. Hearing the loud cracks of three gun shots, we ducked for cover. Seconds later, I peeked out from behind a concrete post and watched the last movements of a handsome, 20-year-old Muslim university student as he lay dying in a pool of blood. His killing had culminated two weeks of violence within 50 yards of our center. There had been several shootouts in which two men were killed, and a number of pedestrians wounded.

Our friends have told us to get out of this war zone. But if we do, that would leave 20,000 Muslims without any Christian witness. Beyond that is the larger issue of our inner spiritual struggle. Will we allow ourselves to be immobilized by fear?

Missionaries all over are vulnerable to senseless acts of terrorism and violence. That is a prime question raised by people we are trying to recruit for service in the Philippines. Never before have we had to conduct seminars for missionaries on violence and survival.

I'm not calling for needless bravado, but I am concerned when guarantees of safety seem to predominate over our desire to preach Christ and teach the Scriptures. After all, Jesus challenges us to be liberated from the fear that binds us to inaction. We can't expect evangelistic success if we sequester ourselves in our mission homes.

DISTRACTIONS

Living hassles

When Julie and I went to a rural area of Bangladesh as new missionaries in 1962, our supervisor told us, "The miracle will be that you can even exist in this primitive village, much less accomplish anything for God." And that's the way it was. Never will I forget those years filled with the hassles of marketing, cleaning the smoking burner of our kerosene refrigerator in the middle of countless dark nights, and pumping up our Coleman lanterns hundreds of times.

Missionaries can easily capitulate to the mundane. The demands of survival force us away from our ministries. Unorganized people give in all too easily and allow myriads of details to dominate their lives. Keeping your car running and your house in order become more of a priority than evangelism.

There's much help on the market for disorganized missionaries. Leaders need to require their people to read books and attend seminars on time management.

Computers, video, and television

Recently, I proposed to a group of missionaries that we talk about Jesus as much as we talk about computers. Embarrassed smiles prevailed. High tech can be either a useful tool or a major distraction. Right now, I surmise that the amount of time and money spent by missionaries on their computers is disproportionate to their value in terms of ministry accomplishments. They are so taken up with the "latest and the greatest" that they forget that computers are a means to an end, and not ends in themselves.

Videos and television represent a different temptation. Of course, missionaries need recreation and diversion, but we need to guard against pure escapism. Our challenge is to master those instruments that can be used for good, and not to allow them to drain away our time and energy.

Fellowship

All of us need interaction in the field. We need reinforcement and edification from each other. Often, our isolation intensifies this legitimate need. I remember in our early days jokingly suggesting that we would buy plane tickets for people to get to Bangladesh, if they would only come visit us in our rural village.

But good and wholesome things often carry their own perils. Let me suggest some prime dangers: marathon talking sessions with colleagues, excessive breaks, and prolonged trips to city centers. They can all be used to dodge the tough work we need to do. It's much easier to talk about out reach than to do it. Our missionary enterprise has its share of makers of grandiose plans who do so to avoid doing undesirable tasks.

How shall we handle this cause of underactivity? We can't be too hard on our colleagues who genuinely seem to need a great deal of fellowship. But our leaders must keep on stressing the imperative of getting assigned jobs done. If we really enjoy our work, then we'll find the proper balance between fellowship and ministry.

Family

How often have you heard people rank their duties this way: God first, family second, work third? That's a neat package, but it seldom matches the real world. There's no question that God comes first, but if family dominates our time, then we need to rethink our call to our work. I have always urged proper time and care for one's family, but I'm afraid many missionaries are victims of family priority overkill. It has become an obsession with them, so now we need to come back to a reasonable balance between family and ministry responsibilities.

Conclusion

Robertson McQuilkin, president of Columbia Bible College and Seminary, often speaks about the need to maintain a creative tension between all the demands of our lives. Both hyperactive and underactive missionaries need to move toward the balanced 20 percent in my original estimation above. I do not call for ceaseless activity that allows no time for reflection or re-creation. At the same time, we must guard against both wrong attitudes and distractions that lead us to become unproductive.

Jesus himself perfectly exemplified both zeal and compassion. At the same time, he took time to pray, to meditate, to have fellowship, and to be refreshed. If we can achieve the balance he did, the missions community will not suffer from lazy underachievers.

RESPONSE

~

WHY THE OPPORTUNITY
FOR UNPRODUCTIVENESS*

by Clyde Cook

I have been a fan of Phil Parshall for many years. His books have stimulated my thinking and this article is no exception. He has done all of us a service by raising this sensitive issue.

There is no question that the missionary enterprise, like any other industry, has people who are not very productive. Phil has done a good job outlining some of the reasons for this, and his reasons match my own experience in the field and in missions management. I remember one missionary who had the finest tropical fish collection on the island, the fruit of hundreds of hours of scuba diving. Instead of fishing for men and women in a responsive field, he simply fished for fish.

Why the opportunity for unproductiveness? Let me underscore Phil's point about accountability. Missions, perhaps more than any other ministry, can have little accountability. Often working alone, without measurable objectives, many times using home as an office, and being thousands of miles from headquarters, many missionaries find a great chance to be lazy. Anyone can write an interesting letter once a month—

* Reprinted by permission of *Evangelical Missions Quarterly* (Box 794, Wheaton, IL 60189, USA)

often about family—which gives the illusion of active ministry. Not even a visit of a few days or hours by the general director makes for accountability.

When I was president of Overseas Crusades, I tried a modified program of management by objectives (MBO), because the reports from the field simply summarized the number of meetings or activities. All I could tell was how busy the missionaries were, not whether our objectives of stimulating and mobilizing the church for evangelism were being accomplished. Management by objectives helped us to focus on what we really wanted to accomplish, so we could lay plans to meet those objectives. It was not easy to move from busyness reports to such a system of accountability, but it worked because, with a few exceptions, we were a team of highly motivated, productive men and women who really wanted to make our lives count.

However, I do feel somewhat uncomfortable with the way Phil Parshall arbitrarily divided up the entire missions community. There is no objective survey data that I know of to support his 30-20-50 breakdown. These numbers really are his subjective guesses, based on personal observation only.

Also, if we do classify missionaries, a productivity scale might be more helpful than simply labeling them hyperactive (which could be taken as a pejorative label) or underactive, i.e., lazy. In other words, only 20 percent of all missionaries, according to Parshall, are "balanced," or, to use my term, productive.

One further comment about living hassles. This is not always capitulating to the mundane. You can have a very productive time-management-oriented missionary working against an event-oriented culture. In our time-oriented culture, I can list four or five errands to do in the morning and get them done. In one trip to the supermarket I can get not only our groceries, but also vegetables and meat and hardware and toothpaste. Then I can stop at the post office and the cleaners and be home in an hour. But when I lived in the Philippines, I had to go one place for our groceries, another for meat, and another for vegetables. The post office stop took an hour. Since this is an event-oriented culture where relationships are important, I had to spend time with people and not race from one stop to the next.

But how do we enhance missionary productivity? Here are a few suggestions?

1 Reward productivity

Basing salaries on productivity is not a bad idea, if an equitable way of evaluating productivity is set up. This is difficult in a Christian organization, because compassion, forgiveness, tolerance, and love are high in our value system, while accountability and productivity are not as high. One of the toughest jobs I have had as president of Biola was to implement a rank-structure promotion based on productivity rather than on longevity.

2 Select carefully

Exercise care in the selection process. Has the candidate been productive? Define what the mission objectives are and see if the candidate has a track record in a similar ministry. Also, have similar standards for the missionaries. It is difficult for a missionary to take those he or she is discipling beyond where the missionary is. On the field where there might be one or two missionaries with less preparation than the others, a great deal of time can be used up by the others to train the unprepared missionaries.

3 Build in accountability

In addition to management by objectives, which encourages accountability, have a team approach so there is encouragement to be productive. Lone Rangers can pretty well do as they please. If you work by yourself, make sure that you set up a system of accountability which could include having an office outside your home. Having an office helps in two ways: it's a self-disciplinary tool, and it improves your standing in the eyes of the public so that you are not perceived as either retired or loafing around the house. For those in sending churches, check the materials of the Association of Church Missions Committees (Box ACMA, Wheaton, Ill. 60189), which help to work out methods of accountability, so you can be sure you are supporting productive missionaries.

Phil Parshall has raised an important issue and I hope that his discussion will lead to further evaluations by both missionaries and mission executives about productivity, so that we can be and do everything God wants.

"A Small Family is a Happy Family"*

Birth control is not only a matter for international, political, economic, and religious debates. This writer believes missionaries and their work could be helped by a voluntary decision to keep their families small.

by Phil Parshall

The caption, "A Small Family is a Happy Family," is written on billboards in beautiful script beneath a picture of a lovely Bengali family of husband, wife and two small children. These ads are strategically placed in hundreds of locations throughout Bangladesh. The message is clear: No longer is the norm of six children per family acceptable in the context of the harsh realities of life in one of the poorest nations of the world.

* Reprinted by permission of *Evangelical Missions Quarterly* (Box 794, Wheaton, IL 60189, USA)

Perhaps I can be accused of taking "acculturation" too far by seeking to apply these exhortations to missionary families. However, my thesis for this article seeks to do just that. Is there not a place for voluntarily limiting the size of the family unit of those who have "forsaken all" to go to the ends of the earth to preach the gospel of Jesus Christ? Would not an objective and pragmatic evaluation of missionary life lead us to consider seriously the value of putting a "hold" on procreation at two children, or less!

BIBLICAL OVERVIEW

"Lo, children are an heritage from the Lord; and the fruit of the womb is his reward. . . . Happy is the man who hath his quiver full of them."

Psalm 127:3,5

"Thy wife shall be as a fruitful vine by the sides of thine house; thy children like olive plants round about thy table."

Psalm 128:3

Records of parents with multiple children in Old Testament times abound. There is no exhortation toward small families among the children of Israel. Conversely, one uncovers statements like the above in Psalms that indicate "the more the merrier!" One rationale is that this small race of God's chosen people was sorely in need of quantitative growth. Enemies were poised on the borders of Palestine ready to attack. A large standing army was crucial to survival.

In the New Testament we find a total lack of guidance on the subject. Jesus does express appreciation toward the wee world and even uses children illustratively to introduce a teaching regarding the Kingdom of God. Yet, we receive no command, explicit or implied, on the subject of a God-sanctioned numerical "ideal" for a Christian family.

Jesus does set forth revolutionary teaching on the subject of discipleship. Peter, James, and John were so captivated by the overpowering presence of Jesus on the seashore that they forsook "all" (including families) and followed Him. Luke 10 describes the sending forth of the seventy without family, purse or even shoes. In Luke 14:26, discipleship is reserved for those willing to forsake even wife and children. Matthew 19:12 affirms the existence of a special breed of people known as eunuchs who voluntarily became so "For the kingdom of heaven's sake."

Paul, in his unmarried state, expresses a desire in 1 Corinthians 7:5 for all men to be as himself. In verse 29 he continues the theme, "The time is short; it remaineth that both they that have wives be as though they had none." Paul, in verse 35, summarizes by encouraging the Corinthians to remain unmarried so that they "may attend unto the Lord without distraction."

So, scripturally, we find a measure of liberty in family matters. There are no clear commands regulating size of families. But we are confronted with the demands of discipleship that seem to move God's called ones into a life of self-denial and some form of privation "for the Kingdom of God's sake." The application of these principles will be extremely varied.

Advocacy of Large Families

Children are a great joy and delight. Many parents have strong feelings that God desires them to have a large number of children. They look forward to the diversity of personality that comes from each new addition to the family. The family becomes a buttress against the harsh realities of mission field life.

Many missionaries anticipate the tranquility of retirement when they can be surrounded by the presence of a large number of children and grandchildren. At last, they can experience a more normal, Western type existence in the presence of a host of loved ones.

There are a few missionaries who have strong convictions against the use of birth control methods. This is an issue of conscience and must be respected. However, I noted how one missionary's "convictions" changed after the birth of his fourth child in five years of married life!

Pragmatic Concerns

It has been a deep personal grief to me to see so many missionaries leave the mission field in their prime of life and service because of "family reasons." After gaining valuable experience in an alien culture and after finally becoming fluent in a foreign language, the missionary is forced to leave his area of expertise to return to his homeland. Generally, missionaries with larger families are the most vulnerable. The following are practical arguments against large families for missionaries serving on the foreign mission field.

1   Expense

In these days of inflation, it is not unusual to find families with support figures of $15,000 per year working in a country like Bangladesh, where the per capita income is less than $100 per annum. One missionary known to me is paying $6,000 per year just for the education of his children.

A large family creates a demand for at least a three-bedroom house with garden facility. In contrast, parents with one or two children can more easily adjust to a small apartment. This is a rather important factor in life-style identification with the Christians of one's host country. How overwhelmed these nationals become when confronted with our massive array of Western gadgets, toys, electronic goods, etc. Still fresh in my mind is the story of the enraged Thai Christian who found out that the foreign missionary was paying more for dog food on a monthly basis than he was paying the Thai for his work as a full-time mission evangelist!

It is staggering to consider what a round trip America-Bangladesh fare costs for parents and four children. A quick calculation reveals this would pay the salary for one of Bangladesh's top M.A. foreign-trained, pastors for a period of twelve years! There is no practical way to avoid completely this problem, but a smaller number of fares to be purchased would indeed be a help. Some years back, our mission was on a "pool" system of all funds. A single lady of our mission, without bitterness or rancor, one day said to me, "Phil, many of us singles have given up any real hope of marriage to come out here and serve the Lord. Would it not be appropriate for couples to purposefully limit their family size as an act of dedication to Christ? Their work would be more effective and money saved would be very significant." A rather provocative observation.

2   Education

Apart from expense, there are other issues involved in the education of missionary kids. In Pakistan, almost all mothers of school age children go up to the hill station in Murree for four months so they can be with their kids. This leaves a difficult choice for the husband. He can fight it out in the intense 120-degree heat (Fahrenheit) of the plains separated from his family, or he can spend an extended time in the hills each year. Even one child creates this dilemma—but for fewer years than if one has four children.

Separation creates real emotional trauma. A number of families have been forced by circumstances to send their children to schools in two different countries. One mother is trying to teach four children at home while one attends a local school.

More than any other cause, children's education is the outstanding reason why missionaries leave the field during the most useful years of their lives. My observations lead me to conclude that the smaller the family, the less likely the dropout potential.

3 Inconvenience to others

Nothing is "simple" or "easy" in the mission field—at least in an under-developed country. Life is complicated and frequently frustrating. For instance, having a baby almost certainly involves a family dislocation of one month in Bangladesh. Going to a reputable doctor will necessitate a day's journey for people in the interior. At each step, it is seen that assistance from others is needed for accommodation, emergencies, purchases, etc. How much more difficult it is to feed and bed down a family of six compared to four.

It is a bit naive to think our family is no one's business but our own. In countless areas our lives interrelate in the mission field. No one is an island unto himself.

A POSITIVE PROPOSAL

In Bangladesh, out of 28 couples married 15 years or longer, I find 22 of them have three children or more. Ten of these couples have four children each. For these couples and for the reader who finds himself in a similar situation, it is a *fait accompli*! But, for the newlyweds and the "contemplators" of matrimony, I offer the following postulate:

Is not a norm of two children an "ideal" for missionaries? If these children are close together, they will provide fun and fellowship for each other. Their schooling needs will also be quite similar. Expenses will be minimized. There will not be great inconvenience caused to others in the mission. And, finally, the chances of being forced to return home because of problems relating to one's children are reduced significantly compared to a family of four kids.

My wife and I, in view of the above arguments, made a calculated decision 15 years ago to limit our family to one child. Our 12-year-old Lindy has been a tremendous delight to our hearts over these years in this turbulent land of Bangladesh. I personally have had no regrets concerning our decision. However, I do see the value of the second child, particularly for families in situations where there are no other foreign children residents.

It is recognized that there is no way to be legalistic on this subject. There does, however, seem to be a need to rethink norms and consider alternatives seriously.

ON FINANCIAL INDIGENEITY*

~

(As practiced by James O Fraser)

James encouraged voluntary and unpaid preachers to go out on evangelism around the vast unreached areas of the border mountains. They were to go where the Spirit of God guided them and trust him to provide for them. If they left families behind, the local Christians were to provide for them while the trip lasted.

He did not pay his helpers either. When volunteers offered to carry his things or bring books to the village James did not pay them. No one was to gain money by serving the Lord.

Out of their poverty James let the people buy their own gospels, hymn books, notebooks, and pencils. If they had no money at all they had to save up.

When the people wanted to build a meeting place he left them to it. The buildings themselves were not regarded as of prime importance anyway, but they kept the rain off their heads. All the materials and labor were their own, right down to the oil in the lamps. If they could not afford oil and were out of pine chips they prayed and sang in the dark. James paid for nothing.

Although indigenous principles are widely accepted in the work of missions today, the idea was relatively new in the 1920's. Not that James was its pioneer by any means. It was in discussion with other workers that the idea came to him to start with.

---

* From *Mountain Rain* by Eileen Crossman, OMF Books, 1982, pp. 174-175

We do not consider ourselves rich as compared with other Europeans out here, but we are rolling in wealth compared with these poor tribespeople, and are tempted to feel mean, burdening them in any way. But I am convinced that we ought to do it. So I let them carry my baggage on their backs from village to village, sometimes as far as twenty miles, and never offer payment. They do not expect it, any more than they expect to be paid for the hospitality I always accept when staying among them. They expect to do these things for their foreign teacher, as for their own evangelists. Would I then be doing them a kindness to encourage a mercenary spirit where there is none to begin with?

So strongly did he feel about the idea of paying converts to preach the Gospel, he called it a "vicious system."

It is the line of least resistance, but is something like the broad road that leads to destruction. No! Far better let our work go slowly, and tread the narrow way of self-support. We shall never regret it . . .

What I want to see everywhere is the spirit of SACRIFICE for the Lord Who bought us with His blood—a desire to prove not what we can get but what we can give—and my heart burns as I write it.

ANALYSIS OF QUESTIONNAIRE ON MISSIONARY SPIRITUALITY

by Phil Parshall

Eight hundred evangelical missionaries serving in 32 different countries with 37 mission societies received this form; 390 missionaries returned the form within the stipulated time, which represents close to a 50% return rate; 46% of the respondents were under 40 while 54% were over 40. 49% are male and 51% female. 76% are married.

Magazines read most frequently are *Time* [84], *Moody Monthly* [78], *Christianity Today* [72], *Reader's Digest* [56], *Newsweek* [53], and *Evangelical Missions Quarterly* [52].

The greatest spiritual struggle in life was defined as: having adequate devotions [118], maintaining spiritual victory [60], and overcoming lust [31]. The things liked most about being a Christian are: assurance of salvation [133], the presence of God in one's life [68], and experiencing God's peace [49]. Least liked areas in the Christian life are: the continuing battle with sin [60], and problems with other Christians [52]. Comments included, "I don't like being identified as a religious fanatic"; and "How can I live up to the expectations of other people?"

On innerancy, 96% of the respondents believe in it; 15 of them would not tell their colleagues and mission leaders if they ceased to believe in it; 70 expressed doubt if they would, and 35 did not answer the question; 48 missionaries defined it as a subject they preferred not to discuss.

Comments included, "If I were to doubt it, what point would there be in living?" "Not unless asked, I suppose"; "Not to all but to some"; and "I would reveal it only to thinking colleagues."

At the end, 79 missionaries commented that the questionnaire was helpful to them, though some said it was painful. One described it as "the trauma of transparency." Another said, "A study of missionary spirituality is in order and overdue"; 58 had a problem with the 4 main categories. They desired "sometimes" or "almost-always" type of options.

I have had the responses computer analyzed into 9 different categories according to various ages and sex. This will form the basis of analytical observations in my book,* as well as in an article or two.

Please note the number of responses given to each question as well as the percentages, which are in parentheses. You may feel free to xerox this analysis and share it with other interested parties.

---

* The Cross and the Crescent, Tyndale, 1989

ANALYSIS OF QUESTIONNAIRE ON MISSIONARY SPIRITUALITY

NUMBER OF PEOPLE RESPONDING			
387	Your age:	180 (46.5) Under 40	207 (53.5) Over 40
387	Sex:	190 (49.1) Male	197 (50.9) Female
384	Married:	294 (76.6) Yes	90 (23.4) No

		0 – 5	6 – 10	11 – 15	over 15
384	How many years have you served abroad as a missionary?	116 (30.2)	83 (21.6)	57 (14.8)	128 (33.4)
378	Are you presently assigned to a foreign field? 311 (82.3) Yes 67 (17.7) No				

		CHECK THE APPROPRIATE COLUMN:			
		ALWAYS	FREQUENTLY	INFREQUENTLY	NEVER
386	Does your mind wander when you pray?	13 (3.4)	257 (66.6)	115 (29.8)	1 (0.2)
387	Do you enjoy prayer?	69 (17.8)	264 (68.2)	54 (14.0)	0 (0.0)
386	Do you pray out of a sense of duty?	5 (1.3)	134 (34.7)	217 (56.2)	30 (7.8)
386	Do you question the validity of prayer?	1 (0.3)	11 (2.8)	117 (30.3)	257 (66.6)
381	Does unanswered prayer bother you?	1 (0.3)	46 (12.1)	253 (66.4)	81 (21.2)
381	Does God give specific answers to your prayers?	21 (5.5)	311 (81.6)	49 (12.9)	0 (0.0)
300	If married, do you have family devotions together?	76 (25.3)	151 (50.3)	64 (21.3)	9 (3.1)
390	Is Bible reading a joy?	88 (22.6)	271 (69.5)	29 (7.4)	2 (0.5)
382	Do Bible "problems" bother you?	2 (0.5)	18 (4.7)	244 (63.9)	118 (30.9)
381	Is your Bible reading New Testament oriented?	4 (1.0)	231 (60.6)	107 (28.1)	39 (10.3)
388	Do you use a commentary as you read the Bible?	4 (1.0)	70 (18.0)	224 (57.7)	90 (23.3)
390	Do you enjoy church attendance?	135 (34.6)	212 (54.4)	42 (10.8)	1 (0.2)
387	Are you stimulated spiritually by sermons?	32 (8.3)	278 (71.8)	75 (19.4)	2 (0.5)
388	Does Christian music minister to you?	98 (25.3)	262 (67.3)	26 (6.7)	2 (0.7)
390	Do you enjoy secular rock music?	1 (0.3)	20 (5.1)	102 (26.2)	267 (68.4)
389	Do you listen to classical music?	24 (6.2)	203 (52.2)	150 (38.6)	12 (3.0)
390	Do you appreciate soft background music?	84 (21.5)	220 (56.4)	73 (18.7)	13 (3.4)
389	Do you question God regarding evil and suffering?	3 (0.8)	30 (7.7)	238 (61.2)	118 (30.3)

NUMBER OF PEOPLE RESPONDING		ALWAYS	FREQUENTLY	INFREQUENTLY	NEVER
390	Are you ever discouraged about life?	1 (0.3)	64 (16.4)	276 (70.8)	49 (12.5)
390	Does the danger of nuclear war bother you?	3 (0.8)	18 (4.6)	160 (41.0)	209 (53.6)
388	Is Christ's return a dynamic reality to you?	136 (35.1)	166 (42.8)	82 (21.1)	4 (1.0)
388	Do you ever wish you hadn't been born?	1 (0.3)	7 (1.8)	61 (15.7)	319 (82.2)
390	Are you fearful of the future?	1 (0.3)	20 (5.1)	233 (59.7)	136 (34.9)
388	Are you afraid to die?	0 (0.0)	9 (2.3)	156 (40.2)	223 (57.5)
388	Do you have absolute assurance of eternal life with Christ?	350 (90.2)	26 (6.7)	2 (0.5)	10 (2.6)
388	Do you have intellectual doubts about Christianity?	2 (0.5)	12 (3.1)	138 (35.6)	236 (60.8)
384	Do you ever feel you are preaching a message you don't fully believe?	1 (0.3)	14 (3.6)	120 (31.2)	249 (64.9)
382	Do you ever feel you are asking people to be better Christians than you are?	6 (1.6)	112 (29.3)	198 (51.8)	66 (17.3)
390	Is anger a problem to you?	4 (1.0)	66 (16.9)	275 (70.5)	45 (11.6)
387	Do you love your missionary colleagues?	69 (17.8)	305 (78.8)	13 (3.4)	0 (0.0)
389	Are you ever emotionally tense?	6 (1.5)	124 (31.9)	248 (63.8)	11 (2.8)
383	Is it easy for you to relax in the Lord?	28 (7.3)	272 (71.0)	81 (21.1)	2 (0.6)
382	Can you forgive missionaries who have hurt you?	145 (38.0)	226 (59.2)	11 (2.8)	0 (0.0)
390	Is frustration a part of your life?	9 (2.3)	155 (39.7)	222 (56.9)	4 (1.1)
387	Do you have sexual fantasies of lust?	3 (0.8)	57 (14.7)	215 (55.6)	112 (28.9)
389	Do you read sexually stimulating literature?	0 (0.0)	4 (1.0)	127 (32.6)	258 (66.4)
384	Do you attend R rated movies?	0 (0.0)	1 (0.3)	61 (15.9)	322 (83.8)
387	Do you attend X rated movies?	0 (0.0)	0 (0.0)	12 (3.1)	375 (96.9)
389	Do you love national Christians on the mission field?	101 (26.0)	276 (71.0)	11 (2.8)	1 (0.2)
384	Do you love national non-Christians on the mission field?	55 (14.3)	277 (72.1)	51 (13.3)	1 (0.3)
350	Are national Christians more spiritual than missionaries?	1 (0.3)	190 (54.3)	152 (43.4)	7 (2.0)
386	Are you happy with the policies of your mission board?	79 (20.5)	294 (76.2)	12 (3.1)	1 (0.2)
384	Do you enjoy visits from mission leadership?	182 (47.4)	180 (46.9)	20 (5.2)	2 (0.5)
387	Do you ever feel you would like to be something other than a missionary?	1 (0.3)	38 (9.8)	207 (53.5)	141 (36.4)
387	Do you ever wish you had more academic degrees?	14 (3.6)	74 (19.1)	185 (47.8)	114 (29.5)

NUMBER OF PEOPLE RESPONDING		ALWAYS	FREQUENTLY	INFREQUENTLY	NEVER
370	Do you enjoy deputation?	51 (13.8)	211 (57.0)	96 (25.9)	12 (3.3)
385	Is pride a problem to you?	14 (3.6)	154 (40.0)	205 (53.2)	12 (3.2)
389	Do you wish you had more money?	12 (3.1)	92 (23.6)	223 (57.4)	62 (15.9)
387	Do you enjoy giving away money?	79 (20.4)	262 (67.7)	45 (11.6)	1 (0.3)
		MINUTES: 0 – 10		**11 – 30**	
377	On an average how much time do you spend in prayer each day?	101 (26.7)		229 (60.7)	
378	On an average how much time do you spend reading the Bible each day?	69 (18.3)		264 (69.8)	
381	How many Christian-type books do you read each month?	0 = 81 (21.3)	1 = 169 (44.4)	2 = 85 (22.3)	
384	How many secular books do you read each month?	0 = 205 (53.4)	1 = 113 (29.4)	2 = 32 (8.3)	
		YES		**NO**	
379	Do you understand the doctrine of inerrancy?	368 (97.1)		11 (2.9)	
373	Do you fully subscribe to inerrancy?	358 (96.0)		15 (4.0)	
344	Is it a subject you prefer not to discuss?	48 (14.0)		296 (86.0)	
376	Have you experienced healing in answer to prayer?	254 (67.6)		122 (32.4)	
379	Have you had a charismatic-type experience?	91 (24.0)		288 (76.0)	
389	Have you ever spoken in tongues?	66 (17.0)		323 (83.0)	
296	Do you feel post-salvation sanctification experiences can be biblically valid?	255 (86.1)		41 (13.9)	
382	Have you remained sexually moral since becoming a missionary?	372 (97.4)		10 (2.6)	
365	Are all non-born-again people in the world going to Hell when they die?	357 (97.8)		8 (2.2)	
343	If your answer is yes, do you believe they deserve to go to Hell?	333 (97.1)		10 (2.9)	
358	If your answer is they are going to Hell, does this bother you?	332 (92.7)		26 (7.3)	
388	Do you drink alcoholic beverages?	100 (25.8)		288 (74.2)	
383	Have you taken tranquilizers since becoming a missionary?	77 (20.1)		306 (79.9)	
387	Do you own property?	129 (33.3)		258 (66.7)	
385	Did answering this questionnaire bother you?	147 (38.2)		238 (61.8)	

PART SIX

RESEARCH

ITEMS

WHAT IS THE QURAN?

by Toby Lester

In 1972, during the restoration of the Great Mosque of Sana'a, in Yemen laborers working in a loft between the structure's inner and outer roofs stumbled across a remarkable gravesite, although they did not realize it at the time. Their ignorance was excusable: mosques do not normally house graves, and this site contained no tombstones, no human remains, no funereal jewelry. It contained nothing more, in fact, than an unappealing mash of old parchment and paper documents—damaged books and individual pages of Arabic text, fused together by centuries of rain and dampness, gnawed into over the years by rats and insects. Intent on completing the task at hand, the laborers gathered up the manuscripts, pressed them into some twenty potato sacks, and set them aside on the staircase of one of the mosque's minarets, where they were locked away—and where they would probably have been forgotten once again, were it not for Qadhi Isma'il al-Akwa', then the president of the Yemeni Antiquities Authority, who realized the potential importance of the find.

Al-Akwa' sought international assistance in examining and preserving the fragments, and in 1979 managed to interest a visiting German scholar, who in turn persuaded the German government to organize and fund a restoration project. Soon after the project began, it became clear that the hoard was a fabulous example of what is sometimes referred to as a "paper grave"—in this case, the resting place for, among other things, tens of thousands of fragments from close to a thousand different parchment codices of the Quran, the Muslim holy scripture. In some pious Muslim circles it is held that worn-out or damaged copies of the Quran must be removed from circulation; hence the idea of a grave, which both preserves the sanctity of the texts being laid to rest and ensures that only complete and unblemished editions of the scripture will be read.

Some of the parchment pages in the Yemeni hoard seemed to date back to the seventh and eighth centuries A.D., or Islam's first two centuries—they were fragments, in other words, of perhaps the oldest Qurans in existence. What's more, some of these fragments revealed small but intriguing aberrations from the standard Quranic text. Such aberrations, though not surprising to textual historians, are troublingly at odds with the orthodox Muslim belief that the Quran as it has reached us today is quite simply the perfect, timeless, and unchanging Word of God.

The mainly secular effort to reinterpret the Quran—in part based on textual evidence such as that provided by the Yemeni fragments—is disturbing and offensive to many Muslims, just as attempts to reinterpret the Bible and the life of Jesus are disturbing and offensive to many conservative Christians. Nevertheless, there are scholars, Muslims among them, who feel that such an effort, which amounts essentially to placing the Quran in history, will provide fuel for an Islamic revival of sorts—a reappropriation of tradition, a going forward by looking back. Thus far confined to scholarly argument, this sort of thinking can be nonetheless very powerful and—as the histories of the Renaissance and the Reformation demonstrate—can lead to major social change. The Quran, after all, is currently the world's most ideologically influential text.

LOOKING AT THE FRAGMENTS

The first person to spend a significant amount of time examining the Yemeni fragments in 1981 was Gerd-R. Puin, a specialist in Arabic calligraphy and Quranic paleography based at Saarland University, in Saarbrücken, Germany. Puin, who had been sent by the German government to organize and oversee the restoration project, recognized the antiquity of some of the parchment fragments, and his preliminary inspection also revealed unconventional verse orderings, minor textual variations, and rare styles of orthography and artistic embellishment. Enticing, too, were the sheets of the scripture written in the rare and early Hijazi Arabic script: pieces of the earliest Qurans known to exist, they were also palimpsests—versions very clearly written over even earlier, washed-off versions. What the Yemeni Qurans seemed to suggest, Puin began to feel, was an evolving text rather than simply the Word of God as revealed in its entirety to the Prophet Muhammad in the seventh century A.D.

Since the early 1980s more than 15,000 sheets of the Yemeni Qurans have painstakingly been flattened, cleaned, treated, sorted, and assembled; they now sit ("preserved for another thousand years," Puin says) in Yemen's House of Manuscripts, awaiting detailed examination. That is something the Yemeni authorities have seemed reluctant to allow, however. "They want to keep this thing low-profile, as we do too, although for different reasons," Puin explains. "They don't want attention drawn to the fact that there are Germans and others working on the Qurans. They don't want it made public that there is work being done at all, since the Muslim position is that everything that needs to be said about the Quran's history was said a thousand years ago."

To date just two scholars have been granted extensive access to the Yemeni fragments: Puin and his colleague H.-C. Graf von Bothmer, an Islamic-art historian also based at Saarland University. Puin and von Bothmer have published only a few tantalizingly brief articles in scholarly publications on what they have discovered in the Yemeni fragments. They have been reluctant to publish partly because until recently they were more concerned with sorting and classifying the fragments than with systematically examining them, and partly because they felt that the Yemeni authorities, if they realized the possible implications of the discovery, might refuse them further access. Von Bothmer, however, in 1997 finished taking more than 35,000 microfilm pictures of the fragments, and has recently brought the pictures back to Germany. This means that soon von Bothmer, Puin, and other scholars will finally have a chance to scrutinize the texts and to publish their findings freely—a prospect that thrills Puin. "So many Muslims have this belief that everything between the two covers of the Quran is just God's unaltered word," he says. "They like to quote the textual work that shows that the Bible has a history and did not fall straight out of the sky, but until now the Quran has been out of this discussion. The only way to break through this wall is to prove that the Quran has a history, too. The Sana'a fragments will help us to do this."

Puin is not alone in his enthusiasm. "The impact of the Yemeni manuscripts is still to be felt," says Andrew Rippin, a professor of religious studies at the University of Calgary, who is at the forefront of Quranic studies today. "Their variant readings and verse orders are all very significant. Everybody agrees on that. These manuscripts say that the early history of the Quranic text is much more of an open question than many have suspected: the text was less stable, and therefore had less authority, than has always been claimed."

COPYEDITING GOD

By the standards of contemporary biblical scholarship, most of the questions being posed by scholars like Puin and Rippin are rather modest; outside an Islamic context, proposing that the Quran has a history and suggesting that it can be interpreted metaphorically are not radical steps. But the Islamic context— and Muslim sensibilities—cannot be ignored. "To historicize the Quran would in effect delegitimize the whole historical experience of the Muslim community," says R. Stephen Humphreys, a professor of Islamic studies at the University of California at Santa Barbara. "The Koran is the charter for the community, the document that called it into existence. And ideally—though obviously not always in reality—Islamic history has been the effort to pursue and work out the commandments of the Koran in human life. If the Koran is a historical docu-ment, then the whole Islamic struggle of 14 centuries is effectively meaningless."

The orthodox Muslim view of the Quran as self-evidently the Word of God, perfect and inimitable in message, language, style, and form, is strikingly similar to the fundamentalist Christian notion of the Bible's "inerrancy" and "verbal inspiration" that is still common in many places today. The notion was given classic expression only a little more than a century ago by the biblical scholar John William Burgon.

> The Bible is none other than *the voice of Him that sitteth upon the Throne!* Every Book of it, every Chapter of it, every Verse of it, every word of it, every syllable of it . . . every letter of it, is the direct utterance of the Most High!

Not all the Christians think this way about the Bible, however, and in fact, as the *Encyclopaedia of Islam* (1981) points out, "the closest analogue in Christian belief to the role of the Kur'an in Muslim belief is not the Bible, but Christ." If Christ is the Word of God made flesh, the Quran is the Word of God made text, and questioning its sanctity or authority is thus considered an outright attack on Islam—as Salman Rushdie knows all too well.

The prospect of a Muslim backlash has not deterred the critical-historical study of the Quran, as the existence of the essays in *The Origins of the Quran*

(1998) demonstrate. Even in the aftermath of the Rushdie affair the work continues: In 1996 the Quranic scholar Günter Lüling wrote in *The Journal of Higher Criticism* about "the wide extent to which both the text of the Quran and the learned Islamic account of Islamic origins have been distorted, a deformation unsuspectingly accepted by Western Islamicists until now." In 1994 the journal *Jerusalem Studies in Arabic and Islam* published a posthumous study by Yehuda D. Nevo, of the Hebrew University in Jerusalem, detailing seventh- and eighth-century religious inscriptions on stones in the Negev Desert which, Nevo suggested, pose "considerable problems for the traditional Muslim account of the history of Islam." That same year, and in the same journal, Patricia Crone, a historian of early Islam currently based at the Institute for Advanced Study, in Princeton, New Jersey, published an article in which she argued that elucidating problematic passages in the Quranic text is likely to be made possible only by "abandoning the conventional account of how the Qur'an was born." And since 1991 James Bellamy, of the University of Michigan, has proposed in the *Journal of the American Oriental Society* a series of "emendations to the text of the Quran"—changes that from the orthodox Muslim perspective amount to copyediting God.

Crone is one of the most iconoclastic of these scholars. During the 1970s and 1980s she wrote and collaborated on several books—most notoriously, with Michael Cook, *Hagarism: The Making of the Islamic World* (1977)—that made radical arguments about the origins of Islam and the writing of Islamic history. Among *Hagarism*'s controversial claims were suggestions that the text of the Quran came into being later than is now believed ("There is no hard evidence for the existence of the Koran in any form before the last decade of the seventh century"); that Mecca was not the initial Islamic sanctuary ("[the evidence] points unambiguously to a sanctuary in north-west Arabia . . . Mecca was secondary"); that the Arab conquests preceded the institutionalization of Islam ("the Jewish messianic fantasy was enacted in the form of an Arab conquest of the Holy Land"); that the idea of the *hijra*, or the migration of Muhammad and his followers from Mecca to Medina in 622, may have evolved long after Muhammad died ("No seventh-century source identifies the Arab era as that of the *hijra*"); and that the term "Muslim" was not commonly used in early Islam ("There is no good reason to suppose that the bearers of this primitive identity called themselves 'Muslims' [but] sources do . . . reveal an earlier designation of the community [which] appears in Greek as 'Magaritai' in a papyrus of 642, and in Syriac as 'Mahgre' or 'Mahgraye' from as early as the 640s").

Hagarism came under immediate attack, from Muslim and non-Muslim scholars alike, for its heavy reliance on hostile sources. ("This is a book," the authors wrote, "based on what from any Muslim perspective must appear an inordinate regard for the testimony of infidel sources.") Crone and Cook have since backed away from some of its most radical propositions—such as, for example, that the Prophet Muhammad lived two years longer than the Muslim tradition claims he did, and that the historicity of his migration to Medina is questionable. But Crone has continued to challenge both Muslim and Western orthodox views of Islamic history. In *Meccan Trade* and the *Rise of Islam* (1987) she made a detailed argument challenging the prevailing view among Western (and some Muslim) scholars that Islam arose in response to the Arabian spice trade.

Gerd-R. Puin's current thinking about the Quran's history partakes of this contemporary revisionism. "My idea is that the Quran is a kind of cocktail of texts that were not all understood even at the time of Muhammad," he says. "Many of them may even be a hundred years older than Islam itself. Even within the Islamic traditions there is a huge body of contradictory information, including a significant Christian substrate; one can derive a whole Islamic *anti-history* from them if one wants."

Patricia Crone defends the goals of this sort of thinking. "The Quran is a scripture with a history like any other—except that we don't know this history and tend to provoke howls of protest when we study it. Nobody would mind the howls if they came from Westerners, but Westerners feel deferential when the howls come from other people: who are you to tamper with *their* legacy? But we Islamicists are not trying to destroy anyone's faith."

Not everyone agrees with that assessment—especially since Western Quranic scholarship has traditionally taken place in the context of an openly declared hostility between Christianity and Islam. (Indeed, the broad movement in the West over the past two centuries to "explain" the East, often referred to as Orientalism, has in recent years come under fire for exhibiting similar religious and cultural biases.) The Quran has seemed, for Christian and Jewish scholars particularly, to possess an aura of heresy; the nineteenth-century Orientalist William Muir, for example, contended that the Quran was one of "the most stubborn enemies of Civilization, Liberty, and the Truth which the world has yet known." Early Soviet scholars, too, undertook an ideologically motivated study of Islam's origins, with almost missionary zeal: in the 1920s and in 1930 a Soviet publication titled *Ateist* ran a series of articles explaining the rise of Islam in Marxist-Leninist terms. In *Islam and Russia* (1956), Ann K.S. Lambton summarized much of this work, and wrote that several Soviet scholars had theorized that "the motive force of the nascent religion was supplied by the mercantile bourgeoisie of Mecca and Medina"; that a certain S.P. Tolstov had held that "Islam was a social-religious movement originating in the slave-owning, not feudal, form of Arab society"; and that N.A. Morozov had argued that "until the Crusades Islam was indistinguishable from Judaism and . . . only then did it receive its independent character, while Muhammad and the first Caliphs are mythical figures. "Morozov appears to have been a particularly flamboyant theorist: Lambton wrote that he also argued, in his book *Christ* (1930), that "in the Middle Ages Islam was merely an off-shoot of Arianism evoked by a meteorological event in the Red Sea area near Mecca."

Not surprisingly, then, given the biases of much non-Islamic critical study of the Quran, Muslims are inclined to dismiss it outright. A particularly eloquent protest came in 1987, in the *Muslim World Book Review*, in a paper titled "Method Against Truth: Orientalism and Qur'anic Studies," by the Muslim critic S. Parvez Manzoor. Placing the origins of Western Quranic scholarship in "the polemical marshes of medieval Christianity" and describing its contemporary state as a "cul-de-sac of its own making," Manzoor orchestrated a complex and layered assault on the entire Western approach to Islam. He opened his essay in a rage.

> The Orientalist enterprise of Qur'anic studies, whatever its other merits and services, was a project born of spite, bred in frustration and nourished by vengeance: the spite of the powerful for the powerless, the frustration of the "rational" towards the "superstitious" and the vengeance of the "orthodox" against the "non-conformist." At the greatest hour of his worldly-triumph, the Western man, coordinating the powers of the State, Church and Academia, launched his most determined assault on the citadel of Muslim faith. All the aberrant streaks of his arrogant personality—its reckless rationalism, its world-domineering phantasy and its sectarian fanaticism—joined in an unholy conspiracy to dislodge the Muslim Scripture from its firmly entrenched position as the epitomé of historic authenticity and moral unassailability. The ultimate trophy that the Western man sought by his dare-devil venture was the Muslim mind itself. In order to rid the West forever of the "problem" of Islam, he reasoned, Muslim consciousness must be made to despair of the cognitive certainty of the Divine message revealed to the Prophet. Only a Muslim confounded of the historical authenticity or doctrinal autonomy of the Qur'anic revelation would abdicate his universal mission and hence pose no challenge to the global domination of the West. Such, at least, seems to have

been the tacit, if not the explicit, rationale of the Orientalist assault
on the Qur'an.

Despite such resistance, Western researchers with a variety of academic and
theological interests press on, applying modern techniques of textual and historical criticism to the study of the Quran. That a substantial body of this scholarship now exists is indicated by the recent decision of the European firm Brill
Publishers—a long-established publisher of such major works as *The Encyclopaedia of Islam* and *The Dead Sea Scrolls Study Edition*—to commission the first-ever
Encyclopaedia of the Qur'an. Jane McAuliffe, a professor of Islamic studies at the
University of Toronto, and the general editor of the encyclopedia, hopes that it
will function as a "rough analogue" to biblical encyclopedias and will be "a turn-
of-the-millennium summative work for the state of Quranic scholarship." Articles for the first part of the encyclopedia are currently being edited and prepared
for publication later this year.

The *Encyclopaedia of the Qur'an* will be a truly collaborative enterprise,
carried out by Muslims and non-Muslims, and its articles will present multiple
approaches to the interpretation of the Quran, some of which are likely to challenge traditional Islamic views—thus disturbing many in the Islamic world, where
the time is decidedly less ripe for a revisionist study of the Quran.

The Testimony
of the Quran

The Testimony of the Quran concerning other holy books

a) God's Word is unchangeable
    1   6:116
    2   10:64
    3   18:27

b) Concerning the Taurat (Genesis-Deuteronomy)
    1   5:44
    2   6:92
    3   40:53
    4   46:12

c) Concerning the Injil
    1   5:46-47

d) Concerning canceled or annulled scriptures
    1   2:106 (concerning the Quran!)
    2   22:52

e) The Quran supports the earlier holy books
    1   3:3
    2   35:31
    3   46:12, 30

f) Various related topics
    1   Command to obey the earlier books, 5:68
    2   The Quran for those who have received no earlier revelations, 32:3

3   The Taurat is referred to as Furkan, 2:53; 21:98

4   Command to believe in all the holy books, 4:136; 42:15

II   The Prophets and their Sins in the Quran

a)   The Quran's testimony concerning the Prophets.
1   Adam, 2:36, 37; 7:19-23
2   Noah, 11:47
3   Abraham, 26:82 (cf. Genesis 20:1-13)
4   Moses, 28:15, 16 (cf. Exodus 2:11-13)
5   Jonah, 37:139-146 (cf. Jonah 1)
6   David, 38:24, 25 (cf. 2 Samuel 11, 12)
7   Muhammad, 40:55; 47:19; 48:1-2

b)   Who is the only prophet without sin according to the Quran?
3:46; 19:17,19

III   The Prophet Muhammad and "Intercession" in the Quran

a)   What is the Prophet Muhammad's work and responsibility?
1   He is only a messenger and giver of a holy book, 3:144; 15:89;
17:93, 105; 18:110; 22:49; 27:92; 29:50; 33:40, 45; 35:23, 24,
37; 36:6; 38:4; 50:2; 50:50, 51; 67:8-9, 26; 79:45
2   He has brought nothing new, 41:43; 46:9
3   The work of a "rasul" is merely to bear God's messages, 95:55;
16:35; 29:18

b)   Who was he sent to? 12:2; 26:192-196; 42:7

c)   What will be the position of those of his followers who do not
follow God's laws? 39:41; 72:20-23; 27:92

d)   Testimony concerning the Prophet's intercession
1   He has neither the power to help nor to hinder anyone, 7:188;
42:48; 72:21

    2   Even though he makes intercession 70 times it will not be accepted for anyone, 9:80

  e) On the day of judgment no intercession will be accepted, 2:48, 123.

IV Jesus Christ in the Quran

  a) His titles
    1   Christ, 3:45; 4:171
    2   The word of God, 3:39; 4:171; 19:34
    3   The Spirit of God, 4:171

  b) His birth, 3:45-51; 19:16-34

  c) His special works, qualities and honor
    1   The second Adam, 3:59 (cf. 1 Corinthians 15:21; Romans 5:12-19)
    2   His holy and sinless character, 19:19; 3:46 (cf. John 8:46; Hebrews 4:15)
    3   He is a grace from God, 19:21 (cf. John 1:17; Hebrews 7:25; 1 Peter 3:18)
    4   Honor to his mother, 3:42
    5   Honor to him, 3:45
    6   His miracles, 3:49
    7   He was taken up alive into heaven, 3:55; 4:158

  d) Which Prophet is given the greatest honor in the Quran? Does the Quran have anything bad to say about Christ?

V The Disciples of Christ in the Quran

  a) What religion did they follow?
    1   3:52 (they were submitted to God, i.e., Muslims)
    2   5:111

b) What will be their situation on the day of judgment?
   1   2:62
   2   5:68-69, 8
   3   57:37
   4   3:55

c) What sort of relationship do they have with Muslims?
   1   5:82
   2   5:5

d) What is their character?
   1   5:82
   2   57:27

AN ABRIDGED QURANIC CONCORDANCE

The following topics and verses, as found in Muhammad Marmaduke Pickthall's *The Meaning of the Glorious Koran*, have been compiled in order to assist the student of Islam in quickly locating some of the more popular and relevant Quranic subjects. I have chosen Pickthall's work because of its wide popularity and general acceptance among Muslims.

PHIL PARSHALL

Allah

4:171	Allah is only one God and do not say "three." Far removed is it from Allah to have a son.
14:4	He leads astray whom He will.
112:1-4	God does not beget nor is begotten.
29:46	God of Islam and Christianity is the same.
3:54	Allah is the best of schemers.
5:72 & 73	Trinity.
57:4 & 13:2	God mounts the Throne.
22:61	Allah hears and sees.
4:164	Allah spoke directly to Moses.
48:10	The Hand of Allah.
38:76	God has two hands.
2:163	God is one God.
4:78	Predestination. All is from Allah.
15:26	Man created out of black mud.
15:27	Jinn was created out of fire.
25:59	Six-day creation.
40:60	Allah answers prayer.

God's Word

6:115-116; 10:65	Scripture is revealed from the Lord in truth and there is nothing that can change his words.
10:95	Muhammad is to check with those who received prior Scripture.
41:43	Nothing is said to Muhammad that was not said to the messengers before him.
3:69-72	Some of the people of the scripture caused people to go astray.
2:106	Allah abrogates and causes his word to be forgotten.

Muhammad

3:31	Muhammad is a model to be followed and then Allah will forgive man's sins if they follow Muhammad.
67:1-5	Pickthall notes pages 405-406; Bukhari Vol. 3, Page 387-388 Describes the private life of Muhammad and comments on polygamy and stresses the humanness of Muhammad.
33:28-34	Model behavior of Muhammad's wives.
33:50-52	Multiple wives.
33:53	Muhammad's wives cannot remarry.
33:37-38	Adopted son Zeyd divorces his wife and Muhammad marries her and God pronounces it legal.
17:1	Muhammad's night journey.
7:157	Muhammad can neither read nor write.
7:157	Muhammad is described in the Torah and the Gospel.
61:6	Muhammad is prophesied by Jesus. His name will be "praised one," i.e., "Ahmed."
47:19	Muhammad is to ask forgiveness for his sin.

Women

4:177	Inheritance laws. Male receives twice as much as the female.
24:31	Modesty.
33:59	Women to draw cloaks around them.
2:222	Menstruation is an illness.
2:223	Women are a tilth to cultivate so go to them as you will.
23:1-7	Permitted to have sex with slaves.
24:60	Older women can discard clothing (the word "outer" is an addition).
4:129	One cannot deal equally between wives.
4:3	Can marry up to four wives, but you must do justice to them.
37:22-23	Women seem to be judged on the basis of their husband's sins.
2:230	If a Muslim divorces his wife, he cannot remarry her until she marries another husband and divorces him.
2:235	Sex can be had only after uttering a certain ritual of words.
4:124	Women believers will enter Paradise.
4:34	Men are in charge of wives. They can be admonished, banished to another bed, and also scourged.
4:24	Can marry captives who are already married.
4:25	*Muta* or temporary marriage.

Heaven

18:31-32	Gardens of Eden and thrones.
37:41-49	Wine and women.
76:12-21	Being served by youths of everlasting youth.
71:15	Seven heavens.
44:51-54; 52:20	Weddings in heaven
47:15	Rivers of wine.

Hell

18:30	Showers of molten lead.
8:50	Smiting of faces and backs.
19:68-72	Everyone goes to hell for a time.
10:56	Skins are consumed and exchanged.
2:217	The apostate goes to hell.

Jesus

19:15-35	Jesus is virgin born and a perfect man and a faultless son.
5:116	Here is the idea of the trinity being God, Mary, and Jesus.
5:110	Jesus giving life to a clay bird, healing the blind and the leper, and raising the dead.
3:45; 4:171	Jesus as a word from Allah.
3:37-59	Various good verses on Jesus
5:75	Jesus only a messenger of God.
4:157-158	Jesus not crucified, but taken to heaven by Allah.
43:61	The "hour" refers to Christ's return.

Miscellaneous

4:103	Worship forms and "fixed hours."
2:256	No compulsion in religion.
24:2	100 stripes for the adulterer and adulteress.
4:15-17	House confinement for adultery. Requires four witnesses.
2:177	Righteousness described. It is not just turning faces to East or West to worship.
4:43	Do not pray when drunk.
5:38-39	Cut off hands of men and women thieves.
2:142-144	Turn toward Mecca in prayer. No longer turn toward Jerusalem.
96:19	Prostration in prayer.
2:216-217, 244	Religious warfare is ordained for Muslims
4:28	Man was created weak

20:130	Five times of prayer.
5:5	Christian food and Christian women are permissible for Muslims.
19:97-98	Gog and Magog.
9:5-6	"Slay the idolaters," or they can repent and pay the poor tax.
3:103	Hold fast to the cable of Allah
3:118	Only be friends with Muslims.
5:51	Do not take Jews and Christians as friends.
29:9	Salvation by belief and good works.
54:1-3	The splitting of the moon.
22:34-37	Qurbani (sacrifice) Festival.
5:6	Ablutions.
2:183-187	Rules for the Ramadan Fast.
2:253	Holy Spirit.
3:110	Muslims are the best community.
5:3	Forbidden foods including blood and swine.
5:45	Eye for an eye.
36:47-52	Judgment and Resurrection Day.

CHAPTER 26

A QURANIC VIEW
OF THE BIBLE

by Tom Wright

Ask any knowledgeable Muslim what he thinks of the Bible that we have today and he will almost certainly say that it has been corrupted. They will acknowledge that the original writings of Moses, David, and Jesus were accurate, but that the Jews and Christians have changed them. They will point to the myriad of different translations in a given language and the fact that we do not possess any of the original manuscripts. If they are especially informed, they will quote from Ahmed Deedat's booklet *Is the Bible God's Word?* in which numerous arguments are made for the supposed large number of errors in the Bible. It is beyond the scope of this paper to delve into this apologetic, but I refer any reader to John Gilchrist's booklet, *The Textual History of the Qur'an and the Bible*, a reply to Deedat's work. It is quite good. In this paper I want to look at the Quranic witness itself about the Bible (the Taurat and the Injil), and see how this can be used as a bridge in witness to Muslims. In addition, we will make a brief reference to the ancient manuscript evidence for the accuracy of our Bible today.

QURANIC WITNESS FOR THE BIBLE

I have compiled 40 different quranic texts that testify to the reliability of the Bible. There are almost certainly more, but for a listing of these 40, please see "Quranic Testimony about the Bible" on pages (364-367).

The first kind of texts deal with God's giving of the various Scriptures. There are 12 texts that state that Moses received the Pentateuch (Taurat) directly from God, two state that David received the Psalms (Zabur) directly from God, and three that state that Jesus received the Gospel (Injil) from God. As mentioned, there are probably more. An example of these is Surah 57:27 "Then We made Our apostle to follow in their footsteps, and We sent Isa son of Marium afterwards, and We gave him the Injeel."

Then we have texts that indicate that the Quran verifies the earlier Scriptures. There are 11 of these, the following being a representative example: Surah 4:47, "O you who have been given the Book! believe that which We have revealed verifying what you have." Notice here that this verse not only says that the Quran verifies the earlier Scriptures, but it verifies the ones they *have* at the time of Muhammad!

Next we have three texts that assert that the Scriptures cannot be changed. This is very important, because this is what Muslims accuse the Jews and Christians of having done. Surah 6:115 reads, "And the word of your lord has been accomplished truly and justly; there is none who can change His words." Surah 18:27 says, "And recite what has been revealed to you of the Book of your Lord; there is none who can alter His words."

In addition we have texts (at least three of them) that exhort Muhammad and all Muslims to believe *all* the Scriptures. An example of this is Surah 29:46, "And do not dispute with the followers of the Book except by what is best, except those of them who act unjustly, and say: We believe in that which has been revealed to us and revealed to you, and our God and your God is One, and to Him do we submit."

Finally, we have several significant miscellaneous texts on the subject. One of the most fascinating is Surah 10:94, "But if you (Muhammad) are in doubt as to what We have revealed to you, ask those who read the Book before you." Notice that Muhammad is instructed to take his doubts to the Jews and Christians who read the Book before him. This would certainly indicate that the Bible present at the time must have been uncorrupted, or why else would God tell him to go to those who read the Book, for confirmation? Another text admonishes the Jews and Christians to carefully follow their Scriptures, Surah 5:68, "Say: O followers of the Book! you follow no good till you keep up the Taurat and the Injeel and that which is revealed to you from your Lord." If these had been corrupted, why would God tell them to follow the corrupted Scriptures?

So we see that God revealed all the Scriptures to his prophets, he reportedly verified their reliability through the Quran, and we see that the Scriptures cannot be changed. Muhammad was instructed to believe in all the revealed Scriptures, and indeed, if he was in doubt, he was to go to those who had read the Scriptures before him! By the Quran's own testimony, the Scriptures at the time of Muhammad were reliable, and indeed could not be changed! Nevertheless, Muslims are convinced they have been changed. Why?

QURANIC WITNESS AGAINST THE BIBLE

There are two major kinds of texts that Muslims use to show that the Bible we have has been changed or is no longer valid. The first of these are numerous texts indicating that the Jews had mishandled the Scriptures. The second is their doctrine on abrogation. In terms of the first, there isn't space to go into depth on this. L Bevan Jones catalogs these texts and then notes: "Two facts emerge from a consideration of these passages: (1) the people against whom Muhammad brings these charges are Jews, not Christians; no such complaint is made against the latter in any part of the Qur'an; (2) even so, in no case are the Jews charged with having tampered with the text of their Scriptures." He goes on to explain that these "corruptions" refer not to an alteration of the written biblical text itself but to a verbal corruption, that is, in the meaning or interpretation of the text. For support he refers to a 19th century eminent Indian Muslim scholar, Sir Sayyid Ahmad Khan who wrote, "What we have to consider is whether all the copies of the Scriptures, scattered throughout Christendom and Judaism, did really go forth with corruption. . . . Other more learned doctors of our faith have stated their deliberate conviction that no such corruption took place in the Scriptures." Sayyid then refers to Bukhari who said that "there is no man who could corrupt a single word of what has proceeded from God, so that the Jews and Christians could corrupt only by misrepresenting the meaning of the words of God." Ibn Abbas, a nephew of Muhammad is quoted, saying in essence the same thing.

The reason Muslims assert so strongly that the Bible has been corrupted is that: 1) they know that there are doctrinal differences between the Bible and the Quran—this is their solution; 2) Surah 61:6 that says that the Bible had predicted the coming of Ahmad but that this had been removed. It is very important to them to believe in the supposed biblical foretelling of Muhammad's coming.

In response one can give all the above-cited arguments. But further, one must ask, when was it changed and for what reason? To the first question there are three possibilities: 1) before Muhammad—but the Quran contradicts this. Furthermore, there would be no reason to remove Muhammad's name from the Bible before Muhammad even arrives on the scene! 2) during Muhammad's lifetime, supposedly to deny Muhammad's prophethood—but how could all the Scriptures have been changed? They existed in at least six different languages in different parts of the world. Certainly Muslims could have discovered this wholesale changing of the Bible and cried "foul." Further, why would the Jews have done this with Muhammad and not done it with the obvious Old Testament prophecies about Jesus, that which also gave them problems? It doesn't make any sense! 3) After the time of Muhammad—but we have many ancient biblical manuscripts that predate Muhammad to show that the Bible we have today is the same as what was present before the time of Muhammad, including entire Greek Bibles (Codex Vaticanus—350 A.D.; Codex Sinaiticus—380 A.D.; Codex Alexandrinus—450 A.D.). See Josh McDowell's books for more evidence on this.

As mentioned above, the second argument is abrogation, mentioned in Surah 2:106, "Whatever communications We abrogate or cause to be forgotten, We bring one better than it or like it. Do you not know that Allah has power over all things?" Muslims would like to think that the Quran abrogates the entire Bible. But as we saw in Surah 5:68 Jews and Christians are admonished to continue to strictly follow them. The doctrine of abrogation is somewhat of an embarrassment to some Muslims as it seems to make God kind of wishy-washy. Certainly God's nature cannot change and the major doctrinal differences between Islam and Christianity concerning Christology and salvation cannot be explained away by abrogation.

CONCLUSION

Despite the fact that Muslims try to totally discredit our current Bible, there is tremendous evidence from the Quran itself, as well as logical argumentation to support the accuracy and authority of our Bible. Due to space constraints, only a portion of this has been presented. I believe that using the Quran to build a bridge to our Bible can enable the sincere God-seeker in Islam to discover the truth and salvation found only in the Bible.

QURANIC TESTIMONY ABOUT THE BIBLE

Testimony of the Taurat

1   Surah 32:23—"And certainly We gave the Book to Musa, so be not in doubt concerning the receiving of it, and We made it a guide for the children of Israel."

2   Surah 21:48—"And certainly We gave to Musa and Harouna [Aaron] the Furqan and a light and a reminder for those who would guard against evil."
    (NOTE: Furqan means "illumination." The Quran is also referred to as Furqan— Surah 3:3).

3   Surah 25:35; Surah 11:110; Surah 37:117; Surah 40:55; Surah 41:45; Surah 45:16; Surah 5:44; Surah 2:87; Surah 2:63; Surah 6:91.

Testimony of the Zabur

1   Surah 17:57—"We have made some of the prophets to excel others and to Dawood [David] We gave a Scripture."

2   Surah 4:163—"And We gave to Dawood [David] Psalms."

Testimony of the Injil

1   Surah 5:46-48— "And We sent after them in their footsteps Isa, son of Marium, verifying what was before him of the Taurat and We gave him the Injeel in which was guidance and light, and verifying what was before it of Taurat and a guidance and an admonishment for those who guard (against evil).

And the followers of the Injeel should have judged by what Allah revealed in it; and whoever did not judge by what Allah revealed, those are they that are the transgressors. And We have revealed to you the Book with the truth, verifying what is before it of the Book and a guardian over it."

2   Surah 19:30—"He said [Jesus in the cradle]: surely I am a servant of Allah; He has given me the Book and made me a prophet."

3   Surah 57:27—"Then We made Our apostle to follow in their footsteps, and We sent Isa son of Marium afterwards, and We gave him the Injeel."

Scriptures Unchangeable

1   Surah 6:115—"And the word of your lord has been accomplished truly and justly; there is none who can change His words, and He is the Hearing the Knowing."

2   Surah 10:64—"They shall have good news in this world's life and in the hereafter; there is no changing the words of Allah; that is the mighty achievement."

3   Surah 18:27—"And recite what has been revealed to you of the Book of your Lord; there is none who can alter His words; and you shall not find any refuge besides him."

Quran Supports Earlier Books

1   Surah 3:3—"He has revealed to you the Book with truth, verifying that which is before it, and he revealed the Taurat and the Injeel aforetime, a guidance for the people, and He sent the Furqan."

2   Surah 46:12—"And before it the Book of Musa was a guide and a mercy; and this is a Book verifying (it) in the Arabic language that it may warn those who are unjust and as good news for the doers of good."

3   Surah 4:47—"O you who have been given the Book! believe that which We have revealed verifying what you have."
[NOTE that here it verifies the Scriptures existing at the time of Mohammad. Also: the Rodwell Koran, Everyman's Library Edition reads: "confirmatory of the Scripture which is in your hands"].

4   Surah 2:89—"And when there came to them a Book from Allah verifying that which they have."

5   Surah 35:31; Surah 46:30; Surah 10:37; Surah 6:92; Surah 2:41; Surah 2:91; Surah 2:97.

Commands to Believe All the Holy Books

1   Surah 4:136—"O you who believe! believe in Allah and His Apostle and the Book which He has revealed to His Apostle and the Book which He revealed before."

2   Surah 42:15—"To this then go on inviting, and go on steadfastly on the right way as you are commanded, and do not follow their low desires and say: I believe in what Allah has revealed of the Book, and I am commanded to do justice before you: Allah is our Lord and your Lord; we shall have our deeds and you shall have your deeds; no plea need there be (now) between us and you: Allah will gather us together, and to Him is the return."

3   Surah 29:46—"And do not dispute with the followers of the Book except by what is best, except those of them who act unjustly, and say: We believe in that which has been revealed to us and revealed to you, and our God and your God is One, and to Him do we submit.

Miscellaneous

1   Surah 10:94—"But if you are in doubt as to what We have revealed to you, ask those who read the Book before you."

[NOTE: Mohammad is here instructed to go to Christians and Jews who had read the Scriptures before; therefore the current Scriptures must have been reliable!]

2   Surah 40:56—"Surely (as for) those who dispute about the communications of Allah without any authority that has come to them, there is naught in their breasts but (a desire) to become great."
[NOTE: those who dispute about God's communication are said to be proud!]

3   Surah 7:170—"And (as for) those who hold fast by the Book and keep up prayer, surely we do not waste the reward of the right doers."
[NOTE: The Book here refers to pre-Quranic Scriptures, probably the Taurat. Those who follow the Taurat will be rewarded!]

4   Surah 5:68—"Say: O followers of the Book! you follow no good till you keep up the Taurat and the Injeel and that which is revealed to you from your Lord; and surely that which has been revealed to you from your Lord shall make many of them increase in inordinancy and unbelief; grieve not therefore for the unbelieving people."
[NOTE: Jews and Christians instructed to obey their books!]

5   Surah 32:3—"Or do they say: He has forged it? Nay! it is the truth before you, that they may follow the right direction."
[NOTE: This says that the Quran was given to those who had not received earlier revelation!]

6   Surah 41:43—"Naught is said to you but what was said indeed to the apostles before you."
[NOTE: Nothing was said to Mohammad that was not said to previous prophets].

ARABIC WORDS

These well-known Arabic words should be memorized and woven into your conversations with Muslims. They will be appreciated and are good bridge material. Your phonetics and spelling may vary, so check these with a local person.

AH-LUL-KITAB — *People of the Book, e.g.,* Christians, Jews, and Muslims. Also Kitabi is used in certain places.

AL-HAMDU-LI'LLAH — *Praise belongs to God; Praise the Lord.*

ALIM — Muslim teacher.

ALLAHU AKBAR — *God is Great.* A very common saying.

AS-SALAM-ALAI-KUM — *Peace be upon you.* A greeting.

ALAI-KUM SALAM — *And upon you be peace.* Response to the greeting.

AYAT — Verse of the Quran.

AZAN — The call to prayer.

BARAKAH — Blessing.

BISMILLAH-AR-RAHAMANER-RAHIM — *In the name of God the compassionate, the merciful.* Very important phrase to know as it is so often stated, particularly at the beginning of an activity.

DAR-UL-HARB — The world outside of Islam.

DAR-UL-ISLAM — The household of Islam.

DHIKR — Ceremony centering around the recitation of the names and attributes of God.

DOHA — Spontaneous prayer.

EID — Islamic festival.

EID-UL-FITR — Feast at the end of the Ramadan Fast.

HADITH — The Traditions; deeds and sayings of the Prophet.

HAJJ — Pilgrimage to Mecca.

HAJJI — One who has completed the pilgrimage to Mecca.

HALAL — That which is allowed.

HARAAM — That which is not allowed, forbidden actions (food or dress).

HIJRA — Flight of the Prophet from Mecca to Medina. The beginning of the Muslim lunar calendar (622 A.D. in our calendar).

IMAM — Muslim priest. Same as *Alim* or its plural, *Ulama.*

IMAN — *Faith.*

INJIL — Literally, the four Gospels, but also generally refers to the New Testament.

INSHA-ALLAH — *God willing.* An often repeated phrase.

JIHAD — Muslim *holy war.*

JINN — Harmful or helpful spirit beings.

KAABA — The cube-like building in the center of the mosque at Mecca which contains the black stone.

KAFIR — Idolators; enemies of Islam.

KALIMA — The Creed; *La-ilaha-il-lal-laho Muhammad-ur-Rasul-Ullah* (There is no deity but God, and Muhammad is the Apostle of God).

KHALIFA — *Caliph* or system of successors in Islam.

MADRASSA — Muslim school associated with the mosque.

MASJID — Mosque.

RAMADAN — Ninth month in the Muslim calendar, the month of fasting.

SALAT — The five daily obligatory prayers.

SHARIAT — Islamic code of law.

SUFI — Follower of mystical Islam.

SURAH — A term used for the chapters of the Quran. We can also use it for chapters of the Bible.

TORAH — The Law of Moses.

TORAH, ZABUR, and INJIL — *The Bible.*

UMMAH — The community of Islam.

WAZU — Ritual ablutions before prayer.

ZABUR — The Psalms of David.

ZAKAT — Almsgiving; 2½ percent of income given by Muslims to charity.

Proper Names

ADAM — Adam; *Sufi-Ullah*, The Chosen of God.

HOWWA — Eve.

AYUB — Job.

NUH — Noah; *Nabi-Ullah*, the Preacher of God.

IBRAHIM — Abraham; *Khalil-Ullah*, the Friend of God.

HAJAŘ — Hagar, mother of Ishmael.

SAARAH — Sarah, wife of Ibrahim.

ISHAQ — Isaac.

ISMAIL — Ishmael.

MUSA — Moses; *Kalim-Ullah*, one who conversed with God.

DAUD — David.

SULAIMAN — Solomon.

YAHYA — John the Baptist.

ISA — Jesus.

ISA-AL-MASIH — Jesus *the Messiah.*

ISA RUH ULLAH — Jesus, *the Spirit of God.*

ISA, ALAI-SALAM — Jesus, *upon Him be peace.*

MUHAMMAD (S.M.) *or* (pbuh) — *Muhammad, peace be upon Him.*

SHAITAN — Satan.

CHAPTER 27

Is it Fitting for Christians to Use the Name *Isa Al Masih?*

Focus on Indonesia

by John Travis

In these days, the Lord is doing a new thing among the world's one billion Muslims. Like never before in history, the church of Jesus Christ is beginning to think seriously about sharing the love of God and salvation through the Messiah with Muslim neighbors. As Christians begin to share their faith with Muslims, and sensitively seek ways to approach the difficult spiritual, theological, and social barriers which exist, it is often the case that the words we use do not communicate the message we hope to convey. In fact, the words we use in and of themselves can become stumbling blocks to a true understanding of the Gospel. One worker in a Muslim land states:

> We began to realize that people were stumbling over the stumbling block of language and culture, and not the stumbling block of the cross.

There will always be those with rebellious hearts, from both Muslims and Christian backgrounds, who will stumble over the cross of death to self, and refuse to accept Jesus as Lord and Savior (1 Peter 2:8). Yet our responsibility as ambassadors of Christ is to find the most relevant way to communicate the precious message of salvation, clearing the path to the cross of all other stumbling blocks.

Jesus Christ is both our creed and our faith. His name, not our religion, is what we desire to lift up before our Muslim friends and neighbors. Indeed, God himself exalts the name of Jesus:

> Therefore God exalted him to the highest place and gave him the name that is above every name, that at the name of Jesus every knee should bow, in heaven and on earth and under the earth, and every tongue confess that Jesus Christ is Lord to the glory of God the Father.
>
> Philippians 2:9-10

In light of this Scripture passage, it behooves us to approach the use of the name of our Savior with much prayer and careful consideration. Whenever the Gospel enters an unevangelized culture, the proclaimer of the Gospel must consider carefully what name or term should be used when referring to Jesus, our Lord and Savior. Throughout the world, not only in Christian but in Hindu, Buddhist, Muslim and Animist settings as well, we encounter a myriad of names and titles used to refer to Jesus Christ, the Messiah from Nazareth. *Isa Al Masih* is one of these names.

Indonesia, which has the world's largest Muslim population, is at least 15 percent Christian. Traditionally, Indonesia has used both the terms *Isa Al Masih* and *Yesus Kristus* in its many Bible translations. The first complete Isa Al Masih Bible in Malay (Indonesian) was printed in 1733, and many more, in a number of regional languages, followed. The tradition of using either *Isa* or *Yesus* continued until the Second World War. Most translations since the 1940s however have favored the use of *Yesus Kristus*. Although *Isa* had been used for over two centuries, today the vast majority of Christians and Bible translations use *Yesus*. The purpose of this article is not to advocate that Christians who have grown up using the term *Yesus* in their churches stop using this beloved name and replace it with another term for Jesus. The purpose rather is to show that in light of linguistic, religious, historical, and cultural considerations, especially involving outreach to Muslims, there is a definite place for the name *Isa Al Masih* in our witness today.

WHERE DID THE NAME *ISA AL MASIH* COME FROM?

In Matthew 1:21 the angel commands Joseph to give the name Jesus to the child born of Mary. The name Jesus means "the Lord saves" and in Hebrew is pronounced "*Yeshua.*" Jesus was given the title Messiah, the Anointed One promised by God, which in Hebrew is pronounced "*Meshia.*" Even to this day, many American Jews who have come to faith in Christ call Jesus "*Yeshua Meshia*" instead of Jesus Christ. The name *Yesus Kristus* is based on the Greek name "*Iesous Christos,*" which is the Greek rendering of the Hebrew "*Yeshua Meshia.*"

The Arabs of Mohammed's day (7th century) were not speakers of Greek and were most probably not blessed with the presence of a complete version of the Scriptures in their own mother tongue. As the Arabs interacted with local Jews and Christians, they learned of Jesus the Messiah. Most likely through transliteration, his name in Arabic became *Isa Al Masih,* the addition being the characteristic Arabic "*Al.*" It is clear that the Greek "*Iesous Christos*" and the Arabic "*Isa Al Masih*" refer to the same historical figure, Jesus the Messiah from Nazareth.

HOW IS *ISA AL MASIH* REPRESENTED IN THE QURAN?

It is amazing how God in his sovereignty has left a witness to the Savior even in the book of another faith. Although the Quran implies that *Isa* was not crucified (sura 4:157) and says that he is not the Son of God (9:30), it does state the following about *Isa Al Masih;* his birth was announced by an angel as good news (3:45), he was born of a virgin (3:47), his birth is a sign from God (23:50), his virgin birth is light and blessing from God (19:21), he was ministered to by the Holy Spirit (2:87), he was given wisdom by God (3:48), he brought blessing wherever he went (19:31), he healed the blind and the lepers (3:49), he raised the dead (3:49), every word he spoke was given to him by God (5:117), he confirmed the Taurat (3:50), he was given the Injil (the New Testament) (5:46), his book is to be believed (3:84), to obey him is the straight path (43:61), he died and was raised again to life (19:33), he ascended to God (4:158), he is the Word of God (4:171), he is the Spirit of God (4:171), he is holy (19:19), he is important both on earth and in eternity (3:45), his followers are more honored than unbelievers both now and on the Last Day (3:55), and he will be a witness on the Last Day for those who believe in him (4:159).

WHAT ARE THE OBJECTIONS TO THE USE OF THE NAME *ISA* ?

Many advocate using the name *Isa Al Masih* when sharing the Good News of salvation with Muslims. Notice the tremendous amount of common understanding we share with our Muslim neighbors regarding the birth, work, and life of Jesus! The Muslims go to great and heroic lengths to try to prove that Mohammed is spoken of in the Bible. The Christian, on the other hand, begins the discussions with a wealth of biblically accurate information concerning the Savior already clearly written in the Muslim book. Many Christians however have never considered using the name *Isa*, or are opposed to its use. The reasons why some Christians object to using *Isa Al Masih* fall into two main arguments.

The first is that *Isa* of the Quran is not the same Jesus of the Bible that we love and adore. The Quran affirms much, but it does not teach that he is the Savior nor that he is divine. The second is that in Indonesia the Bible is already translated into a number of different versions and the Christian population has a long-standing tradition of using the name *Yesus Kristus*. Let us examine these arguments.

The First Objection

Argument number one: *Isa* of the Quran is not seen as the Savior crucified, nor is he divine, therefore it is better to use a different name, specifically *Yesus Kristus*, to avoid confusion.

This is the most common reason given by Christians for the exclusive use of the term *Yesus Kristus*. It is true, most Muslims do not begin to understand who *Isa* really is, and even hold false concepts about him. But the question must be asked: Does changing his name from *Isa* to *Yesus* change the false concepts that Muslims hold? Be assured, our Muslim friends don't think that the person called *Yesus Kristus* is Savior and Lord either! Just because we call him *Tuhan Yesus* (Lord Jesus), doesn't mean it will help them believe he is *Tuhan* (Lord). It could even be argued that in a number of ways the Quran's presentation of *Isa Al Masih* is much closer to biblical truth than the common Muslim understanding of the Christian *Yesus Kristus*. If a Muslim has heard the name *Yesus* at all, he usually has three misconceptions which become major stumbling blocks, namely, that *Yesus Kristus* is the physical offspring of God's union with Mary, that he is indeed one of the three gods worshipped by Christians, and lastly that he is a religious leader for a limited group but not for the whole world. Which base is therefore more reasonable to build upon when talking to Muslims: their view of *Isa Al*

Masih, which although lacking is largely biblical, or their view of the Christian *Yesus Kristus*, of whom their understanding is almost wholly unbiblical and even blasphemous?

There is also a major inconsistency in our thinking when we choose to use *Yesus* rather than *Isa* on the basis that the understanding of *Isa* is incomplete. Do Christians believe that the Muslim understanding of God, heaven, prayer, and revelation is complete? Certainly not, yet these four words, "*Allah*," "*surga*," "*doa*" and "*wahyu*," originally from the Quran, are freely used in our Bible translations and in our Christian services! What has happened is that we've taken the Arabic term and added or given new meaning to it. Why can't this be the case with the name *Isa*?

L. Bevon Jones in an article regarding the use of the name *Isa*, expresses it this way: "The conclusion to be drawn is clearly this—that we should gratefully receive, and without hesitation use the name for Jesus which the Muslims offer us and fill it, **for their sakes, with a new content**" (emphasis ours).

The Second Objection

The second argument often put forth is that of tradition and precedent, specifically that we already have the Bible and other Christian literature not only in Indonesian, but in Javanese, Sundanese, Balinese, etc., and that the name for the Savior is always some form of *Jesus Kristus*. Why should we change now?

It is for the sake of Muslims outside the Savior that we consider using the name *Isa Al Masih*! We want as many Muslims as possible to hear and receive the Good News of salvation, without having to learn Christian expressions first, which may in and of themselves become stumbling blocks to their receiving Christ.

Many Muslims are prejudiced against Christianity, viewing it as a foreign religion and western institution, but they may not be prejudiced against the Prophet *Isa Al Masih*. Evangelicals all affirm that salvation is in Jesus, not in religion. Therefore our goal should be to emphasize Jesus, and present him in the clearest way possible. The following case study from Bangladesh perhaps most vividly illustrates this point.

THE BEST SELLING BOOK IN ONE MUSLIM LAND

In other parts of the world, with the purpose of drawing Muslim readers, the United Bible Society and others are producing some very attractive and relevant Bible texts which make use of familiar terminology, artwork, printing, and type of cover. The most famous of these translations is the one now being used in Bangladesh, a place where thousands of Muslims are turning to Christ.

The Bible and Christian workers have been in Bangladesh for over 200 years. In fact, the New Testament is available in at least 16 of Bangladesh's languages. Yet, until just recently, the 87 percent Islamic majority essentially shunned reading the Bible. But an amazing thing has happened in the last decade! A new translation of the New Testament designed for Bengali Muslims has become, according to missiologist Dr. Phil Parshall, the NUMBER ONE SELLING BOOK in the country with thousands of Muslims reading it! This innovative Muslim Bengali New Testament published by the United Bible Societies in cooperation with Dr. Viggo Olsen, uses the term *Isa* when referring to Jesus. The beauty of this translation is that by the use of relevant terms, Muslims are seeing it as their book instead of as a book for Christians only.

Already in Indonesia, we have various translations of the Bible in the Indonesian language to accommodate the needs of differing audiences. The standard LAI translation, simply called *Alkitab*, is used in most church services. The *Kabar Baik Bible* (Good News Bible) and the *Firman Allah yang Hidup Bible* (Living Bible) address readers who are more comfortable with every-day Indonesian. Another translation of the New Testament has been published especially for children. If special editions of the Scriptures, each true to God's Word, yet each making use of unique terminology, artwork, printing, and cover styles are useful for various audiences, would it not make sense to create an edition of the Scriptures especially for Muslim readers, using the name *Isa* and other familiar terminology?

The Quran says that if Muslims are unsure about what has been sent down from God, they should ask the people who read the holy books which were sent down by God before the Quran (sura 10:94). According to the Quran, what are those holy books sent down beforehand? They are the *Taurat* (first five books of the Old Testament), the *Jabur* and the book of the Prophets (the Psalms and the rest of the Old Testament), and the *Injil* (the New Testament).

Therefore, should we not make every effort to erase the foreignness of the Bible for the sake of our Muslim neighbors? We can replace "*perjanjian Baru*" (New Testament) with "*Kitab Suci Injil*" (The Holy Injil), "*Mazmur*" (Psalms) with "*Kitab Suci Jabur*" (The Holy Jabur), "*Yesus Kristus*" with "*Isa Al Masih*," "*Raja Solomon*" (King Solomon) with "*Nabi Sulaiman*" (the prophet *Sulaiman*), and so forth, so that Muslims will be more inclined to read the true book of life, hopefully seeing the Scriptures as a part of their own religious heritage. When the living and active Word of God is read and studied, the One who is called *Isa Al Masih* will be clearly seen as Savior and Lord.

TEN REASONS FOR USING THE NAME *ISA AL MASIH*

Let us consider ten reasons for using the name *Isa Al Masih* among those with a Muslim heritage.

Isa is the most widely used name for Jesus in the world. The Arabic name *Isa Al Masih* is used by the world's one billion Muslims, followed in second place by the English name Jesus Christ, used by 700 million speakers of English. Let us use and fill with saving knowledge the name for Jesus already on the lips of one billion people!

In terms of historical reference, *Yesus Kristus* and *Isa Al Masih* are the same person. By using the name *Yesus* we cannot erase the name *Isa* from 1,300 years of Muslim literature and thinking. By using *Isa Al Masih* an interesting topic of discussion could arise with our Muslim friends: Just what does "*Al Masih*" mean? We could explain that *Al Masih* (Messiah) means Prophet, Priest and King. As our Priest, he didn't just bring an animal as a sacrifice for sin, but being perfect, he offered himself to God on our behalf.

We show respect for the redeemable aspects of the listener's heritage, beginning our witness on common ground. As Samuel Zwemer, the great missionary to Muslims once said in the early part of this century, "To help our Muslim brothers answer the question, 'What do you think of Christ?', we must lead them up to higher truth by admitting all of the truth which they possess.'"

The use of the name *Isa Al Masih* is proving to be an effective tool of evangelism in other parts of the Muslim world. Many tracts and other evangelistic literature are being written with a Muslim audience in mind, including quite a few in English, which refer to Jesus as *Isa*.

Isa Al Masih is already a national term in Indonesia. Holidays such as *Kenaikan Isa Al Masih* (The Ascension of Isa the Messiah) and *Wafat Isa Al Masih* (The Death of Isa the Messiah, *i.e.*, Good Friday), give us a place to begin our witness. The author has been able to share the life of the Messiah with Muslims because the name *Isa* is used for Christian holidays. The Islamic sounding name of the holiday gives credence to its meaning in the Muslim mind.

There is strong historical precedent for using the name *Isa* in the Indonesian context. As stated earlier in this article, *Isa* had been used in many Bible translations prior to the 1940s. A number of denominations included hymns using

Isa in their hymnals even as recently as the 1960s. A Javanese evangelist in the 1800s named Tunggul Wulung won over 1,000 Muslims to Christ. He preached salvation in the name of *"Ratu Adil Isa Rohollah"* (The Just King Isa, the Spirit of God). Even today there are at least two denominations in Indonesia which use *Isa Al Masih* rather than *Yesus Kristus* in their church's official name (one is the Gereja Isa Al Masih found in Jakarta and Bandung).

Since it is believed that the Quran has always existed in heaven in the Arabic language, it would follow that Muslims believe the name *Isa Al Masih* has always existed as well. In the eyes of our Muslim neighbors, the name *Isa Al Masih* is not of human origin, but is a God-given name. Let us therefore begin to share the Holy Gospel with them, using this name for the Savior which is already considered acceptable and holy to the Muslim.

As Christians, words in and of themselves hold no spiritual power. We do not use mantras. The name of Jesus in one particular language is not superior to his name in another language. It is our relationship with God through Jesus himself, not the particular name by which we call him, that endues us with salvation, power over Satan, and life eternal.

The use of terms relevant to the hearer is in keeping with Scriptural principles outlined in Acts 15:19 and 1 Corinthians 9:19-23. It can lessen barriers and help create bridges rather than walls; discussion rather than arguments and heated debate.

One of the most compelling reasons to use the name *Isa Al Masih* with those of Muslim heritage is its potential effect on the unsaved relatives and neighbors of the new believer. Those still outside *Al Masih* must be brought along the same journey to the Savior that the new believer has traveled. Would it not be better for the new believer to go home and **begin** his testimony with, "I have a new and closer relationship with God after coming to a deeper understanding of what he has done for us through the work of *Isa Al Masih*," instead of, "Jesus Christ is now my Lord, and I have entered the Christian religion." By using the name of *Isa Al Masih*, we are giving the new believer a tool of sensitive and patient witness. Is it possible that a more sensitive approach on the part of new believers could minimize some of the persecution and hostility that they must face? Could it be that many more souls would come into the Kingdom in response to the eternal Gospel, if it were expressed in familiar terms?

CONCLUSION

Are we advocating that in a country such as Indonesia, the name *Yesus Kristus* completely be replaced by the name *Isa Al Masih?* No, we are not. The term *Yesus Kristus* is as precious to the Christian as the name *Isa Al Masih* potentially is to the Muslim. But as Christians called to be "all things to all men so that by all possible means some might be saved" (1 Corinthians 9:22), we must be the flexible ones. Among the Sundanese, for example, there are at most 10,000 professing Christians out of a population of 32 million Muslims. Therefore for every 3,000 Sundanese, one is a Christian. If a movement to Jesus is going to take place, we need Bibles, booklets, videos and tapes that Muslims will take interest in and pass on to other Muslims. We believe that a film or video called "*Yesus Kristus*" would rarely be shared by Muslims with Muslims. But a film called "*Kisah Nabi Isa Al Masih*" (The Account of the Prophet Isa the Messiah) might be. The existing translations of the New Testament at times touch the Muslim heart. Remembering what is happening in Bangladesh, a new innovative translation, using familiar names, terms and artwork would touch the Muslim heart all the more!

Although there are millions of Christians in Indonesia, the harvest among Muslims is only beginning. As this new work emerges, let us keep an open mind to new approaches. Let us, with fervent prayer, tears, and deep love for our Muslim neighbors, break out of our narrow church world and reach into their world, in ways and terms that will make sense to them. Let us encourage, support and pray for our brothers in Christ who are called by God to approach our Muslim neighbors in new and sensitive ways with the Good News of salvation through *Isa Al Masih*. May the name of God our Lord, his Eternal Word made flesh, and his Holy Spirit be magnified and lifted up among Muslims in Indonesia and everywhere in the world.

Note: *Since the original writing of this article in 1990, a change has taken place in Indonesia. Although* **Yesus Kristus** *is still the most commonly used term for Jesus in Bible translations, from 1994 onward there have been a number of Bibles published using the name* Isa Al Masih.

Thoughts on the Use of *Allah* for the Name of God

by Howie Brant, SIM

1   SIM has not yet taken any official position on the use of the name *Allah* in our translation or church planting ministry. No one should assume that because it is done one way in one country, that this is SIM policy throughout the mission.

2   At SIM's Consultation On Muslim Evangelism we did discuss this issue but could not come to any consensus. It was left in the category of questions which should be decided at the field level.

3   It may be helpful to limit the question to its linguistic component.

   a)   By using *Allah* as the name for God, one is NOT implying that everything said about Allah in the Quran is true or in keeping with Scripture.

We readily acknowledge that the Quran is filled with misconceptions and distortions of many truths, including the concept of God.

b) By the same token, one must recognize that some of the things said about Allah in the Quran are true about the God of the Bible.

c) The fundamental question then, is not whether or not the Quran teaches the truth about Allah/God, but rather, what is the best method for correcting those mistaken notions about him.

d) We are not without biblical precedent in this question. For when Paul dealt with the Athenians (Acts 17) he chose to use the name "Theos" for God even though the Athenians had attached a number of misconceptions to that name.

   In fact, the first part of his message to them was specifically aimed at correcting those very misconceptions.

4   It would be very difficult to carry out the process of "changing the name" for each misconception of the Quran.

a) Should we no longer call Jesus *"Isa"* because there are lies about him in the Quran?

b) Should we no longer call Mary "Mariam" because there are lies about her as well?

c) Is it wrong to talk about paradise as "genet," or do we need to find a different word for "hell" because there are misconceptions about these eternal abodes?

5   The purpose of using the name *Allah* with the Muslim is an attempt to find some common ground as a point of departure for discussion about the true God. If the Muslim believes that Allah is the Eternal Creator, the Sovereign Lord of the universe, and the Judge of all mankind, then those may be starting points for discussion. We must agree that the One to whom we attach those characteristics is, indeed, the One whom we call God!

6   The use of the common word for the Supreme Deity in languages around the world is not new or novel. In animistic sectors, missionaries have most often

used the local name of the Supreme Deity or Creator as the name for the God of the Bible—even though there may have been many misconceptions attached to it.

The problem has come, however, when this name has been used uncritically and without ever examining the theological baggage with which it comes.

7   The danger, then, in using the name *Allah* (or whatever other name God may be called) is in accepting the name without redefining its true meaning. In fact, if one does not give careful attention to this process of redefinition, believers will most certainly have a mistaken concept of God.

8   One could argue that it is not only Muslims or animists who have mistaken concepts of God. A. W. Tozer in his book, *The Knowledge of the Holy,* said, "It is my opinion that the Christian conception of God current in the middle years of the twentieth century is so decadent as to be utterly beneath the dignity of the Most High God and actually constitute, for professed believers, something amounting to a moral calamity" (Tozer 1961:10).

Tozer goes on to call believers back to a true knowledge of that One who is holy. Should we, then, change our name for God, because our understanding of him has been dim and sometimes misinformed?

9   The bottom line here is that even if we change the name for God, we still have not solved the problem of a distorted view of him. We must adopt either one of two methods. Either we correct mistaken concepts about the name *Allah,* or we must teach new concepts about the new name we use for God.

The suggestion that we use the common ground as the beginning point in our discussion about the true God, simply follows the logic of all great teachers in starting with the known and progressing to the unknown.

Ultimately, even if we call Allah/God something else, we do not solve the problem of a mistaken perception of God. As soon as the Muslim learns our new name for God, he will immediately attach all his old concepts of Allah to that God anyway.

Whichever way we go, we still have to reconstruct the Muslim's notion of Deity. Introducing yet another name for him, may simply make that process one step more difficult.

10 SIM policy on this question should not insist that the name *Allah* be used in all Muslim cultures. (The Tuareg team, for example, have found a Tamashek word for God which predates the coming of Islam. They are using that name for God in their shafighna script translations.)

By the same token, we recommend that our evangelists and translators should be free to use the name *Allah* for God where they feel this is the best method of teaching new biblical truth about Deity.

PART SEVEN

Reasons,

Rationale

and

Responses

WHY MUSLIMS
ARE ANGRY?

by Phil Parshall

Well, first off, let it be stated that not all Muslims are angry, and certainly not all are even beginning to approach the threshold of *Jihad* so often attributed to them by Western media critics. Caricatures of the wild-eyed, long-nosed, straggly-bearded Muslim terrorist abound in cartoons placed prominently at the top center of editorial pages. Gullible readers extrapolate the truth of the fringe to embrace the whole of the 1.2 billion Muslim community. That is no more fair than it is to accuse 1.8 billion Christians of being represented by the Bible-quoting, cultic extremist, David Koresh.

But there is truth to the postulate that a lot of Muslims are less than enamored with the actions and attitudes of the Western, so-called "Christian" world. No, they are not ready to hijack a jet or blow up a school bus full of Israeli kids, but as one who has lived among Muslims for many years, I find they have an almost knee-jerk reaction of satisfaction when the West suffers.

To even begin to understand the last remaining great stand-off of our age, we must focus on the nature of the Muslim world view.

Firstly, it is historical. Muhammad, the reputed spokesman of Allah lived in a specific place during an identifiable period of time (570-632 A.D.). Therefore, all current events are to be evaluated as they relate to the historical revelation given by God to Muhammad (the Quran). In addition, the words and deeds of the Prophet (the Traditions or *Hadith*) are to be maximally, even meticulously followed. A historical perspective that focuses on Allah, Muhammad, the Quran, and the Traditions absolutely permeates the worldview of the contemporary Muslim. To compromise this allegiance (or to explore religious alternatives) would be to arrogantly deny the very reality of God.

Secondly, the Muslim worldview is integrative. Politics, economics, social issues, education, and religion are parts of a cohesive whole. Think of a popcorn ball with individual pieces of popcorn held together by a gooey mixture of caramel. The autonomous units of popcorn represent various components of worldview which are held in place, not by caramel, but by the religion of Islam. What gives meaning and direction to a Muslim's total life is to be voluntarily submissive to the rule of Allah in every aspect of his or her life. Contrast this with the average Westerner who individualizes a personal worldview to the extent that we often follow the age-old maxim for relational harmony by avoiding talk of politics and religion. To a Muslim, such a thought borders on a denial of the God who creates and sustains.

Thirdly, the Muslim worldview has a binding sociological effect. "I am, therefore we are; we are, therefore I am" as originally applied to African tribalism helps us to understand the cohesive nature of Islamic society. The word *ummah* (community) is such a meaningful, pregnant concept which leads to personal as well as group fulfillment. How enjoyable it is for the Muslim to think of himself or herself as members of a supportive, universal, Allah-sanctioned community of truth.

With these understandings locked in place, reflect a bit on these historical happenings which have contributed to alienation between the Muslim and the Western world:

- From 1096 to 1300 AD, European Crusaders embarked on a "Christian Jihad," a holy war waged against the Muslim occupiers of Palestine. No matter that the Muslims had been in the land for 450 years. The liberators for Jesus with crosses emblazoned on their breastplates of armor rode in on horses of conquest. They slaughtered, pillaged, burned homes, and in some cases raped young women. This violation was aimed not only at Muslims, but also at the Jews of the land. At all costs, the

Palestine of Jesus' birth and crucifixion must be in the possession of the Christians. The Crusaders miserably failed in their efforts. But the nauseating memory of that terrible, historical moment powerfully lingers on in the Muslim consciousness.

- It has been estimated that 90 percent of the Muslim world was, at one time or another, ruled by Western colonial nations during the period from 1700 to 1960. To the Muslim, not only was this a human rights violation, but it was also a form of religious imperialism. For behind the colonial soldiers came the propagating missionary who no longer had to solicit visa and residence permits from obstructive Muslim rulers. Never mind that significant development projects were completed throughout Islamic lands. The Muslims were convinced the missionaries had only one goal in view, and that was to see their Islamic religion destroyed and replaced by Christianity. Added to this concern was the perceived economic rape of their natural resources by colonial overlords. The era of colonial rule is of recent enough historical vintage to qualify as a potent ongoing force in Muslim distrust of the West.

- Palestine. Volumes could be written (and have been) about this explosive subject. At the close of World War II, Hitler's genocidal nightmare had been played out with up to six million Jews brutally slaughtered. The world gasped in horror. The "New Nation of Israel" became the shrill cry and demand of the surviving Jews. But wait. What about the millions of Muslims who had been residing in Palestine since 650 A.D.? Isn't there some significance connected to a 1300 year sojourn in a land? The world didn't seem to think so. The United Nations voted Israel into existence in 1948.

  Some Muslims thought of another alternative. Germans were the oppressors. So let a new Jewish nation be carved out of Germany. After all, the Muslims were not the violators. Why should they now be penalized because of the Nazis' dastardly deeds? No one listened. Jews (with Christian support) pointed to the Old Testament and said, "The land is ours." Muslims angrily refuted the relevance of a religious book not their own. And so the grinding war of attrition began—and continues.

  Terrorism becomes the weapon of choice. To many Muslims, negotiations are futile and only aimed at winning unfair concessions from their camp. What remains are acts which will grab the attention of a world which is basically passive and just wishes the status quo would be accepted. Throughout the Muslim world the greatest ongoing deterrent to peaceful co-existence between the 1.2 billion Muslims and the West is the Palestinian issue.

- Lastly, a word needs to be said about the cultural clash between the Islamically-influenced Muslim world and the Christian-influenced West. Muslims live under a set of religious legalisms that prescribe personal and corporate behavior. To many, this is liberating. They now know the will of Allah and how to relate to him.

  The Westerner, however, loves choice, liberty, grace, if you will. Legalisms are confining and restrictive. Live the generalized, non-specific golden rule and all will be well, so goes the Westerner's code of life. But, therein lies the seeds of conflict. Muslims look aghast at a culture run amuck with drug and alcohol abuse, pornography, prostitution and a 50 percent divorce rate. I'm not saying Muslims do not have societal problems, but by and large the above mentioned are minimal compared to the West. And what irritates Muslims most is the cultural export of Western "sins" into their midst, thereby corrupting their young people.

Solutions? Certainly there are no easy answers. But an appropriate beginning for Christians is to humanize Muslims and seek to understand their perspectives. Perhaps an attitude of empathy and even humility on our part would be a good start in reducing the tensions that have so often led to Muslim anger.

NEIL A. ARMSTRONG
31 N. BROADWAY
LEBANON, OHIO 45036
TELEPHONE 513-932-6853

July 14, 1983

Mr. Phil Parshall
Director
Asian Research Center
International Christian Fellowship
29524 Bobrich
Livonia, Michigan 48152

Dear Mr. Parshall:

Mr. Armstrong has asked me to reply to your letter and
to thank you for the courtesy of your inquiry.

The reports of his conversion to Islam and of hearing
the voice of Adzan on the moon and elsewhere are all
untrue.

Several publications in Malaysia, Indonesia and other
countries have published these reports without verification. We apologize for any inconvenience that this
incompetent journalism may have caused you.

Subsequently, Mr. Armstrong agreed to participate in a
telephone interview, reiterating his reaction to these
stories. I am enclosing copies of the United States
State Department's communications prior to and after
that interview.

Sincerely,

Vivian White
Administrative Aide

CHAPTER 30

MANUFACTURING *KUFR*

Christian Missionaries in the Muslim World
(A Muslim Critique)

In the Washington Post, February 22nd, the CIA admitted a "controversial loophole" that permits the agency to "employ clerics and missionaries for clandestine work overseas."

During famines, you will find them swarming to our lands under the cloak of 'aid' or 'relief' work. They will bring aid and relief but it isn't given to the Muslims for free—it does have a price.

If you go to a missionary church in a typical African country you'll find that it resembles a mosque more than the arche-typal church. The worshipers stand in rows during prayer and sit on the ground in circles during classes . . . When reciting the Bible they even use a style of recitation exactly the same as the Quranic *Tajweed.* It's all a calculated deception . . .

Perhaps the most insidious method used by the missionaries is to kidnap Muslim children from war-torn countries, and sell them to non-Muslims to raise as disbelievers.

"And from those who call themselves Christians, We took their covenant, but they abandoned a good part of the Message that was sent to them. So We planted amongst them enmity and hatred till the Day of Resurrection (when they discarded Allah's Book, disobeyed Allah's Messengers and His Orders and transgressed beyond bounds in Allah's disobedience), and Allah will inform them of what they used to do." (5:14)

THE 10/40 WINDOW

In evangelical jargon they call it the 10/40 window. The 10/40 window is the rectangle with boundaries of latitudes 10 and 40 degrees north of the equator. To the modern day crusaders of the Christian missions it is exactly what China is to the Coca Cola company—one billion people just dying to hear the message. The 10/40 window takes in the newly independent states of Central Asia, Malaysia, Indonesia, the Middle East, and part of Africa.

This region has become the target of unprecedented efforts by Christian missionaries to convert the Muslims to their religion. Like a cancerous growth, we are seeing Christians gain a foothold in the lands of the believers. The first time, these crusading forces came with swords and suits of armor, this time they arrive with credit cards and million-dollar aid cheques. Employing Faustian machinations, these human *shayateen* are converting many Muslims to their false religion, and serving to inject a virulent poison into the stream of the *Ummah*. The Muslim world is under attack.

Alhamdulillah, Islam has spread all over the world rapidly and with amazing acceptance. As such, the *shirk* and *kufr* of Christianity is under threat. In response, they are 'fighting back' through escalated missionary activity. Christian Aid provides an excellent insight into 'why they do it' in their pamphlet documenting missionary efforts in Nigeria:

"Folake left a successful career in journalism to answer God's call to take the gospel to women in purdah—the practice of keeping Muslim women from being seen by any man other than their husbands. They are practically prisoners in their houses. If they go out, they must be completely covered except for their eyes."

As can be seen from this quote, they are motivated by their desire to mislead our brothers and sisters. They want our sisters to walk around exposing themselves shamelessly in the same manner that *kafir* women do. They want our sisters to leave their homes and wander the streets. They want us to disbelieve in the Revelation, and they want to extinguish the light of truth that is Islam. They are calling us to the worship of *Taghoot*, and thus they are calling us to hellfire.

These missionary groups are present in every corner of the Muslim world. World Vision is perhaps one of the most prolific and probably the organization with which most Australians are familiar, thanks to their sappy media campaign. Many will remember their work during the Somalian famine in which they showed images revealing the Awra of emaciated Muslims, and pleaded with us to give them money. *Alhamdulillah*, the Muslim is kind-hearted and many Muslims donated money to this fund under the illusion it would be used to provide food for the needy. Rest assured that World Vision is not the altruistic humanitarian organization they would have us believe, but rather a *kafir* missionary organization. Their mission is not to alleviate the suffering of those afflicted with hardship, but rather to convert them. In their mission statement, World Vision describe themselves as "an international partnership of Christians whose mission is to follow our Lord and Savior Jesus Christ." World Vision's "Changing Lives" document provides the best insight into their true agenda, and should serve as ample warning to the global Muslim community. "We preach Christ crucified not only through the words we share, but through our deeds . . . (We are) acting as the hand and feet of Jesus . . . In many cases, new churches are emerging where none existed before, and others are being strengthened." In addition to the many millions of dollars tricked out of the public, this organization also receives annually over US$30 million from the US government, United Nations and other multilateral agencies to support their evangelism.

"MUSLIMS: IT'S THEIR TURN"

Almost all of the world's missionary organizations are targeting Muslims. Frontiers, for example, is a major mission group devoted completely to converting believers. They boast that "through creative approaches, patient sowing, and fearless proclamation, more Muslims have come to Christ in the last 25 years than in the previous 1,400 years combined!" The Mesa, Arizona-based group claims to have 500 missionaries in 30 countries, or about 20% of all North American Protestant missionaries serving among Muslims. Frontiers seeks missionaries for the 90's with the motto:

"Muslims. It's their turn. It's all we do. Whatever it takes."

What does it take and what are these "creative approaches"? Murder, sexual assault, kidnapping, and calculated deception are a few. More on this later.

Without a doubt however, the Christians are paying their closest attention to Africa, Indonesia, and Malaysia. Africa in particular is a major target. The Catholic Pope himself has visited Africa on seven separate occasions as part of his announced plan to transform Africa into a Christian continent by the year 2000. Has the plan of our enemies worked? Well, the Council of Muslims in Africa says that in Malawi, for example, the percentage of Muslims has dropped from 66% to 17% in half a century. Similar figures are found in many other African states. In 1900, there were just 9 million Christians in Africa (9% of the population). In 1980, the population had grown to over 200 million! At this current rate of growth, it can be predicted that by the year 2000, there will be 390 million Christians in Africa, or 48% of the population.

METHODOLOGY OF THE MISSIONARY

"O you who believe! Take not as your *Bitanah* (supporters) those outside your religion since they will not fail to do their best to corrupt you. They desire to harm you severely. Hatred has already appeared from their mouths, but what their breasts conceal is far worse. Indeed, we have made plain to you the *ayat* if you understand." (3:118)

The methodology of the Christian missionaries is reflective of the hatred and contempt they hold for Allah and his religion. For instance, when natural disasters or war affects the Muslims, we will find the missionaries salivating at the mouths at the opportunity to convert more believers to their false religion. During famines, you will find them swarming to our lands under the cloak of 'aid' or 'relief' work. They will bring aid and relief but it isn't given to the Muslims for free—it does have a price. The price is to commit apostasy and join the fold of Christianity.

It is also a well-known fact that the missionary organizations work in close conjunction with the CIA in a 'you-scratch-our-back, we'll-scratch-yours' capacity. In the *Washington Post*, February 22nd, the CIA admitted a "controversial loophole" that permits the agency to "employ clerics and missionaries for clandestine work overseas." This said, one can only imagine what evil the two have perpetrated against humanity over the years! It certainly doesn't fit with the image of the Christian as "meek and mild," does it?

By far, the most popular long-term method has been to establish front export businesses in order to gain access to the target country. *Alhamdu-lillah*, many Muslim nations still do not openly allow missionary organizations in. However, often the *Kufar* work around this by starting branch offices of companies overseas or enter as consultants. Cindy Brown, an American *kafir* missionary, speaks with pride of her husband who set up a fake landscaping business in Atlanta, USA: "It's real tough getting into Malaysia because it's such a closed Muslim nation. But the good Lord has been opening doors. We couldn't openly go for a while but then Mike got hired as a consultant with permanent resident status there."

Their photo album shows Mike Bowen landscaping for the Agrigrine Machine & Landscaping Company of Petaling Jaya, Malaysia.

> "The company that hired us is owned by Muslims, but there are some Christians on the Board of Directors who helped us get in. It's kinda funny that a Muslim-owned company has opened the way for us to spread the Gospel in Malaysia. You gotta love the wicked!"

Ahmad Baharrudin of the Malaysian Islamic Study Group, a leading Muslim student organization, says that the problem of apostasy amongst Muslim Malays, especially young sisters, is alarming. "Every year, the Department of Religious Affairs changes many Muslim names to Christian names," says Baharrudin.

THE TOOLS OF THE TRADE

Good old-fashioned Christian deception forms the basis of their evangelism, and the inspiration of their weapons in the war against Islam.

If you go to a missionary church in a typical African country you'll find that it resembles a mosque more than the archetypal church. The worshipers stand in rows during prayer and sit on the ground in circles during classes. The traditional pulpit of the preacher has given way to the minibar. When reciting the Bible they even use a style of recitation exactly the same as the Quranic *Tajweed*. It's all a calculated deception to ensnare the unsuspecting Muslim into thinking that Christianity is 'not so bad' and 'is just like Islam.'

They have developed material specifically targeting Muslims, for instance the widely distributed *Shahadat Al-Qur'an* book. In this and other books, they quote the Quranic verse (An-Nisaa:171) referring to Jesus (AS) as a Prophet, a Word, and a Spirit. They then apply their own satanic *tafseer* and claim that this refers to the trinity! Of course, this is a lie because Allah blew in Adam (AS) and gave His Word to others besides Jesus (AS) such as Muhammad (s.a.w.). In addition, they publish fabricated stories of Muslims who 'discovered the truth' and became Christian. These stories are distributed in pamphlets and also via radio stations, and act to weaken the *Iman* of the Muslim community.

The Christian missionaries are also attempting to draw many Muslims into their trap through redefining Christianity to something more acceptable to the norms of the believers. In Africa especially, they have made some startling concessions to try and confuse and ensnare the ignorant. For instance, they hold their services on Fridays (*Jumu'ah*) and they even allow polygamy. You will also find the missionaries use Islamic expressions such as *"bismillah" "Jesus Alaihi Salam"* and *"Allah Subhanah"* to deceive the Muslims. They might even go so far as to say that Islam is indeed a religion from God, however Christianity was not abrogated!

It should not be surprising that many Muslims who fall into these traps do not even realize it. For instance, the Christian missionaries are taught not to inform the Muslims that they believe Jesus (AS) is the son of Allah. Instead, they might say he is the "spirit of Allah" which is closer to the Islamic understanding.

The "educational aid" provided by these "humanitarian" organizations is a myth. World Vision's "educational aid" consists of, according to their documentation, "Bible studies, Christian literature, Sunday School classes, and spiritual counseling." A course in *Kufr*! Of course, they also give a few classes in conventional subjects such as English (albeit only to such a level that the young Muslim can succumb to the manipulation of Western media), maths, *et al*. However, the overall thrust of this educational experience is not to produce educated individuals, so much as it is to produce obedient Christians.

In its most extreme form, the Christian church has developed institutions within schools and universities to ensnare Muslims. In recent years, Egyptian Muslims have had a problem with some American missionary organizations capturing young Muslim girls, and pressuring them to participate in immoral activities and then photographing them. They then use these photos to black-mail the sisters into taking part in Christian activities such as Sunday school, camps, and so forth. There are now Christian terrorist groups in Egypt that operate with the tacit approval of the state, and the funding of the American and

European missions; these are usually spread in the country areas with large Christian concentrations.

Perhaps the most insidious method used by the missionaries is to kidnap Muslim children from war-torn countries, and sell them to non-Muslims to raise as disbelievers. This problem reached endemic proportions in Bosnia where Christian aid organizations were kidnapping young   Muslim children with alarming frequency. Currently, there is a fight in England where Hassan Keranovic, a Bosnian, has attempted to reclaim his granddaughter, Edita, who was kidnapped. She was then sent to England to be raised to pray to a man who, on the day of judgment, will weep that so many took him as a God. Even though the British court ruled the adoption as invalid, they still ordered the child to stay with her adoptive parents because of the 'trauma' of losing her 'new family.' Usually, these children are under 3-years old so they are not old enough to know anything about their religion (Islam), and thus accept Christianity, and grow up praying to the cross and idols. A similar incident occurred some years ago in Albania where a missionary group bought an orphanage of Muslim children in order to turn them into disbelievers.

CONCLUSION

"If a good befalls you, it grieves them, but if some evil overtakes you, they rejoice at it. But if you remain patient and become Al-Muttaqun not the least harm will their cunning do to you. Surely, Allah surrounds all that they do." (2:120)

The root of the problem is a failure on our part—a failure to implement Islam correctly on a personal and governmental level. An exposition of this problem is really an article in itself, however, I will attempt to address some of these weaknesses succinctly.

Our personal failures to practice Islam have meant that many Muslims have been easily led astray by the *Shaytan*. In Africa and Indonesia, for instance, the belief of the common Muslim is a mesh of Islam and paganism. This lack of understanding of true Islam has meant that the well-read Christian missionary could use his or her superior knowledge of our religion to present 'evidence' from our own sources. This evidence naturally twisted and contorted, however, to the ignorant Muslim it is often highly convincing, and casts serious doubt into their hearts. Evidence has come to surface recently in the form of training manuals for Christian missionaries that detail how to do just this.

As an *Ummah* we have failed many of our brothers and sisters in Islam. The fact that there are many sections of the Muslim community with vast wealth and many sections in abject poverty is an indication of this failure. It sets a scene whereby the Christian missionary can come in, and 'save' the Muslim from poverty and destitution by providing food, money, clothing and so forth. Of course, the price for this is *kufr*, but when your family is starving, then that price begins to look more and more like a bargain. Muslims need to support the development of parallel aid organizations that can work instead of the *kafir* groups bringing aid to our brothers and sisters in need. By doing so we can force the *kafir* "out of the market," and ensure that our brothers and sisters are given Muslim aid and Muslim *da'wah insha'Allah*.

Muslims have been tricked by the emotive pleas for funds issued by World Vision and their ilk. Unknown to most believers who contribute to these groups, they are contributing money to turn their brothers and sisters into apostates. Muslims must be made aware that the Red Cross, World Vision, Salvation Army, Christian Aid, and others are simply evangelist groups. As such it is incumbent on us not to support them, and to work in every way possible to halt the damage they're doing.

On a governmental level there is an incumbent duty for the Islamic State to protect the religion of Islam from attack. The state's foreign policies should prohibit the visitation of missionaries, and severe measures should be taken against those caught calling to *taghoot*. Of course, many governments are working in conjunction with the Christian missionaries, and *kafir* powers. For example, the Egyptian apostate regime of Mubarak was pressured by the Coptic minority to remove Quran and Hadith from the curriculum of the school system. Another state that has been working in cooperation with our enemies is Uzbekistan. In fact the Uzbek government has shamelessly revealed itself as an open enemy of Allah and the truth. It is truly hard to believe that Uzbekistan is the same land that gave birth to both *Imam* Bukhari and Tirmidhi. Straight from the horse's mouth (Christian Aid) we hear:

> "In fact, when radical Muslim missionaries began coming into Uzbekistan in 1991 to foment change and revolution, the government arrested them as subversives. As of January, 71 were still in jail, but there are no Christians in prison for their faith. Uzbek authorities seem interested in maintaining religious tolerance and don't want one group to get dominance of the other."

In terms of deterrent, the biggest deterrent is to come down hard on these *kufar*. Just like drug dealers pushing drugs in our neighborhoods, the missionaries are pushing *kufr*. Weigh the effects of drugs against the effects of apostasy and one finds that whilst the effects of drugs are limited to Dunia, the effects of apostasy will carry a person all the way to Hellfire.

IS THE BIBLE
GOD'S WORD?

*by Ahmed Deedat**

WHAT THEY SAY

Christians Confess

Dr. W. Graham Scroggie of the Moody Bible Institute, Chicago, one of the most prestigious Christian evangelical missions in the world, answering the question— "Is the Bible the Word of God?" (also the title of his book), under the heading: It is Human, yet Divine. . . . says on page 17:

> "Yes, the Bible is human, though some, out of a zeal which is not according to knowledge, have denied this. Those books have passed through the **minds of men**, are written in the **language of men**, were penned by the **hands of men**, and bear in their style the **characteristics of men**." (Highlighting is mine).

---

* The author is a leading apologist for Islam and antagonist against Christians.

Another erudite Christian scholar, Kenneth Cragg, the Anglican Bishop of Jerusalem, says on page 277 of his book, *The Call of the Minaret*:

> "Not so the New Testament . . . There is condensation and editing; there is choice, reproduction and witness. The Gospels have come through the mind of the Church behind the authors. They represent experience and history."

If words have any meaning, do we need to add another word of comment to prove our case? No! But the professional propagandists, after letting the cat out of the bag, still have the face to try to make their readers believe that they have proved beyond the shadow of any doubt that the Bible is the "irrefutable Word of God." Their semantic gymnastics—equivocating, and playing with words—is amazing!

Both these Doctors of Religion are telling us in the clearest language humanly possible that the Bible is the handiwork of man, all the while pretending that they are proving to the contrary. An old Arab saying goes:

"IF SUCH ARE THE PRIESTS, GOD BLESS THE CONGREGATION."

With this sort of drivel, the hot-gospeller and the Bible-thumper is "inspired" to harry the "heathen." A theological student—a not-yet-qualified young evangelist—from the University of Witwatersrand, became a frequent visitor to the Newtown Mosque in Johannesburg, with the "noble" thought of "witnessing" to the members of its congregation. When I was introduced to him, (and having learned his purpose), I invited him to lunch at my brother's residence—a stone's-throw from the Mosque. While discussing the authenticity of the Bible over the dinner table and sensing his stubborn dogmatism, I put out a feeler: "Your Professor Geyser, (The Head of the Department of Theology) does not believe the Bible to be the Word of God." Without the slightest surprise he answered, "I know." Now I personally had no knowledge of the Professor's conviction about the Bible. I had only assumed so from a controversy which raged around him about the "Divinity of Christ." He had taken issue with the orthodox believers on this point some years ago. I continued further, saying, "Your lecturer does not believe the Bible as being "God's Word." The young evangelist, responded again, "I know," but he continued this time with the words, "but I believe that it is the Word of God!" There is no real remedy for such people. Even Jesus bewailed this sickness:

". . . seeing they see not; and hearing they hear not, neither do they understand."

Matthew 13:13

Al-Quran, the Holy book of God, also condemns this mulish mentality:

"Deaf, dumb and blind, they will not return (to the path)."

(Holy Quran 2:18)

These pages are now addressed to those sincerely humble souls, who are genuinely interested in seeking the Light of God, and who wish to be guided by it. As for the other, with a sickness in their souls, the facts presented herein can only increase the disease of their hearts.

THE MUSLIMS STANDPOINT

Presumptuous Christians

Whether Catholic, Protestant or a "cultist," of the thousand-and-one-sects-and-denominations-of-Christianity, never will you find a missionary who will not, *prima facie*, presuppose that his potential convert accepts his "Holy Bible" as the book of final authority on every religious opinion. The only answer the prospective proselyte has is to quote verses from the Bible which are contradictory to the missionary's or debate their interpretations.

The Dogged Question

When the Muslim proves his point from the Christian's own Holy Scripture, and when the professional priest, parson or predikant cannot refute the arguments—the inevitable Christian evasion is—"Do you accept the Bible as God's Word?" On the face of it, the question seems to be an easy one, but a simple "Yes" or "No" cannot be given as an answer. You see, one has first to explain one's position. But the Christian will not give one the opportunity. He gets impatient, "Answer— 'Yes or No!'" he insists. The Jews did the same to Jesus two thousand years ago, except that surprisingly he was not straitjacketed, as is the fashion today!

The reader will readily agree that things are not always either BLACK or WHITE. Between these two extremes there are various shades of GREY. If you say "Yes" to his question, then it would mean that you are prepared to swallow everything HOOK, LINE and SINKER, from Genesis to Revelation from his Bible. If you respond with a "No," he quickly unhooks himself from the facts you have presented, and rallies support from his co-religionists in the audience with: "You see, this man does not believe in the Bible! What right has he to expound his case from our Book?" With this hydra-like somersault he rests content that he has safely evaded the issue. What is the Muballigh to do? He has to explain his position vis-à-vis the Bible, as he ought to do.

Three Grades of Evidence

We Muslims have no hesitation in acknowledging that in the Bible, there are three different kinds of witnessing recognizable without any need of specialized training. These are:

1   You will be able to recognize in the Bible what may be described as "**The Word of God**."

2   You will also be able to discern what can be described as the "**Word of a Prophet of God**."

3   And you will most readily observe that the bulk of the Bible are the records of eyewitnesses or ear witnesses, or people writing from hearsay. As such they are the "**words of a historian**."

You do not have to hunt for examples of these different types of evidences in the Bible. The following quotations will make the position crystal clear:
The FIRST type:

> "I will raise them up a prophet . . . and I will put my words in . . . and he shall speak unto them all that I shall command him."
>
> Deuteronomy 18:18

> "I, even I, am the Lord, and besides **me** there is no saviour."
>
> Isaiah 43:11

"Look unto **me**, and be ye saved, all the ends of the earth: for **I** am God, and there is none else."

Isaiah 45:22

Note the first person pronoun singular (in bold typeface) in the above references, and without any difficulty you will agree that the statements seem to have the sound of being GOD'S WORD.

The SECOND type:

"**Jesus cried** with a loud voice, saying 'Eloi, Eloi, lama sabachtani? . . .'"

Matthew 27:46

"And **Jesus answered** him, 'The first of all the commandments is, Hear, O Israel; the Lord our God is one Lord.'"

Mark 12:29

"And **Jesus said** unto him, 'Why callest thou me good? There is none good but one, that is God.'"

Mark 10:18

Even a child will be able to affirm that: Jesus "**cried**," Jesus "**answered**," and Jesus "**said**," are the words of the one to whom they are attributed, *i.e.*, the WORDS OF A PROPHET OF GOD.

The THIRD type:

"And seeing a fig tree afar off having leaves, **he**, (Jesus) came, if haply **he** (Jesus) might find anything thereon: and when **he** (Jesus) came to it, **he** (Jesus) found nothing but leaves . . ."

Mark 11:13

The bulk of the Bible is a witnessing of this THIRD kind. These are the words of a **third** person. Note the (bold faced) pronouns. They are not the Words of God or of His prophet, but the WORDS OF A HISTORIAN.

For the Muslim it is quite easy to distinguish the above types of evidence, because he also has them in his own faith. But of the followers of the different religions, he is the most fortunate in this that his various records are contained in **separate** Books!

ONE: The first kind—THE WORD OF GOD—is found in a
                Book called **The Holy Quran**.

TWO: The second kind—THE WORDS OF THE PROPHET OF GOD,
                (Muhammad, may the peace and blessings of Allah be
                upon him) are recorded in the Books of Tradition called
                The Hadith.

THREE: Evidence of the third kind abounds in different volumes
                of Islamic history, written by some of high integrity and
                learning, and others of lesser trust-worthiness, but the
                Muslim advisedly keeps his Books in separate volumes!

The Muslim keeps the above three types of evidence jealously apart, in their
proper gradations of authority. He never equates them. On the other hand, the
"Holy Bible" contains a motley type of literature which composes the embarrassing kind, the sordid, and the obscene—all under the same cover—A Christian is forced to concede equal spiritual import and authority to all, and is thus
unfortunate in this regard.

THE MULTIPLE BIBLE VERSIONS

It will now be easy for us to analyze a Christian's claim about his Holy Book.

Separating the Wheat from the Chaff

Before we scrutinize the various versions, let us clarify our own belief regarding
the Books of God. When we say that we believe in the **Tauraat**, the **Zaboor**, the
Injeel and the **Quran**, what do we really mean? We already know that the Holy
Quran is the infallible Word of God, revealed to our Holy Prophet Hazrat Muhammad Mustapha (Peace be upon him) word for word, through the agency of the
Archangel Jibraeel, (known as Gabriel in English), and perfectly preserved and
protected from human tampering for the past fourteen hundred years! Even hostile
critics of Islam have grudgingly vouched for the purity of the Holy Quran:

> "There is probably in the world no other book which has remained
> twelve centuries (now fourteen) with so pure a text."
>
> Sir William Muir

The **Tauraat** we Muslims believe in is not the "Torah" of the Jews and the Christians, though the words—one Arabic, the other Hebrew—are the same. We believe that whatever the Holy Prophet Moses (Peace be upon him) preached to his people, was the revelation from God Almighty, but that Moses was not the author of those "books" attributed to him by the Jews and the Christians.

Likewise, we believe that the **Zaboor** was the revelation of God granted to Hazrat Dawood (David) (Peace be upon him), but that the present Psalms associated with his name are not that revelation. The Christians themselves do **not** insist that David is the sole author of "his" Psalms.

What about the **Injeel?** INJEEL means the "Gospel" or "good news" which Jesus Christ preached during his short ministry. The "Gospel" writers often mention that Jesus went about preaching the Gospel (the **Injeel**):

> "And Jesus went . . . preaching the **gospel** . . . and healing every disease among the people."
>
> Matthew 9:35

> ". . . but whoever shall lose his life for my sake and the **gospel's** the same shall save it."
>
> Mark 8:35

> ". . . preached the **gospel** . . ."
>
> Luke 20:1

The "gospel" is a frequently-used word, but what Gospel did Jesus preach? Of the 27 books of the New Testament, only a small fraction can be accepted as the words of Jesus. The Christians boast about the Gospels according to St. Matthew, according to St. Mark, according to St. Luke and according to St. John, but there is not a single Gospel **"according"** to (St.) Jesus himself! We **sincerely** believe that everything Christ (May the peace and blessings of God be upon him) preached was from God. That was the **Injeel**, the good news and the guidance of God for the Children of Israel. In his lifetime Jesus never wrote a single word, nor did he instruct anyone to do so. What passes off as the "gospels" today are the works of anonymous hands!

The question before us is: **"Do you accept that the Bible is God's Word?"** The question is really in the form of a challenge. The questioner is not simply seeking enlightenment. The question is posed in the spirit of a debate. We have every right to demand in a similar vein—"Which Bible are you talking about?" we may ask. "Why, there is only ONE Bible!" he mutters.

The Catholic Bible

Holding the "**Douay**" Roman Catholic Version of the Bible aloft in my hand, I ask, "Do YOU accept THIS Bible as the Word of God?" For reasons best known to themselves, the Catholic Truth Society have published their Version of the Bible in a very short, stumpy form. This Version is a very odd proportion of the numerous Versions in the market today. The Christian questioner is taken aback. "What Bible is that?" he asks. "Why, I thought you said that there was only ONE Bible." I remind him. "Y-e-s," he murmurs hesitantly, "but what Version is that?" "Why, would that make any difference?" I inquire. Of course it does, and the professional preacher knows that it does. He is only bluffing with his "ONE Bible" claim.

The Roman Catholic Bible was published at Rheims in 1582, from Jerome's Latin Vulgate and reproduced at Douay in 1609. As such the RCV (Roman Catholic version) is the oldest Version that one can still buy today. Despite its antiquity, the whole of the Protestant world, including the "cults" condemn the RCV because it contains seven extra "books" which they contemptuously refer to as the "**apocrypha**," i.e. of DOUBTFUL AUTHORITY. Notwithstanding the dire warning contained in the Apocalypse, which is the last book in the RCV (renamed as "**Revelation**" by the Protestants), it is "revealed":

> "... If any man shall add to these things (or delete) God shall add unto him the plagues written in this Book."
>
> Revelation 22:18-19

But who cares! They do not really believe! The Protestants have bravely **expunged seven whole books** from their Book of God! The outcasts are:

The Book of Judith
The Book of Tobias
The Book of Baruch
The Book of Esther, etc.

The Protestant Bible

Sir Winston Churchill has some pertinent things to say about the *Authorized Version* (AV) of the Protestant Bible, which is also widely known as the "*King James Version*" (KJV).

> "The authorized version of the Bible was published in 1611 by the will and command of His Majesty King James the 1st whose name it bears till today."

The Roman Catholics, believing as they do that the Protestants have mutilated the Book of God, are yet aiding and abetting the Protestant "crime" by forcing their native converts to purchase the Authorized Version (AV) of the Bible, which is the only Bible available in some 1500 languages of the lesser developed nations of the world. The Roman Catholics milk their cows, but the feeding is left to the Protestants! The overwhelming majority of Christians—both Catholics and Protestant—use the *Authorized* (AV) or the *King James Version* (KJV) as it is alternatively called.

Glowing Tributes

First published, as Sir Winston says, in 1611, and then revised in 1881 (RV), and now re-revised and brought up to date as the *Revised Standard Version* (RSV) 1952, and now again re-re-revised in 1971 (still RSV for short). Let us see what opinion Christendom has of this most revised Bible, the RSV:

> "The finest version which has been produced in the present century."
> *Church of England* Newspaper

> "A completely fresh translation by scholars of the highest eminence."
> *Times Literary Supplement*

> "The well-loved characteristics of the Authorized Version combined with a new accuracy of translation."
> *Life and Work*

> "The most accurate and close rendering of the original."
> *The Times*

The publishers (Collins) themselves, in their notes on the Bible at the end of their production, say on page 10:

> "This Bible (RSV), is the product of **thirty-two scholars**, assisted by an advisory committee representing fifty co-operating denominations."

Why all this boasting? To make the gullible public buy their product? All these testimonies convince the purchaser that he is backing the right horse, with the purchaser little suspecting that he is being taken for a ride.

"The World's Best Seller"

But what about the *Authorized Version* of the Bible (AV), the "World's Best Seller"? These revisers, all good salesmen, have some very pretty things to say about it. However, their page iii, paragraph six of the Preface of the RSV reads:

> "The *King James Version* (alternative description of AV) has with good reason been termed **'the noblest monument of English prose.'** Its revisers in 1881 expressed admiration for **'its simplicity, its dignity, its power, its happy turns of expression . . . the music of its cadences, and the felicities of its rhythm.'** It entered, as no other book has, into the making of the personal character and the public institutions of the English-speaking peoples. We owe to it an incalculable debt."

Can you, dear reader, imagine a more magnificent tribute being paid to the "Book of Books" than the above? I, for one, cannot. Let the believing Christian, now steel himself for the unkindest blow of all from his own beloved Lawyers of Religion; for in the very same breath they say:

> "Yet the King James Version has **grave defects**. And that these defects are **so many and so serious** as to call for revision . . ."

This is straight from the horse's mouth, *i.e.* the orthodox Christian scholars of "**the highest eminence.**" Another galaxy of Doctors of Divinity are now required to produce an encyclopedia explaining the cause of those GRAVE AND SERIOUS DEFECTS in their Holy Writ and their reasons for eliminating them.

FIFTY THOUSAND ERRORS (?)

The Jehovah's Witnesses in their *Awake!* Magazine, dated 8 September 1957, carried this startling heading—"50,000 Errors in the Bible?"

While I was still formulating the theme of this booklet, I heard a knock at my door one Sunday morning. I opened the door. A European gentleman stood there, grinning broadly. "Good morning!" he said. "Good morning," I replied.

He was offering me his *Awake* and *Watchtower* magazines. Yes, a Jehovah's Witness! If a few had knocked at your door previously, you will recognize them immediately. The most supercilious lot of people who ever knocked at people's doors! I invited him in.

As soon as he settled down, I produced the full reproduction. Pointing to the monograph at the top of the page, I asked, "Is this yours?" He readily recognized his own. I said, "It says: 50,000 Errors in the Bible, is it true?" "What's that!" he exclaimed. I repeated, "I said, that it says that there are 50,000 errors in your Bible." "Where did you get that?" He asked. (This was published 23 years ago, when he was perhaps a little nipper.) I said, "Leave the fancy talk aside—is this yours?" pointing again to the monograph—*Awake!* He said, "Can I have a look?" "Of course," I said. I handed him the page. He started perusing. They (the Jehovah's Witnesses) are trained. They attend classes, five times a week in their "Kingdom Halls." Naturally, they are the fittest missionaries among the thousand-and-one-sects-and-denominations of Christendom. They are taught that when cornered, do not commit yourself to anything, do not open your mouth. Wait for the Holy Ghost to inspire you with what to say.

I silently kept watching him, while he browsed the page. Suddenly he looked up. He had found it. The "Holy Ghost" had tickled him. He began, "The article says that '*most of those errors have been eliminated.*'" I asked, "If **most** are eliminated, how many remain out of 50,000? 5,000? 500? 50? Even if 50 remain, do you attribute those errors to God?" He was speechless. He excused himself by suggesting that he will come again with some senior member of his church. That will be the day!

If I had this booklet ready, I would have offered him, saying—"I would like to do you a favour, give me your name and address, and your tele-phone number. I will loan you this booklet—*Is the Bible God's Word?* for 90 days. I want a written reply!" If you do this, and a few other Muslims do the same, they and the other missionaries will never darken your doors again. I believe that this publication will prove the most effective talisman to date. *Insha-Allah!*

This "cult" of Jehovah's Witnesses which is so strong in its condemnation of the orthodox Trinitarians, for playing with the "Word of God," is itself playing the same game of semantic gymnastics. In the article under review—"50,000 Errors in the Bible?" they say:

> "There are probably 50,000 errors . . . errors that have **crept** into the Bible text . . . 50,000 **such serious** (?) errors . . . most of those **so-called** errors . . . *as a whole* the Bible is accurate." (!)

We do not have the time and space to go into the tens of thousands of—grave or minor—defects that the authors of the *Revised Standard Version* (RSV) have attempted to revise. We leave that privilege to the Christian scholars of the Bible. Here I will endeavour to cast just a cursory glance at a "half-a-dozen" or so of those "minor" changes.

> "Therefore the Lord himself shall give you a sign: Behold, a virgin shall conceive, and bear a son, and shall call his name Immanuel."
>
> Isaiah 7:14, *AV*

The indispensable "VIRGIN" in the above verse has now been replaced in the RSV with the phrase "a young woman," which is the correct translation of the Hebrew word ALMÁH. *Almáh* is the word which has occurred all along in the Hebrew text, and not BETHULAH which means "VIRGIN." This correction is only to be found in the English language translation, as the RSV is only published in this tongue. For the African and the Afrikaner, the Arab and the Zulu, in fact, in the 1500 other languages of the world, Christians are made to continue to swallow the misnomer "VIRGIN."

Begotten, Not Made

"Jesus is the only begotten son of God, BEGOTTEN not MADE," is an adjunct of the orthodox catechism, leaning for support on the following:

> "For God so loved the world, that he gave his only **begotten** son, that whosoever believeth in him should not perish, but have everlasting life."
>
> John 3:16, *AV*

No priest worth his cloth would fail to quote "the only BEGOTTEN of the Father!" when preaching to a prospective convert. But this fabrication—"BEGOTTEN"—has now been unceremoniously excised by the Bible Revisers, without a word of excuse. They are as silent as church mice and would not draw the reader's attention to their furtive excision. This blasphemous word "begotten" was another of the many such interpolations in the "Holy Bible." God Almighty condemned this blasphemy in the strongest terms soon after its innovation. He did not wait for 2000 years for Bible scholars to reveal the fraud.

400

"And they say: '(God) Most Gracious has begotten a son!' Indeed ye have put forth a thing most monstrous! At it the skies are ready to burst, and the earth to split asunder, and the mountains to fall down in utter ruin, that they should invoke a son for (God) Most Gracious. For it is not consonant with the Majesty of (God) Most Gracious that He should beget a son."

Holy Quran 19:88-92

The Muslim World should congratulate the "Fifty cooperating denominations" of Christendom and their Brains Trust, the "Thirty-two scholars of the highest eminence" for bringing their Holy Bible a degree nearer to the quranic truth.

"He (God Almight) begets not nor is he begotten."

Holy Quran 112:3

"Christian Mes-a-mathics"

"For there are three that bear record in heaven, the Father, the Word, and the Holy Ghost: and these three are one."

1st Epistle of John 5:7, AV

This verse is the closest approximation to what the Christians call their Holy Trinity in the encyclopedia called the *Bible*. This keystone of the Christian faith has also been scrapped from the RSV without even a semblance of explanation. It has been a pious fraud all along and well-deservedly has it been expunged in the RSV for the English-speaking people. But for the 1499 remaining language groups of the world who read the Christian concoctions in their mother tongues, the fraud remains. These people will never know the truth until the Day of Judgment. However, we Muslims must again congratulate the galaxy of D.D.'s who have been honest enough to eliminate another lie from the English (RSV) Bible, thus bringing their Holy Book yet another step closer to the teachings of Islam. For the Holy Quran says:

"... And don't say 'trinity':
Desist: it will be better for you:
For Allah is one God: ..."

Holy Quran 4:171

The Ascension

One of the most serious of those "grave defects" which the authors of the RSV had tried to rectify concerned the Ascension of Christ. There have been only two references in the Canonical Gospels of Matthew, Mark, Luke and of John to the most stupendous event in Christianity—OF JESUS BEING TAKEN UP INTO HEAVEN. These two references were obtained in every Bible in every language, prior to 1952, when the RSV first appeared. These were.

> "So then the Lord Jesus, after he had spoken to them, was **taken up into heaven**, and sat down at the right hand of God."
>
> Mark 16:19

> "While he blessed them, he parted from them, and was **carried up into heaven**."
>
> Luke 24:51

You will be shocked to note that Mark 16 ends at verse 8, and after an embarrassing expanse of blank space the missing verses appear in "small print" as a footnote at the bottom of the page. If you can lay your hands on a RSV 1952, you will find the last six words of 4b above, i.e., "AND WAS CARRIED UP INTO HEAVEN" replaced by a tiny "a" to tell you to see the footnote if you please, where you will find these missing words. Every honest Christian has to admit that he does not consider any footnote in any Bible as the Word of God. Why should the paid servants of Christianity consign the mightiest miracle of their religion to a mere footnote?

The Donkey Circus

The above facts are a staggering confession by Christendom that the "inspired" authors of the Canonical Gospels did not record a single word about the ASCEN-SION of Jesus. Yet these "inspired" authors were unanimous in recording that their Lord and Savior rode a donkey into Jerusalem as his mission drew to a close.

> ". . and they sat him thereon." (The donkey)
>
> Matthew 21:7

". . . and they set Jesus thereon" (The donkey)

Luke 19:35

". . . and he sat upon him." (The donkey)

Mark 11:7

". . . Jesus . . . sat thereon." (The donkey)

John 12:14

Could God Almighty have been the author of this incongruous situation—going out of His Way to see that all the Gospel writers did not miss their footing recording His "son's" donkey ride into the Holy City—and yet "inspiring" them to blackout the news about His "son's" heavenly flight on the wings of angels?

Not for long!

The hot-gospellers and the Bible-thumpers were too slow in catching the joke. By the time they realized that the cornerstone of their preaching—THE ASCENSION OF JESUS—had been undermined as a result of Christian biblical erudition, the publishers of the RSV had already raked in a net profit of 15,000,000 dollars! (fifteen million). The propagandists made a big hue and cry, and with the backing of two denominational committees out of the fifty, forced the publishers to reincorporate the interpolations into the "INSPIRED" Word of God. In every new publication of the RSV after 1952, the expunged portion was "RESTORED TO THE TEXT."

It is an old, old game. The Jews and the Christians have been editing their "Book of God" from its very inception. The difference between them and the ancient forgers is that the ancient forgers did not know the art of writing "prefaces" and "footnotes," otherwise they too would have told us as clearly as our modern heroes have about their tampering, and their glib excuses for transmuting forged currency into glittering gold.

> "Many proposals for modification were submitted to the committee by individuals and by two denominational committees. All of these were given careful attention by the committee.
>
> "Two passages, the longer ending of Mark (16:9-20) . . . and Luke 24:51 are restored to the text."
>
> Preface — Collins' page vi and vii

"Why 'restored'?" Because they had been previously expunged! Why had the references to the Ascension been expunged in the first place? The **most** ancient manuscripts had no references to the Ascension at all. They were interpolations similar to 1 John 5:7 about the Trinity. Why eliminate one and re-instate the other? Do not be surprised! By the time you lay your hands on a RSV, the "Committee" might also have decided to expunge the whole of their invaluable Preface. The Jehovah's Witnesses have already eliminated 27 revealing pages of their Foreword to their *New World Translation of the Christian Greek Scriptures*, (this is their way of saying—New Testament).

The Rev. C. I. Scofield, D.D. with a team of eight consulting editors, also all D.D.'s, in the *Scofield Reference Bible*, thought it appropriate to spell the Hebrew word "**Elah**" (meaning **God**) alternatively as "Alah." The Christians had thus swallowed the camel—they seemed to have accepted at last that the name of God is Allah—but were still straining at the gnat by spelling Allah with one "L"! References were made in public lectures to this fact by the author of this booklet. Believe me, the subsequent *Scofield Reference Bible* has retained word for word the whole commentary of Genesis 1:1, but has, by a clever sleight-of-hand, blotted out the word "Alah" altogether. There is not even a gap where the word "Alah" once used to be. This is in the Bible of the orthodox! One is hard pressed to keep up with their jugglery.

DAMNING CONFESSIONS

Mrs. Ellen G. White, a "prophetess" of the Seventh Day Adventist Church, in her *Bible Commentary Vol. 1*, page 14, has this confession to make about the fallibility of the "Holy Bible."

> "The Bible we read today is the work of many copyists who have in most instances done their work with marvellous accuracy. But copyists have **not been infallible**, and God most evidently has **not seen fit** to preserve them altogether from error in transcribing."

In the following pages of her commentary, Mrs. White testifies further:

> "I saw that God had especially guarded the Bible," (from what?) "yet when copies of it were few, learned men had in some instances

changed the words, thinking that they were making it plain, when in reality they were **mystifying** that which was plain, by causing it to lean to their **established views,** which were governed by tradition."

Developed Sickness

The mental malady is a cultivated one. This authoress and her followers can still trumpet from rooftops that "Truly, the Bible is the infallible Word of God." "Yes, it is adulterated, but pure." "It is human, yet divine." Do words have any meaning in their language? Yes, they have in their courts of law, but not in their theology. They carry a "poetic licence" in their preaching

"In their hearts is a disease; and Allah has increased their disease: And grievous is the penalty they (incur), because they are false (to themselves)."

Holy Quran 2:10

The Witnesses

The most vociferous of all the Bible-thumpers are the Jehovah's Witnesses. On page 5 of their Foreword, mentioned earlier, they confess:

"In copying the inspired originals by hand the element of human frailty entered in, and so none of the thousands of copies extant today in the original language are perfect duplicates. The result is that no two copies are exactly alike."

Now you see, why the whole "Foreword" of 27 pages is eliminated from their Bibles. Allah was making them to hang themselves with their own erudition.

Potluck

Out of over four thousand differing manuscripts the Christians boast about, the Church fathers just selected four which tallied with their prejudices and called them Gospels of Matthew, Mark, Luke, and John. We will deal with each of them in their proper place. Here, let us go over the conclusion of the Jehovah's Witnesses' research as recorded in the now expunged Foreword:

> "The evidence is, therefore, that the original text of the Christian Greek
> Scriptures has been tampered with, the same as the text of the LXX
> has been."

Yet this incorrigible cult has the effrontery to publish 9,000,000 (nine million) copies as a First Edition of a 192-page book entitled *Is the Bible REALLY the Word of God?* We are dealing here with a sick mentality, for no amount of tampering, as they say, will "appreciably affect the authenticity of the Bible" (?). This is Christian logic.

A Patient Hearing

Dr. Graham Scroggie in his aforementioned book, pleads on page 29 for the Bible:

> "And let us be perfectly fair as we pursue the subject, (*Is the Bible the
> Word of God?*). Bearing in mind that we are to hear what the Bible
> has to say about itself. In a court of law we assume that a witness will
> speak the truth, and must accept what he says unless we have good
> grounds for suspecting him, or can prove him a liar. Surely the Bible
> should be given the same opportunity to be heard, and should receive
> a like patient hearing."

The plea is fair and reasonable. We will do exactly as he asks and let the Bible speak for itself.

In the first five books of the Bible—Genesis, Exodus, Leviticus, Numbers and Deuteronomy—there are more than 700 statements which prove not only that God is NOT the Author of these books, but that EVEN Moses himself had no hand in them. Open these books at random and you will see:

> "And the **Lord said unto him**, 'Away, get thee down . . .'"

> "And **Moses said unto the Lord**, 'The people cannot come . . .'"

> "And the **Lord said unto Moses**, 'Go on before the people . . .'"

> "And the **Lord spoke unto Moses**, saying . . ."

> "And the **Lord said unto Moses**, 'Get down, charge the . . .'"

It is manifest and apparent that these are neither the Words of God nor of Moses. They indicate the voice of a third person writing from hearsay.

Moses Writes his Own Obituary?

Could Moses have been a contributor to his own obituary before his demise? Did the Jews write their own obituaries?

> "So Moses . . . **died** . . . And he (God Almighty) **buried Him** (Moses) . . . he was 120 years old when he **died** . . . And there arose not a prophet **since** in Israel like unto Moses . . ."
>
> Deuteronomy 34:5-10

We will analyze the rest of the Old Testament presently from other angles.

THE BOOK CHRISTENED, "THE NEW TESTAMENT"

Why "according to"?

What about the so-called New Testament? Why does every Gospel begin with the introduction—ACCORDING TO . . . ACCORDING TO . . . Why "according to"? Because not a single one of the vaunted four thousand copies extant carries its author's autograph! Hence the supposition "according to"! Even the internal evidence proves that Matthew was not the author of the first Gospel which bears his name.

> "And as Jesus passed forth thence, **he** (Jesus) saw a man, named Matthew, sitting at the receipt of custom: and **he** (Jesus) saith unto **him** (Matthew), follow **me** (Jesus) and **he** (Matthew) arose, and followed **him** (Jesus)."
>
> Matthew 9:9

Without any stretch of the imagination, one can see that the "He's" and the "Him's" of the above narration do not refer to Jesus or Matthew as its author, but some third person writing what he saw and heard—a hearsay account. If we cannot even attribute this "book of dreams" (as the first Gospel is also described) to the disciple Matthew, how can we accept it as the Word of God? We are not alone in this discovery that Matthew did not write the "Gospel according to St. Matthew," and that it was written by some anonymous hand. J.B. Phillips concurs with us in our findings. He is the paid servant of the Anglican church, a prebendary of the Chichester Cathedral, England. He would have no reason to lie or betray to the detriment of the official view of his Church! Refer to his introduction to the "Gospel of St. Matthew." Phillips has this to say about its authorship.

> "Early tradition ascribed this gospel to the apostle Matthew, but scholars nowadays **almost all reject this view**."

In other words, St. Matthew did not write the Gospel which bears his name. This is the finding of **Christian scholars** of the highest eminence—not of Hindus, Muslims, and Jews who may be accused of bias. Let our Anglican friend continue:

> "The author, whom we still can conveniently call Matthew."

"**Conveniently**," because otherwise everytime we made a reference to "Matthew," we would have to say—"THE FIRST BOOK OF THE NEW TESTAMENT" chapter so and so, verse so and so. And again and again "The first book . . ." etc. Therefore, according to J.B. Phillips it is **convenient** that we give the book some name. So why not "Matthew"? I suppose it's as good a name as any other! Phillips continues:

> "The author has plainly drawn on the mysterious 'Q' which may have been a collection of oral traditions."

What is this "mysterious 'Q'"? "Q" is short for the German word "*quella*," which means "**sources**." There is supposed to be another document—a common source—to which our present Matthew, Mark, and Luke had access. All these three authors, whoever they were, had a common eye on the material at hand. They were writing as if looking through "one" eye. And because they saw eye to eye, the first three "Gospels" came to be known as the Synoptic Gospels.

Wholesale Cribbing

But what about that "**inspiration**" business? The Anglican prebendary has hit the nail on the head. He is, more than anyone else, entitled to do so. A paid servant of the church, an orthodox evangelical Christian, a Bible scholar of repute, having direct access to the "original" Greek manuscripts, let HIM spell it out for us. (Notice how gently he lets the cat out of the bag): "He (Matthew) has used Mark's gospel freely" which in the language of the schoolteacher—"has been copying wholesale from Mark!" Yet the Christians call this wholesale plagiarism the Word of God?

Does it not make you wonder that an eyewitness and an ear-witness to the ministry of Jesus, which the disciple Matthew was supposed to be, instead of writing his own firsthand impressions of the ministry of "his Lord," would go and steal from the writings of a youth (Mark), who was a 10-year-old lad when Jesus upbraided his nation? Why would an eyewitness and ear-witness copy from a fellow who himself was writing from hearsay? The disciple Matthew would not do any such silly thing. For an anonymous document has been imposed on the fair name of Matthew.

Plagiarism or Literary Kidnapping

Plagiarism means literary theft. Someone who copies *ad verbatim* (word for word) from another's writing and palms it off as his own, is known as a plagiarist. This is a common trait amongst the 40 or so anonymous authors of the books of the Bible. The Christians boast about a supposedly common cord amongst the writers of the 66 Protestant booklets and the writers of the 73 Roman Catholic booklets called the "Holy Bible." Some common cord there is, for Matthew and Luke, or whoever they were, had plagiarized 85% word for word from Mark! God Almighty did not dictate the same wordings to the synoptists (one-eyed). The Christians themselves admit this, because they do not believe in a verbal inspiration, as the Muslims do about the Holy Quran.

This 85% plagiarism of Matthew and Luke pales into insignificance compared to the literary kidnapping of the authors of the Old Testament where a hundred percent stealing occurs in the so-called Book of God. Christian scholars of the calibre of Bishop Kenneth Cragg euphemistically calls this stealing, "reproduction," and takes pride in it.

Perverted Standards

Dr. Scroggie (referred to earlier on) most enthusiastically quotes in his book a Dr. Joseph Parker for his unique eulogy of the Bible:

> "What a book is the Bible in the matter of variety of contents! . . . Whole pages are taken up with obscure names, and more is told of a genealogy than of the day of judgment. Stories are half-told, and the night falls before we can tell where victory lay. Where is there anything (in the Religious Literature of the world) to correspond with this?"

A beautiful necklace of words and phrases undoubtedly! It is much ado about nothing, and rank blasphemy against God Almighty for authorizing such an embarrassing hotch potch. Yet the Christians gloat over the very defects of their book, like Romeo over the "mole" on Juliet's lip!

Nothing less than 100%

To demonstrate the degree of plagiarism practised by the "inspired" Bible writers, I asked my audience during a symposium at the University of Cape Town conducted between myself and Professor Cumpsty, the Head of the Department of Theology, on the subject "Is the Bible God's Word?" to open their Bibles.

Some Christians are very fond of carrying their Bibles under their arms when religious discussions or debates take place. They seem to be utterly helpless without this book. At my suggestion a number of the audience began ruffling the pages. I asked them to open to chapter 37 in the "Book of Isaiah." When the audience was ready, I asked them to compare my "Isaiah 37" with their "Isaiah 37" while I read, to see whether they were identical. I began, reading slowly verses 1,2,3,4,10,15 and so on, until the end of the chapter. I kept on asking after every verse if what I had been reading, was identical with the verses in their Bibles. Again and again they chorused—"Yeh!", "Yeh!" At the end of the chapter with the Bible still open in my hands at the place from which I had been reading, I made the Chairman to reveal to the audience that I was not reading from Isaiah 37 at all but from **2 Kings 19**! There was a terrible consternation in the audience! I had thus established 100% plagiarism in the "Holy Bible." (See next page.)

In other words, Isaiah 37 and 2 Kings 19 are identical word for word. Yet, they have been attributed to two different authors, centuries apart, whom the Christians claim have been inspired by God.

100% PLAGIARISM

II KINGS 19

AND it came to pass, when king Hĕz-ĕ-kĭ'-ăh heard *it*, that he rent his clothes, and covered himself with sackcloth, and went into the house of the LORD.

2 And he sent Ĕ-lĭ'-ă-kĭm, which *was* over the household, and Shebna the scribe, and the elders of the priests, covered with sackcloth, to Isaiah the prophet the son of Amoz.

3 And they said unto him, Thus saith Hĕz-ĕ-kĭ'-ăh, This day *is* a day of trouble, and of rebuke, and blasphemy: for the children are come to the birth, and *there is* not strength to bring forth.

5 So the servants of king Hĕz-ĕ-kĭ'-ăh came to Isaiah.

10 Thus shall ye speak to Hĕz-ĕ-kĭ'-ăh king of Judah, saying, Let not thy God in whom thou trustest deceive thee, saying, Jerusalem shall not be delivered into the hand of the king of Assyria.

11 Behold, thou hast heard what the kings of Assyria have done to all lands, by destroying them utterly: and shalt thou be delivered?

12 Have the gods of the nations delivered them which my fathers have destroyed; *as* Gozan, and Haran, and Rezeph, and the children of Eden which *were* in Thĕl'-ă-sär?

14 ¶ And Hĕz-ĕ-kĭ'-ăh received the letter of the hand of the messengers, and read it: and Hezekiah went up into the house of the LORD, and spread it before the LORD.

15 And Hĕz-ĕ-kĭ'-ăh prayed before the LORD, and said, O LORD God of Israel, which dwellest *between* the chĕr'-ū-bims, thou art the God, *even* thou alone, of all the kingdoms of the earth; thou hast made heaven and earth.

36 So Sĕn-năch'-ĕr-ĭb king of Assyria departed, and went and returned, and dwelt at Nin'-ĕ-vĕh.

37 And it came to pass, as he was worshipping in the house of Nĭś'-rŏch his god, that Ă-drăm'-mĕ-lĕch and Shä-rĕ'-zĕr his sons smote him with the sword: and they escaped into the land of Armenia. And E-sär-hăd'-dǫn his son reigned in his stead.

ISAIAH 37

AND it came to pass, when king Hĕz-ĕ-kĭ'-ăh heard *it*, that he rent his clothes, and covered himself with sackcloth, and went into the house of the LORD.

2 And he sent Ĕ-lĭ'-ă-kĭm, who *was* over the household, and Shebna the scribe, and the elders of the priests covered with sackcloth, unto Isaiah the prophet the son of Amoz.

3 And they said unto him, Thus saith Hĕz-ĕ-kĭ'-ăh, This day *is* a day of trouble, and of rebuke, and of blasphemy: for the children are come to the birth, and *there is* not strength to bring forth.

5 So the servants of king Hĕz-ĕ-kĭ'-ăh came to Isaiah.

10 Thus shall ye speak to Hĕz-ĕ-kĭ'-ăh king of Judah, saying, Let not thy God, in whom thou trustest, deceive thee, saying, Jerusalem shall not be given into the hand of the king of Assyria.

11 Behold, thou hast heard what the kings of Assyria have done to all lands by destroying them utterly; and shalt thou be delivered?

12 Have the gods of the nations delivered them which my fathers have destroyed, *as* Gozan, and Haran, and Rezeph, and the children of Eden which *were* in Tĕ-lăs'-sär?

14 ¶ And Hĕz-ĕ-kĭ'-ăh received the letter from the hand of the messengers, and read it: and Hezekiah went up unto the house of the LORD, and spread it before the LORD.

15 And Hĕz-ĕ-kĭ'-ăh prayed unto the LORD, saying,

16 O LORD of hosts, God of Israel, that dwellest *between* the chĕr'-ū-bims, thou *art* the God, *even* thou alone, of all the kingdoms of the earth: thou hast made heaven and earth.

37 ¶ So Sĕn-năch'-ĕr-ĭb king of Assyria departed, and went and returned, and dwelt at Nin'-ĕ-vĕh.

38 And it came to pass, as he was worshipping in the house of Nĭś'-rŏch his god, that Ă-drăm'-mĕ-lĕch and Shä-rĕ'-zĕr his sons smote him with the sword; and they escaped into the land of Armenia: and Ĕ-sär-hăd'-dǫn his son reigned in his stead.

These verses are culled from the Authorised Version, but you will find the same in every Version.

Who is copying whom? Who is stealing from whom? The 32 renowned Bible scholars of the RSV say that the author of the Book of Kings is "unknown"! These notes on the Bible were prepared and edited by the Right Rev. David J. Fant, Litt. D., General Secretary of the New York Bible Society. Naturally, if the Most Reverend gentlemen of Christendom had an iota of belief about the Bible being the Word of God, they would have said so, but they honestly (shame-facedly?) confess: "AUTHOR — UNKNOWN!" They are prepared to pay lip service to Scriptures which could have been penned by any Tom, Dick or Harry, and expect everyone to regard these as the Word of God—Heaven forbid!

No Verbal Inspiration

What have Christian scholars to say about the "Book of Isaiah?" They say:

> "Mainly credited to Isaiah. Parts may have been written by others."

In view of the confessions of Bible scholars, we will not take poor Isaiah to task. Can we then nail this plagiarism on the door of God? What blasphemy! Professor Cumptsy confirmed at question time, at the end of the aforementioned symposium that the "Christians do not believe in a verbal inspiration of the Bible." So God Almighty had not absent-mindedly dictated the same tale twice! Human hands, all too human, had played havoc with this so-called Word of God—the Bible. Yet, Bible-thumpers will insist that "every word, comma, and full stop of the Bible is God's Word!"

THE ACID TEST

How do we know that a book claimed to be from God is really the Book of God? One of the tests, out of many such tests, is—that a Message emanating from an Omniscient Being MUST be consistent with itself. It ought to be free from all discrepancies and contradictions. This is exactly what the *Last Testament*, the Book of God says:

> Do they not consider the Qur'an (with care)
> Had it been from any other than Allah
> They would have found therein many a discrepancy
> > Holy Quran 4:82

God or the Devil?

If God Almighty wants us to verify the authenticity of His Book (The Holy Quran) with this acid test, why should we not apply the very same test to any other Book claiming to be from Him? We do not want to bamboozle anybody with words as the Christians have been doing. It would be readily agreed from the references, I have given from Christian scholars, that they have been proving to us that the Bible is NOT the Word of God, yet making us believe that they have actually convinced us to the contrary.

A classic example of this sickness was in evidence again only "yesterday." The Anglican synod was in session in Grahamstown. The Most. Rev. Bill Burnett, the Archbishop was preaching to his flock. He created a confusion in his Anglican community. An erudite Englishman, addressing a group of learned English priests and bishops, in their own mother tongue—English, which his learned colleagues drastically misunderstood: to such an extent that Mr. McMillan, perhaps also an Anglican, the Editor of an English daily, *The Natal Mercury*, dated December 11, 1979, had this to say about the confusion the Archbishop had created among his own learned clergy:

"Archbishop Burnett's remarks at the synod were hardly a model of clarity and were widely and dramatically misinterpreted by many of those present."

There is nothing wrong with English as a language, but can't you see that the Christian is trained in muddled thinking in all matters religious? The "bread" in his Holy Communion is not "bread" but "flesh"? The "wine" is "blood"? "Three is one"? and "Human is Divine"? But don't make a mistake, he is not that simple when dealing with the earthly kingdom, he is then most precise. You will have to be doubly careful when entering into a contract with him! He can have you sold out, without your realizing it.

The examples that I shall furnish in substantiating the points I have raised about the contradictions in the so-called Book of God, would be found so easy even for a child to follow and understand.

You will observe that the authors of the books of "Chronicles" and of "Samuel" are telling us the same story about David taking a census of the Jews. Where did David get his "inspiration" to do this novel deed? The author of 2 Samuel 24:1 says that it was the "LORD" God who MOVED (RSV: "incited") David, but the author of 1 Chronicles 21:1 says that it was "Satan" who PROVOKED (RSV:

413

"incited") David to do such a dastardly thing! How could the Almighty God have been the source of these contradictory "INSPIRATIONS"? Is it God or is it Satan! In which religion is the devil synonymous with God! I am not talking about "Satanism," a recent fungus growth of Christianity, in which ex-Christians worship the Devil. Christianity has been most prolific in spawning isms, Atheism, Communism, Fascism, Totalitarianism, Nazism, Mormonism, Moonism, Christian Scientism and now Satanism. What else will Christianity give birth to?

The "Holy Bible" lends itself to all kinds of contradictory interpretations. This is the Christian boast!

> "Some claim and rightly so, that biblical passages have been continuously misused and misappropriated to justify almost every evil known to man."
>
> (From *The Plain Truth*, an American-based Christian Journal under the heading "The Bible—World's Most Controversial Book,"
> July 1975)

Who are the real authors?

As further evidence will be adduced from "Samuel" and "Chronicles," I deem it advisable first to determine their authors instead of suspecting God of those books' incongruities. The revisers of the RSV say:

a) SAMUEL: Author "Unknown" (Just one word.)

b) CHRONICLES: Author "Unknown, probably collected and edited by Ezra."

We must admire the humility of these Bible scholars, but their "poss-ibly's," "probably's" and "likely's" are always construed as ACTUALLY's by their fleeced sheep. Why make poor Ezra or Isaiah the scapegoats for these anonymous writers?

Three or Seven?

Compare both the quotations. 2 Samuel 24:13 tells us—

> "So Gad came to David, AND TOLD HIM, and said unto him, . . ."

These words are repeated word for word in 1 Chronicles 21:11, except the redundant "**and told him**" is removed! But while trimming the useless phrase, the author also pruned the time factor from "**seven**" years to "**three**" years. What did God say to Gad—three or seven years plague—"on both your houses?"

Eight or Eighteen?

Compare the two quotations. 2 Chronicles 36:9 tells us that Jehoiachin was "**eight**" years old when he began to reign, while 2 Kings 24:8 says that he was "**eighteen**" when he began to reign. The "**unknown**" author of KINGS must have reasoned that what possible "evil" could a child of eight do to deserve his abdication, so he generously added 10 years to make Jehoiachin mature enough to become liable to God's wrath. However, he had to balance his tampering, so he cut short his reign by 10 days! Add ten years to age and deduct ten days from his rule? Could God Almighty say two widely differing things on the same subject?

Cavalry or Infantry?

How many chariot riders did David slay? Seven "**hundred**" or seven "**thousand**"? And further, did he slay 40,000 "*horsemen*" or 40,000 "*footmen*"? The implication in the conflicting records between 2 Samuel 10:18 and 1 Chronicles 19:18 is not only that God could not discern the difference between hundreds and thousands, but that He could not even distingush "**cavalry**" from "**infantry**"! It is obvious that blasphemy masquerades in the Christian dictionary as "inspiration"!

Practical Homework

Solomon in his glory began building a royal palace for himself which took him 13 years. We learn this from the 1st Book of Kings, chapter 7. You remember Dr. Parker's boast about "**whole pages being taken up by obscure names**"? Well, for sheer puerility you cannot beat this chapter 7 and Ezekiel chapter 45. You owe it to yourself to read it just once in your lifetime. After that, you will really appreciate the Holy Quran. If you do not own a Bible, and if you are a Muslim, you will get a free copy from the address at the bottom of this page. You may then color the various references from this booklet in your Bible. **Yellow** for all contradictions, use **Red** for pornographic passages, and **Green** for sensible, acceptable quotations as the ones I have mentioned at the beginning of this essay—that is words that you can effortlessly recognize as being those of God and His Holy Messengers. With just this preparation, you will be ready to confute and confuse any missionary or Bible scholar that comes your way!

> "If we perspire more in times of peace, we will bleed less in times of war."
>
> Chiang Kai-Shek

How Hygienic?

Note that the author of 1 Kings 7:26 has counted 2,000 baths in Solomon's palace, but the author of 2 Chronicles 4:5 increases the kingly count by 50% to 3,000! What extravagance and error in the "Book of God"? Even if God Almighty had nothing else to do, would He occupy Himself "inspiring" such trivial contradictory nonsense to the Jews? Is the Bible God's Book? Is it the Word of God?

Piled Contradictions

Before I conclude this series of contradictions, let me give you just one more example. There are hundreds of others in the Bible. It is Solomon again. He really does things in a big way. The ex-Shah of Iran was a nursery kid by comparison! The author of 2 Chronicles 9:25 gives Solomon one thousand more stalls of horses than the number of baths he had given him.

> "And Solomon had four thousand stalls for horses . . ."

But the author of 1 Kings 4:26 had real kingly thoughts about this royal patron. He multiplied Solomon's stalls by 1,000%—from 4,000 to 40,000 stalls of horses! Before some glib evangelist draws the wool over your eyes that the difference is only a nought, a zero—"0'" that some scribe or copyist had inadvertently added a zero to 4,000 to make it 40,000, let me tell you that the Jews in the time of Solomon knew nothing about the zero—"0"! It was the Arabs who introduced the zero to the Middle East and to Europe centuries later. The Jews spelt out their figures in words in their literary works and did not write them in numerals. Our Question is—Who was the real author of this staggering discrepancy of 36,000? Was it God or man?

MOST OBJECTIVE TESTIMONY

The Christian propagandist is very fond of quoting the following verse as proof that His Bible is the Word of God.

> "All Scripture IS given by inspiration of God, and IS profitable for doctrine, for reproof, for correction, for instruction in righteous-ness."
>
> 2 Timothy 3:16, *AV* by Scofield

Note the "IS's" are in capitals. Rev. Scofield is telling us silently that they do not occur in the original Greek. *The New English Bible*, translated by a committee representing the Church of England, the Church of Scotland, the Methodist Church, the Congregational Church, the Baptist Union, the Presbyterian Church of England, etc., etc., **and the British and Foreign Bible Society** have produced the closest translation of the original Greek which deserves to be reproduced here:

> "Every inspired Scripture has its use for teaching the truth and refuting error, or for reformation of manners and discipline in right living."
>
> 2 Timothy 3:16

The Roman Catholics in their *Douay Version*, are also more faithful to the text than the Protestants in their *Authorized Version* (AV). They say:

> "All Scripture, inspired of God, is profitable to teach, to reprove, to correct . . ."

We will not quibble with words. Muslims and Christians are agreed that whatever emanates from God, whether through inspiration or by revelation, must serve one of four purposes:

1. It must either teach us **DOCTRINE**;
2. **REPROVE** us for our error;
3. Offer us **CORRECTION**;
4. Guide us into **RIGHTEOUSNESS**.

I have been asking learned men of Christianity for the past forty years, whether they can supply a FIFTH "peg" to hang the Word of God on. They have failed signally. That does not mean that I have improved upon their performance. Let us examine the "*Holy Bible*" with these objective tests.

Not Far to Seek

The very first book of the Bible—Genesis—provides us with many beautiful examples. Open chapter 38 and read. We are given here the history of Judah, the father of the Jewish race, from whom we derive the names "Judea" and "Judaism." This patriarch of the Jews got married and God granted him three sons, Er, Onan and Shelah. When the first-born was big enough, Judah had him married to a lady called Tamar.

> "But Er, Judah's first-born was wicked in the sight of the Lord; and the Lord slew him."
>
> Genesis 38:7

Under what heading, from the above four principles of Timothy will you place this sad news? The second—"REPROVE" is the answer. Er was wicked so God killed him. A lesson for all, God will destroy us for our wickedness. RE-PROOF!

Continuing with this Jewish history, according to their custom, if a brother died and left no offspring, it was the duty of the other brother to give "seed" to his sister-in-law so that the deceased's name might be perpetuated. Judah, in honor of this custom, orders his second son Onan to do his duty. But jealousy enters his heart. It will be **his seed** but the name will be his brother's! So at the critical moment

> "He spilled it on the ground . . . and the thing he did displeased the Lord: wherefore He slew him also."
>
> Genesis 38:9-10

Again, where does this slaying fit into Timothy's tests? "Reproof!" is the answer again. No prizes are offered for these easy answers. They are so basic. Do wrong and bear the consequence! Onan is forgotten in the "Book of God," but Christian sexologists have immortalized him by referring to "coitus interruptus," as Onanism in their "Books of Sex."

418

Now Judah tells his daughter-in-law, Tamar, to return to her father's house until his third son Shelah attains manhood, when she will be brought back so that he can do his duty.

A Woman's Revenge

Shelah grows up and is, perhaps, married to another woman. But Judah had not fulfilled his obligation to Tamar. Deep in his **heart he** is terrified. He has already lost two sons on account of this "witch,"—

> *"Lest peradventure he (shelah) die also, as his brethren did."*
>
> Genesis 38:11

So Judah conveniently forgets his promise. The aggrieved young lady resolves to take revenge on her father-in-law for depriving her of her "seed" right.

Tamar learned that Judah is going to Timnath to sheer his sheep. She plans to get even with him on the way. She forestalls him, and goes and sits in an open place en route to Timnath. When Judah sees her, he thinks she is a harlot because she had covered her face. He comes up to her and proposes—*"Allow me to come in unto thee; and she said, 'What wilt thou give me, that thou mayest come in unto me?'"* He promises that he would send her a goat kid from his flock. What guarantee could she have that he would send it? What guarantee did she require, Judah queried. "His ring, his bracelet and his staff" is the ready answer. The old man hands these possessions to her, and *"came in unto her, and she conceived by him"* (Genesis 38:16-18).

The Moral Lesson

Before we seek the heading from 2 Timothy 3:16, under which to categorize this filthy, dirty story from the "Book of God," I am tempted to ask, as you would be tempted to ask: what is the moral (?) lesson that our children will learn from Tamar's sweet revenge? Of course we do tell our children fables, not really for their entertainment value, but that through them some moral may be imparted. *The Fox and the Grapes, The Wolf and the Lamb, The Dog and His Shadow,* etc. However simple or silly the story, a **moral** is aimed at.

'Christian Parental Dilemmas'

Dr. Vernon Jones, an American psychologist of repute, carried out experiments on groups of schoolchildren to whom certain stories had been told. The heroes of the stories were the same in the case of the different groups of children, but the heroes behaved contradictorily [in] each group. [In] one group "St. George," [slew] the dragon [and] emerged a very brave figure, but [in] another group, [fled] in terror . . . seeking shelter in his mother's lap. "These stories made certain slight but permanent changes in character, even in the narrow classroom situation," concluded Dr. Jones.

How much more permanent damage the rapes and murders, incests, and bestialities of the "Holy Bible" has done to the children of Christendom, can be measured from reports in our daily newspapers. If such is the source of Western morality, it is no little wonder, then, that Methodists and Roman Catholics have already solemnized marriages between homosexuals in their "Houses of God." And 8,000 "gays" (an euphemistic term for sodomites) parade their "wares" in London's Hyde Park in July 1979, to the acclaim of the news and TV media.

You must get that "Holy Bible" and read the whole chapter 38 of Genesis. Mark in "red" the words and phrases deserving this adornment. We have reached verse 18 in our moral (?) lesson—"*and she conceived by him.*"

Can't Hide Forever

Three months later, as things were bound to turn out, news reached Judah that his daughter-in-law, Tamar, had played the "harlot," and that she was with "child by whoredom and Judah said, "Bring her forth, and let her be burnt" (Genesis 38:24). Judah had deliberately spurned her as a "witch," and now he sadistically wants to burn her. But this wily Jewess put one up on the old man. She sent the "ring," the "bracelet," and the "staff," with a servant, beseeching her father-in-law to find the culprit responsible for her pregnancy. Judah was in a fix. He confessed that his daughter-in-law was more "*righteous*" than himself, and "*he knew her again no more*" (verse 26). It is quite an experience to compare the choice of language in which the different versions describe the same incident. The Jehovah's Witnesses in their *New World Translation* translate the last quotation as—"*He had no further intercourse with her after that.*" This is not the last we will hear about in the "Book of God," of this Tamar whom the Gospel writers have immortalized in their "Genealogy of their Lord."

Incest Honored

I do not want to bore you with details, but the end verses of Genesis 38 deal with a duel in Tamar's womb: about the twins struggling for ascendancy. The Jews were very meticulous about recording their firstborns. The firstborn got the lion's share of their father's patrimony. Who are the lucky winners in this prenatal race? There are four in this unique contest. They are "Pharez and Zarah of Tamar by Judah." How? You will see presently. But first, let us have the moral. What is the moral in this episode? You remember Er and Onan: how God destroyed them for their several sins? And the lessons we have learnt in each case was "REPROOF." Under what category of Timothy will you place the incest of Judah, and his illegitimate progeny? All these characters are honored in the "Book of God" for their bastardy. They become the great grandfathers and great grandmothers of the "only begotten son of God." (?)

See Matthew 1:3. In every version of the Bible, the Christians have varied the spelling of these characters' names from those obtained in the Old Testament (Genesis chapter 38) with those contained in the New Testament (Matthew chapter 1) to put the reader off the scent. From Pharez in the "Old" to Pares in the "New," and Zarah to Zara and Tamar to Thamar. But what about the moral? God blesses Judah for his incestous crime! So if you do "evil" (Er), God will slay you; if you spill "seed" (Onan), God will kill you, but a daughter-in-law (Tamar) who vengefully, and guilefully collects her father-in-law's (Judah's) "seed" is rewarded. Under what category will the Christians place this "honor" in the "Book of God"? Where does it fit? Is it . . . your?

1   DOCTRINE?
2   REPROOF?
3   CORRECTION? OR
4   INSTRUCTION INTO RIGHTEOUSNESS?

Ask him who comes and knocks at your door—that professional preacher, that hot-gospeller, that Bible-thumper. Here, he deserves a prize if he can grant an explanation for the correct answer. There is none born who can justify this filth, this pornography under any of the above headings. But a heading has to be given. It can only be recorded under—"pornography"!

Ban the Book!

George Bernard Shaw said,

> "The most dangerous book (the Bible) on earth, keep it under lock and key."

Keep the Bible out of your children's reach. But who will follow his advice? He was not a "B.A." [born again], a "reborn" Christian.

According to the high moral scruples of the Christian rulers of South African who have banned the book, *Lady Chatterley's Lover*, because of a "tetragrammaton"—a four-letter word, they would most assuredly have place a ban on the "Holy Bible," if it had been a Hindu religious Book, or a Muslim religious Book. But they are utterly helpless against their own "Holy Book," their "salvation" depends upon it!

> "Reading Bible stories to children can also open all sorts of opportunities to discuss the morality of sex. An unexpurgated Bible might get an X-rating from some censors."
>
> *The Plain Truth,* October 1977

Daughters Seduce Their Father

Read Genesis 19, verses 30 to the end and mark again in "red" the words and phrases deserving this honor. Do not hesitate and procrastinate. Your "colored" Bible will become a priceless heirloom for your children. I agree with Shaw, to keep the Bible "under lock and key," but we need this weapon to meet the Christian challenge. The Prophet of Islam said that "war is strategy," and strategy demands that we use the weapons of our enemy. It is not what we like and what we do not like. It is what we are forced to use against the "one book" (Bible) professors, who are knocking at our doors with "the Bible says this" and "the Bible says that." They want us to exchange our Holy Quran for their "Holy Bible." Show them the holes in the "holiness" which they have not yet seen. At times these zombies pretend to see the filth for the first time. They have been programmed with selected verses for their propagation.

To continue: "history" has it that, night after night, the daughters of Lot seduce their drunken father with the noble (?) motive of preserving their father's "seed." "Seed" figures very prominently in this "Holy Book": 47 times in the

422

little booklet of Genesis alone! Out of this another incestuous relationship come the **Ammonites** and the **Moabites**, for whom the God of Israel was supposed to have had a special compassion. Later on in the Bible we learn that the Jews are ordered by the same compassionate God to slaughter the Philistines mercilessly —men, women, and children. Even trees and animals are not to be spared, but the Ammonites and the Moabites are not to be "**distressed**" or "**meddled**" with because they are the seed of Lot! (Deuteronomy 2:19)

No decent reader can read the seduction of Lot to his mother, sister, or daughter, not even to his fiancée if she is a chaste and moral woman. Yet you will come across perverted people who will gorge on this filth. Tastes can be cultivated!

Read again and mark Ezekiel 23. You will know what colour to choose. The "whoredoms" of the two sisters, Oholah and Oholibah. The sexual details here puts to shame even the unexpurgated edition of many banned books. Ask your "born-again" Christian visitors, under what category will they classify all this lewdness? Such filth certainly has no place in any "Book of God."

THE GENEALOGY OF JESUS

Watch now how the Christian fathers have foisted the incestuous progenies of the Old Testament upon their Lord and Saviour, Jesus Christ, in the New Testament. For a man who had no genealogy, they have manufactured one for him. And what a genealogy! **Six adulterers and offsprings of incest are imposed upon this holy man of God.** Men and women deserving to be stoned to death according to God's own law, as revealed through Moses, and further to be ostracised and debarred from the House of God for generations.

Ignoble Ancestry

Why should God give a "father" (Joseph) to His "son" (Jesus)? And why such an ignoble ancestry? "This is the whole beauty of it," says the pervert. "God loved the sinners so much that he disdaineth not to give such progenitors for His 'son.'"

Only Two Commissioned

Of the four Gospel writers, God "inspired" only two of them to record the genealogy of His "son." To make it easy for you to compare the "fathers and grandfathers" of Jesus Christ in both the "inspired" lists, I have culled the names only, minus the verbiage. Between David and Jesus, God "inspired" Matthew to record only 26 ancestors for His "son." But Luke, also "inspired," gathered up 41 fore-fathers for Jesus. The only name common to these two lists between David and Jesus is Joseph and that, too, a "supposed" father according to Luke 3:23 (AV). This one name is glaring. You need no fine-tooth comb to catch him. It is Joseph, the carpenter. You will also easily observe that the lists are grossly contradictory. Could both the lists have emanated from the same source, *i.e.* God?

Fulfilling Prophecy?

Matthew and Luke are overzealous in making David the King, the prime ances-tor of Jesus, because of that false notion that Jesus was to sit on the "throne of his father David" (Acts 2:30). The Gospels belie this prophecy, for they tell us that instead of Jesus sitting on his father's (David's) throne, it was Pontius Pilate, a Roman Governor, a pagan who sat on that very throne and condemned its right-ful (?) heir (Jesus) to death. "Never mind," says the evangelist, "if not in his first coming, then in his second coming he will fulfill this prophecy and 300 others beside." But with their extravagant enthusiasm to trace the ancestry of Jesus physically to David, (for this is actually what the Bible says—that of the fruit of his (David's) loins, according to the flesh" (literary, not metaphorically Acts 2:30), both the "inspired" authors trip and fall on the very first step.

Matthew 1:6 says that Jesus was the son of David through Solomon, but Luke 3:31 says that he (Jesus) was the son of David through Nathan. One need not be a gynecologist to tell that by no stretch of the imagination could the seed of David reach the mother of Jesus both through Solomon and Nathan at the same time! We know that both the authors are confounded liars, because Jesus was conceived miraculously, without any male intervention. Even if we concede a physical ancestry through David, both authors would still be proved liars for the obvious reason.

Breaking Prejudice

As simple as the above logic is, the Christian is so emotionally involved that it will not penetrate his prejudiced mind. Let us give him an identical example, but one where he can afford to be objective.

We know from history that Muhammad, the Prophet of Islam, was the son of Abraham through Ishmael, so if some "inspired" writer came along and tried to palm off his "revelation" to the effect that Muhammad was the son of Abraham through Isaac, we would, without any hesitation, brand such a writer as a liar, because the seed of Abraham could never reach Amina (Muhammad's mother) through Ishmael and through Isaac at the same time! The differences of lineage between these two sons of Abraham is the difference between the Jews and the Arabs.

In the case of Muhammad, we would know then that anyone who says that Isaac is his progenitor, was a liar. But in the case of Jesus both Matthew and Luke are suspect. Until the Christians decide which line of ancestors they prefer for their "god," both Gospels will have to be rejected. Christen-dom has been battling tooth and nail with these genealogies for the past 2,000 years, trying to unravel the mystery. They have not given up yet. We admire their perseverance. They still believe that "time will solve the problem."

> "There are claimed contradictions that theologians have not resolved to every atheist's satisfaction. There are textual difficulties with which scholars are still wrestling. Only a Bible illiterate would deny these and other problems."
>
> *The Plain Truth*, July 1975

The Source of Luke's "Inspiration"

We have already nailed 85% of Matthew and Luke to Mark or that "mysterious 'Q.'" Let us now allow Luke to tell us who "inspired" him to tell his "most excellent Theophilus" (Luke 1:3) the story of Jesus. He tells us plainly that he was only following in the footsteps of others who were less qualified than himself, others who had the temerity to write accounts of his hero (Jesus). As a physician, as against fishermen and tax collectors, he was no doubt better equipped to create a literary masterpiece. This he did, because "it seemed good to me also" to "PUT IN ORDER." These are his prominent justifications over his predecessors.

In the introduction to his translation of the "Gospel of St. Luke," a Christian scholar J. B. Phillips, has this to say—

> "On his own admission Luke has carefully compared and edited existing material, but it would seem that he had access to a good deal of additional material, and we can reasonably guess at some of the sources from which he drew."

And yet you call this the Word of God?! Obtain *The Gospels in Modern English*, in soft cover by 'FONTANA' publications. It is a cheap edition. Get it quickly before the Christians decide to have Phillips' invaluable notes expunged from his translation! And do not be surprised if the authors of the RSV also decide to eliminate the "Preface" from their translation. It is an old, old habit. As soon as those who have vested interests in Christianity realize that they have inadvertently let the cat out of the bag, they quickly make amends. They make my current references "past" history overnight!

The Remaining Gospel

Who is the author of "The Gospel of St. John"? Neither God nor St. John! (John 19:35; 21:24-25) Who is his "he" and "his" and "this"? And, his "we know" and "I suppose." Could it be the fickle one who left him in the lurch in the garden, when he was most in need, or the fourteenth man at the table, at the "Last Supper," the one that "Jesus loved"? Both were Johns. It was a popular name among the Jews in the times of Jesus, and among Christians even now. Neither of these two was the author of this Gospel. That it was the product of an anonymous hand, is crystal clear.

Authors in a Nutshell

Let me conclude this "authorship" search with the verdict of those 32 scholars, backed by their 50 cooperating denominations. God had been eliminated from this authorship race long ago. In the RSV by "Collins," invaluable notes on *The Books of the Bible* are to be found at the back of their production. We start with "Genesis"—the first book of the Bible. The scholars say about its "author": "One of the 'five books of Moses.'" Note the words "five books of Moses" are written in inverted commas—" ". This is a subtle way of admitting that this is what people say—that it is the book of Moses, that Moses was its author, but we (the 32 scholars) who are better informed, do not subscribe to that tittle-tattle.

The next four books, "Exodus, Leviticus, Numbers and Deuteronomy:" Author? "Generally credited to Moses." This is the same category as the book of Genesis.

Who is the author of the book of "JOSHUA"? Answer: "Major part credited to Joshua."

Who is the author of the book of "JUDGES"? Answer: "Possibly Samuel."

Who is the author of "RUTH"? Answer: "Not definitely known" and Who is the author of:

1ST SAMUEL? .... Answer: Author "Unknown"

2ND SAMUEL? .... Answer: Author "Unknown"

1ST KINGS? .... Answer: Author "Unknown"

2ND KINGS? .... Answer: Author "Unknown"

1ST CHRONICLES? .... Answer: Author "Unknown, **probably** . . ."

2ND CHRONICLES? .... Answer: Author "**Likely collectively** . . ."

And so the story goes. The authors of these anonymous books are either "**unknown**" or are "**probably**" or "**likely**" or are of "**doubtful**" origin. Why blame God for this fiasco? The Long-suffering and Merciful God did not wait for two thousand years for Bible scholars to tell us that He was not the Author of Jewish peccadilloes, prides and prejudicès; of their lusts, wranglings, jealousies, and enormities. He said it openly what they do:

> "And woe to those who write the book with their own hands and then say: 'This is from Allah.' To traffic with it for a miserable price! So woe to them for what their hands do write, and woe to them for what they earn thereby!"
>
> Holy Quran 2:79

We could have started the thesis of this book with the above Quranic verse and ended with it, with the satisfaction that God Almighty had Himself delivered His verdict on the subject "Is the Bible God's Word?" but we wished to afford our Christian brethren an opportunity to study the subject as objectively as they [could] wished. Allowing believing Christians, "reborn" Christians, and their own Holy Book the Bible to testify against their "better" judgment.

What about the Holy Quran? Is the Quran the Word of God? The author of this humble publication has endeavored to answer this question in a most scientific manner in his book *Al'Quran—The Ultimate Miracle*, available absolutely free of charge from the "Centre" on request.

EPILOGUE

The reader must by now be convinced, that is, if he has an open mind, that the Bible is not what it is claimed to be by the protagonists of Christianity.

For nearly four decades people have asked me as to how I have such an "in-depth" knowledge of the Bible and Christianity.

Frankly speaking, my present position as a Muslim "expert" on Judaism and Christianity is not of my own volition. I have been forced into being what I am.

Early Provocation

It was in 1939 when I was working as a shop assistant at Adams Mission near a Christian seminary by that name, producing preachers and priests, that I and my fellow Muslim workers were the targets of young aspiring men of the cloth. Not a day passed when these young Christians did not harass me or my brothers-in-faith, through insults which they piled on Islam, the Holy Prophet and the Quran.

Being a sensitive young man of 20, I spent sleepless nights in tears for not being able to defend the one dearer to me than my own life, **that mercy unto all mankind**—Muhammad (P.B.U.H.) I resolved to study the Quran, the Bible and other literature. My discovery of the book *Izharul Haq* was the turning point in my life. After a short while I was able to invite the trainee missionaries of Adams Mission College, and cause them to perspire under the collar until they developed a respect for Islam and its Holy Apostle.

Muslims under Constant Attack

It made me ponder as to how so many unwary Muslims are being constantly assaulted by Christian evangelists who carry out a door-to-door campaign, and being invited in by the proverbially hospitable Muslim, I thought of how the merciless missionary munched the *samoosas*, and punched the wind out of the Muslim with snide remarks against his beliefs.

Determined to bring home to the Muslims their right to defend themselves, and to arm them with enough knowledge to counter the hot gospeller, the door to door peddler of Christianity and the shameless insulter of Islam and its Holy Apostle; I humbly undertook to deliver lectures to show the Muslim masses that they had nothing to fear from the assaults of the Christians.

My lectures were also an invitation to the Christians to witness the truth of Islam and the fabrications which had penetrated the true teachings of Jesus (P.B.U.H.).

Attack Not New

Christian Missionaries in the past hundred years and more have challenged Muslims on many aspects and quite a number of these challenges have, to my knowledge, gone answered or have been only partly answered. Perhaps by the will of Allah my contribution in this field can also be answers, or part answers to the challenges of the detractors of Islam. It is of supreme importance that we do not go by default.

One such challenge comes to mind viz. Geo G. Harris, the author of *How to Lead Muslims to Christ*. This missionary who tried to convert the Muslims of China says in the usual arrogant and condescending manner of the West-erner on page 19 under the heading "The Theory of Charge of Corruption":

"We now come to the most serious charge by the Moslem world against our Christian Scriptures. There are three aspects of this charge.

1   That the Christian Scriptures have been so changed and altered that they bear little, if any, resemblance to the glorious Injil praised in the Qur'án. This can be answered by the asking of one of the following questions: Wherein have these been so changed or altered? Can you obtain a copy of a true Injil and show it that I may compare it with mine? At what date in past history was the unaltered Injil in circulation?

2   That our Gospels have suffered corruption. The following five questions are definite, and we have a perfect right to ask them:
a)   Was such a corruption or alteration intentional?
b)   Can you point out in my Bible one such passage?

c) How did this passage read originally?

d) When, by whom, how or why was it corrupted or altered?

e) Was such, corruption of the text or of the meaning?

3 That our Gospels are "faked" substitutes for the original Injil. Or that our Gospels are the handiwork of men, not the noble Injil which descended upon Jesus. A little questioning will usually reveal the true situation, that usually the Muslim making the charge is woefully ignorant of the Bible or New Testament as it actually existed in the past or exists today.

Before going on to the latter half of this discussion a reminder is important that as soon as the objector is willing to sense the flimsiness of such a charge, we should press home some teaching from our Scriptures, that our effort may be positive, and not negative."

Have Muslims the Answer?

Have we as Muslims no answers for these questions? If you, gentle reader have read this book you will admit that Geo G. Harris has no feet to stand on. I have been able to give actual pages from the Bible to disprove his assertions.

Muslims Challenged

On page 16 of Geo G. Harris' book he teaches his comrades a basic missionary rule in order to corner the Muslim prospective:

"In this chapter it is assumed that the question of the authenticity and genuineness of our Scriptures has been raised by the Mohammadan. When this is the case, before we undertake defence of our position we should bear in mind a basic rule. The burden of proof rests with the Muslim."

Praise be to Allah that in my 40 years of disproving the authenticity of the Bible which the Christians have so boldly asked for, I have been able to win the day.

Remember, we Muslims do not go door to door peddling our religion. Whereas Christians of different denominations encroach upon our privacy and peace and take advantage of our hospitality to harass the unwary Musalmán.

Those who are afraid to project the truth when they are provoked by these Christians, who even go to the extent of insulting our beloved Nabee Muhammad (S.A.W.) should reexamine their *Eimaan*.

The lectures I hold are to sound out these slinking missionaries who "attack" the home and hearth of the unsuspecting Muslim who goes about minding his own business.

The lectures are also aimed at restoring the damaged dignity of the Muslim who has been ruffled by the ruthless attacks of the Christian peddler. Ask the poor Muslims of Chatsworth, Hanover Park, or Riverlea as to how they were subjected to the tyranny of certain missionaries.

If this humble little contribution of mine, "Is the Bible God's Word?" finds a place in the Muslim home as a bulwark against the missionary menace, my effort would be amply rewarded.

A greater reward would be if even one sincere disciple of Jesus (on whom be peace) were to be led to the truth, and be removed from fabrications and falsehood.

The greatest reward of course lies with Allah Almighty whom I supplicate for guidance and mercy and pray and crave that He accepts my effort which I dedicate to Him in all humility.

ZWIMMING FOR MUSLIM SOULS

(A Muslim critique of the Samuel Zwemer Institute for Muslim Studies)

by Nahid Khan

Just when you thought it was safe to go out in hijab or a kufi, the Zwemers emerge. They may be coming to your neighborhood soon.

Pasadena, CA is home to the Rose Bowl, Tournament of Roses Parade, the NASA Jet Propulsion Laboratory, and little old ladies. Unknown to most Muslims, however, something else calls Pasadena 'home.' It's the U.S. Center for World Mission, an umbrella organization for many Protestant missionaries.

Spread over several blocks in the northeastern corner of the city are branch organizations and affiliated offices. These include the William Carey International University, an institution currently training about 75 student missionaries to work in Asia and Africa. There's a K-12 Christian day school, the Reynolds Christian Academy, and the International Theological Seminary. Scattered around them are a variety of agencies such as the Christian Education Association International, the Presbyterian Center for Mission Studies, and the Samuel Zwemer Institute for Muslim Studies.

Why would an evangelical Protestant Missionary center be engaged in Muslim studies? To figure out how to convert Muslims to Christianity, obviously. And it has the programs that it believes can do exactly that. However, what the Zwemer Institute and other missionaries focusing on Muslims, do is only underscore what the growing Muslim community in North America and elsewhere needs: First, a widespread basic teaching of Islam throughout the rank and file of the Muslim community and, second, a way to swiftly respond to confusion tactics—from within or outside 'Muslim' rank.

Without this, we only keep the missionaries—like the Zwemers—in business.

* * *

Founded in 1978 from the First North American Conference on Muslim Evangelization, the Zwemer Institute takes its name from Samuel Zwemer, a missionary who worked in the Muslim world from the 1890s to the 1940s. He initiated a worldwide network of Christian missionary efforts directed at Muslims, and organized the first two conferences ever held for this end —at Cairo in 1906 and Lucknow in 1911. He literally wrote the book (really 13 books) on evangelizing Muslims.

As its founder and former executive director, Don McCurry, puts it, the Zwemer Institute serves as "a nerve center and coordinating hub that conducts research, trains people for working with Muslims, and, in general, promotes the cause of Muslim evangelization. It sees itself as a servant organization to the whole Christian movement . . . reaching unreached Muslims for Christ." (McCurry, by the way, spent 18 years as a missionary in Pakistan.)

The Institute prints and distributes flyers and publishes a quarterly newsletter. A recent flyer boldly reads: MUSLIMS STRATEGIZE TO CONVERT AMERICANS TO ISLAM! Thousands of Americans have ALREADY converted to Islam!

They also produce brochures, pamphlets, books, films, videotapes, posters, maps, and other materials to help Christians proselytize Muslims, and also to interest Muslims in Christianity. Convenient 9-hour long "Muslim Awareness Seminars" are available for church groups.

Regular classes on Islam are conducted primarily for student ministers and missionaries enrolled at the Institute, the William Carey International

University, and the Fuller Theological Seminary's School of World Mission (located less than two miles away). The offerings include:

> Introduction to Islam
> Revelation, the Koran and Muslim Tradition
> Folk Islam
> Current Trends in Islam
> Approaches to Islam
> Muslim Evangelism
> Cross-Cultural Communication in Muslim Societies
> Church Planting in Muslim Contexts
> Initiating Cultural Change in Muslim Contexts

It also offers practical "field experience" in proselytizing Arabs, Iranians, Pakistanis, Afghans, and even transient Muslim students.

The Institute conducts research on Muslim ethnic groups, history, and culture, and the state of Islamic faith and practice—all in cooperation with other Christian studies institutes throughout the world. It gauges and suggests methods for improving the effectiveness of current Christian mission strategies, identifying Muslims having no Christian mission effort directed at them.

Almost all of the staff members that oversee academic affairs, research, and the training of local missionary teams hold degrees in Islamic studies, Arab studies, or Asian and African history, and have experience in 'witnessing' to Muslims, abroad or in the States, with groups like World Vision, United Presbyterian Missions, Campus Crusade for Christ, or the Overseas Missionary Fellowship. The Institute's current executive director is Robert C. Douglas, Ph.D. in Social Ethics from the University of Southern California, and M.A. in Missions to Muslims from the Fuller Theological Seminary. His resumé includes missionary stints in Libya, Egypt, and Lebanon. Although the Zwemer Institute is not controlled by one church denomination, strong ties to the Presbyterian Church are evident.

Though some of the Institute's funding comes from mission agencies which use its services, much support comes from churches throughout North America. Zwemer staff regularly travel in the country visiting churches to publicize their activities and solicit donations.

* * *

While Zwemer hums with activities and Islam continues to be a growth religion in the States, as it is in the world, missionary efforts, and institutes pumping them, will go on to strategize and re-strategize for Muslims. Questions arise,

Should we be overly concerned?
What should our response be?
Should we respond at all?

The time has come, I think, to start answering the inquiries.

Rather than worry, some say, we should just do our own positive work. We must simply reach Muslims in this country and in others, and convey the right information about Islam to them and to nonMuslims.

This is the normal protocol. Not a response to the fantasies of Evangelicals, or the fear of their work and institutions, but the norm borne out of the fear of Allah. The prey of Christian missions aren't merely those who may fall out of faith—which are few, indeed—as a result of missionary methods. That is, those who apostatize to Christianity are generally not so much the victims of tactics as they are of a prevalent and more frightening reality: basic, knowledge about Islam is not at all basic and is even non-existent for far too many Muslims in America and elsewhere. For many believers, belief is a habit, and not so much the [product of] rational choice. Articulating Islam is cumbersome and incoherent not for language, but because of spiritual illiteracy. Just like a limping gazelle in the sight of a hungry lion, so must a weak Muslim look to a Christian missionary.

What's the program of response? At the moment, not much or underdeveloped, but all fingers seem to be pointing toward Islamic centers and publishing houses as part of the solution.

The Islamic center suddenly becomes the obvious choice. Evening Quran and Islamic studies classes at the local center—weeknights—should at least be an option for adults. A variety of education programs for the local community can be devised. These must be aimed at all ages, language groups, levels of knowledge, ability, and motivation, and for both sexes. Islamic center libraries should play a vital role in providing a sound knowledge base, particularly to those who prefer individual study to group learning. At this point, there are not many centers around the continent which offer regular adult classes on weeknights. Tsk. Tsk.

Developing support systems for educating Muslims and for presenting our message to nonMuslims are important. Islamic schools everywhere are a must, as are various types of institutions of Islamic learning and higher education in Islamic studies.

Another area of great need is literature.

"We need to produce a wide spectrum of *Da'wa* literature for non-Muslims, new Muslims, and old Muslims, from a myriad of positions," says Ihsan Bagby, director of Tarbiyyah at ISNA's Islamic Teaching Center in Plainfield, IN. "Telling stories of conversions to Islam is one good idea."

We need to do foundational educational and inspirational work across the communications board—radio, television, documentary films, slide shows, video and audio tapes. Several cities in North America have local weekly radio programs about Islam.

The point is the Muslim community has a collective responsibility to deal with challenges that face it. With this missionary thing (as George Bush might say) the challenge is really a double-edged one. On one hand, we must present Islam and, on the other, present it right, not in an offensive, jabbing way.

The emphasis should always be on presenting our own positive and beautiful message, regardless of the circumstances. Even when these circumstances include encounters with Christian missionaries. Unfortunately, many such encounters degenerate into attacks on Christianity under the dubious pretext that Islam is being defended, or proven.

There seems to be some competitive enjoyment in ever-pointing out the contradictions of the Bible or arguing about the illogic of Christianity. Muslims tend to focus on this as if they're in a wrestling match where points have to be scored, and the match itself has to be won.

That's not *Da'wa*. That's not inviting to Allah. And inviting, not disputing, is what we're supposed to be doing. Allah says:

> "Dispute not with the People of the Book, except with better means" (29:46).

and

> "Invite all to the way of thy Lord with wisdom and beautiful preaching, and argue with them in ways that are best" (16:125).

We must never forget this.

* * *

In this corner, we have Ahmad Deedat, weighing in at . . .

Ahmad Deedat is a popular source of information about Christianity for Muslims. His knowledge of the Bible is remarkable. His arguments are good to know, too. It is comforting to know there are Ahmad Deedats in the world. But we shouldn't depend solely on such information.

Muslims must not only be prepared to rebut Christianity, we must positively present Islam and Islamic life. By offering mere polemics, we don't necessarily convey the message. We have to use *hikma*, wisdom, and avoid arguing unnecessarily. Of course, if they start to attack—which incidentally was the norm—we must defend Islam.

This can be done without being insulting. And the trade-off for this approach is not naivete.

We should also keep ourselves well-informed of the activities, methods, arguments, and goals of Zwemer-like institutions. One reason is the negative religious influence of Christian missionaries in the Muslim world, where they've promoted secularization, and caused a great deal of religious confusion among many people from the upper socio-economic classes in Muslim countries. There is also exploitation of poverty and famine conditions that find many Muslim nations where Christian missionary efforts have been more or less successful by dangling a literal carrot from the end of a cross.

But because so few Muslims have ever been converted out of Islam, most Muslims don't take the missionary threat very seriously, as the Christians do Islam's *da'wa*. Generally, the attitude is incredulous: "How could any missionary possibly convert Muslims to Christianity?"

We have to realize missionaries today are aware. They know our histories, our cultures, how we think, what we believe in, where we disagree with Christianity, where we disagree with each other, and the evidence we give for our beliefs. They have thought long and hard to devise clever counter-arguments against Islam—something most Muslims aren't yet aware of.

"Some Muslims automatically dismiss all Christian arguments as farfetched, and believe all Christians, including missionaries, have no knowledge of Islam," says Bagby. "But their arguments are based on a study of Islam. They're not totally ignorant, and we can't dismiss their arguments as totally fanciful."

We can't dismiss their latest methods either. They no longer directly attack the personality of Prophet Muhammad, peace be upon him, in an attempt to avoid turning Muslims off. But they are using distorted and self-serving interpretations of the Quran in order to convince Muslims it supports Christian viewpoints.

Many of these missionaries employ false contrasts between Islam and Christianity, in order to make their beliefs look good, and Islam seem inadequate. They hope to give Muslim listeners doubts about Islam, or to make us feel dissatisfied with our beliefs. For example, they claim Islam emphasizes God's power and teaches He is stern and distant, while Christianity emphasizes He is loving, forgiving and personal.

To try to prove everyone needs salvation through Jesus, they denigrate the Islamic teaching that humans are created without original sin. They point to the evil we see around us every day asking, Isn't it obvious humans are naturally sinful?

In a further attempt to unsettle Muslims, missionaries commonly argue that Islam does not guarantee forgiveness or entry into Heaven, something Christianity claims to give. While these arguments don't affect Muslims who are firm in their faith and knowledgeable, they may confuse the weak and less knowledgeable.

"A response is required, and it requires some thought," notes Bagby. "We should be developing our own counter-arguments to their positions on Islam."

To do this, Muslim community leaders need to be acquainted with the writings of missionaries to Muslims. Such works reveal what they're thinking, what strategies they're using, where they disagree with each other, and their own frank evaluations of the tactics being employed, particularly weaknesses and flaws. Some relevant titles include:

- *Islam: A Survey of the Muslim Faith* by George C. Fry and James R. King
- *Islam: A Christian Perspective* by Michael Nazir-Ali
- *How to Respond to Islam* by Philip Lochhaas
- *A Christian's Response to Islam* by William Miller
- *The Great Islam Debate* by Josh McDowell
- *How to Share the Good News with Your Muslim Friend* by Max R. Kershaw
- *Share Your Faith with a Muslim* by Charles R. Marsh
- *Sharing Your Faith with a Muslim* by Abdiyah Akbar Abdul-Haqq
- *Sharing the Gospel with Iranians*, edited by Don McCurry
- *Biblical Approach to the Muslims* by John Elder
- *Theological Principles in the Towrah, the Zabur, the Injil, and the Quran; The Gospel and Islam*, edited by Don McCurry

- *New Paths in Muslim Evangelism: Evangelical Approaches to Contextualization* by Phil Parshall

For an even more revealing encounter, Muslims should attend lectures by Zwemer Institute staff and other missionaries to Muslims held by local churches. Scan the religion sections of newspapers for announcements, and attend as a group. Showing up at a Zwemer Institute Muslim Awareness Seminar or McCurry's Reaching Your Muslim Neighbors Seminar held at a local church would be even better, in terms of learning what their methods are.

But keep in mind that the goal is learning, not confronting. Since the program is being held at churches, arguments would be inappropriate, and show bad manners.

If you attend one of these programs, you will be told that Muslims are imprisoned in darkness because our faith "cannot meet the deepest needs of the human heart in these crisis times." Such statements will be followed by a subtle but sly ridiculing of Islamic teachings and practices. The fewer Muslims present, the more overt the ridicule will be, because of the inherent two-facedness of such activity.

There's more to be said about all of this.

Should we have anything like the Zwemer Institute? I think not. We do not want an institute that distorts or misrepresents other religions. It is not in the spirit of Islam to distort and misrepresent other peoples' faiths.

But there should be institutes for *Da'wa*. One such institutes is ISNA's Islamic Teaching Center at Plainfield, Indiana, where Bagby is located. Its main activity is distributing literature that introduces Islam to nonMuslims and new Muslims—in the form of pamphlets, booklets, books, and the Islamic Correspondence Course—and producing informational videos.

> "We give talks on Islam throughout the country, hold dialogues with people of other faiths, and help local Muslim communities organize these types of activities. We encourage and train people to become involved in *da'wa* by holding one-day training programs for communities."

Sounds a little bit like the Zwemer Institute. But Bagby insists there's a big difference.

"As our name indicates, our function is to teach Muslims and non-Muslims, to provide correct information on Islam, and to bring nonMuslims to the point where they can make a decision about which spiritual path they wish to follow, and which religion they wish to embrace.

"Our idea of 'proselytizing' is different because we feel people must rationally and with their own free choice come to Islam, in contrast to a more agressive approach that is emotional, and wishes to take this freedom of choice out of people's hands which is typical of the fundamentalist type of movement the Zwemer Institute reflects."

Some see the Zwemer Institute as more of a challenge to Muslims than a danger, or a worry. They're free to work for their religion, and we're free to work for ours. So we should look at what kind of work we're doing for Islam, remembering that if the truth is presented in its true form it will prevail over falsehoods.

Many articles are written by Muslims on Christian missionary activities, causing people to get very angry. But after the anger subsides, few respond to the challenge.

Few see Christian missions as a danger simply because Muslims in America and in the Muslim world are faced with so many bigger threats. The dangers of missionary activity pale before the onslaught of secularization and materialism, communism, poverty, and war, and natural catastrophes, just to name a few.

And the ever increasing conversions and reversions to Islam from Christianity, *al-hamdu-lillah*, give Muslims some reason to discount the Christian missionary threat.

But such negligence has served only to strengthen Christian missionary influence in Muslim areas of the world, who claim to have converted thousands of Muslims principally in Indonesia and some Asian countries. To counter this alarming trend, Muslims must respond to the new strategies and tactics being developed and tested in places such as the Zwemer Institute. . . . which should not be too difficult, since nothing works like the truth.

BEYOND THE MOSQUE: CHRISTIANS WITHIN MUSLIM COMMUNITY

(A book review written by a Muslim in an Islamic Journal)

Phil Parshall continues to propagate the gospel of *contextualization*, albeit less enthusiastically. Parshall's primary emphasis is on deriding the importance of the concept of the Muslim *Ummah*. This is done so that it will eventually become easier for missionaries to gain converts to Christianity, as anyone who leaves the fold of Islam is automatically precluded from retaining membership within the Islamic *Ummah*.

With appalling hypocrisy, Parshall attempts to accentuate the gaps that exist between the normative and actual practices of the *Ummah* in Islam, while at the same time he minimizes the similar divergencies that continue to exist on the side of Christianity. Such divergencies have in the past provided for great Christian luminaries such as Saint Augustine to officially condone slavery as a right and proper "Christian" institution. They have also allowed both American and South African churches to first tactfully, and then openly, express support for the very concept of white racial superiority right up to the 20th century C.E.

The author offers to contrast the Iran-Iraq war as proof of the supposedly bitter divisions that are forever destined to pit Muslims against one another, with the "spirit of brotherhood" that he has witnessed engulfing Muslim converts to

Christianity. Parshall refuses to acknowledge that "Christian brotherhood" can just as easily be theoretically negated by attributing to Christianity the mindless killings that, in the same period, occurred among Catholics and Protestants in the Northern Ireland territory.

As an active Christian missionary stationed in Manila, Philippines, Parshall takes upon himself to demonstrate that the difficulties and hardships that face the Muslim people are a direct consequence of Islam. Therefore, he argues, the only possible solution is for Muslims to completely abandon Islam, and to become Christians. The absolute falsehood of such a thesis is clear if one looks at "the difficulties and hardships" that face Christian people—in Central and South America, in Africa, in the Philippines. It is clear, too, when one objectively assesses the Christian record of condoning slavery, aggressive intolerance to other religions, and recurring wars that have been undertaken in the name of Christ in Europe and from it into Africa, the Americas and Asia.

The author rationalizes the inability of Christian missionary organizations such as Frontiers International the Arab World Team, and Operation Mobilization to gain Muslim converts by blaming 'Islam.' He states that due to sociological factors, economic repercussions, and even threats of physical violence, "very few Muslims have been willing to pay such a high price to follow Christ." Following this very reductionist argument to its logical end, one would come to ridiculous conclusions that some one billion Muslims identify themselves with Islam only because it is temporarily expedient for them to do so!

The author, on a number of occasions, endeavours to deride Islam with a series of negative comments and examples. Although, to be fully expected from a Christian missionary, it is nonetheless always disconcerting to see the Holy Quran attributed as the work of the *Shaitan* as Parshall does. Another prominent example of this style of comment is the claim that "blind faith is a cornerstone of Islam." The most immediate response to such an accusation is that if this is true of Islam, it is certainly just as prevalent, if not more so, in Christianity.

The last quarter of *Beyond the Mosque* is devoted to *contextualization* as a concept, both in terms of theory and actual practice. Suffice it to say that Mr. Parshall is a vigorous proponent of *contextualization* but slightly wary of abandoning more traditional Christian practices in favour of methods that would be easily digestible by converts living in a predominantly Islamic environment. As evidence of his belief in *contextualization*, he relates certain personal experiences that include fasting during the entire month of Ramadan, and celebrating the two Islamic 'Eids as "special" Christian holidays.

It is not the purpose of this review to exaggerate the strength of Christian missions in Islamic countries and/or environments. Indeed, if not for the response of people which is exceedingly dismal—and more specifically Muslims—to the Christian missionary call, "innovations" such as *contextualization* would not be necessary. Nevertheless, *contextualization* is becoming a formidable weapon in the burgeoning arsenal of the Christian missionary movement, and one that we should not ignore. Although the survival of Islam has been assured by Allah (*s.w.t.*), the continuance, or some would argue, the reemergence of the Muslim *Ummah* is not so easily assured. Without an unbreakable bond of love, empathy, and *'ilm* that extends to all areas of the globe, Muslims may find it increasingly difficult to flourish in an environment where Christian missionaries are so fervently active—for while all these missionaries are religious, they are not scrupulous about truth.

PART EIGHT

RESOURCES FOR STRATEGY

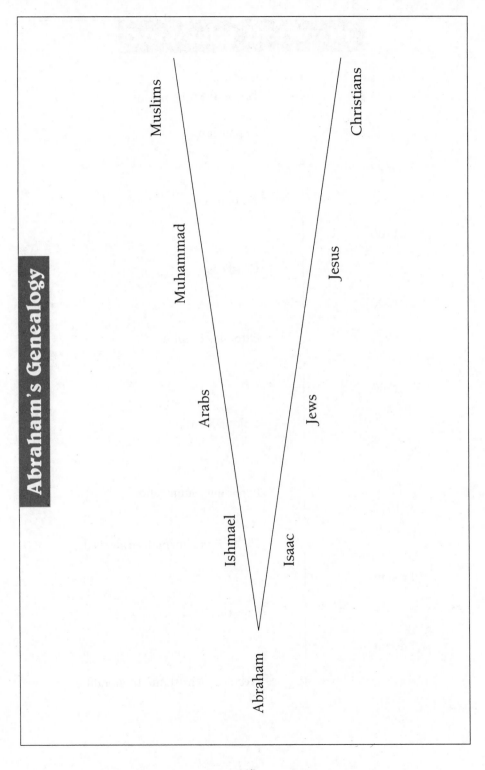

Abraham's Genealogy

Abraham

Ishmael
Isaac

Arabs
Jews

Muhammad
Jesus

Muslims
Christians

Historical Time Line

632 A.D.	Death of Muhammad
	Expansion
750	
	Golden Age
1100	
	Crusades
1300	
	Ottoman Empire
1700	
	Colonialism
1950	
	Economic Subjugation
1970	
	Oil & Fundamentalism Revival
Present	
	Palestine
Present	
	Western "Christian" Immorality

Colonial Influence on
Muslim Populations

1	Great Britain	Egypt, Sudan, half of Libya, Kenya, Sierra Leone, Malawi, Nigeria, Uganda, Gambia, Iraq, Palestine, Jordan, Saudi Arabia, Iran, Yemen, United Arab Emirates, Kuwait, Bahrain, Qatar, Afghanistan, India, Pakistan, Bangladesh, Malaysia
2	France	Algeria, Morocco, Tunisia, Ivory Coast, Senegal, Guinea, Benin, Togo, Mali, Niger, Chad, Gabon, Burkina Faso, Mauritania, Madagascar, Syria, Lebanon
3	Italy	Half of Libya, Eritrea, Somalia
4	Spain	Western Sahara, Guinea-Bissau
5	Germany	Cameroon, Tanzania
6	Dutch	Indonesia
7	U.S.A.	Philippines
8	Portugal	Mozambique

NOTE: Major Muslim people groups in China and the CIS were exempted from Western Colonial occupation.

Overview of Muslim Countries

Very intolerant	Saudi Arabia (83), Sudan (81), Iran (73), Maldives (67), Mauritania (65), Pakistan (64)
Intolerant	Iraq (61), Malaysia (60), Afghanistan (58), Djibouti (58), Oman (58), Egypt (56), Brunei (54), Libya (54), Morocco (54), Algeria (53), Tunisia (53), Kuwait (52), Syria (52), Somalia (52), United Arab Emirates (51), Qatar (48), Comoros (48), Indonesia (47), Turkey (46), Bahrain (45), Bangladesh (44), Yemen (40)
Tolerant	Jordan (32), Mali (25), Niger (25), Senegal (22), Lebanon (21)
Areas where Muslims are under threat	Burma (Araka State), India (Kashmir), Israel, Yugoslavia (Croatia and Bosnia-Herzegovina)
Nations with Muslim-Christian unrest	Nigeria, Ethiopia, Philippines, Azerbaijan-Armenia
Muslim Minorities	Bulgaria, China, Great Britain, France, United States, Central Asian Republics of the former U.S.S.R.

NOTE: Numbers (in brackets) are the Zwemer Religious Tolerance Scale

The Revelation of One True God

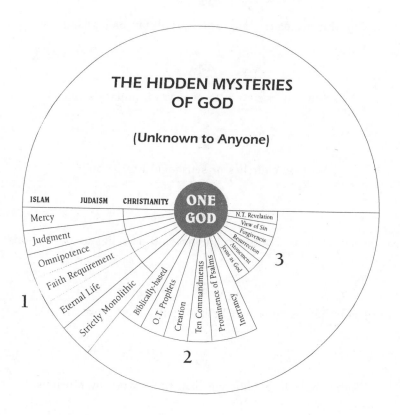

1 Teachings about God common in belief to Christianity, Judaism and Islam

2 Teachings about God common in belief to Christianity and Judaism

3 Teachings about God exclusive to Christianity

Code of Umar

1

Non-Muslim males were to pay a poll tax plus a land tax.

2

Non-Muslims were not to engage in military service.

3

No new churches or synagogues to be built

4

No display of crosses outside churches and no religious processions.

5

Christian's houses could not be built taller than those of Muslims.

6

Clothes were to be different than those worn by Muslims.

7

Non-Muslims were forbidden to ride on horses and had to ride on mules or donkeys.

8

They had to show respect to Muslims; for instance, by giving up their seats to them.

Mystical Islam

Sufism

Mysticism

Folk Islam
Popular Islam
Animistic Influence

Comparison of World Views

CONCEPT	OT HEBREW & MUSLIM	WESTERN CHRISTIAN
1 Unity	Emphasis on unity in all of life	Emphasis on unity only if it has pragmatic value
2 Time	High respect for the past and tradition	*Orientation toward the future
3 Family	Solidarity	*Emphasis on individual
4 Peace	Harmony, integration, Total way of life Internal and external characteristics	Contentment *A segment of life Internal characteristic
5 Honor	All important consideration	High priority
6 Status	A matter associated with wealth, family, name, age	*A result of accomplishment
7 Individualism	Subordination to emphasis on group	*High regard for independence
8 Secularism	A totally unacceptable trend	*A largely acceptable trend
9 Change	An undesirable phenomenon	*A highly desirable phenomenon
10 Equality	A theoretical ideal which is not practised	A theoretical ideal which is not practiced
11 Efficiency	A matter of little or no concern	*An imperative

* In direct contrast to Hebrew-Muslim world view

Concepts of Religious Terminology

VOCABULARY	MUSLIM	EVANGELICAL CHRISTIAN
1 God	Distant, merciful, capricious, vengeful, almighty	Personal, loving, concerned, judgmental, holy
2 Christ	Prophet	God
3 Bible	Revelation from God; changed, corrupted	Revelation from God; authoritative
4 Trinity	God, Mary, Jesus	Father, Son, Holy Spirit
5 Faith	Object: God and Muhammad	Object: Jesus as God
6 Sin	Shame, embarrassment, rebellion against God	Guilt, Rebellion against God (primarily) and man
7 Salvation	Requirement: Faith and works. Provider: God No assurance	Requirement: faith Provider: God in Christ Assurance
8 Sanctification	Emphasis on obedience and ritual	Emphasis on role of Holy Spirit
9 Love	Stresses family	Stresses Community
10 Supernatural power	Belief in spirit world	Belief based on teaching of Bible

Form and Meaning in Official and Popular Islam

FORM	MEANING IN OFFICIAL ISLAM	MEANING IN POPULAR ISLAM
PILLARS		
Confession	proves one is a true Muslim	protection in spaces inhabited by evil
Prayer	bodily pure to worship God	removal by water of demonic pollution and sins
Alms	responsibility to fellow Muslims	precaution against the evil eye
Fasting	sign of communal commitment	veneration of Muhammad and "Night of Power"
Pilgrimage	visit epicenter of the faith	obtaining of blessing and alternative shrines
CREEDS		
One God	monotheistic confession of faith	magical use of the names of God
Angels	Servants of God at his pleasure	possible mediators and powerful in charms
Books	encoding of God's self-revelation	bibliolatry
Apostles	vehicles of God's word to man	possible mediators
Last Day	ethical focus of man's life	acts to gain merit for dead relatives
Predestination	ultimately, all in God's hands	"Night of Power" to try and change destinies

Bill Musk, adapted from *The Unseen Face of Islam*, p. 222

"Image" as Perceived by Muslims

MUSLIM PRIEST	CHRISTIAN MISSIONARY
1 Passive disposition	1 A driver, a doer
2 Subjective in outlook	2 Objective in orientation to life
3 People-oriented	3 Task-oriented
4 Financially poor (with the exception of certain *pirs*)	4 Possessor of a car, camera, computer, tape recorder, etc. Regarded as extremely rich
5 Would not attend drama, watch TV, or go to movies	5 Would do all of these
6 Would not eat in expensive restaurants	6 Would eat in expensive restaurants
7 Would not eat pork	7 Would eat pork
8 Man's clothes identify him as a religious person	8 Clothes identify him as a secular person
9 Wears a beard	9 Infrequently has a beard
10 Wife would either wear a veil or culturally-approved clothes	10 Missionary wives have not always dressed in clothes which would be regarded by Muslims as modest: thus they are identified with the "sinful" actresses as seen on Western movie and TV imports.

"Ministry" as Perceived by Muslims

MUSLIM PRIEST	CHRISTIAN MISSIONARY
1 Mosque is focus of life	Goes to church a few hours a week.
2 Prays openly 5 times a day	Little public prayer
3 Fasts for one month during daylight hours	Seldom, if ever, fasts
4 Constantly uses religious vocabulary	Little use of such
5 Not a giver of relief and financial aid: a recipient of local money only	A dispenser of foreign funds—for relief, jobs, training institutions, hospitals, etc.
6 Has no employees	Has employees with accompanying status
7 Puts little value on non-quranic education	Puts great value on formal, secular education, degrees
8 Memorizes vast parts of the Quran in Arabic	Memorizes very little of the Bible—in any language
9 Involves himself in a healing ministry by pouring consecrated water on the sick, putting charms on the diseased, chanting the Quran, and saying prayers.	Gives a mild prayer for the sick with little faith or conviction. People go to the missionary for medicine, not prayer. Emphasis on the scientific, not the spiritual

Felt Needs in Popular Islam

FELT NEEDS IN POPULAR ISLAM	POPULAR ISLAM'S ANSWERS TO FELT NEEDS	FELT NEEDS MET BY JESUS CHRIST
Fear of the unknown	Idolatry, stone worship, Fetishes, *talismans*, charms	Security in Christ as keeper, guide
Fear of evil spirits	Witchcraft, amulets, exorcism	Exorcism by Christ; power over spirits
Powerlessness before power of shaman	Sorcery; Prophylaxes	Protection from attack; offensive weapon for spiritual warfare
Fear of the future	Angel worship; Divination; Spells	Trust in Christ as Lord of the future
Shame of not being in the in-group	Curse; hair/nail trimmings	Acceptance in the fellowship of believers
Disequilibrium	Magic; divination	Restoration and answered prayer
Sickness	Tree/saint worship; Healing; Magic	Divine healing in Christ's power
Helplessness in crisis	Magic, vows; intercession of saint	Christ answering prayer directly
Meaninglessness of life	Turning to spirit world	Purpose in life as God's child; using gifts, abilities
Vulnerability of women	Occult influence; practices at birth, etc.	Security in Christ; Influence as prayer warriors

Bill Musk (Adapted from *The Unseen Face of Islam*, p. 222)

OFTEN THE PRIMARY BARRIER IN SHARING THE GOSPEL WITH THOSE OF A DIFFERENT CULTURE OR RELIGION IS A SOCIAL BARRIER RATHER THAN A THEOLOGICAL ONE.

MANY OF OUR CHRISTIAN TRADITIONS AND PRACTICES HINDER THE UNDERSTANDING OF THE MEANING OF THE GOSPEL AND THE BEAUTY OF SALVATION THROUGH JESUS.

BIBLICAL AUTHORITY

CHRIST AS GOD

SALVATION IN JESUS

Church architecture
Wedding traditions
Burial traditions (casket)
Prayer forms
Use of the symbol of the Cross
Day and style of worship

Western worship songs
Western-style holidays
Eating pork

Circumcision
Infrequency of fasting
Use of Christian names
Having dogs as pets
Use of pictures of Jesus
Different clothing for worship

Western Denominations
Misunderstood religious terminology
Birth ceremonies

WHAT CAN WE DO TO OVERCOME THIS SITUATION?

Strategy

1   Simple housing
2   National dress
3   Beard for men
4   Selection of target group
5   Muslim dietary practices are adopted
6   Time is regarded as event-oriented
7   Provision for washing before prayer
8   Shoes are removed
9   Worshipers sit on the floor
10 Bibles are placed on folding stands
11 Prayer is emphasized with inquirers and converts. Biblical forms are followed. Muslim prayer is sacramental. Continuance in the mosque is discouraged.
12 Muslim tunes are sung with Christian words. Scripture is chanted.
13 Worshipers embrace in Muslim fashion
14 Days and times of worship are pragmatically regulated.
15 Fasting is an area of liberty.
16 A high profile of religious observance is encouraged.
17 Muslim religious vocabulary is used.
18 The word 'Christian' is avoided (Relationships with the established church).
19 Convert's Muslim name is retained.
20 *Eid-al-Fitr* (end of Fast)
21 *Eid-al-Korban* (end of *Haj*)
22 Christmas and Easter
23 Baptism and initiation
24 Polygamy issue
25 Homogeneous Muslim convert fellowships. Autonomous. Informal. Patterned after the mosque.
26 Overnight training sessions
27 Contextual literature is utilized
28 Healing, dreams, and exorcism
29 Persecution issues
30 Low-key propagation along family and friendship lines
31 Radio
32 Financial assistance perspectives

Cross-Cultural Church Planting Spectrums

C1
Traditional church structure using local Christian language. Reflects western churches in practices and styles.

C2
Traditional church structures and forms but uses Muslim-oriented vocabulary.

C3
Contextualized church structure. Muslim art, culture, and language are reflected in the worship and ecclesiology of the church.

C4
The same as C-3 along with the utilization of biblically acceptable Islamic forms, rituals and ceremonies.

C5
C-4 guidelines to ecclesiology are followed. However, there is an allowance for converts (and missionaries) to be in the mosque as a discreet witness for Christ.

C6
Christians follow C-5, but they also legally and officially become Muslims. In this instance the creed of Islam, "There is no God but Allah and Muhammad is his prophet," is affirmed publicly in the mosque. The Islamic community considers the person to be fully Muslim, and not a Christian. However, the motivation of the Christian is, as an insider, to win the Muslims to Christ.

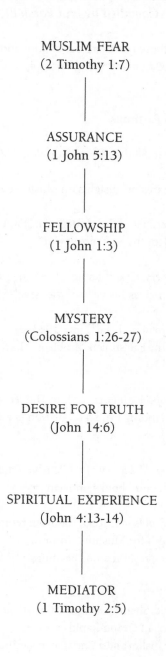

Bridges to Folk Muslims

MUSLIM FEAR
(2 Timothy 1:7)

ASSURANCE
(1 John 5:13)

FELLOWSHIP
(1 John 1:3)

MYSTERY
(Colossians 1:26-27)

DESIRE FOR TRUTH
(John 14:6)

SPIRITUAL EXPERIENCE
(John 4:13-14)

MEDIATOR
(1 Timothy 2:5)

ANNOTATED BIBLIOGRAPHY OF BOOKS OF ISLAM
Compiled by Phil Parshall

(Note: Most of these books are out of print and will have to be borrowed from institutional libraries.)

A   Books by Christian Authors

Abdul-Haqq, Abdiyah Akbar. *Sharing Your Faith With a Muslim*. Bethany Fellowship, 1980.
This Indian scholar shares his insights on Muslim evangelism.

Arberry, A. J. *Sufism: An Account of the Mystics of Islam*. Unwin Paperbacks, 1950.
A simple, clear history of the Sufi movement.

Chacour, Elias, *Blood Brothers*. Grand Rapids, Chosen, 1984.
A Christian Palestinian gives his view of the Israel-Arab conflict. Excellent.

Chapman, Colin. *Whose Promised Land*. Lion, 1983.
The best exposition of the Palestinian "problem" I have seen by a Christian scholar. Very fair and balanced.

Cragg, Kenneth. *The Call of the Minaret*. Oxford University Press, 1956.
Bishop Cragg, an outstanding British scholar on Islam, shares his insights in this introductory book.

Fry, George and James King, *A Survey of the Muslim Faith*. Baker, 1980.
One of the best introductory books on Islam.

Hughes, T. P. *The Dictionary of Islam*. 1895. Has been reprinted and probably available from Fellowship of Faith for Muslims, Toronto.
An absolutely excellent resource on meanings of Muslim terms and practices, even though dated.

Kateregga, Badru and David Shenk. *Islam and Christianity*. Uzima Press, 1980. Also published by Eerdmans in Grand Rapids.
A dialogue between a Muslim and a Christian regarding respective religious beliefs. Outstanding.

McCurry, Don, Editor. *The Gospel and Islam*. MARC, 1979.
A timeless compendium of excellent papers presented by experts in a Lausanne-sponsored consultation in Colorado Springs in 1978.

Mahmoody, Betty. *Not Without My Daughter*. St. Martin's Press, 1987.
An absolutely gripping book about an American woman married to an Iranian Muslim. Highlights religious life and culture of Iran.

Marsh, Charles. *Share Your Faith With a Muslim*. Moody Press, 1975.
Practical suggestions on witnessing to Muslims from a missionary with 45 years of experience in Africa.

Matheny, Tim. *Reaching the Arabs: A Felt Need Approach*. Wm Carey, 1981.
Good insight on how to approach Muslim Arabs in a contextualized manner.

Musk, Bill. *The Unseen Face of Islam*. Available through MARC, Monrovia, CA 1989.
An excellent book on the inside story of Folk Islam.

Parshall, Phil. *New Paths in Muslim Evangelism*. Baker, 1980.
An overview of the contextualized approach to Muslim Evangelism.

_____. *The Cross and the Crescent*. Tyndale, 1989.
A comparison of spirituality as seen through the beliefs and practices of Christians and Muslims.

Rasooli, Jay and Allen Cady. *Dr. Saeed of Iran*. Kregels, 1957.
Biography of one of the great Muslim converts.

Rushdie, Salman. *The Satanic Verses*. Viking, 1988.
Difficult to understand, but made a classic by the Ayatollah's reaction.

Schimmel, Annemarie. *And Muhammad is His Messenger*. University of North Carolina Press, 1985.
A Harvard professor gives a very readable account of how the Prophet is venerated within Folk Islam.

Watt, Montgomery. *Muhammad, Prophet and Statesman*. Oxford University Press, 1961.
A very good exposition of Muhammad's life. A compilation of Watt's *Muhammad at Mecca* and *Muhammad at Medina*.

Willis, Avery. *Indonesian Revival.* Wm. Carey, 1977.
A Southern Baptist missionary analyzes factors relevant in the conversion of two million Muslims to Christ following the 1965 political upheaval in Indonesia.

Wilson, J. Christy, Sr. *Apostle to Islam.* Baker, 1952.
An inspirational and informative biography of the great "Apostle to Islam," Samuel Zwemer.

Woodberry, Dudley, Editor. *Muslims and Christians on the Emmaus Road.* MARC, 1989.
An excellent compendium of papers on various Islamic themes presented by knowledgeable practitioners and academics in a Lausanne-sponsored conference in July of 1987 held in Zeist, The Netherlands.

Zwemer, Samuel. *Raymund Lull.* Revell, 1902.
Zwemer writes about the life of this 13th century missionary to Muslims.

_____. *A Moslem Seeker After God.* Revell, 1920.
Biography of Al-Ghazali, a renowned Muslim mystic and theologian of the eleventh century.

_____. *The Influence of Animism on Islam.* MacMillan, 1920.
A forerunner of books on Folk Islam.

B   Books by Muslim Authors

Asad, Muhammad. *The Road to Mecca.* Simon And Schuster, 1954.
Asad's pilgrimage to faith in Islam.

Hussein, Kamel. *City of Wrong.* Geoffrey Bles, 1959.
An Egyptian surgeon writes a classic on Good Friday from a Muslim perspective.

Nasr, Seyyeed Hossein. *Ideals and Realities of Islam.* Beacon Press, 1966.
The best exposition of Islam I have ever read as written from the perspective of a devout, highly educated Muslim.

Rahman, Fazlur. *Islam.* University of Chicago Press, 1966.
A well known classic written by a now deceased Pakistani professor at the University of Chicago.

C Qurans

Ali, Muhammad. *The Holy Quran*. Specialty Promotions, 1917.
This Pakistani Ahmadiyyah author has produced a Quran with commentary. Non-Ahmadiyyah Muslims refuse to validate this translation.

Ali, Yusuf. *The Holy Quran*. The Islamic Foundation, 1975.
A Pakistani scholar who has produced a translation and commentary widely appreciated by Muslims. Recommended for use in discussions with Muslims.

Arberry, Arthur. *The Koran Interpreted*. Oxford University Press, 1964.
A scholarly work somewhat recognized by Muslims.

Bell, Richard. *The Quran,* Vols. 1 & 2. T. & T. Clark, 1937.
A critical translation by a British scholar. Not accepted by Muslims.

Dawood, N. J. *The Koran*. Penguin Books, 1956.
Not generally known by Muslims.

Irving, T. B. *The Quran*. Amana Books, 1985.
An American Ph.D. (Princeton) convert to Islam who sets forth the "first American version" of the Quran. Not widely respected by Muslims as it was a solitary effort.

Pickthall, Mohammed. *The Meaning of the Glorious Koran*. Mentor Books.
One of the most widely used translations of the Quran. Hard to follow.

D Hadith

al-Bukhari, Muhammad bin Ismail. *Sahih*, Vols. 1-9. Dar Al Arabia.
The best and most authoritative collection of Hadith.

Siddiqi, Abdul. *Sahih Muslim,* Vols. 1-4. Ashraf Printing, 1976.
A translation of the second most authoritative collection of Hadith.

MOBILIZING THE NATIONAL CHURCH FOR MUSLIM EVANGELISM

by Phil Parshall

Some years ago, a zealous American armed with tracts came to my Syrian friend, Yusuf, and requested that he accompany him to the Street Called Straight in Damascus. Standing under the shadow of the wall where tradition has it that the newborn Apostle Paul was lowered in a basket, Sam urged Yusuf to accompany him down the mile-long street as he distributed tracts and called upon people to repent because the Kingdom of God is at hand. Yusuf, with grace, declined the invitation and suggested he would wait for Sam's return in the shadows of St. Paul's wall. Remarkably, Sam returned intact, effusively reporting the calling of God upon his life was wonderfully fulfilled!

Such actions by foreign Christians are one of a number of deterrents that give Christian nationals pause in initiating a witness to their fellow Muslim countrymen. They are, for good reason, hesitant to be associated with a faith that has a fringe element that causes embarrassment and even danger to them. Other concerns that nationals may have include:

- A lack of precedent. The believers have never actually seen a sensitive evangelistic outreach in their town or village.
- Often the church is surrounded by a sea of Muslims. They are intimidated by such an overpowering cultural-cum-religious presence. The normal response is to form a reactionary ghetto in which one feels maximally secure. "Don't rock the boat," becomes the unarticulated maxim. Evangelism has the potential of creating big-time waves.
- "Jihad" is a potent reality in certain Islam-dominated areas of the world. In two islands of the Southern Philippines where there is a large Muslim population, tracts have recently been distributed informing resident Christians they must convert to Islam immediately or face the consequences of Jihad. In such a situation believers are hoping for basic survival. They certainly are not going to upset Muslims even more by evangelistic forays.
- There would be some who would fear the overturning of the established Christian social, cultural, and religious traditions if suddenly a large number of Muslims were converted. Believers are well established in their comfort zone. The whole concept of contextualization is extremely threatening to the status quo. Thus . . . resistance.
- Then there is the issue of foreign financial assistance. Many churches in the Two-Thirds World receive significant gifts from the West. A sharing of these limited resources with a new body of believers may lead to diminished finances within the established church.
- If many Muslims came to Christ, would they seek to control the politics of the existing denominations? Some leaders are intimidated by such a thought.
- Lastly, there is the perennial doubt about the sincerity of Muslim converts. Stories, both factual and apocryphal, abound regarding those who professed and then reverted back to Islam. One or two case studies are extrapolated to embrace all inquirers/converts.

Fortunately, small numbers of active witnessing Christians may be found in many Muslim settings. But, overall their number is small and inadequate. Is there a way out of this conundrum?

2

In 1984, my wife Julie and I came to the Philippines to engage in Muslim evangelism. This was to be within a consortium effort with SEND, OMF, and our mission SIM. We approached the relevant church body for their permission. As they were doing nothing among Muslims, they wholeheartedly endorsed our efforts.

The Philippines has a minority Muslim community of five million or about eight percent of the total population. They are clustered in the southern island of Mindanao as well as in regional centers throughout the Philippines. For various reasons, the Muslims have felt violated by Christians. They are therefore quite militant. Over the past decade a number of missionaries have been kidnapped, a few raped, and several killed. This has given rise to a common saying among Filipino Christians, "The only good Muslim is a dead Muslim." Alienation is pervasive between the two communities.

A number of steps led to a turnaround among evangelical church leaders and members. Perhaps some of these will have transferable value in other Muslim settings.

1   In 1985, as a group of missionaries we commenced a five-day Consultation on Islam. Over the years, we have brought in top practitioners to speak to this group which was attended by 44 persons during the first conference and has grown to over 200 for the most recent one. This has been a powerful tool to challenge Filipinos to the task. Only four nationals attended the initial gathering while 121 were present for the 1999 consultation. It is now largely administered by nationals.

2   In 1989, while the Lausanne Congress was meeting less than a mile away, Filipinos organized a parallel Congress on Evangelism. They used local people as well as Lausanne '89 plenary speakers.

Florentino de Jesus, Sr., a 75-year-old Filipino, spoke and piercingly challenged his own people toward Muslim ministry. Over 1,000 people came forward as he gave the invitation. Sadly, only a few of those have followed through, but it was definitely a watershed moment. De Jesus, now deceased, had led his own C&MA denomination to have the greatest Muslim outreach in the Philippines. We all look on this dear brother as the Samuel Zwemer of the Philippines.

3   In 1991, my colleague and close friend, John Speers, was visiting in Mindanao seeking to better learn a Muslim dialect. With him was his lovely, musically-gifted wife and two children, ages four and two. John was one of the most intelligent and spiritually sensitive missionaries I

have ever known.

At 5:15 p.m., as John was returning from a language learning walk-about, a Muslim came up behind him and, using a homemade pistol, fired a bullet into John's brain. Entry into heaven was immediate.

The story has been told and retold. If an American could so love Filipino Muslims that he would die for them, then how much greater is the responsibility of local believers to engage in a loving witness to the Sons of Ishmael. John's impact has even been greater in death than in life.

4   As missionaries we have sought to model what we have taught. Filipi-nos are very perceptive people. They want to see more than hear. For 16 years, I have had an outreach center in a Muslim area of inner-city Manila. Our street has been described by a local TV station as "the most dangerous street" in this city of ten million people. One persistent Muslim fundamentalist has repeatedly threatened to kill me if I don't close the center. Four afternoons a week I go and show the "Jesus" film and seek to distribute literature. This practical demonstration of involve-ment has challenged a number of Filipinos, some of whom now join me on a voluntary basis.

5   I looked for a man. Who could I disciple by example and friendship? The Lord brought Gene Lara into my life. He is a graduate of the most reputed University and Seminary in the Philippines. Gene at that time pastored the church we attend which is made up of professionals and educators. Over a period of time the Lord worked in Gene to the point he resigned his prestigious church, joined an OMF-related national missionary society, and now works with me in our Reading Center. Gene has influenced scores of people toward Muslim ministry. He is a power-ful speaker and seminar teacher. Before leaving his church he led it into becoming the most involved single body of believers in the country in Muslim outreach. In many ways, he has now become my mentor!

6   A lesson from the above is the necessity of long-term and patient involvement. Our Filipino church had no ministry with Muslims when we started attending there 14 years ago. Slowly that has all wonderfully changed. Amazingly, the godly pastor who followed Gene also resigned after four years and went into full-time Muslims outreach!

Scores of new initiatives have commenced all over the country. Most are community development based. This practical dimension of help is appreciated. Recently, significant numbers of Muslims have turned to Christ in two areas of the country. Enthusiasm and optimism are at an all time high even though the political situation (and resultant danger) is as bad as it has been since the all-out conflict of the early '70s.

I realize the Philippines is unique, both demographically and religiously. Other Islamic countries will have their own contexts. But perhaps some of these strategies will be helpful to others in thinking through options in regard to mobilizing the church toward active engagement in Muslim evangelism.